VIZ GRAPHIC NOVEL

SAMURAI
CRUSADER™
THE KUMOMARU
CHRONICLES

STORY BY **HIROI OJI**
ART BY **RYOICHI IKEGAMI**

CONTENTS

This volume contains the SAMURAI CRUSADER installments from
MANGA VIZION Vol. 1, No. 1 through half of Vol. 1, No. 8 in their
entirety.

STORY BY HIROI OJI
ART BY RYOICHI IKEGAMI

English Adaptation/James D. Hudnall & Lillian Olsen
Touch-Up Art & Lettering/Wayne Truman
Cover Design/Viz Graphics
Editor/Annette Roman
Assistant Editor/Toshifumi Yoshida

Senior Editor/Trish Ledoux
Editor-in-Chief/Satoru Fujii
Publisher/Seiji Horibuchi

Printed in Canada

Published by Viz Communications, Inc.
P.O. Box 77010 • San Francisco, CA 94107

10 9 8 7 6 5 4 3 2 1
First printing, May 1996

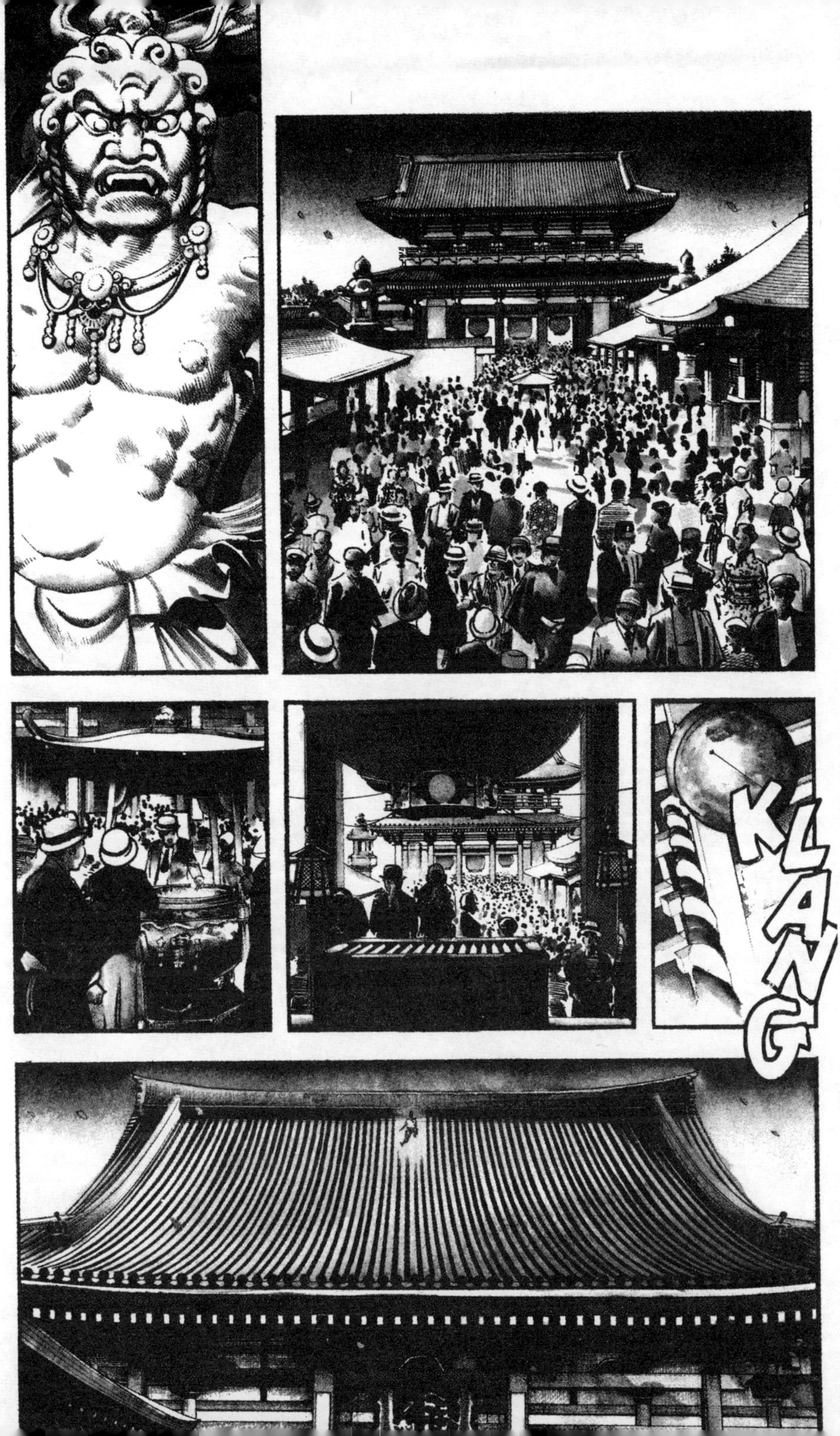
KLANG

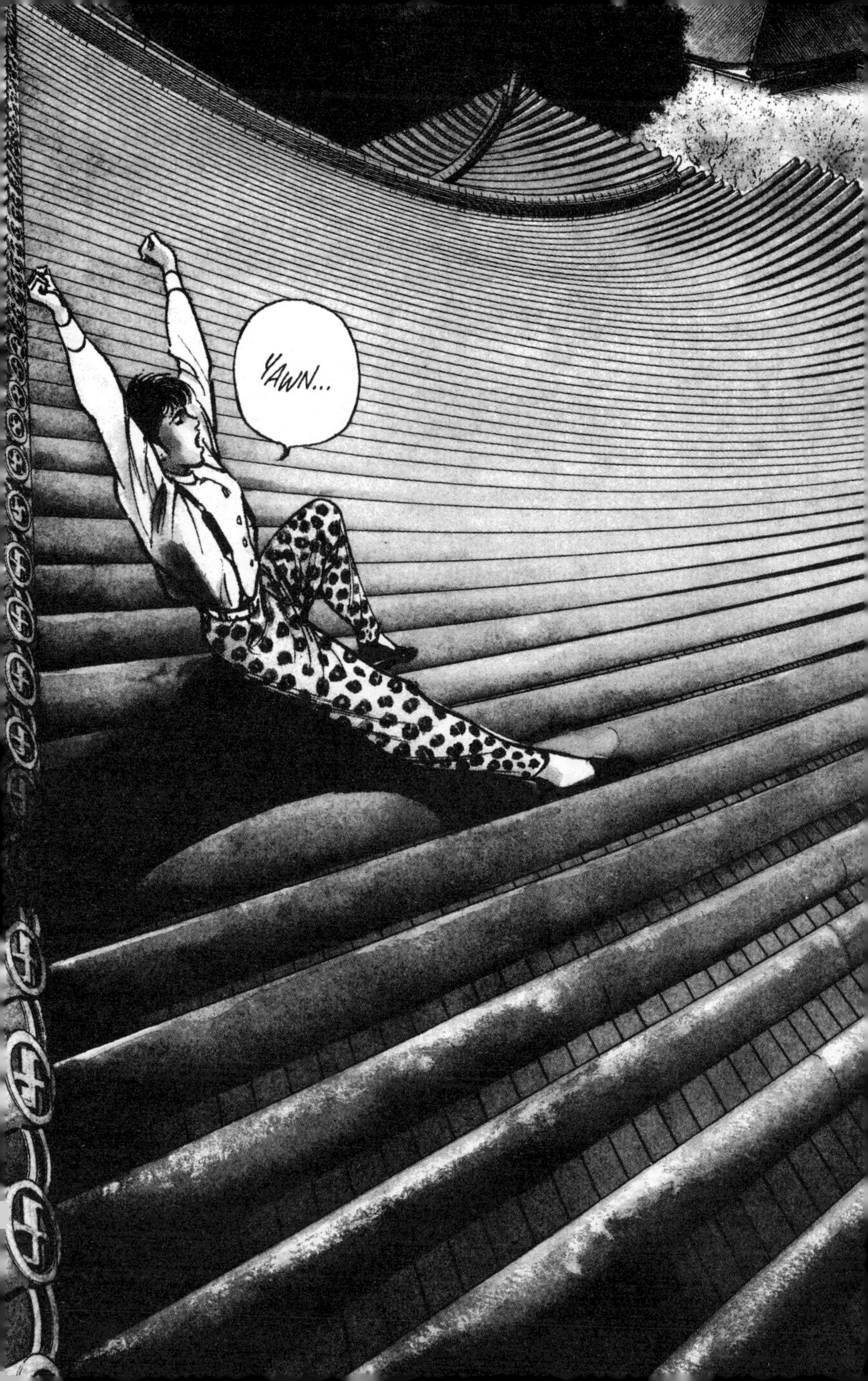
YAWN...

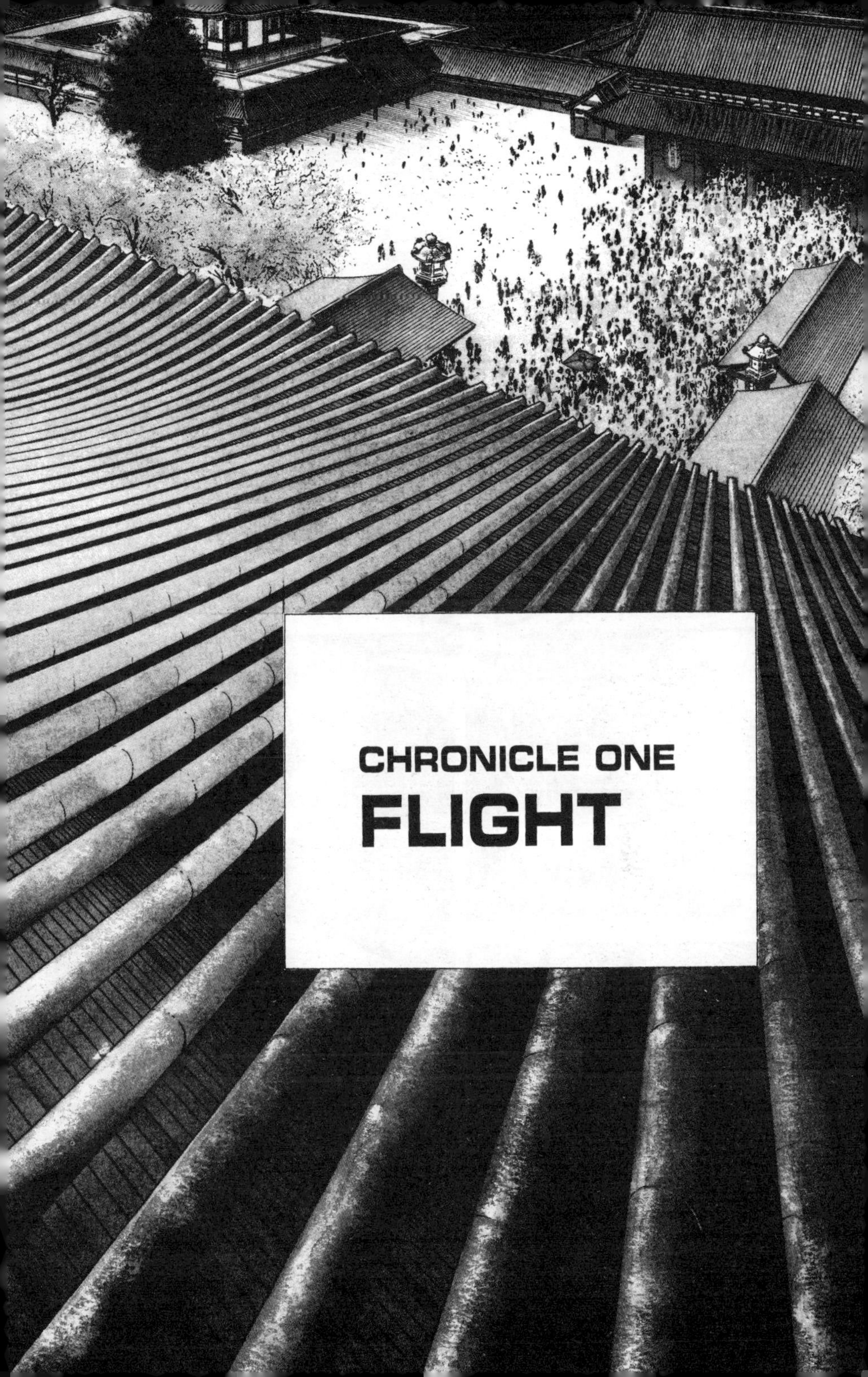
CHRONICLE ONE
FLIGHT

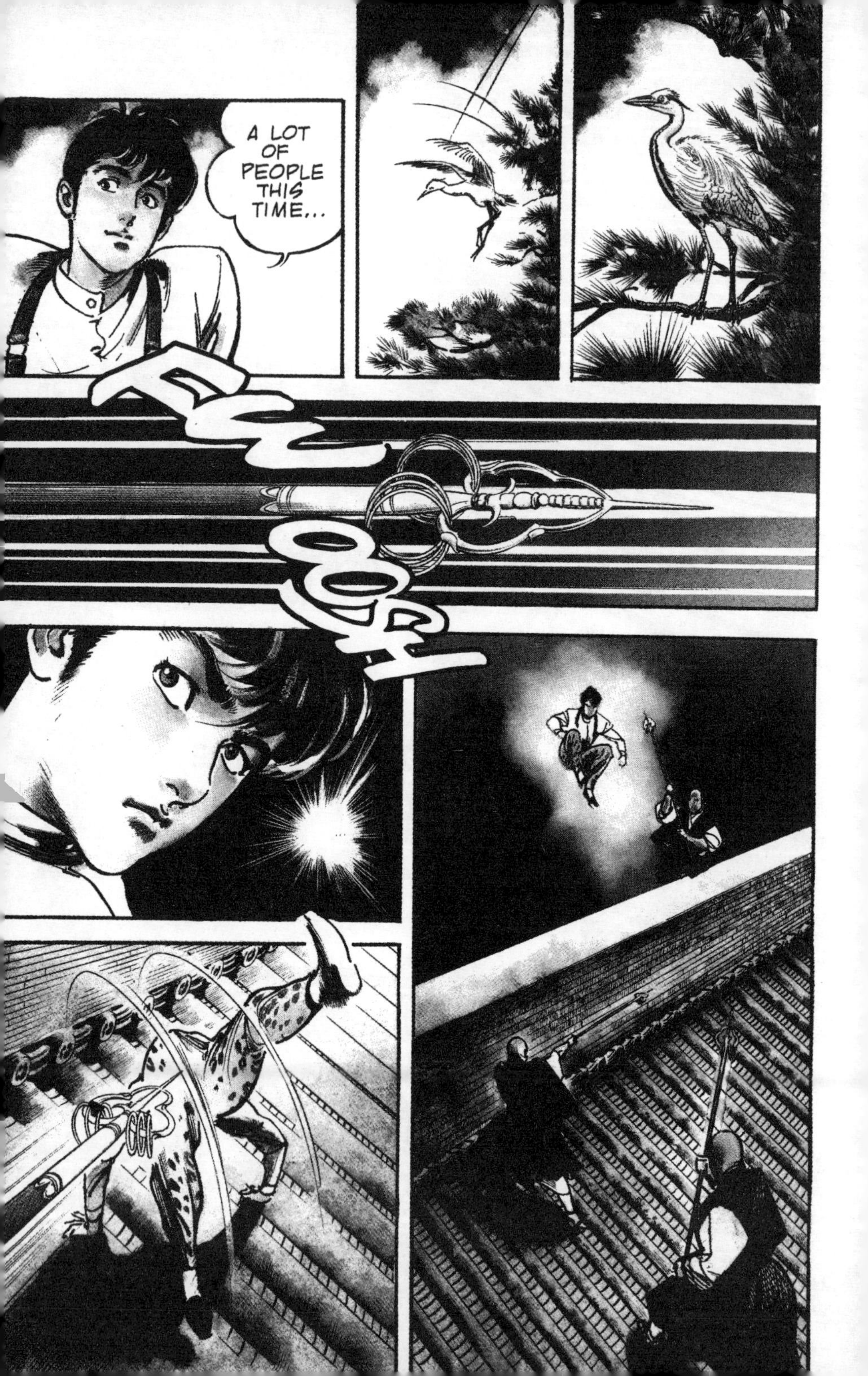
A LOT OF PEOPLE THIS TIME...
FWOOSH

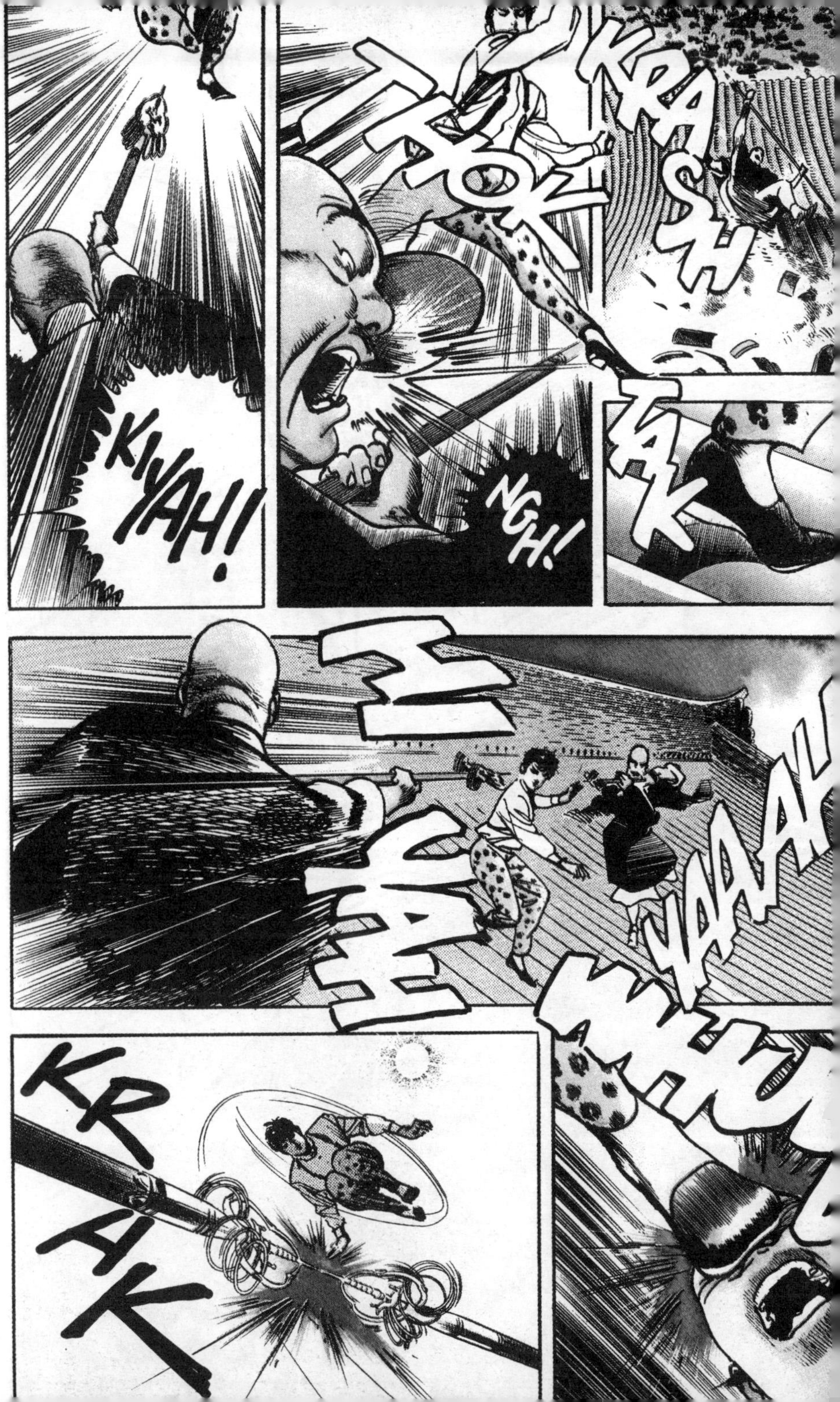
KI-YAH!
THOK
NGH!
KRASH
TAK
WHAM
KRAK

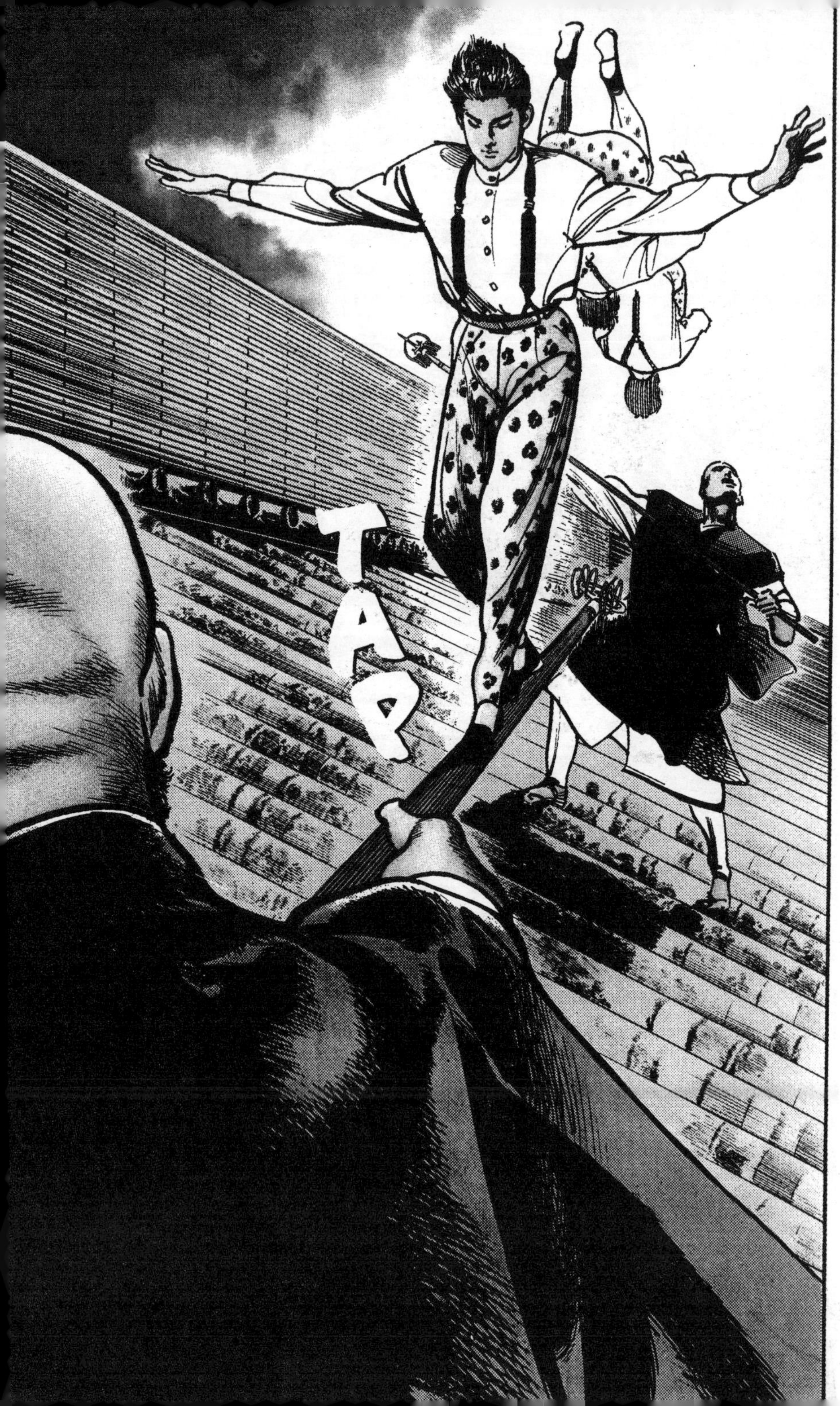
TAP

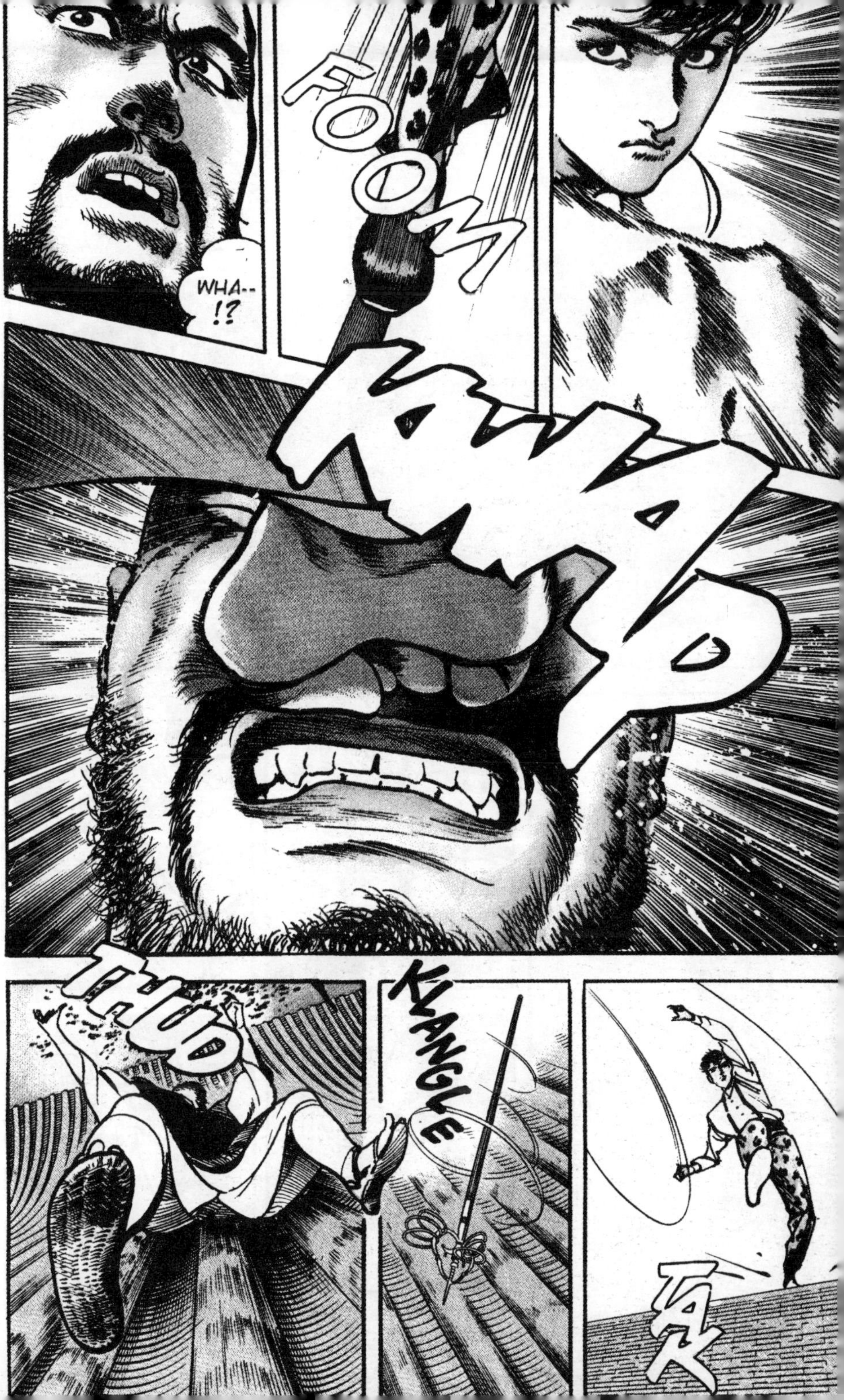
WHA-- !?
FOOM
KWAP
THUD
KLANGLE
TAK

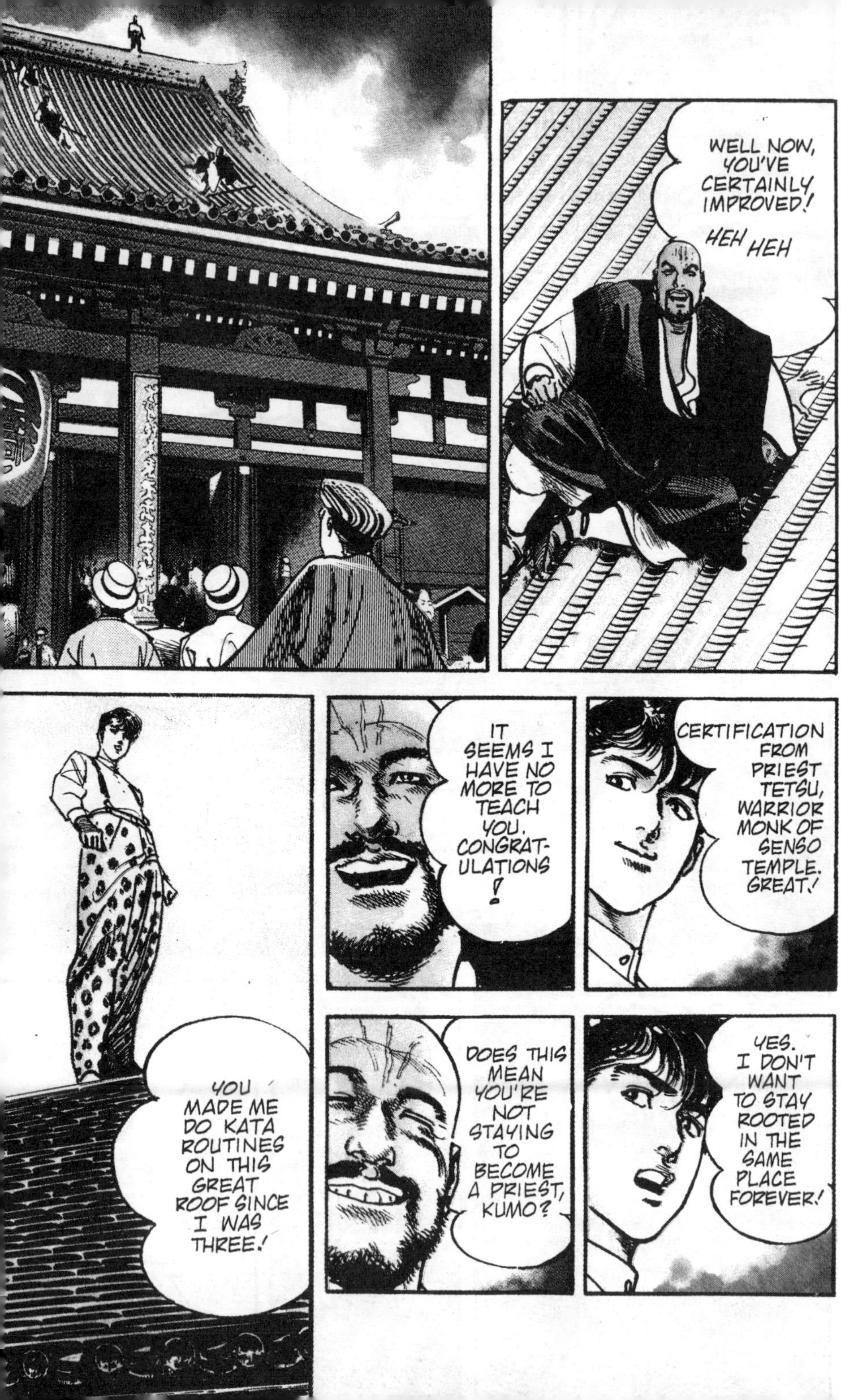

WELL NOW, YOU'VE CERTAINLY IMPROVED!
HEH HEH
YOU MADE ME DO KATA ROUTINES ON THIS GREAT ROOF SINCE I WAS THREE!
IT SEEMS I HAVE NO MORE TO TEACH YOU. CONGRATULATIONS!
CERTIFICATION FROM PRIEST TETSU, WARRIOR MONK OF SENSO TEMPLE. GREAT!
DOES THIS MEAN YOU'RE NOT STAYING TO BECOME A PRIEST, KUMO?
YES. I DON'T WANT TO STAY ROOTED IN THE SAME PLACE FOREVER!

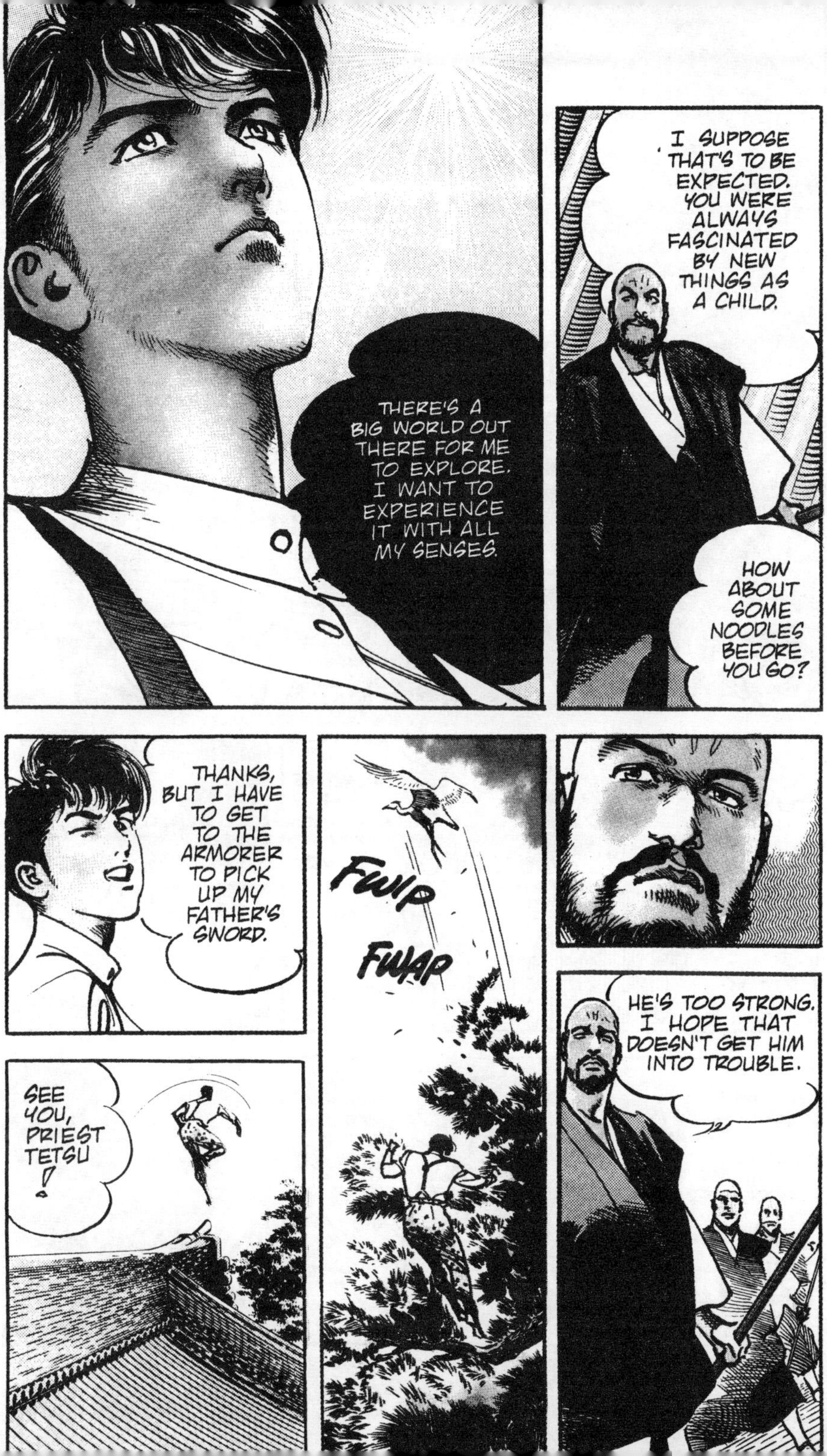
THERE'S A BIG WORLD OUT THERE FOR ME TO EXPLORE. I WANT TO EXPERIENCE IT WITH ALL MY SENSES.
I SUPPOSE THAT'S TO BE EXPECTED. YOU WERE ALWAYS FASCINATED BY NEW THINGS AS A CHILD.
HOW ABOUT SOME NOODLES BEFORE YOU GO?
THANKS, BUT I HAVE TO GET TO THE ARMORER TO PICK UP MY FATHER'S SWORD.
SEE YOU, PRIEST TETSU!
FWIP
FWAP
HE'S TOO STRONG. I HOPE THAT DOESN'T GET HIM INTO TROUBLE.

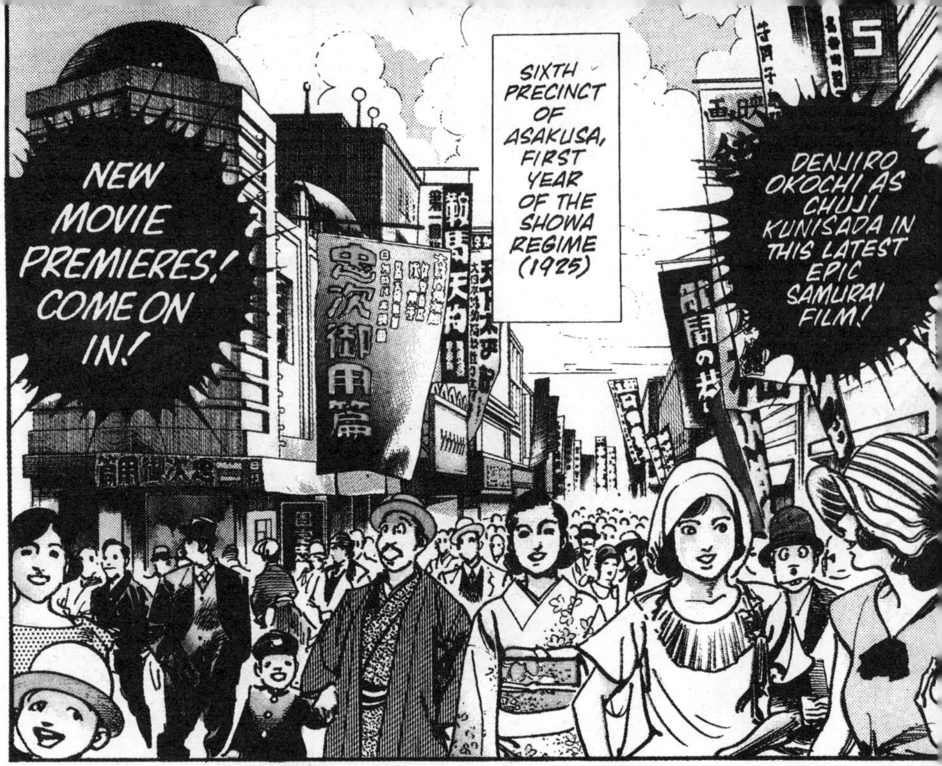
SIXTH PRECINCT OF ASAKUSA, FIRST YEAR OF THE SHOWA REGIME (1925)
NEW MOVIE PREMIERES! COME ON IN!
DENJIRO OKOCHI AS CHUJI KUNISADA IN THIS LATEST EPIC SAMURAI FILM!

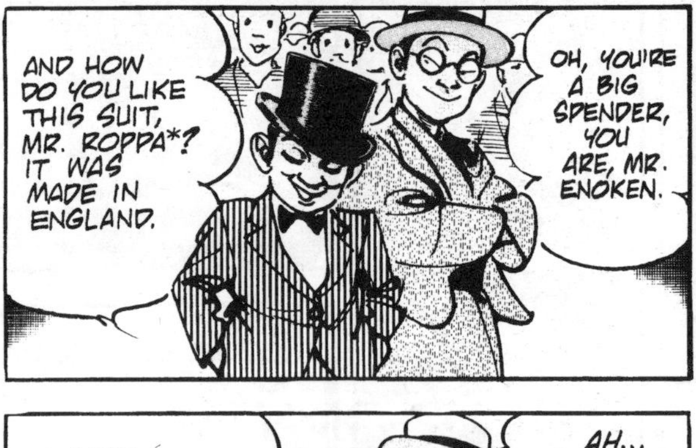
AND HOW DO YOU LIKE THIS SUIT, MR. ROPPA*? IT WAS MADE IN ENGLAND.
OH, YOU'RE A BIG SPENDER, YOU ARE, MR. ENOKEN.

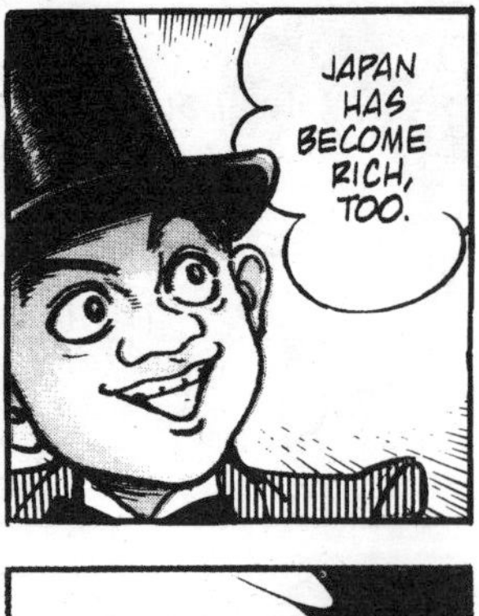
JAPAN HAS BECOME RICH, TOO.

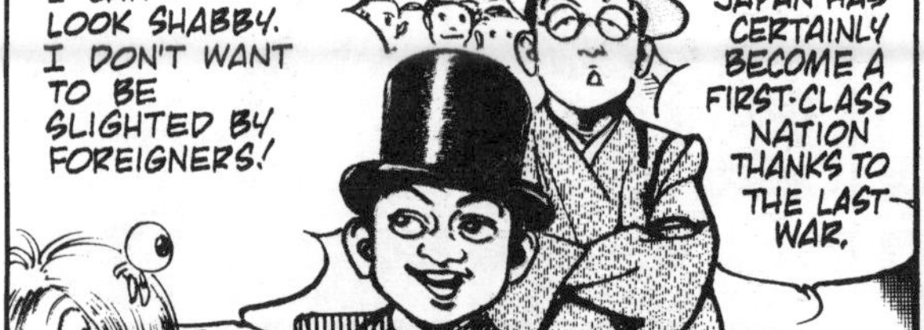
I CAN'T LOOK SHABBY. I DON'T WANT TO BE SLIGHTED BY FOREIGNERS!
AH... JAPAN HAS CERTAINLY BECOME A FIRST-CLASS NATION THANKS TO THE LAST WAR.

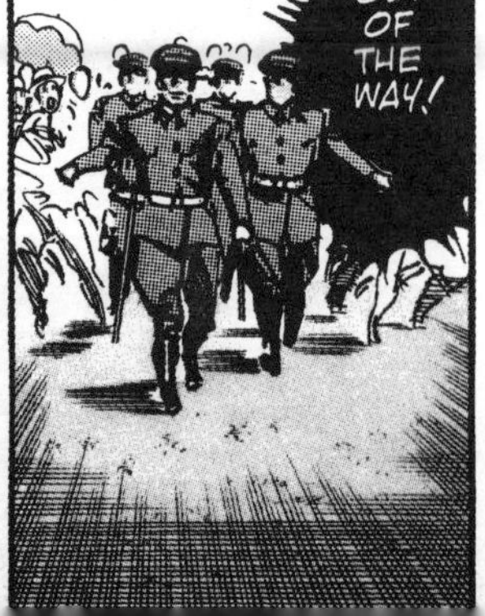
OUT OF THE WAY!

*ROPPA AND ENOKEN WERE POPULAR JAPANESE COMEDIANS IN THE '20s AND '30s.

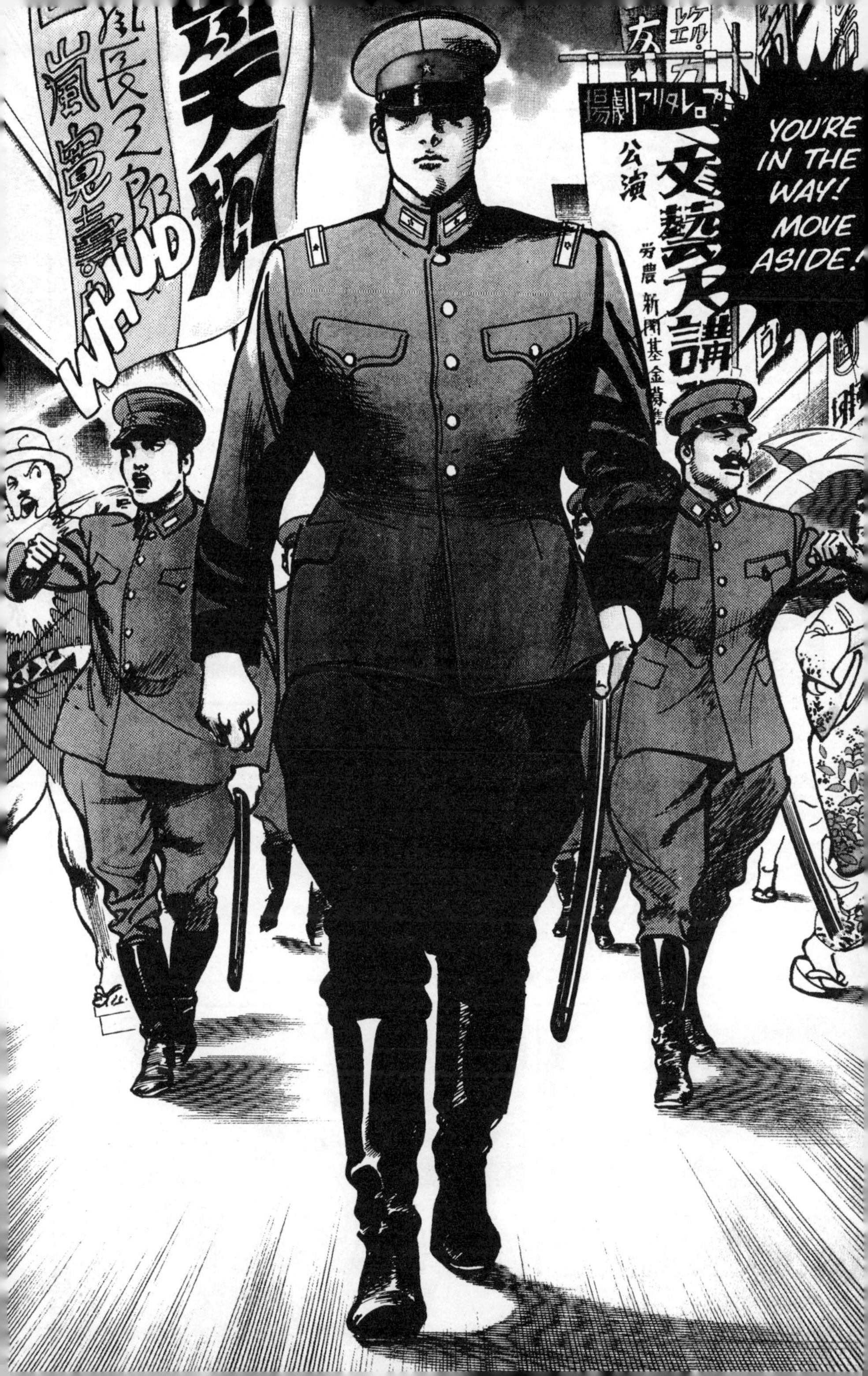
WHUD
YOU'RE IN THE WAY! MOVE ASIDE!
プロレタリア劇場
公演
労農新聞基金募集

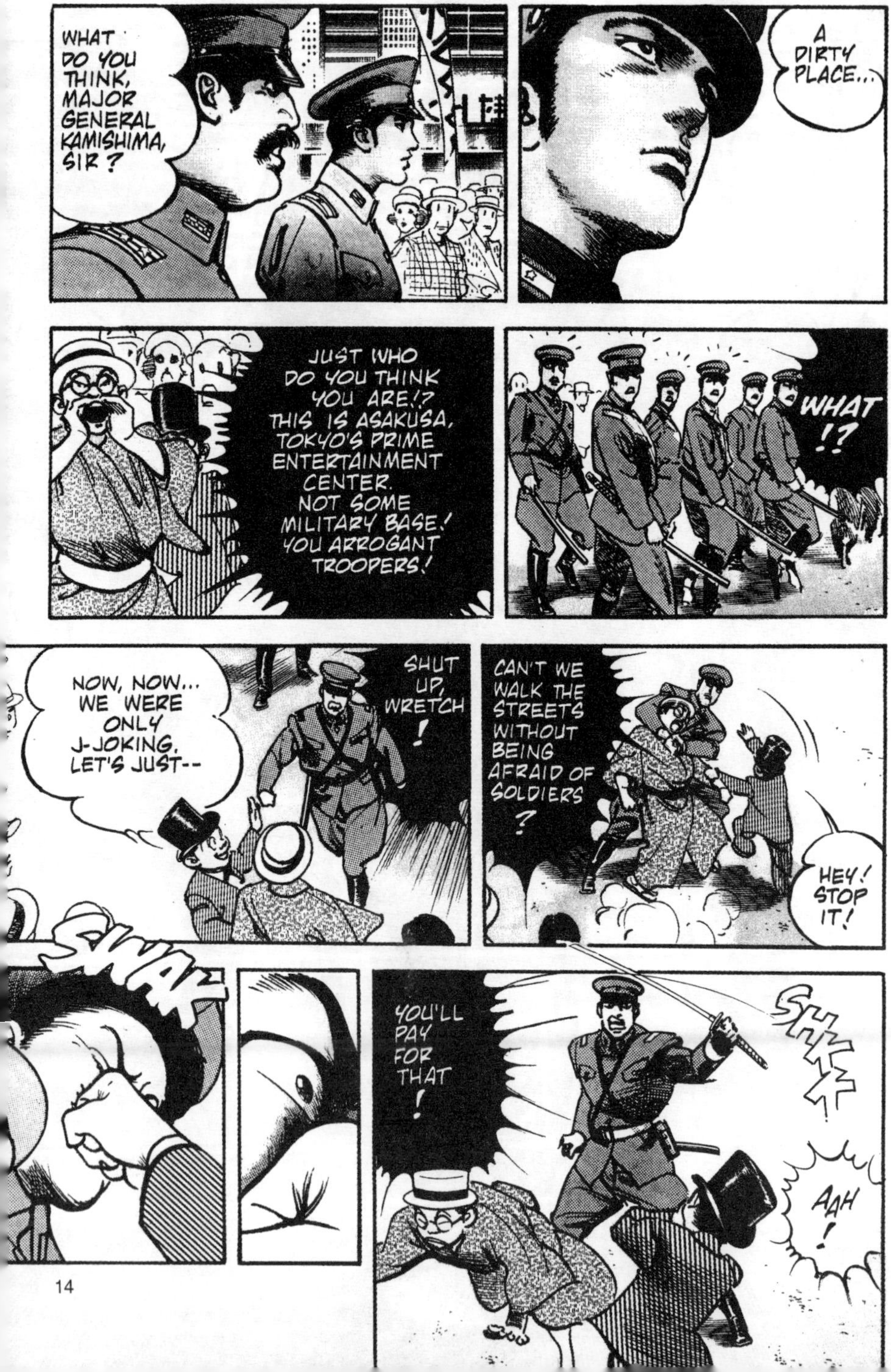
WHAT DO YOU THINK, MAJOR GENERAL KAMISHIMA, SIR?
A DIRTY PLACE...
JUST WHO DO YOU THINK YOU ARE!? THIS IS ASAKUSA, TOKYO'S PRIME ENTERTAINMENT CENTER. NOT SOME MILITARY BASE! YOU ARROGANT TROOPERS!
WHAT!?
NOW, NOW... WE WERE ONLY J-JOKING. LET'S JUST--
SHUT UP, WRETCH!
CAN'T WE WALK THE STREETS WITHOUT BEING AFRAID OF SOLDIERS?
HEY! STOP IT!
SWAK
YOU'LL PAY FOR THAT!
SHKK
AAH!

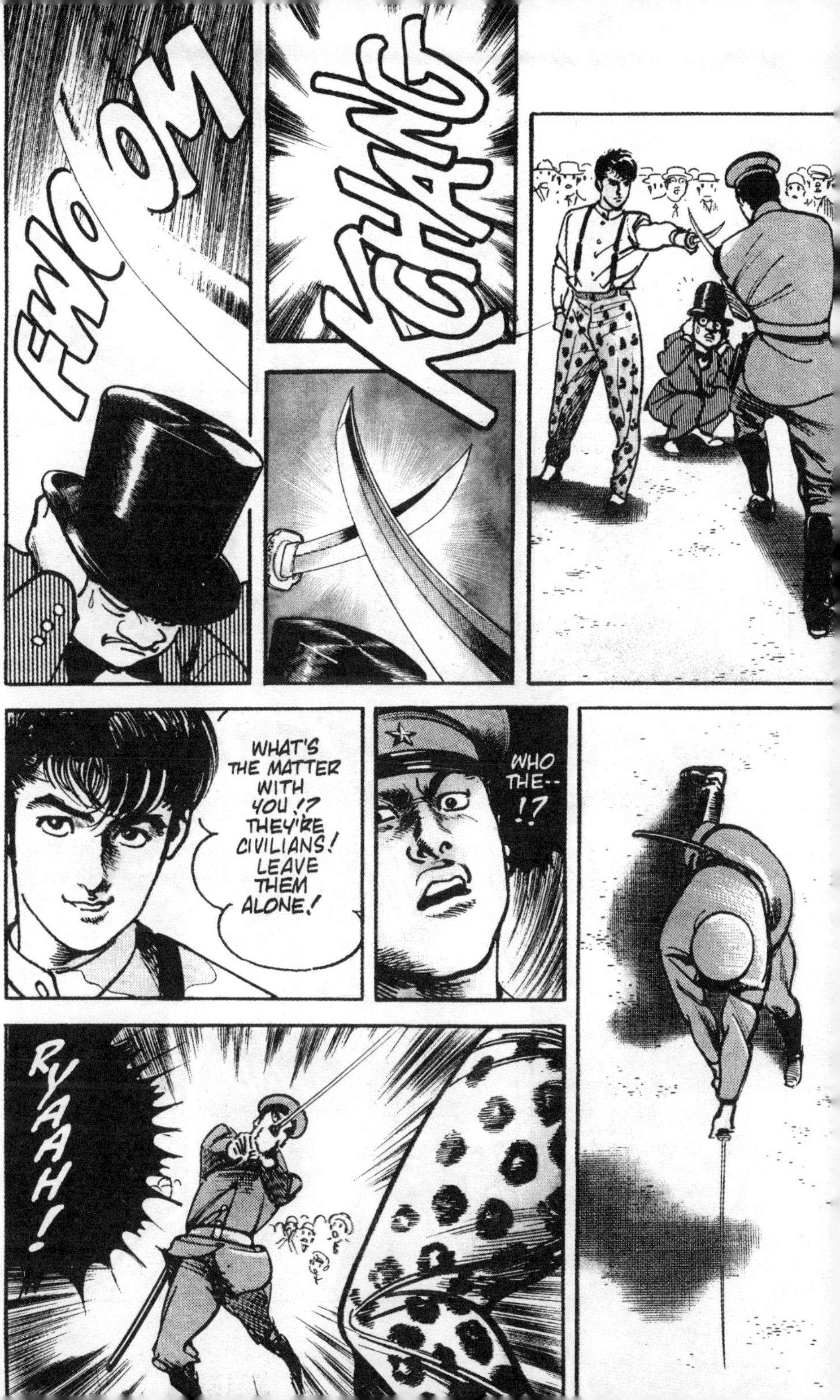
FWOOM
KCHANG
WHAT'S THE MATTER WITH YOU!? THEY'RE CIVILIANS! LEAVE THEM ALONE!
WHO THE-- !?
RYAAAH!

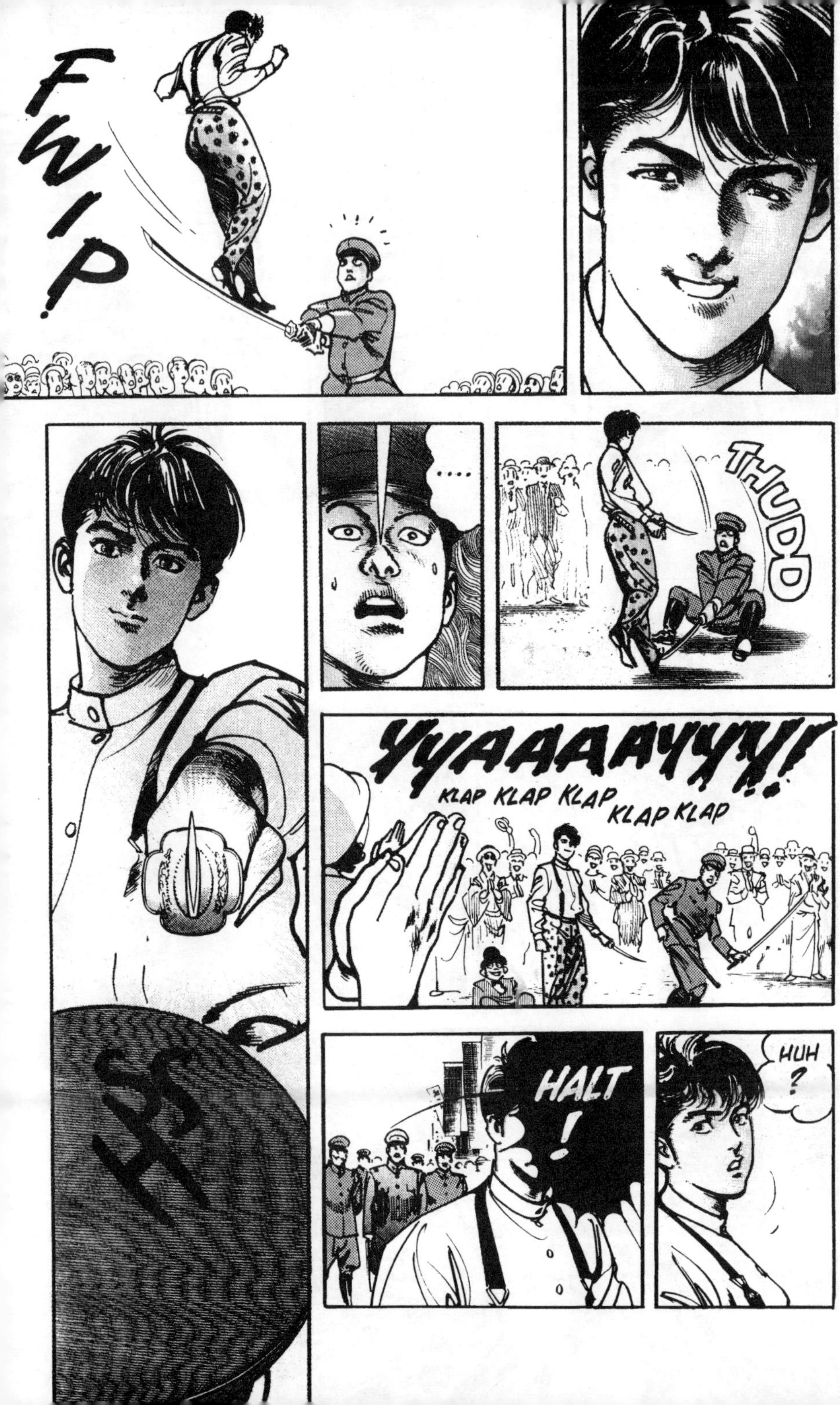
FWIP
....
THUDD
YYAAAAYYY!!
KLAP KLAP KLAP KLAP KLAP
HALT!
HUH?

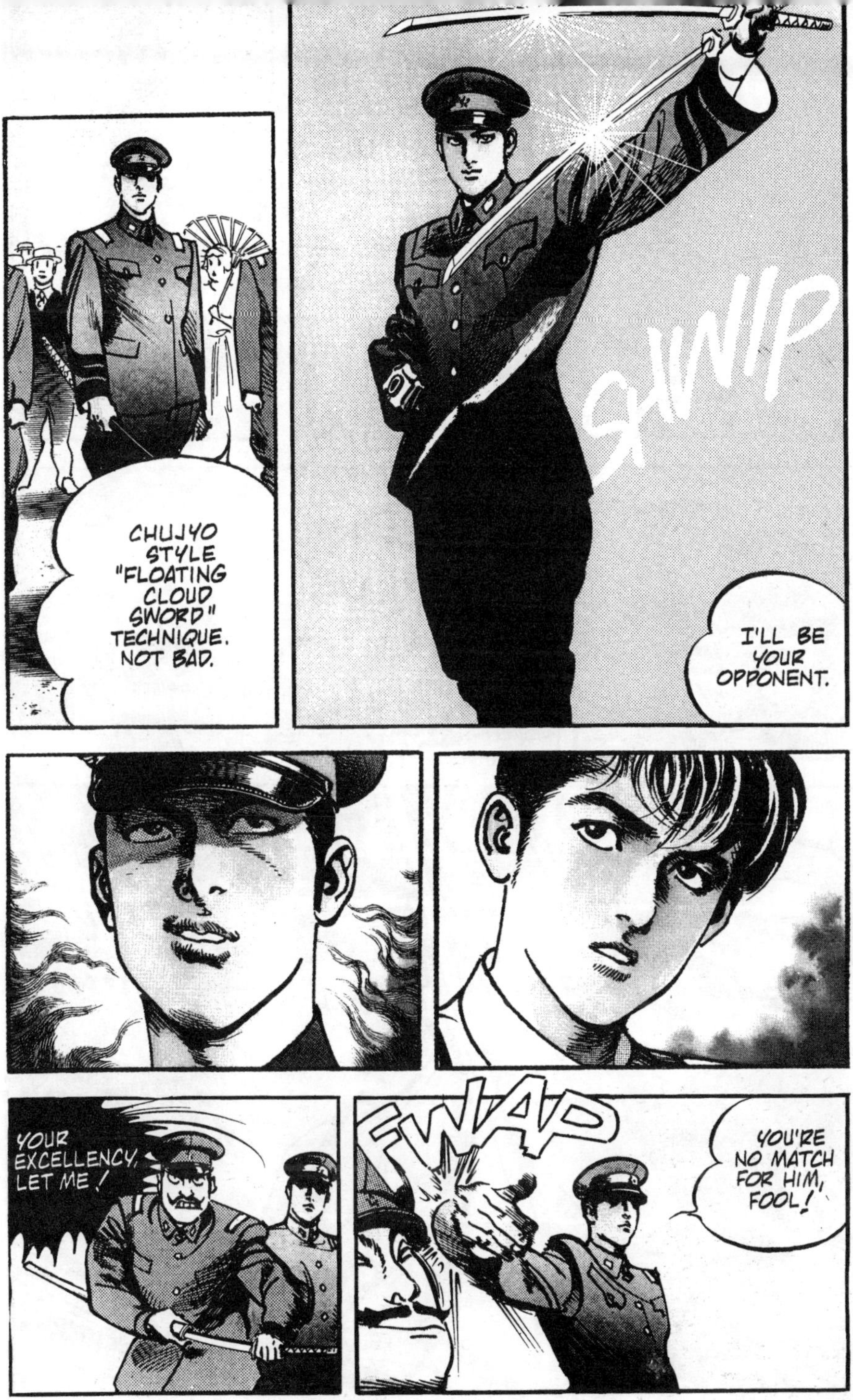
CHUJYO STYLE "FLOATING CLOUD SWORD" TECHNIQUE. NOT BAD.
SHWIP
I'LL BE YOUR OPPONENT.
YOUR EXCELLENCY, LET ME!
FWAP
YOU'RE NO MATCH FOR HIM, FOOL!

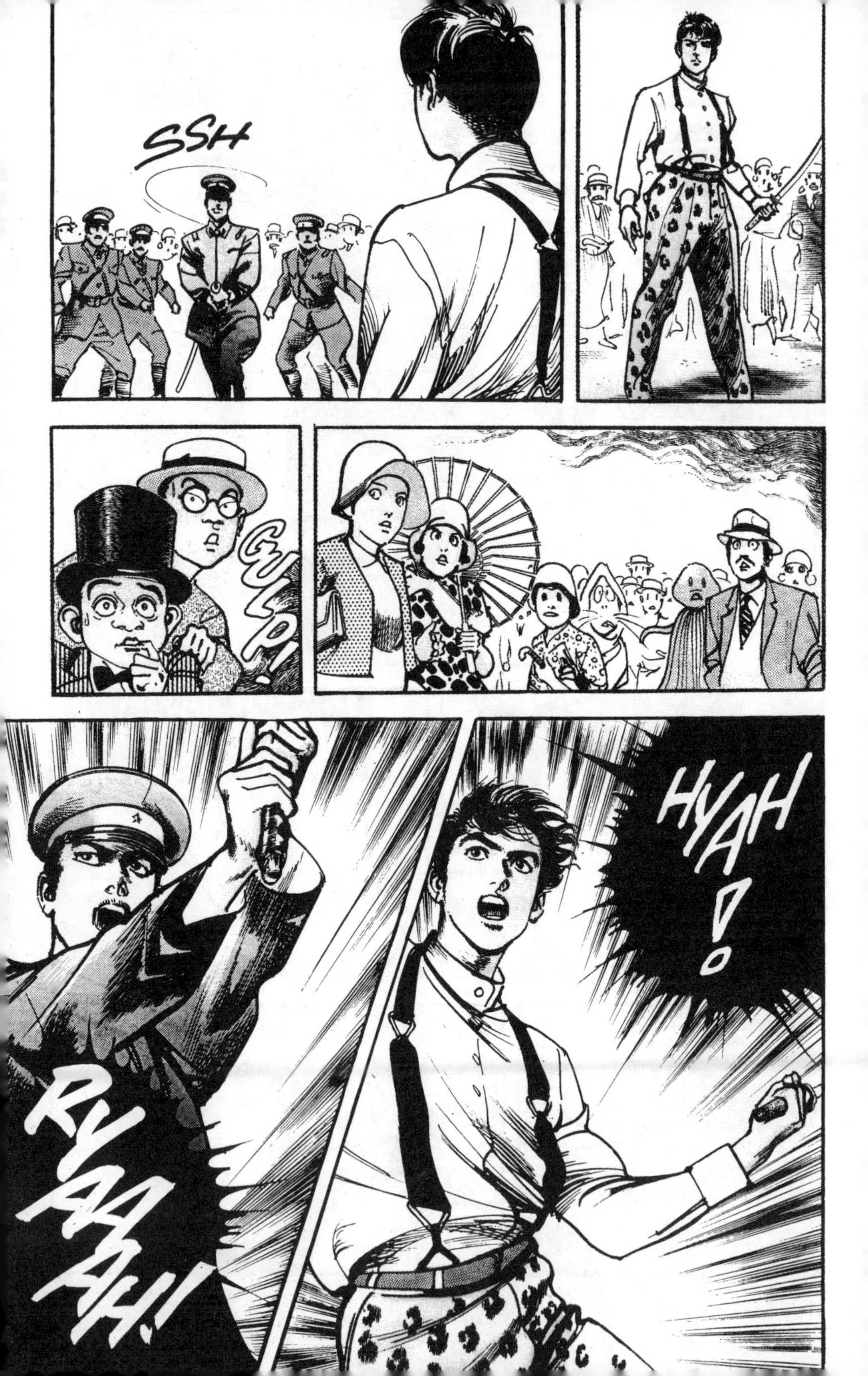
SSH
GULP!
HYAH!
RYAAAH!!

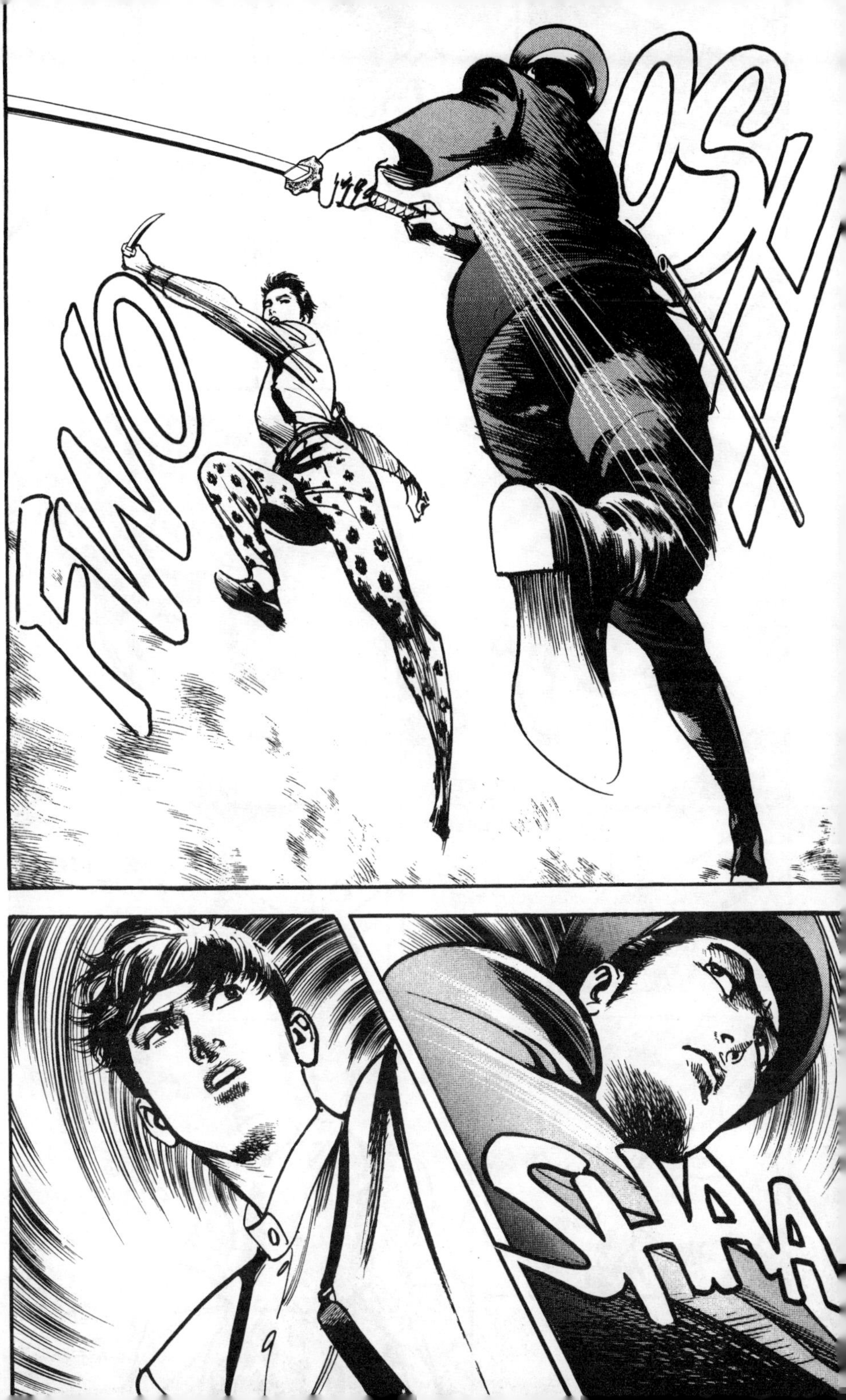
FWO
OSH
SHAA

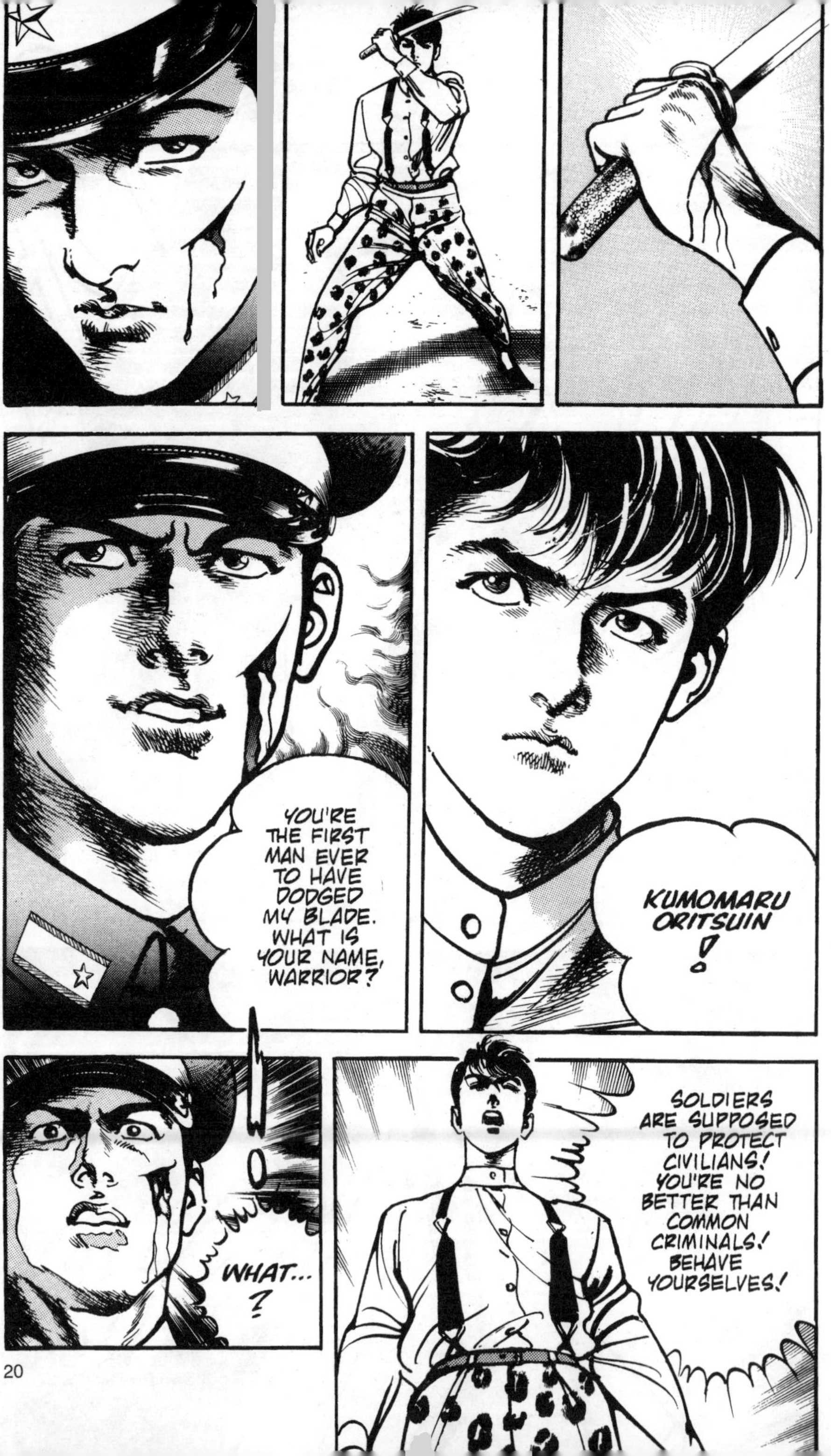
YOU'RE THE FIRST MAN EVER TO HAVE DODGED MY BLADE. WHAT IS YOUR NAME, WARRIOR?
KUMOMARU ORITSUIN!
WHAT...?
SOLDIERS ARE SUPPOSED TO PROTECT CIVILIANS! YOU'RE NO BETTER THAN COMMON CRIMINALS! BEHAVE YOURSELVES!

SILENCE, BRAT! I NEVER SHOW MERCY! EVEN TO AN ORITGUIN!

THE POLICE! THEY'RE COMING!

SIR, THE POLICE COULD BE A PROBLEM FOR US

SHUNK

YOU'RE DEATH HAS BEEN POSTPONED FOR NOW. BUT I WILL NOT FORGET YOUR NAME, KUMOMARU!

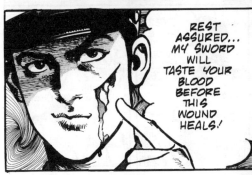

REST ASSURED... MY SWORD WILL TASTE YOUR BLOOD BEFORE THIS WOUND HEALS!

TSK! WHAT HORRIBLE SOLDIERS!

IT'S A GOOD THING THE POLICE SHOWED UP!

LAP

PHEW! THERE ARE SOME PRETTY STRONG PEOPLE IN THE WORLD!

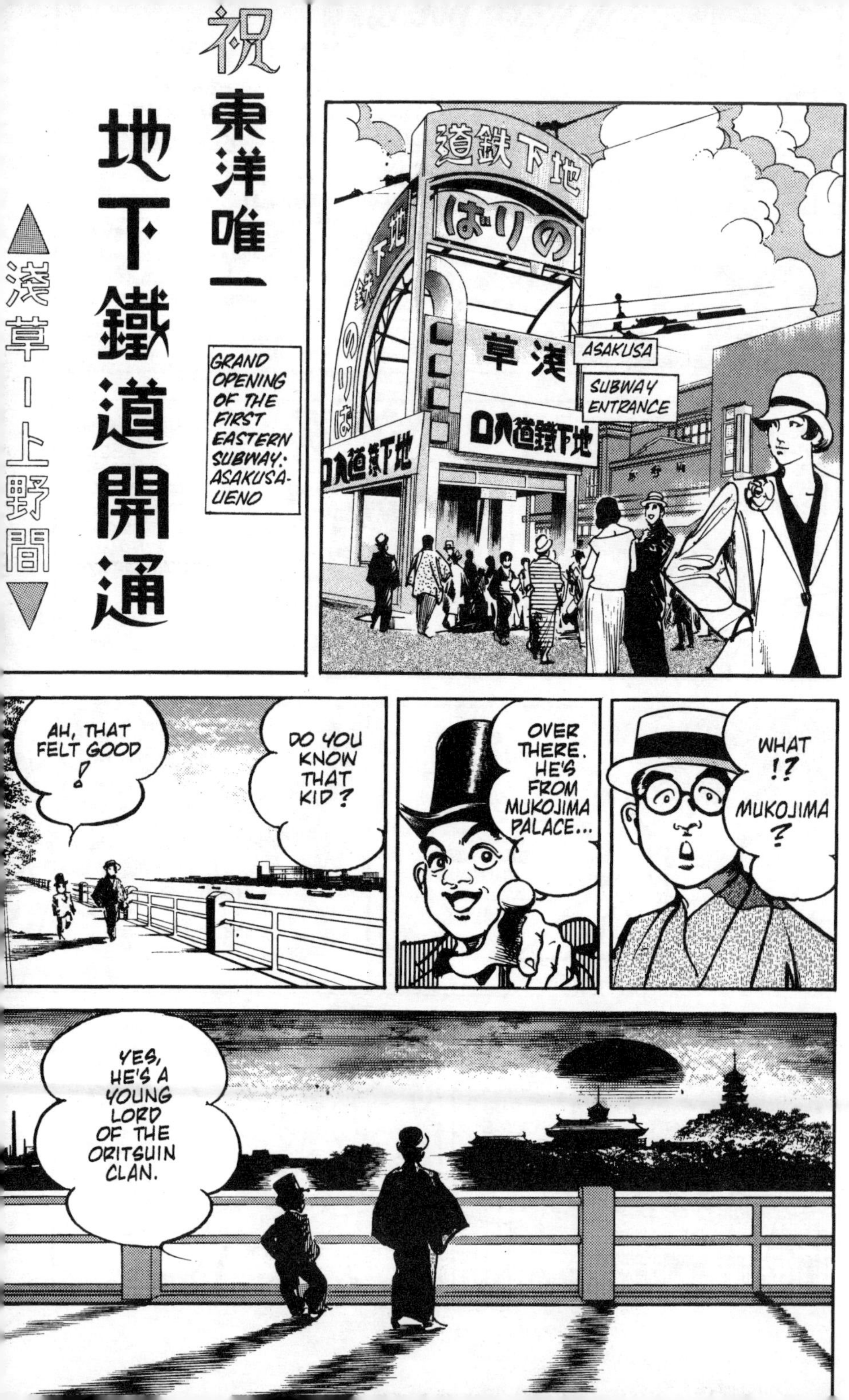
祝
東洋唯一
地下鐵道開通
▲淺草ー上野間▼
GRAND OPENING OF THE FIRST EASTERN SUBWAY: ASAKUSA-UENO
ASAKUSA
SUBWAY ENTRANCE
AH, THAT FELT GOOD!
DO YOU KNOW THAT KID?
OVER THERE. HE'S FROM MUKOJIMA PALACE...
WHAT!? MUKOJIMA?
YES, HE'S A YOUNG LORD OF THE ORITSUIN CLAN.

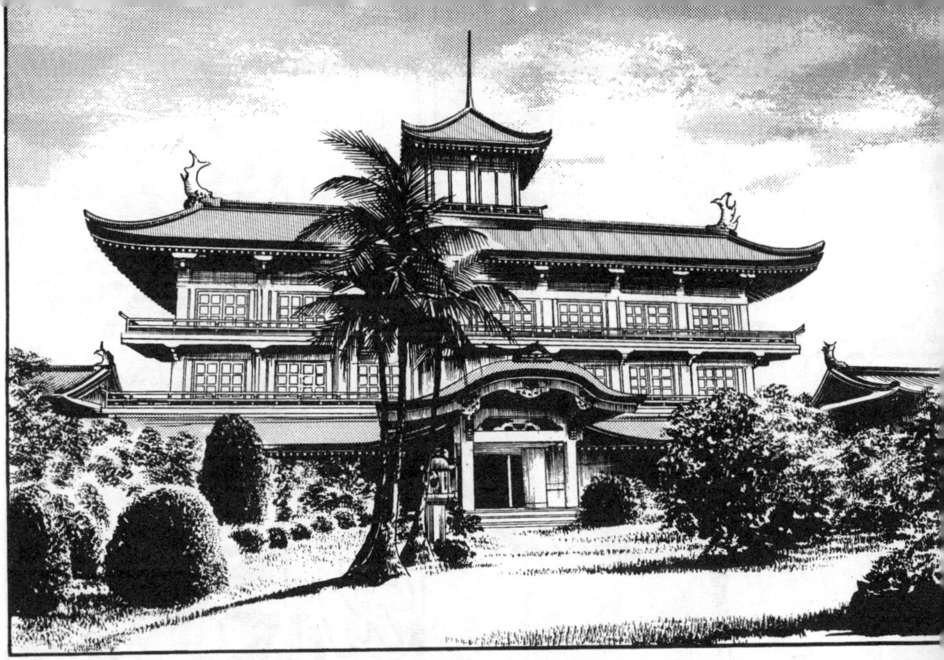

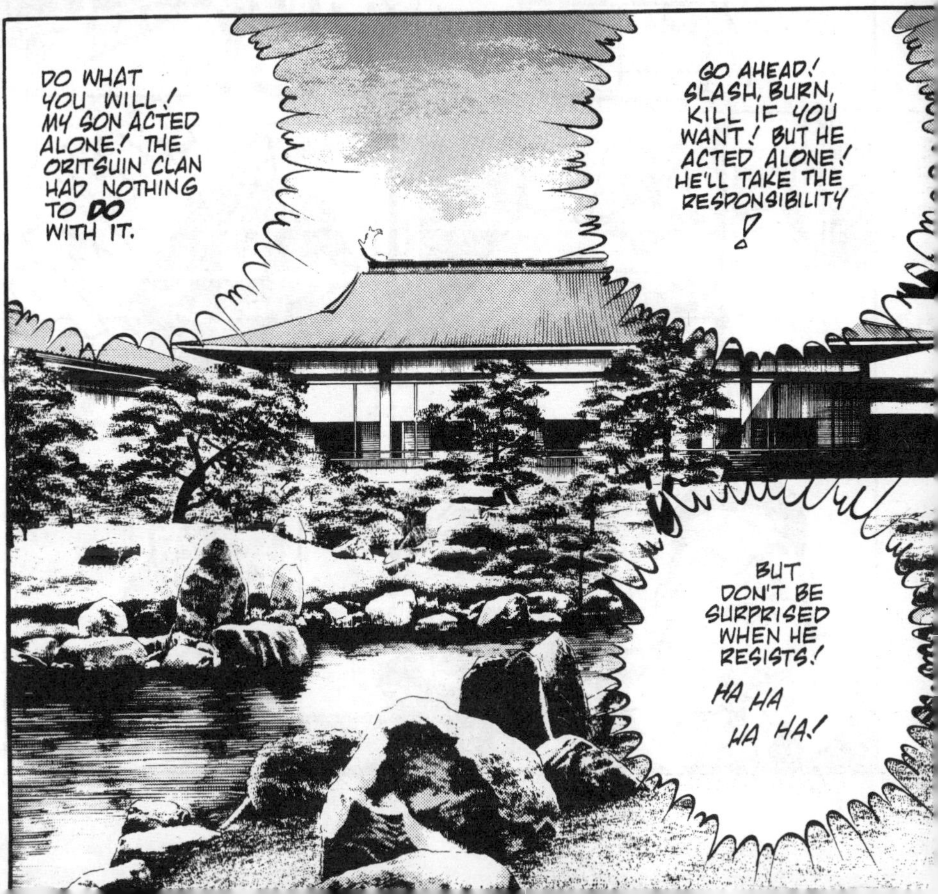
DO WHAT YOU WILL! MY SON ACTED ALONE! THE ORITSUIN CLAN HAD NOTHING TO DO WITH IT.
GO AHEAD! SLASH, BURN, KILL IF YOU WANT! BUT HE ACTED ALONE! HE'LL TAKE THE RESPONSIBILITY!
BUT DON'T BE SURPRISED WHEN HE RESISTS!
HA HA HA HA!

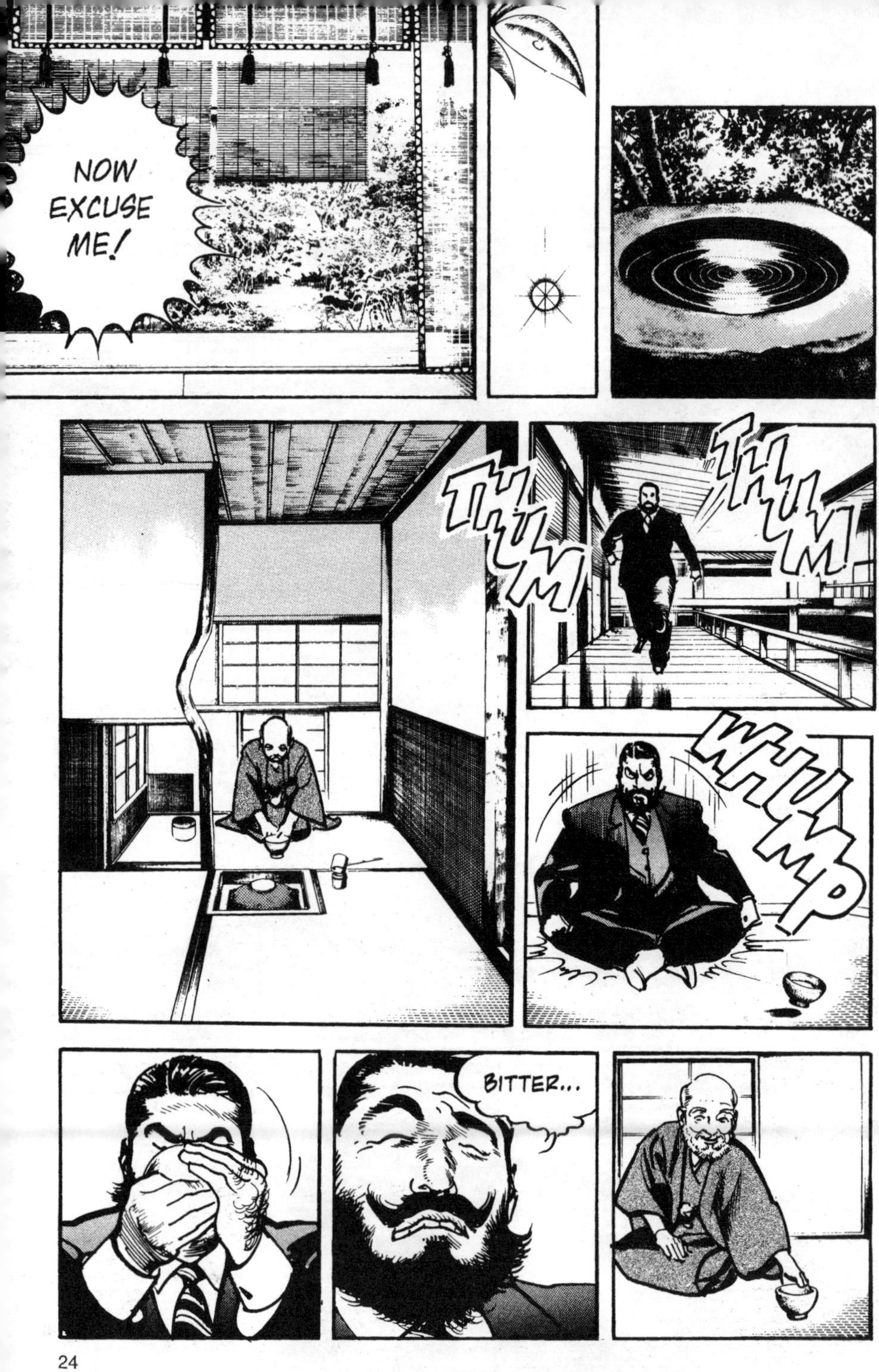
NOW EXCUSE ME!
THUM
THUM
WHUMP
BITTER...

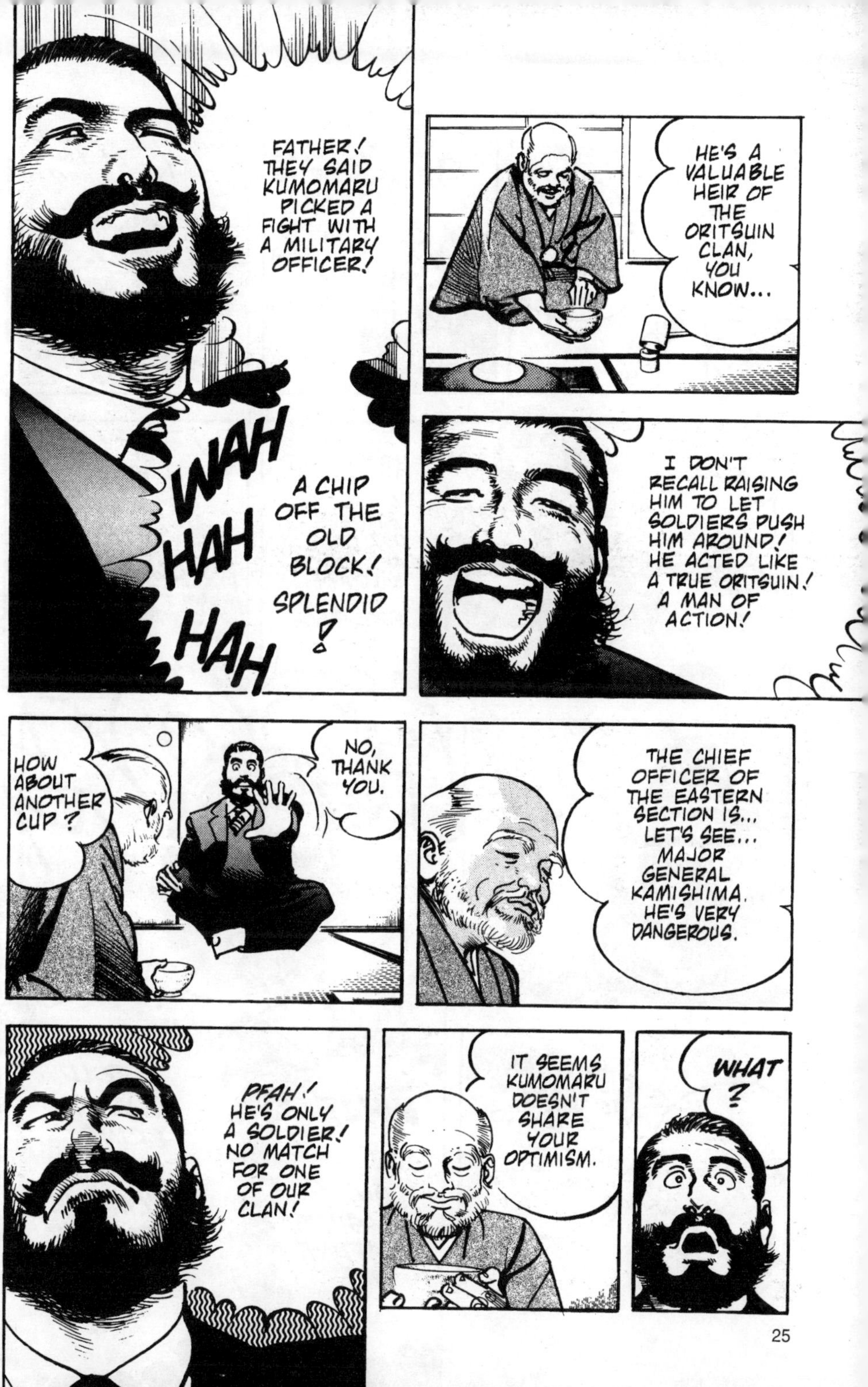
FATHER! THEY SAID KUMOMARU PICKED A FIGHT WITH A MILITARY OFFICER!
WAH HAH HAH
A CHIP OFF THE OLD BLOCK! SPLENDID!
HE'S A VALUABLE HEIR OF THE ORITSUIN CLAN, YOU KNOW...
I DON'T RECALL RAISING HIM TO LET SOLDIERS PUSH HIM AROUND! HE ACTED LIKE A TRUE ORITSUIN! A MAN OF ACTION!
HOW ABOUT ANOTHER CUP?
NO, THANK YOU.
THE CHIEF OFFICER OF THE EASTERN SECTION IS... LET'S SEE... MAJOR GENERAL KAMISHIMA. HE'S VERY DANGEROUS.
PFAH! HE'S ONLY A SOLDIER! NO MATCH FOR ONE OF OUR CLAN!
IT SEEMS KUMOMARU DOESN'T SHARE YOUR OPTIMISM.
WHAT?

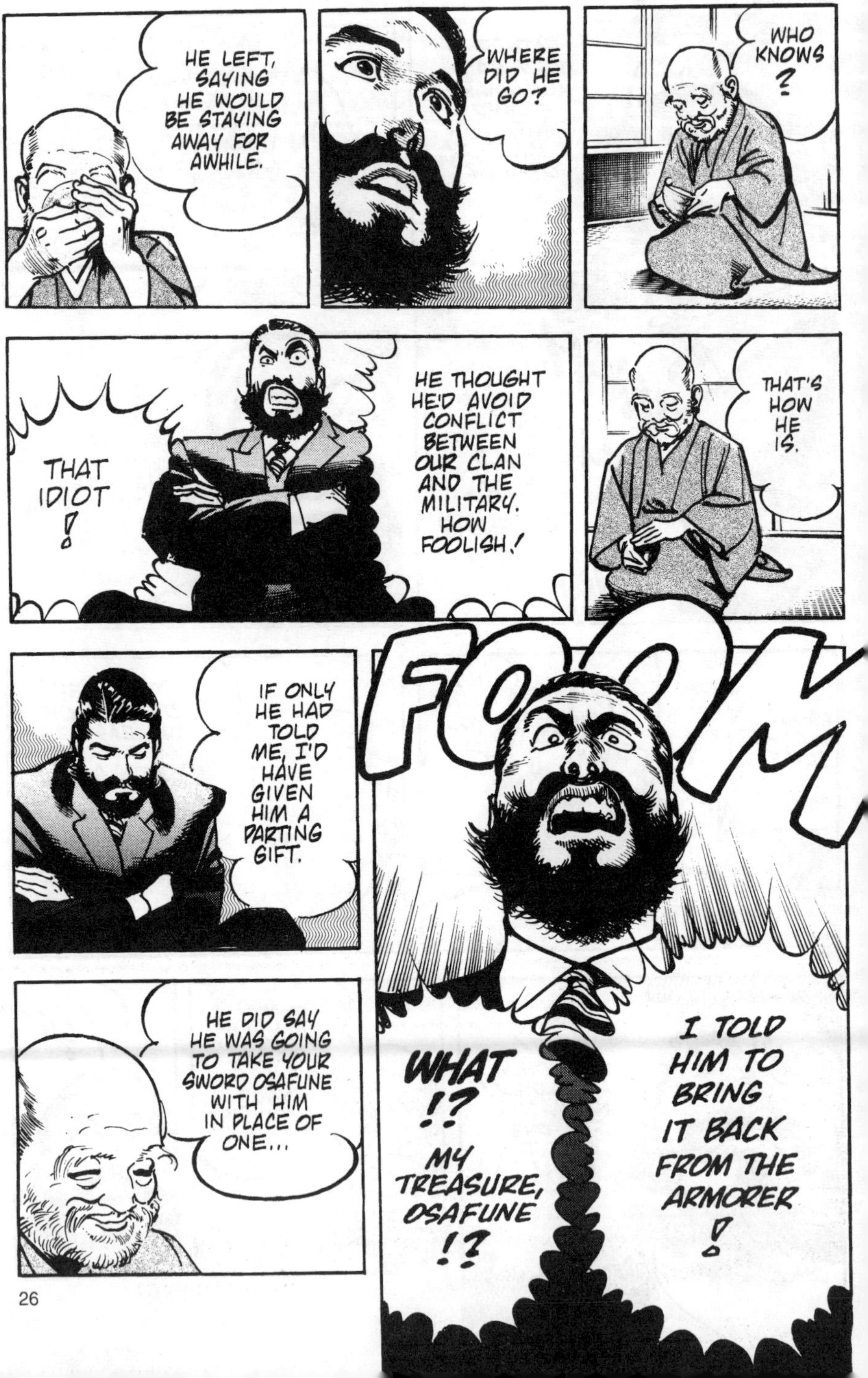
HE LEFT, SAYING HE WOULD BE STAYING AWAY FOR AWHILE.
WHERE DID HE GO?
WHO KNOWS?
THAT IDIOT!
HE THOUGHT HE'D AVOID CONFLICT BETWEEN OUR CLAN AND THE MILITARY. HOW FOOLISH!
THAT'S HOW HE IS.
IF ONLY HE HAD TOLD ME, I'D HAVE GIVEN HIM A PARTING GIFT.
FOOM
HE DID SAY HE WAS GOING TO TAKE YOUR SWORD OSAFUNE WITH HIM IN PLACE OF ONE...
WHAT!? MY TREASURE, OSAFUNE!?
I TOLD HIM TO BRING IT BACK FROM THE ARMORER!

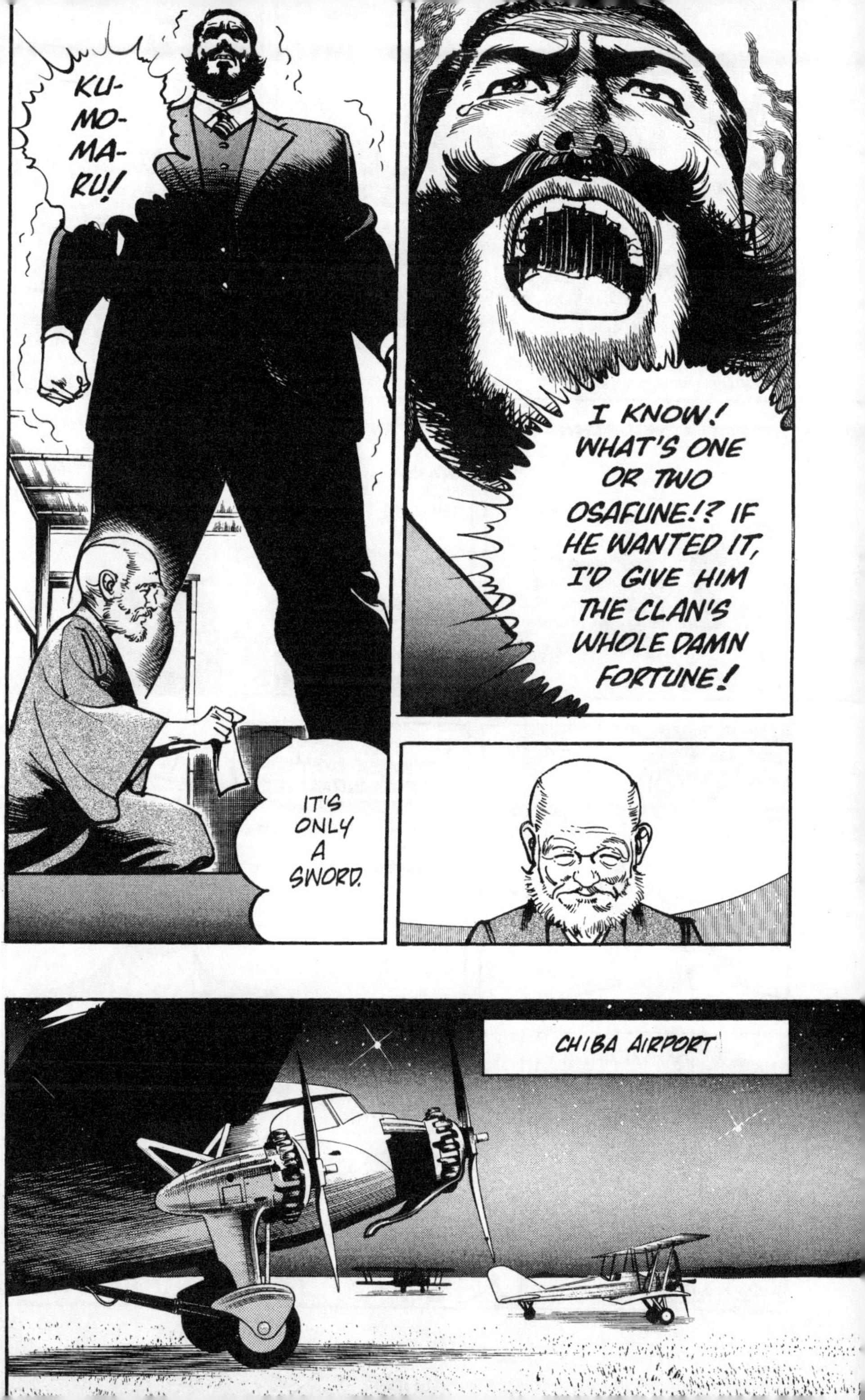
KU-MO-MA-RU!
IT'S ONLY A SWORD.
I KNOW! WHAT'S ONE OR TWO OSAFUNE!? IF HE WANTED IT, I'D GIVE HIM THE CLAN'S WHOLE DAMN FORTUNE!
CHIBA AIRPORT

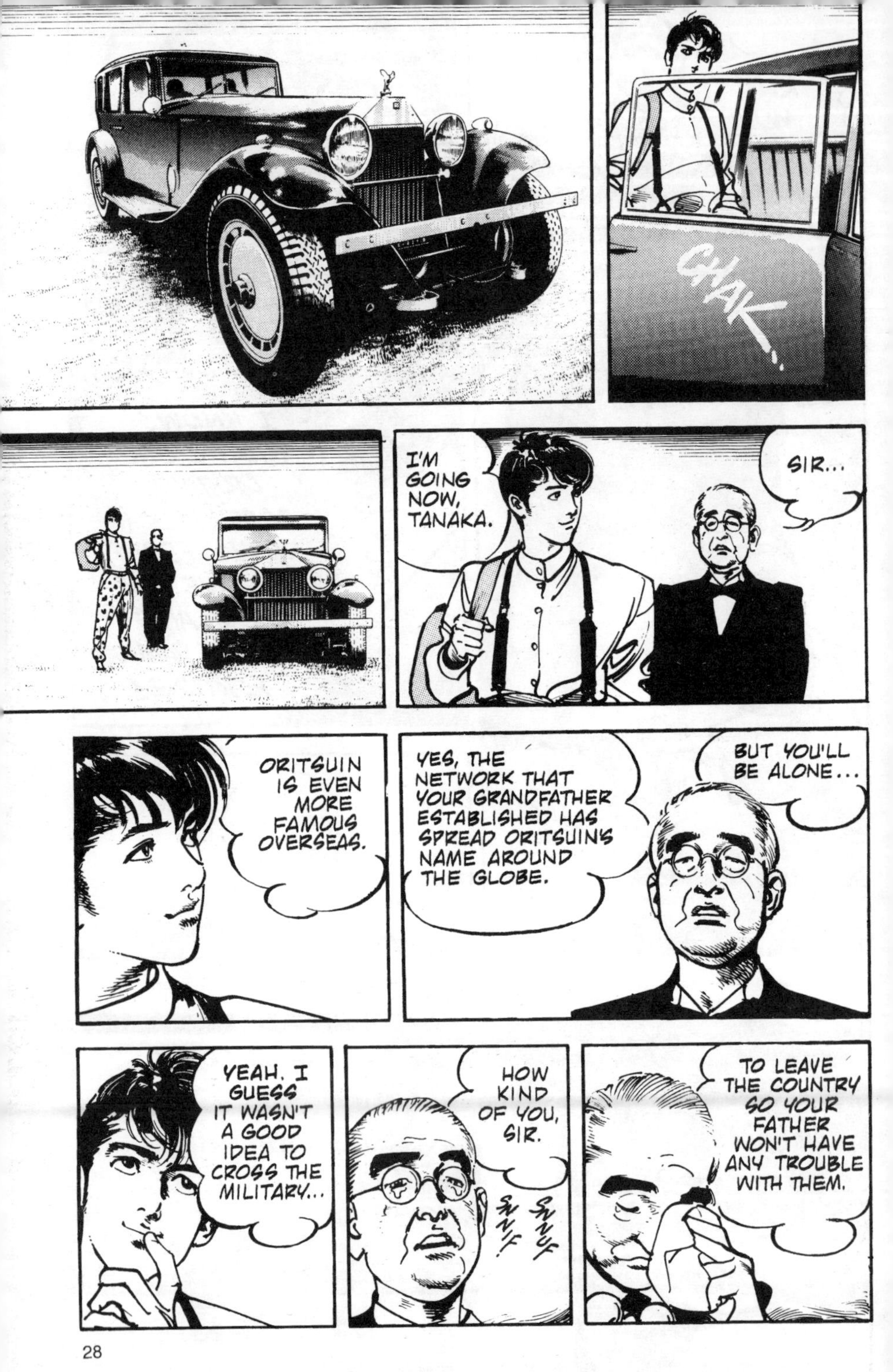
CHAK
I'M GOING NOW, TANAKA.
SIR...
ORITSUIN IS EVEN MORE FAMOUS OVERSEAS.
YES, THE NETWORK THAT YOUR GRANDFATHER ESTABLISHED HAS SPREAD ORITSUIN'S NAME AROUND THE GLOBE.
BUT YOU'LL BE ALONE...
YEAH. I GUESS IT WASN'T A GOOD IDEA TO CROSS THE MILITARY...
HOW KIND OF YOU, SIR.
SNNUF
SNNIF!
TO LEAVE THE COUNTRY SO YOUR FATHER WON'T HAVE ANY TROUBLE WITH THEM.

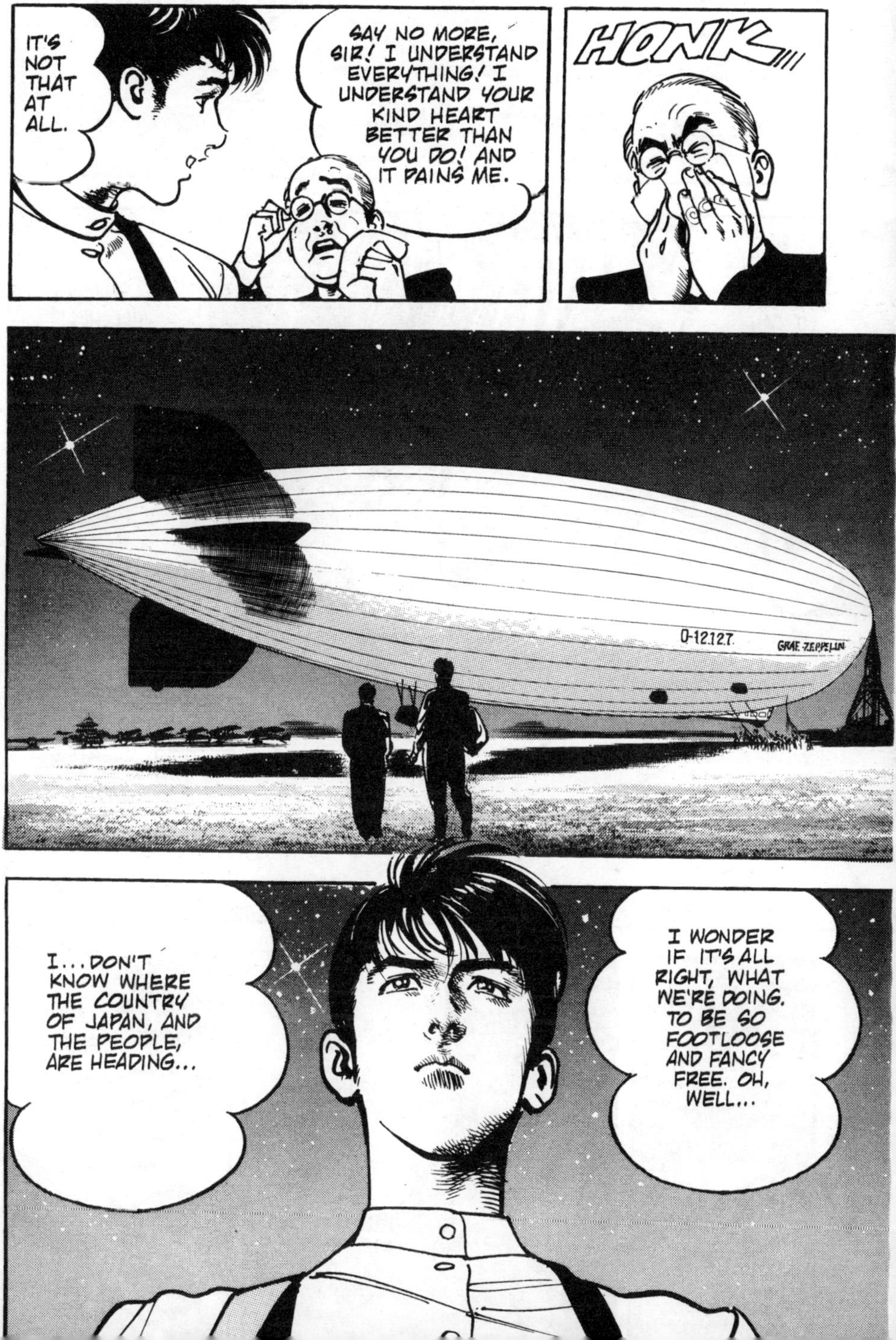
IT'S NOT THAT AT ALL.
SAY NO MORE, SIR! I UNDERSTAND EVERYTHING! I UNDERSTAND YOUR KIND HEART BETTER THAN YOU DO! AND IT PAINS ME.
HONK
D-12127.
GRAF ZEPPELIN
I...DON'T KNOW WHERE THE COUNTRY OF JAPAN, AND THE PEOPLE, ARE HEADING...
I WONDER IF IT'S ALL RIGHT, WHAT WE'RE DOING. TO BE SO FOOTLOOSE AND FANCY FREE. OH, WELL...

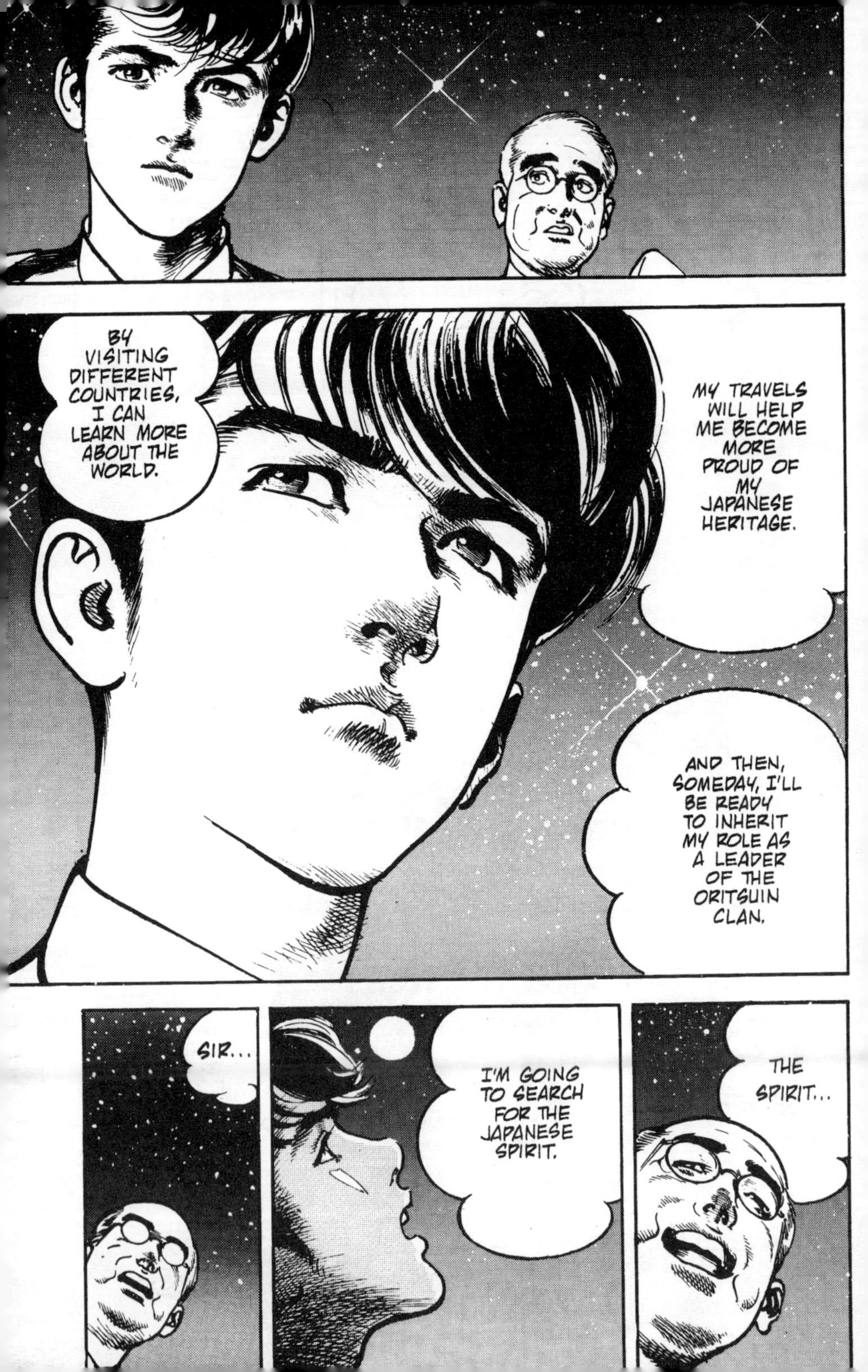
BY VISITING DIFFERENT COUNTRIES, I CAN LEARN MORE ABOUT THE WORLD.
MY TRAVELS WILL HELP ME BECOME MORE PROUD OF MY JAPANESE HERITAGE.
AND THEN, SOMEDAY, I'LL BE READY TO INHERIT MY ROLE AS A LEADER OF THE ORITSUIN CLAN.
SIR...
I'M GOING TO SEARCH FOR THE JAPANESE SPIRIT.
THE SPIRIT...

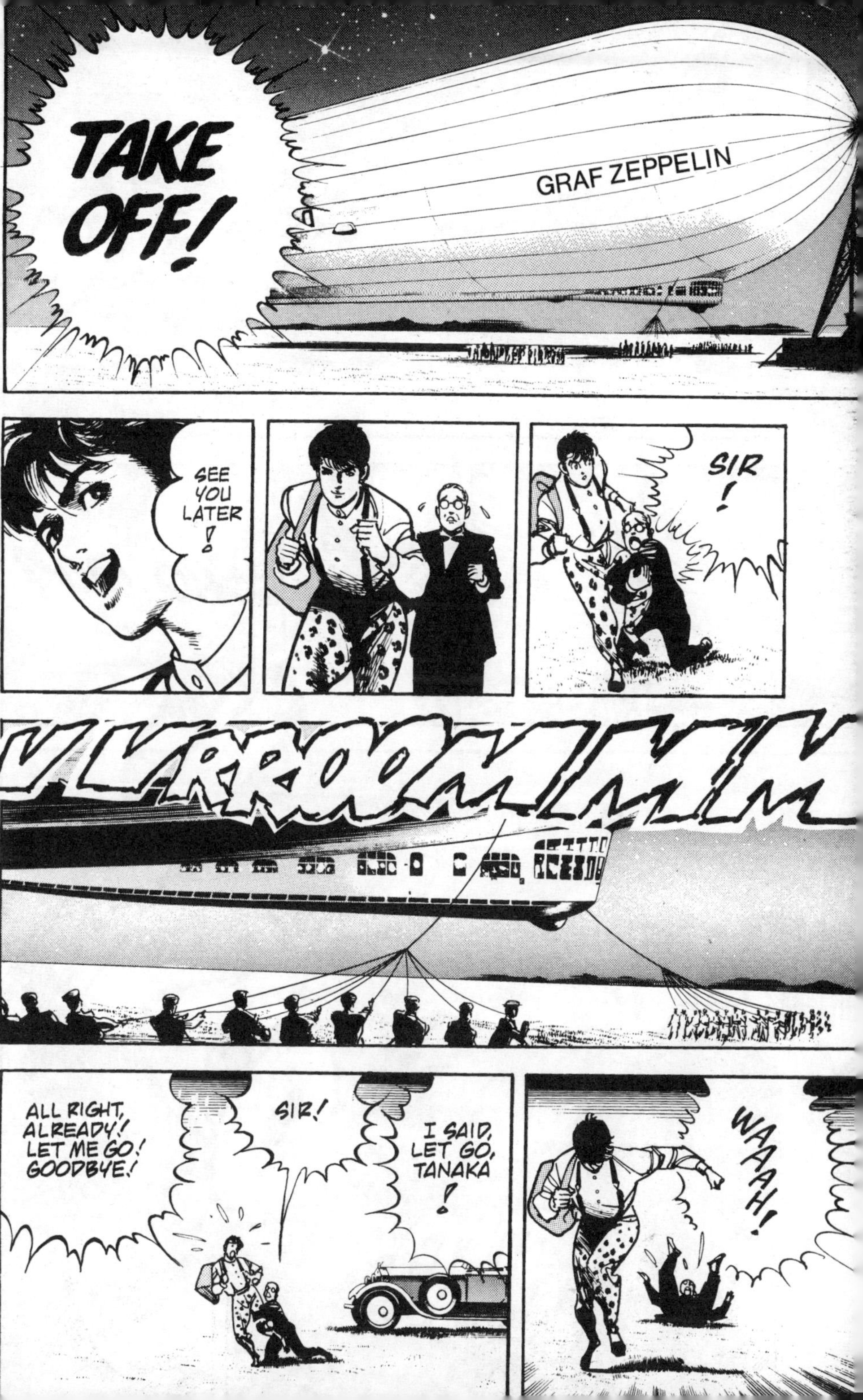
TAKE OFF!
GRAF ZEPPELIN
SEE YOU LATER!
SIR!
VVROOMMMM
ALL RIGHT, ALREADY! LET ME GO! GOODBYE!
SIR!
I SAID, LET GO, TANAKA!
WAAAH!

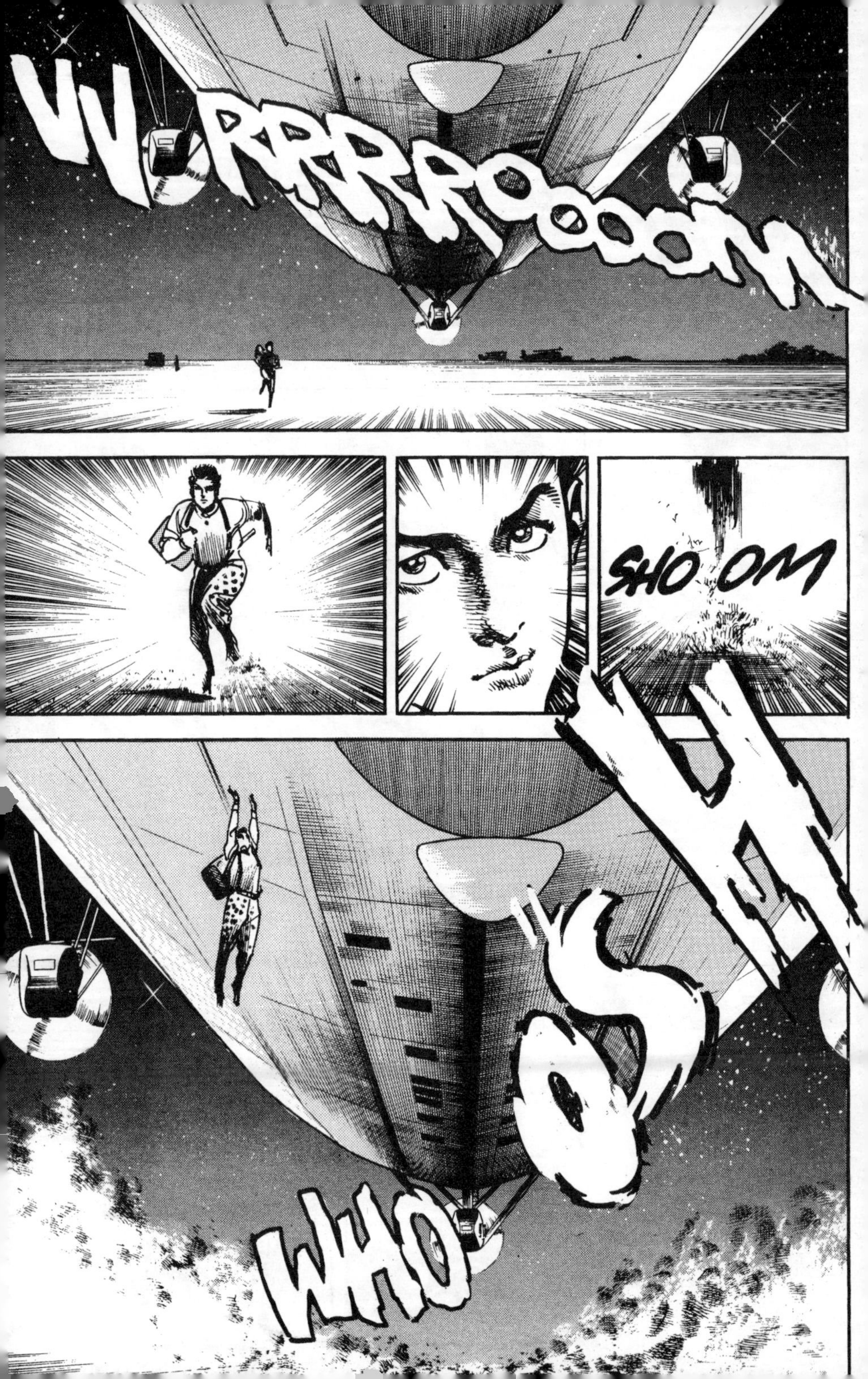
VVRRRROOOOM
SHOOM
WHOOSH

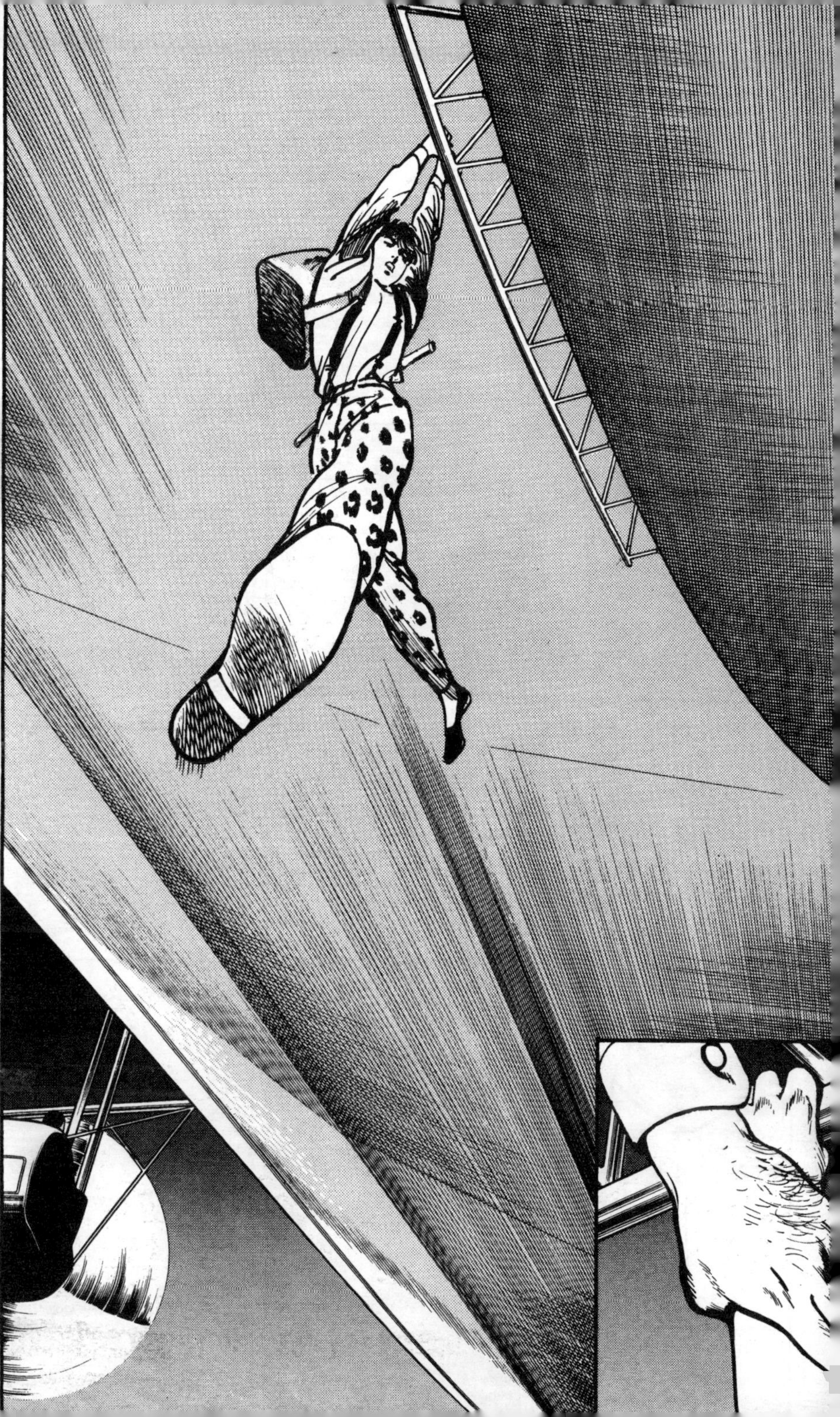

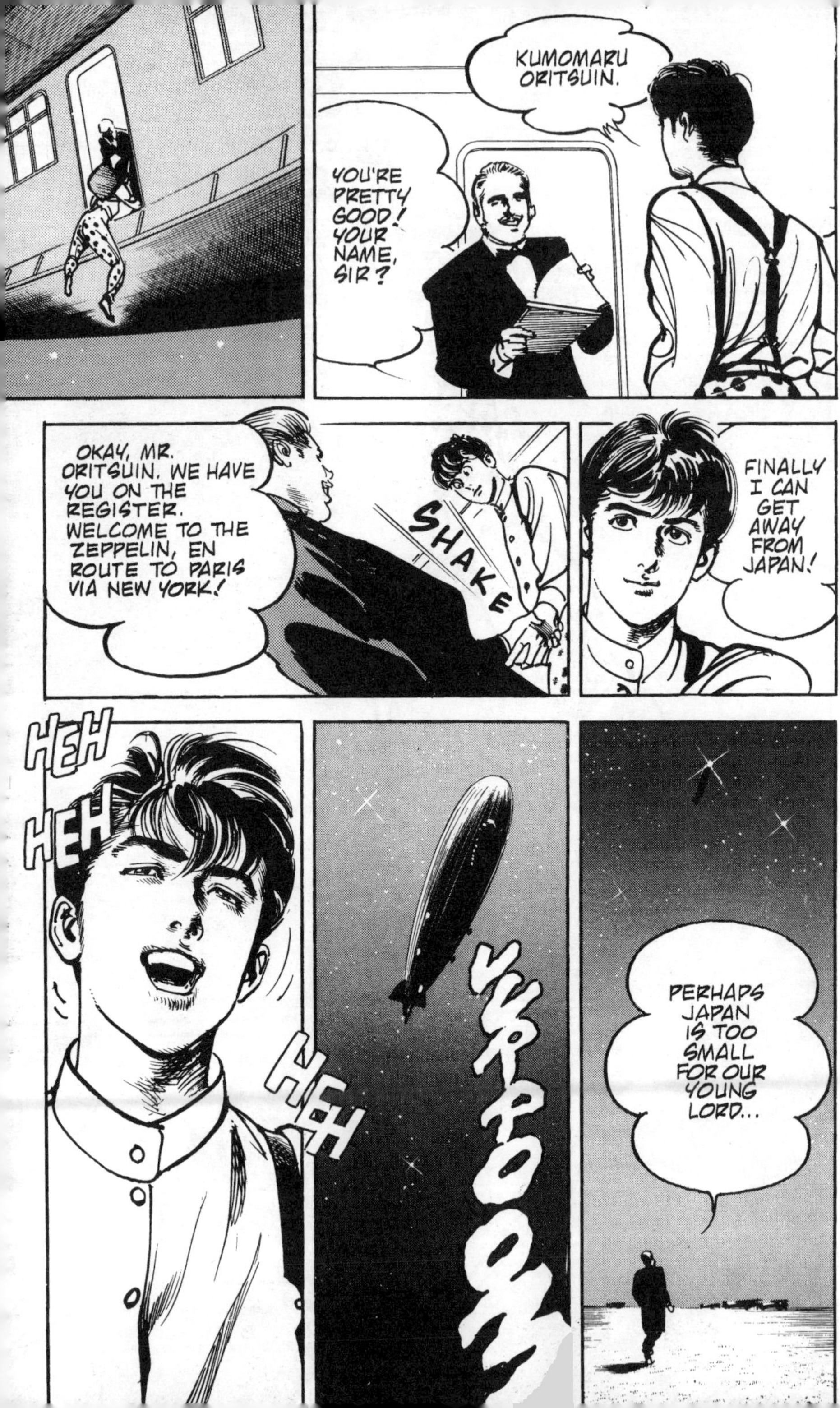
YOU'RE PRETTY GOOD! YOUR NAME, SIR?
KUMOMARU ORITSUIN.
OKAY, MR. ORITSUIN. WE HAVE YOU ON THE REGISTER. WELCOME TO THE ZEPPELIN, EN ROUTE TO PARIS VIA NEW YORK!
SHAKE
FINALLY I CAN GET AWAY FROM JAPAN!
HEH HEH
HEH HEH
VVROOOM
PERHAPS JAPAN IS TOO SMALL FOR OUR YOUNG LORD...

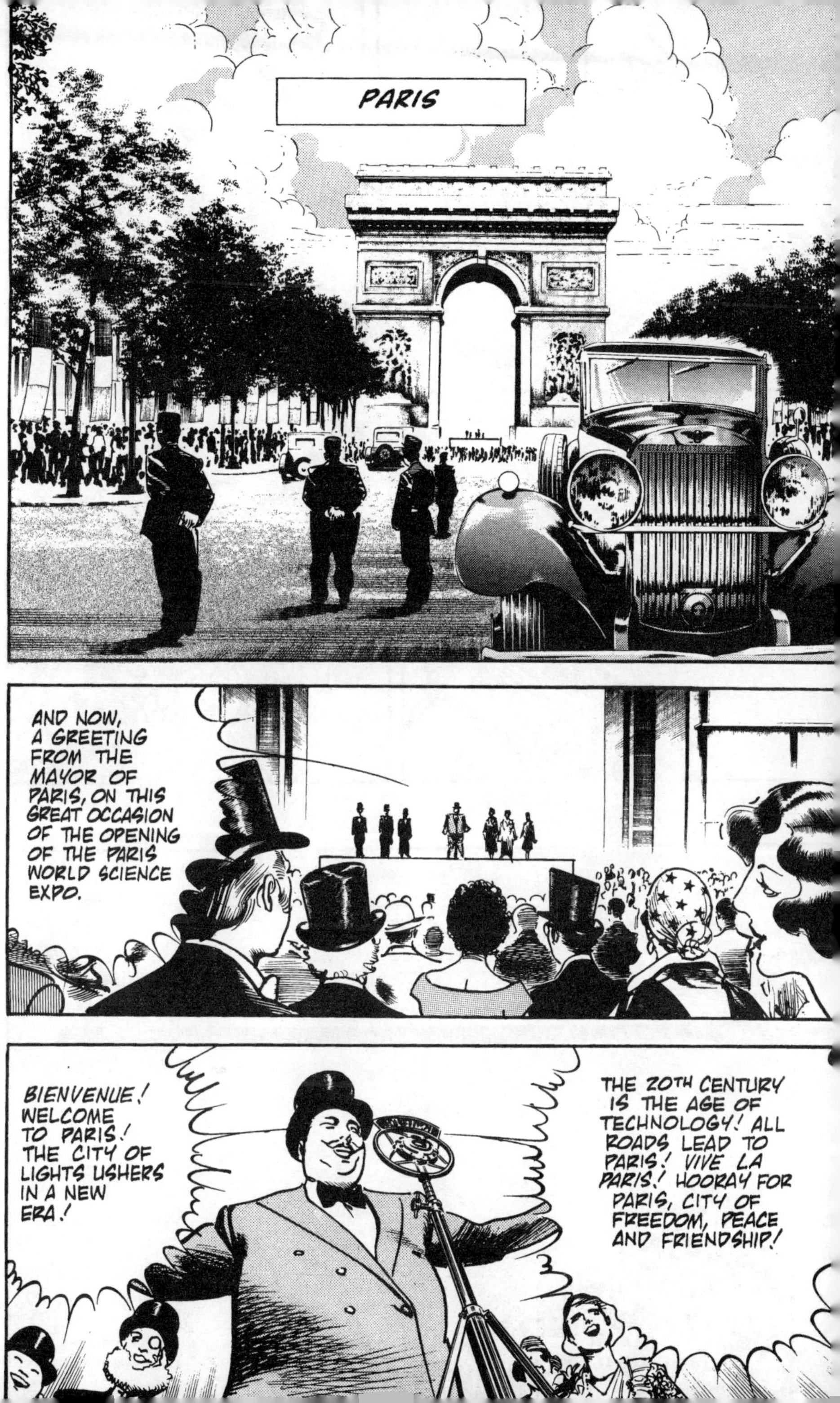
PARIS
AND NOW, A GREETING FROM THE MAYOR OF PARIS, ON THIS GREAT OCCASION OF THE OPENING OF THE PARIS WORLD SCIENCE EXPO.
BIENVENUE! WELCOME TO PARIS! THE CITY OF LIGHTS USHERS IN A NEW ERA!
THE 20TH CENTURY IS THE AGE OF TECHNOLOGY! ALL ROADS LEAD TO PARIS! VIVE LA PARIS! HOORAY FOR PARIS, CITY OF FREEDOM, PEACE AND FRIENDSHIP!

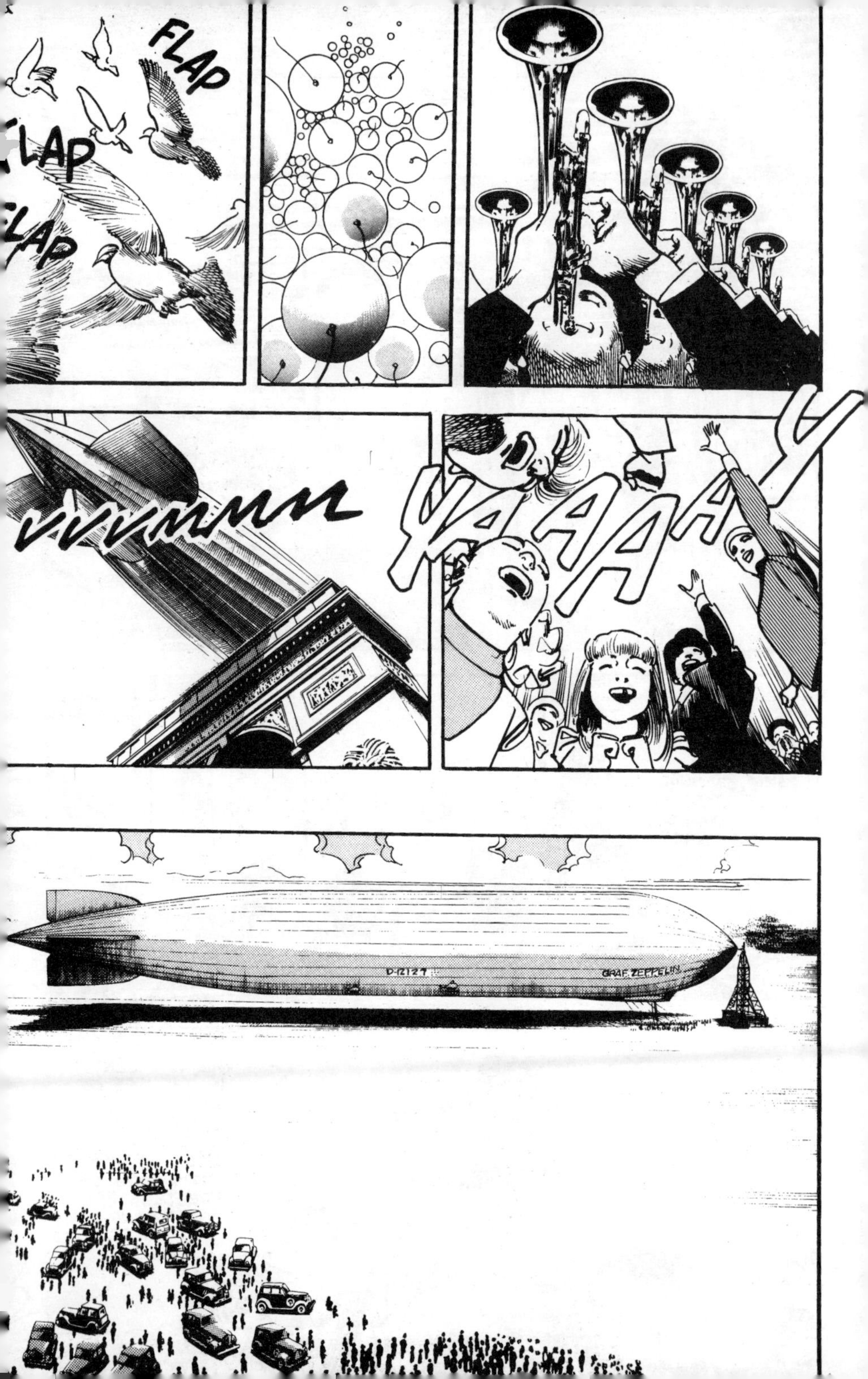
FLAP
FLAP
FLAP
VVVMMMM
YAAAAY
D-IZ127
GRAF ZEPPELIN

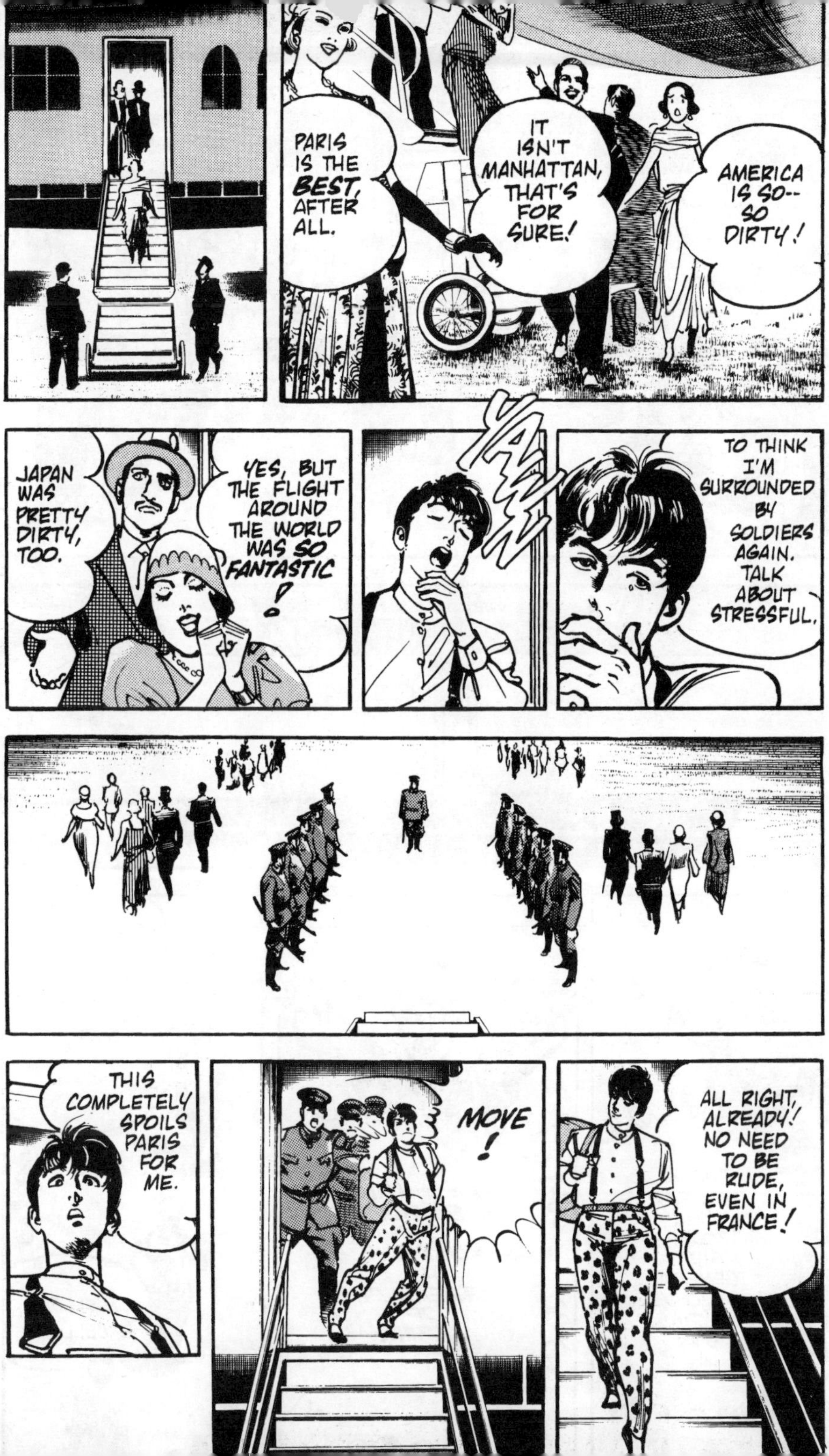
PARIS IS THE BEST, AFTER ALL.
IT ISN'T MANHATTAN, THAT'S FOR SURE!
AMERICA IS SO-- SO DIRTY!
JAPAN WAS PRETTY DIRTY, TOO.
YES, BUT THE FLIGHT AROUND THE WORLD WAS SO FANTASTIC!
YAWN
TO THINK I'M SURROUNDED BY SOLDIERS AGAIN. TALK ABOUT STRESSFUL.
THIS COMPLETELY SPOILS PARIS FOR ME.
MOVE!
ALL RIGHT, ALREADY! NO NEED TO BE RUDE, EVEN IN FRANCE!

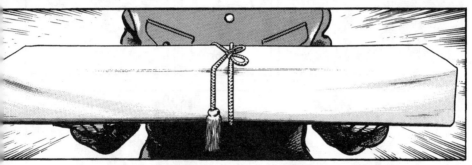

THANK YOU FOR YOUR TROUBLE, SIR! GENERAL KUJO IS WAITING, SIR!

PRESENTING THE SWORD OF KUSANAGI, THE TREASURE OF JAPAN!

WE SHALL ESCORT YOU TO THE EXPOSITION CENTER, SIR.

EXCELLENT... EXCELLENT...

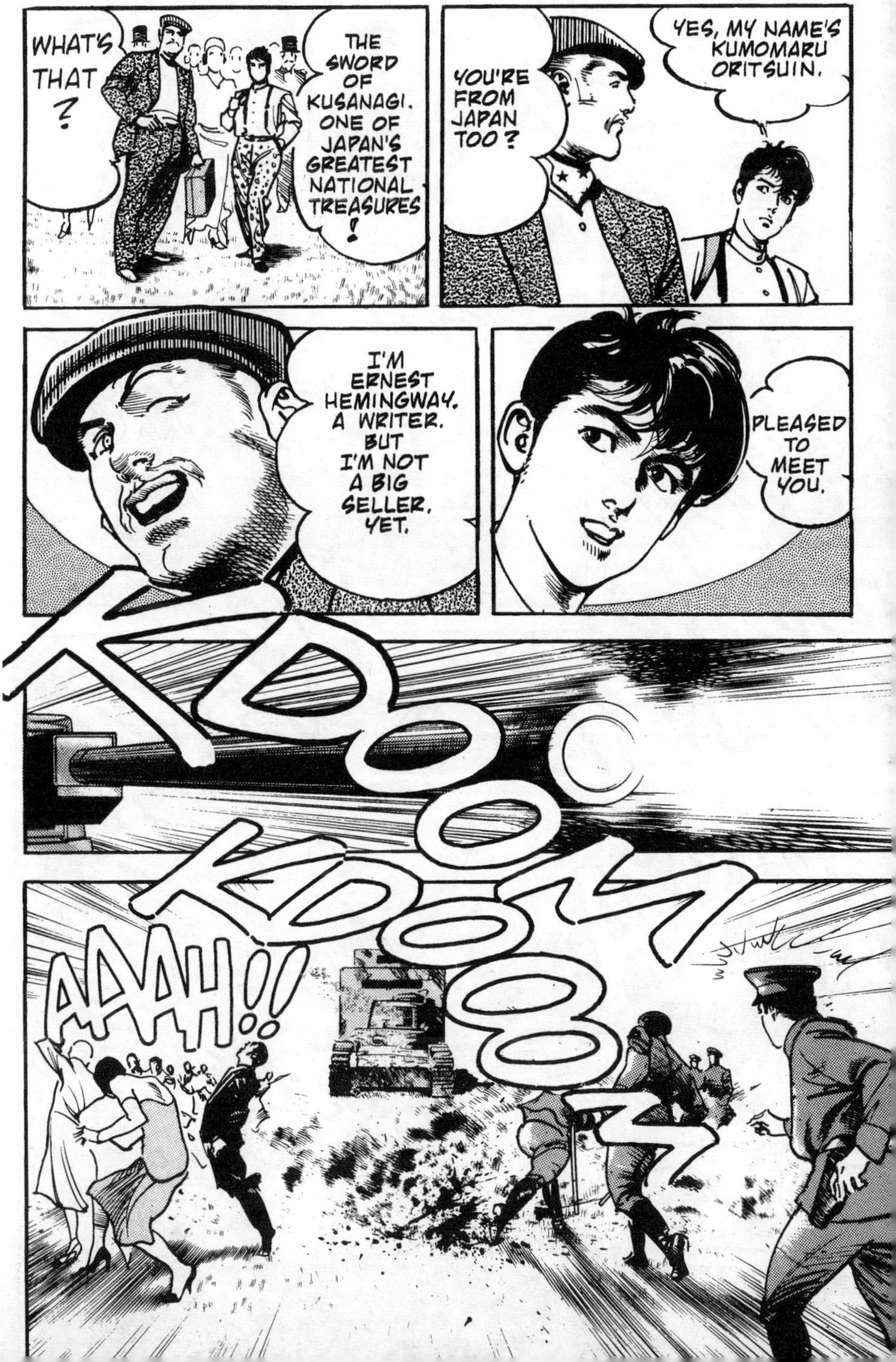
WHAT'S THAT ?
THE SWORD OF KUSANAGI. ONE OF JAPAN'S GREATEST NATIONAL TREASURES !
YOU'RE FROM JAPAN TOO ?
YES, MY NAME'S KUMOMARU ORITSUIN.
I'M ERNEST HEMINGWAY. A WRITER. BUT I'M NOT A BIG SELLER, YET.
PLEASED TO MEET YOU.
KDOOM
KDOOOM
AAAH!!

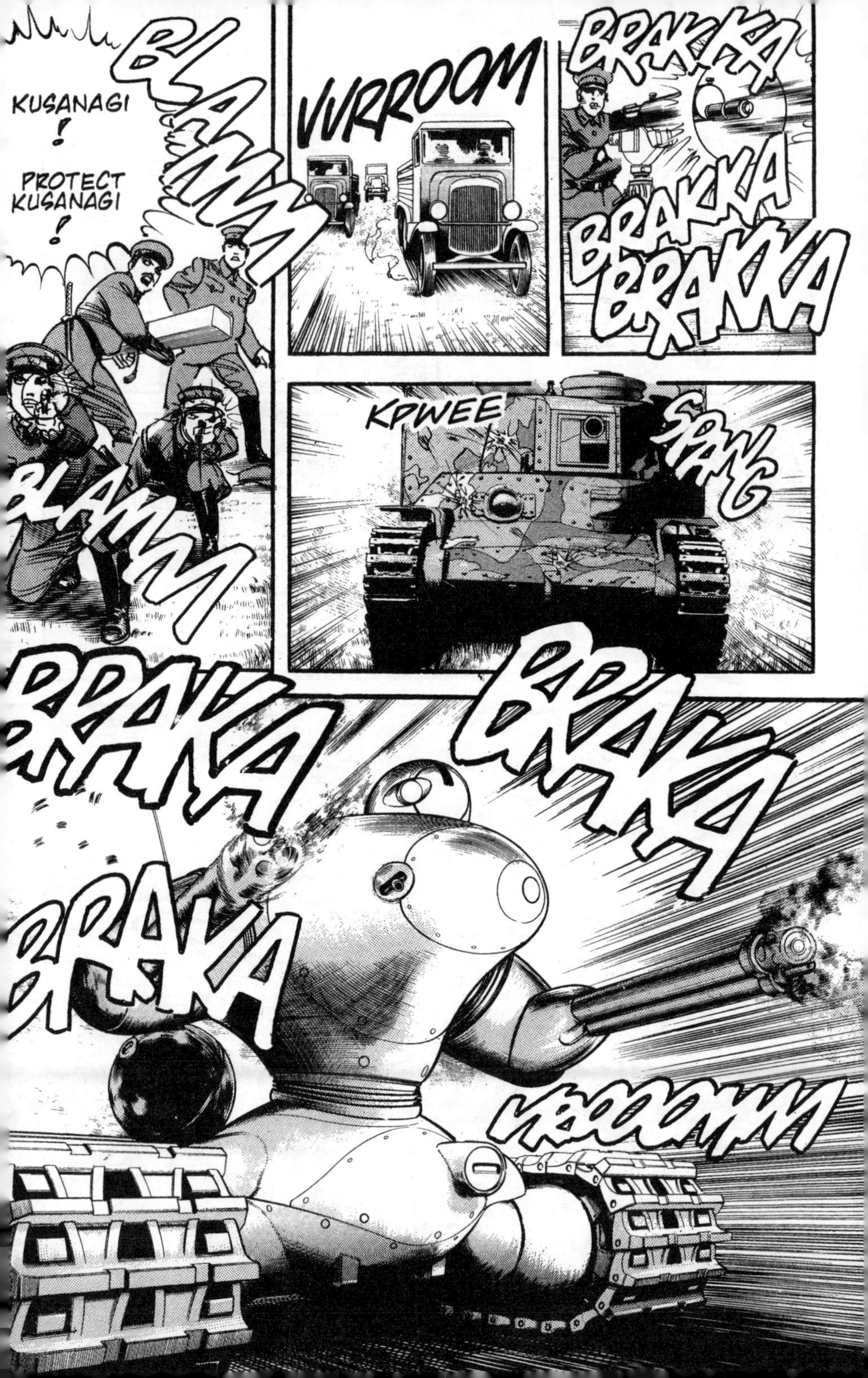

BLAMM
KUSANAGI!
PROTECT KUSANAGI!
BLAMM
VVRROOM
BRAKKA
BRAKKA
BRAKKA
BRAKKA
KPWEE
SPANG
BRAKA
BRAKA
BRAKA

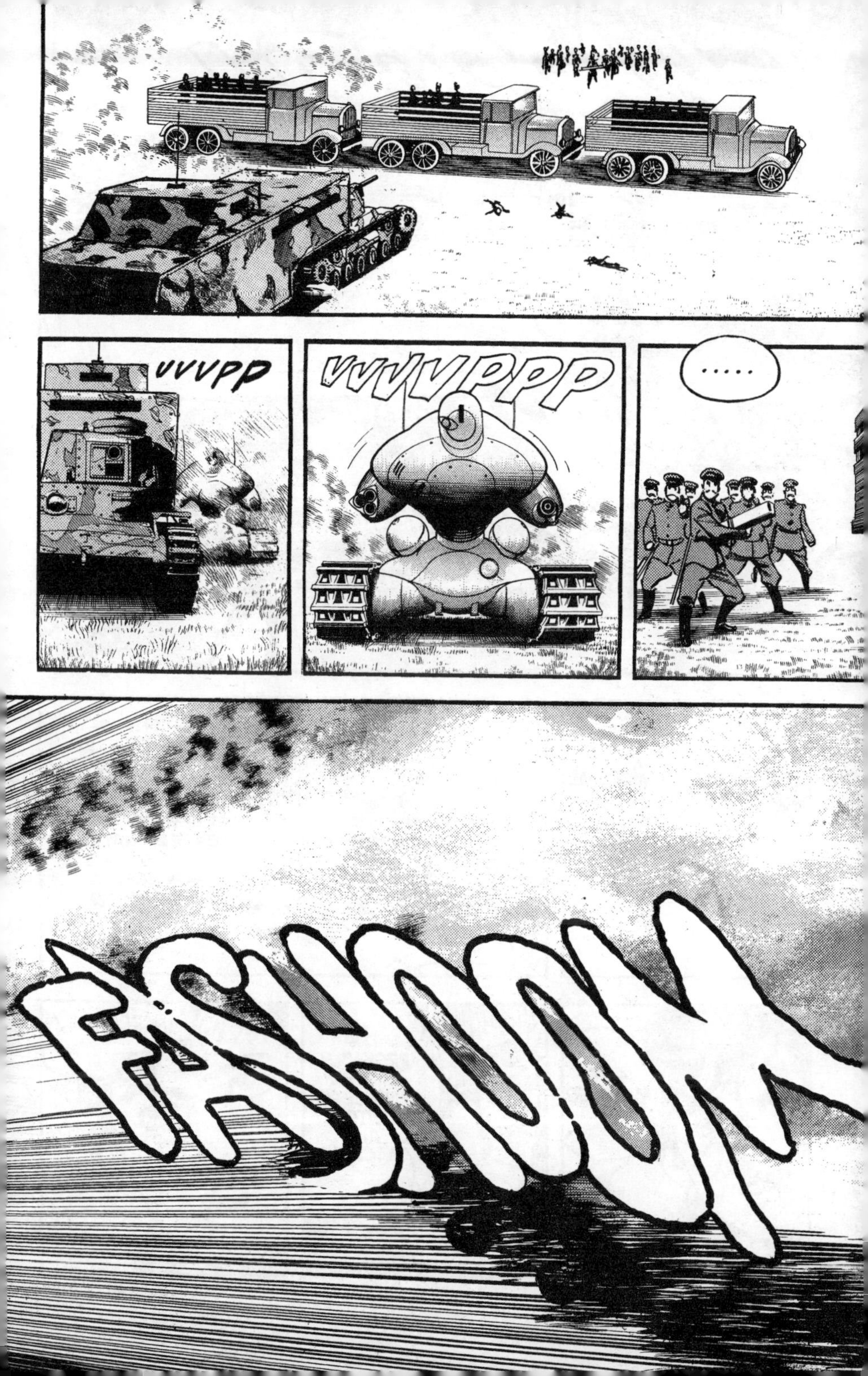
VVVPP
VVVVPPP
......
FSHOOM

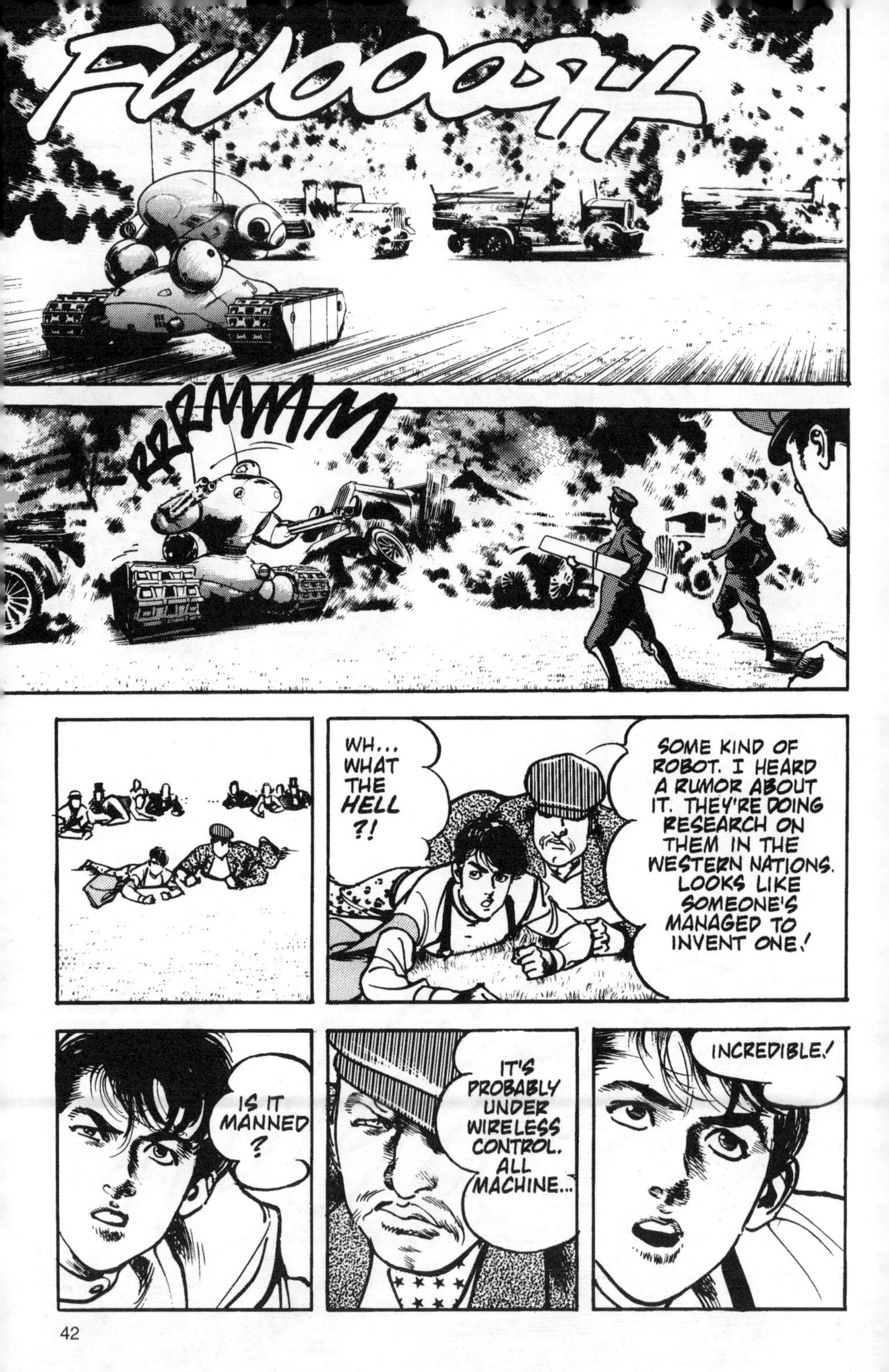
FWOOSH
RRRMMM
WH... WHAT THE HELL ?!
SOME KIND OF ROBOT. I HEARD A RUMOR ABOUT IT. THEY'RE DOING RESEARCH ON THEM IN THE WESTERN NATIONS. LOOKS LIKE SOMEONE'S MANAGED TO INVENT ONE!
IS IT MANNED ?
IT'S PROBABLY UNDER WIRELESS CONTROL. ALL MACHINE...
INCREDIBLE!

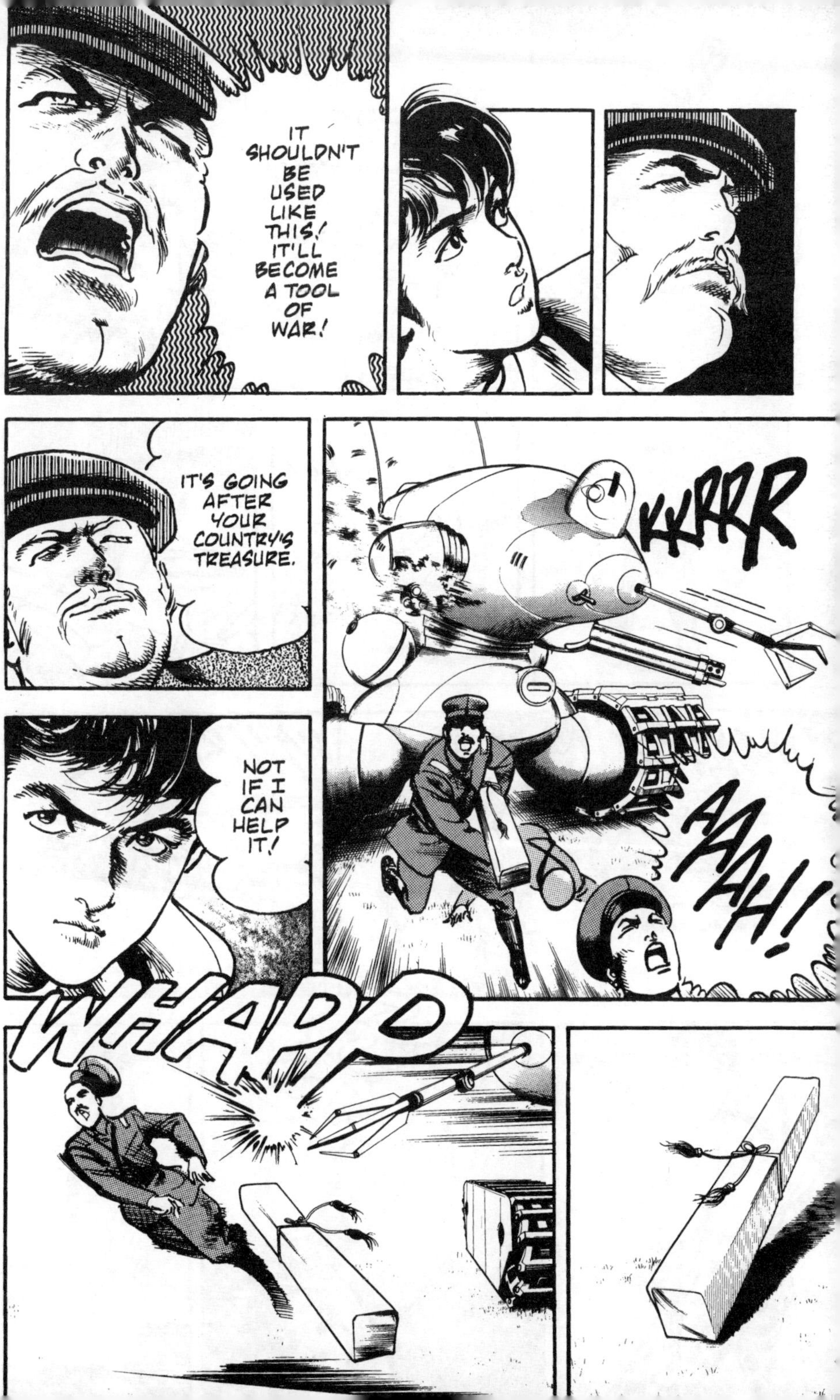
IT SHOULDN'T BE USED LIKE THIS! IT'LL BECOME A TOOL OF WAR!
IT'S GOING AFTER YOUR COUNTRY'S TREASURE.
KKRRR
AAAH!
NOT IF I CAN HELP IT!
WHAPP

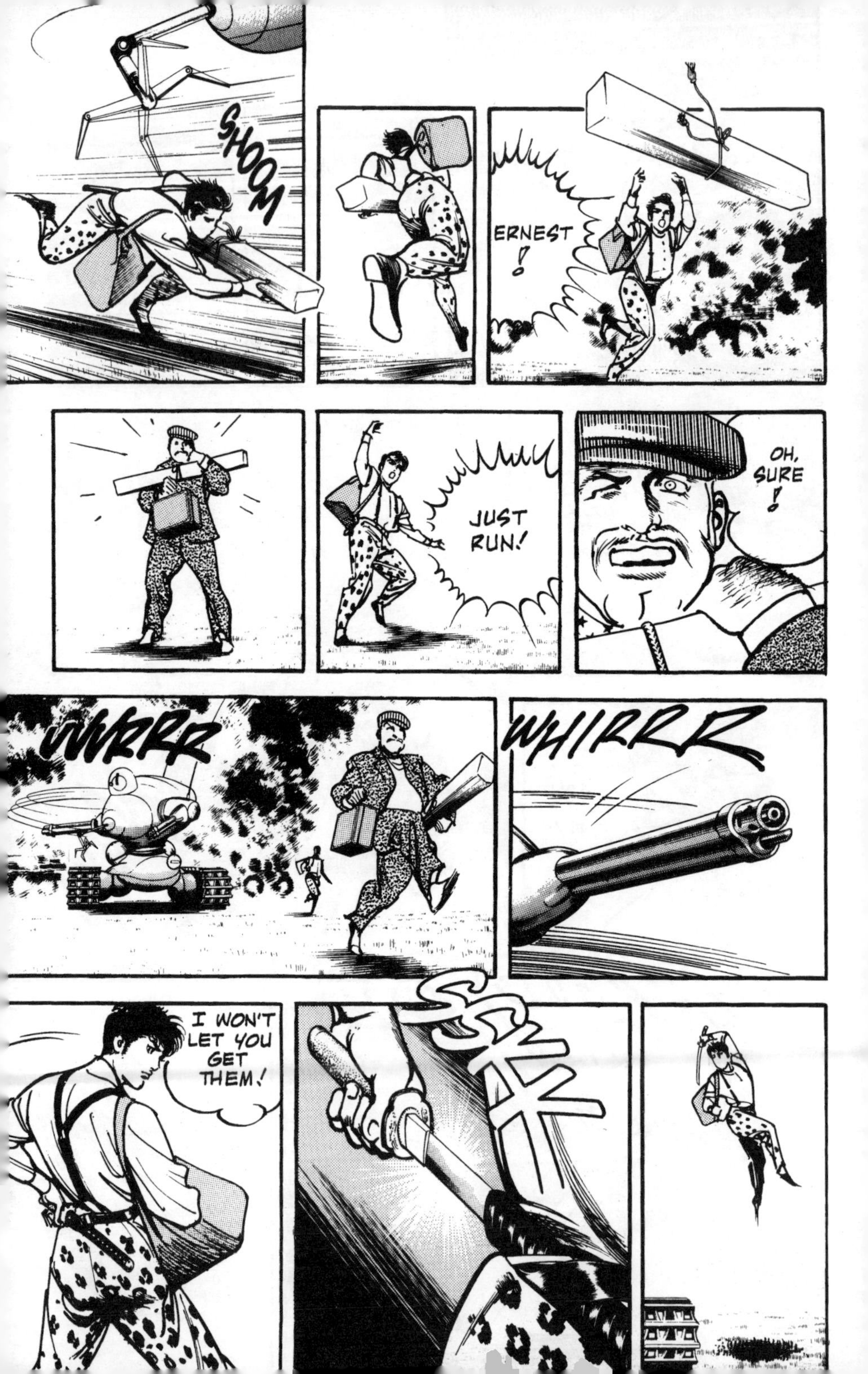
SHOOM
ERNEST!
JUST RUN!
OH, SURE!
VWRRR
WHIRRR
I WON'T LET YOU GET THEM!
SSHK

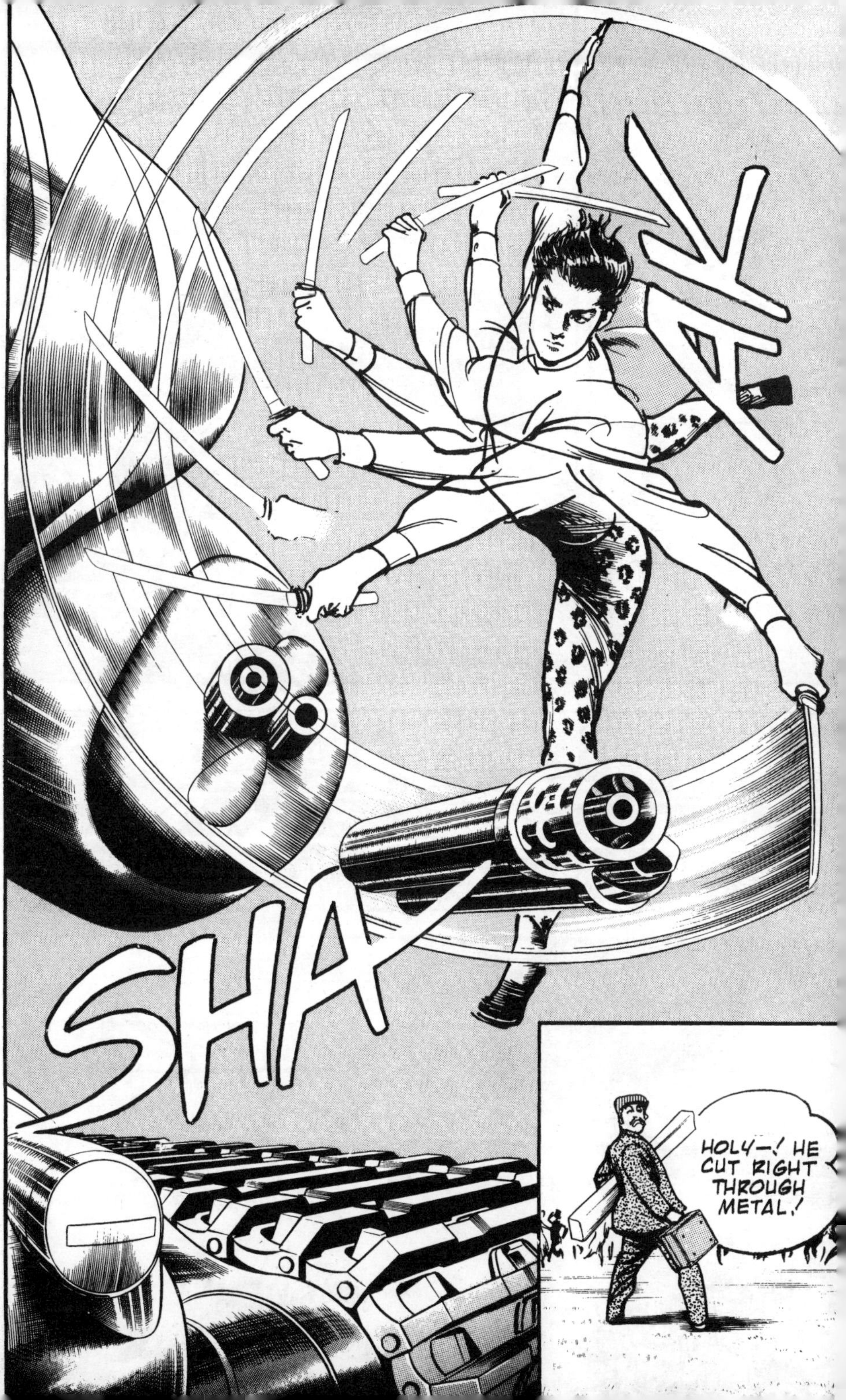
SHAK
SHA
HOLY—! HE CUT RIGHT THROUGH METAL!

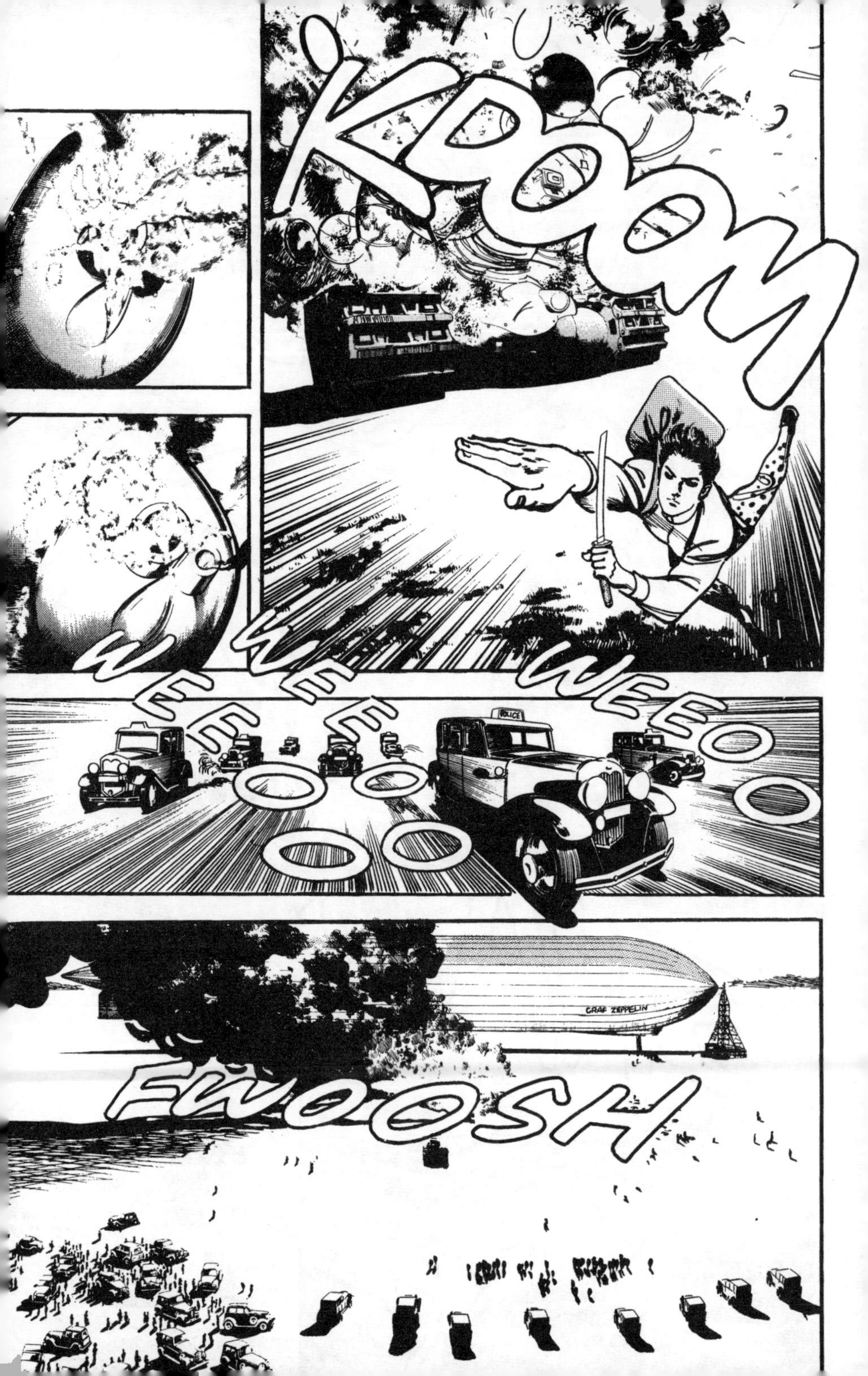
KBOOM
WEEOO WEEOO WEEOO
POLICE
GRAF ZEPPELIN
FWOOSH

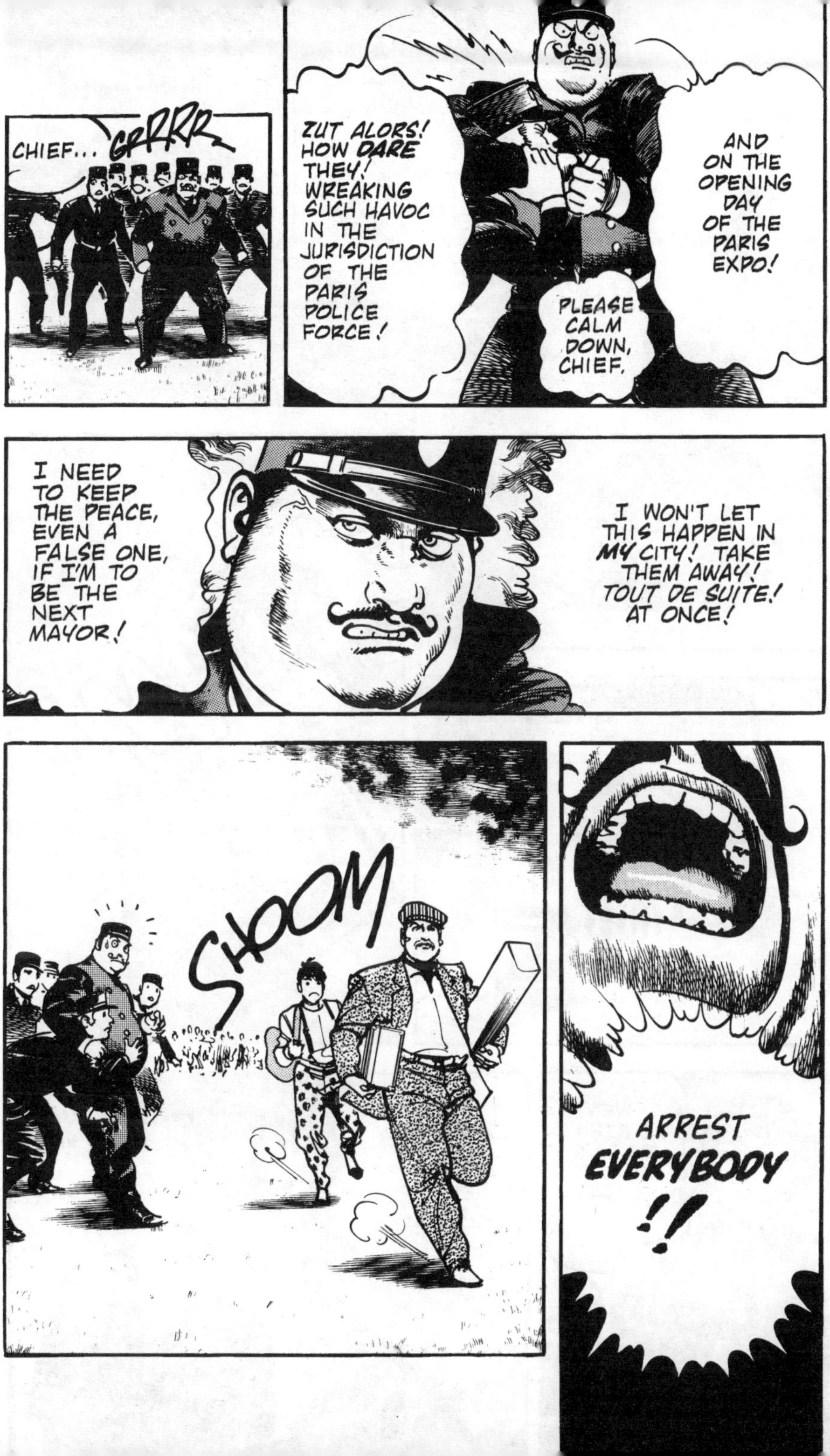
CHIEF...
GRRRR
ZUT ALORS! HOW DARE THEY! WREAKING SUCH HAVOC IN THE JURISDICTION OF THE PARIS POLICE FORCE!
AND ON THE OPENING DAY OF THE PARIS EXPO!
PLEASE CALM DOWN, CHIEF.
I NEED TO KEEP THE PEACE, EVEN A FALSE ONE, IF I'M TO BE THE NEXT MAYOR!
I WON'T LET THIS HAPPEN IN MY CITY! TAKE THEM AWAY! TOUT DE SUITE! AT ONCE!
SHOOM
ARREST EVERYBODY!!

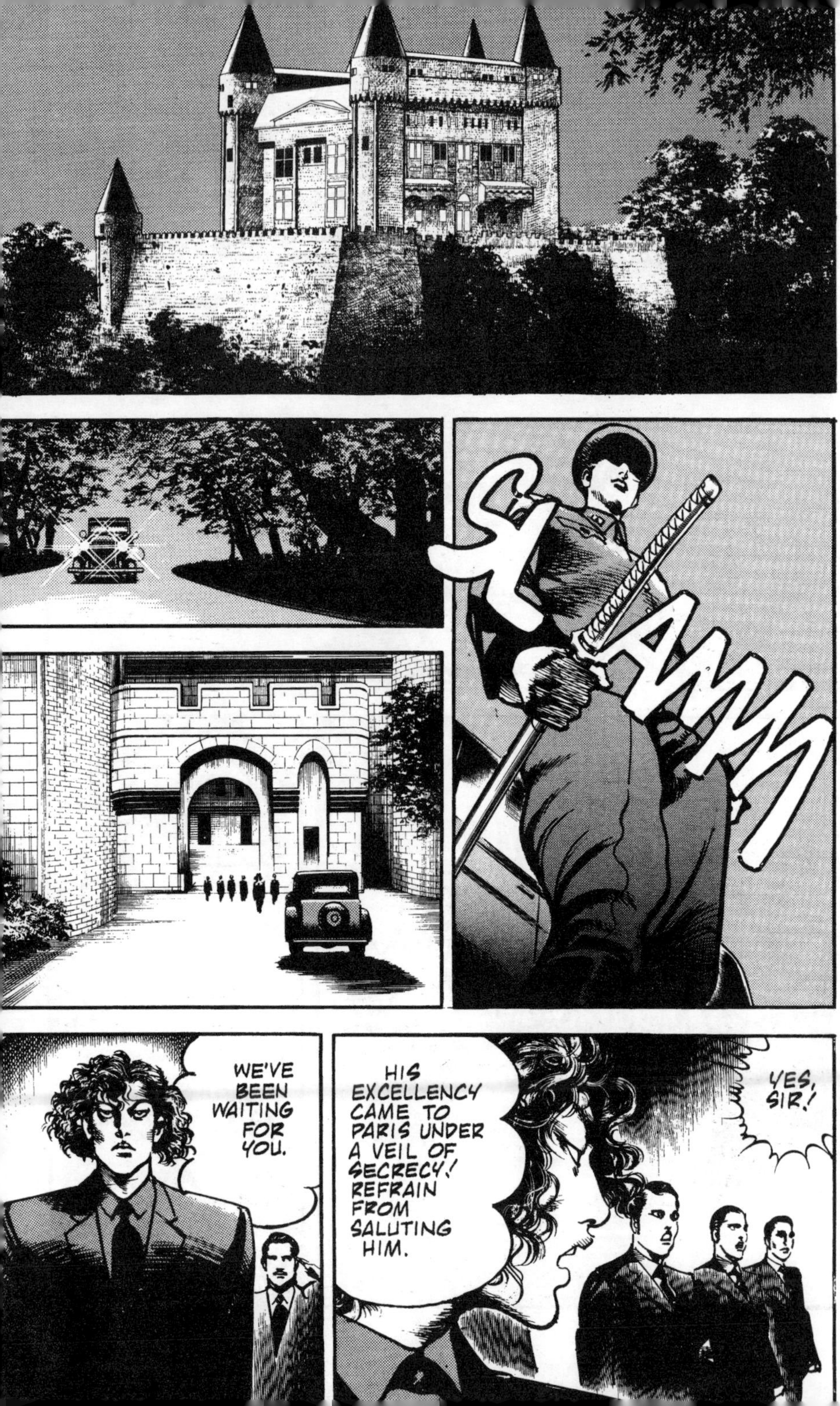
SLAMM
WE'VE BEEN WAITING FOR YOU.
HIS EXCELLENCY CAME TO PARIS UNDER A VEIL OF SECRECY! REFRAIN FROM SALUTING HIM.
YES, SIR!

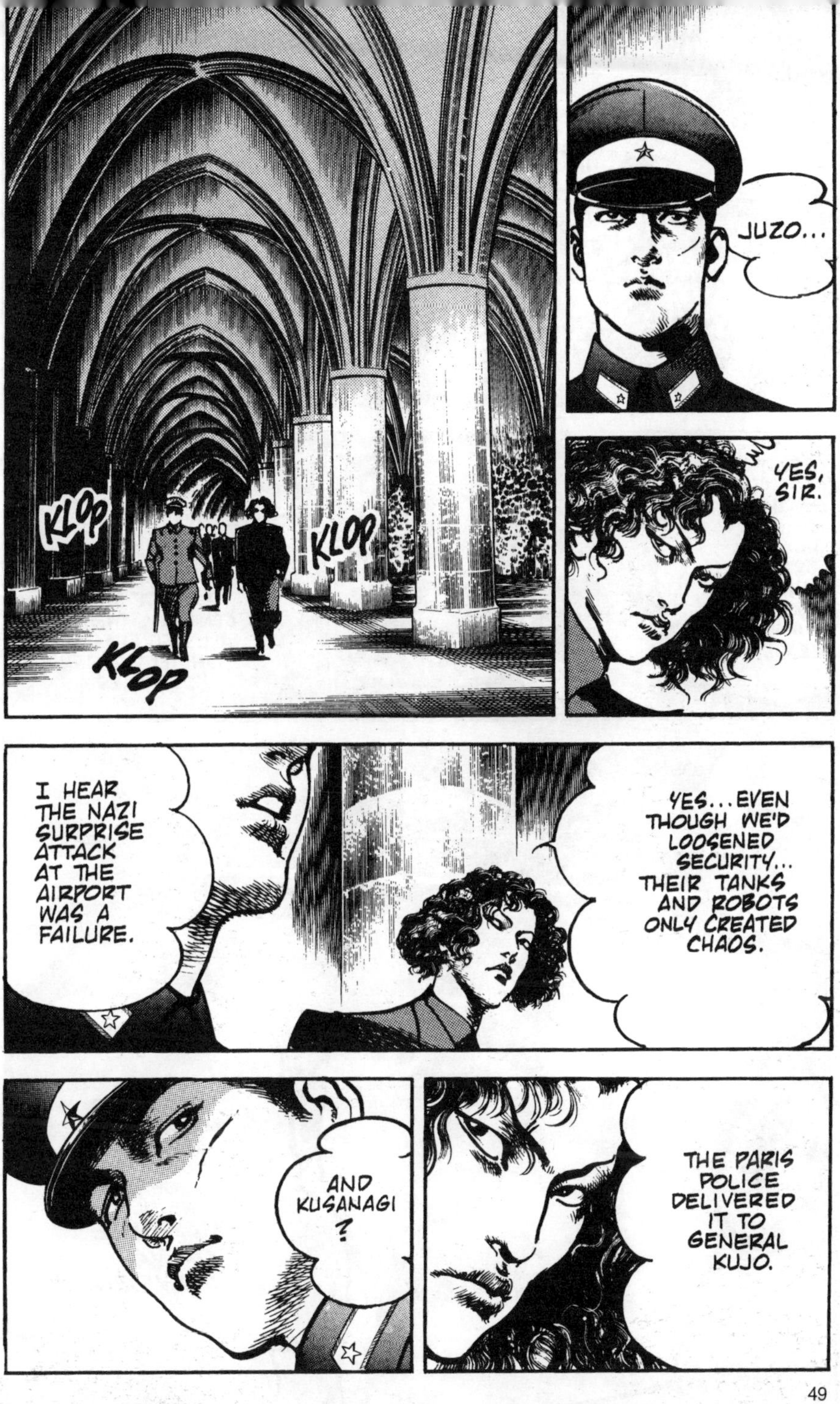
KLOP
KLOP
KLOP
JUZO...
YES, SIR.
I HEAR THE NAZI SURPRISE ATTACK AT THE AIRPORT WAS A FAILURE.
YES...EVEN THOUGH WE'D LOOSENED SECURITY... THEIR TANKS AND ROBOTS ONLY CREATED CHAOS.
AND KUSANAGI?
THE PARIS POLICE DELIVERED IT TO GENERAL KUJO.

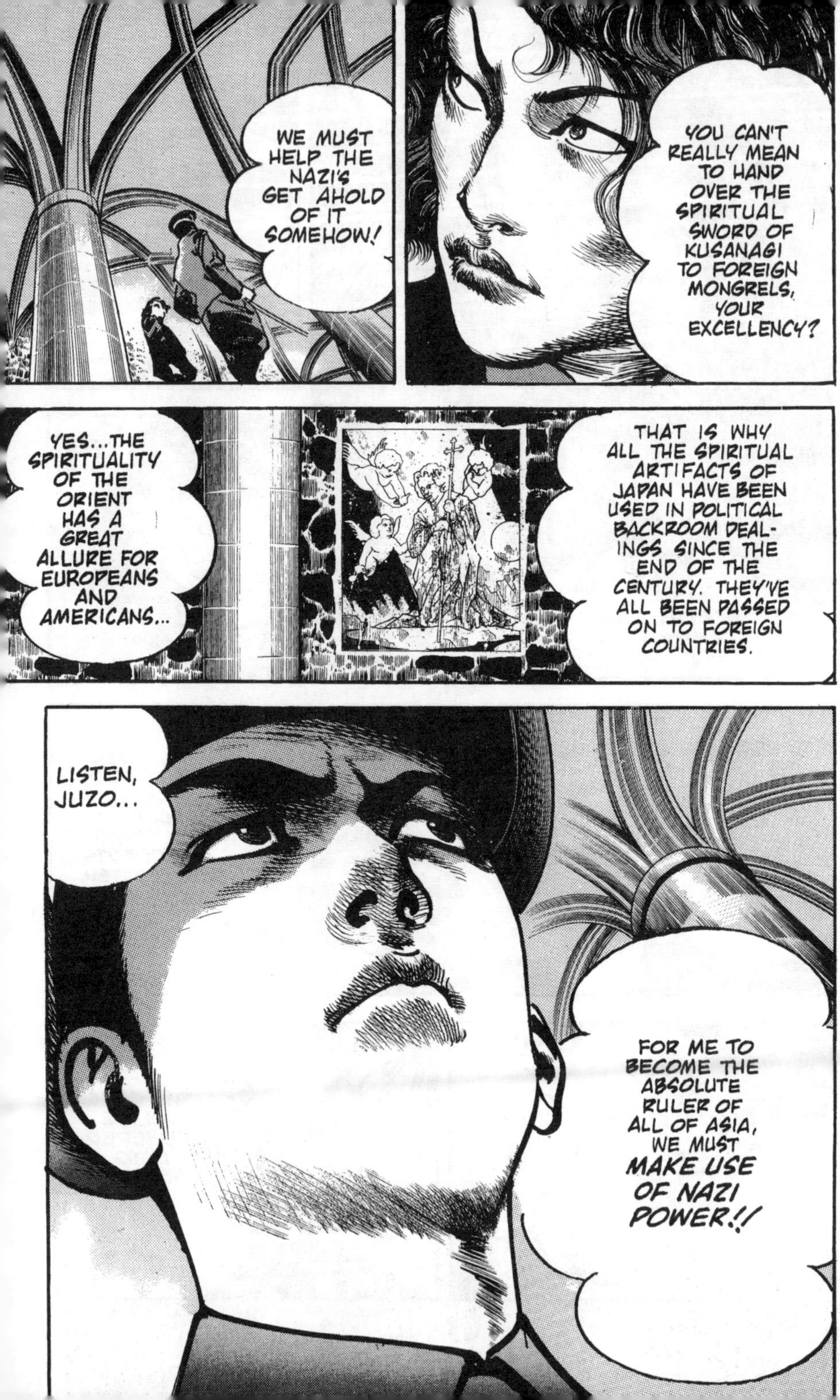
WE MUST HELP THE NAZI'S GET AHOLD OF IT SOMEHOW!
YOU CAN'T REALLY MEAN TO HAND OVER THE SPIRITUAL SWORD OF KUSANAGI TO FOREIGN MONGRELS, YOUR EXCELLENCY?
YES...THE SPIRITUALITY OF THE ORIENT HAS A GREAT ALLURE FOR EUROPEANS AND AMERICANS...
THAT IS WHY ALL THE SPIRITUAL ARTIFACTS OF JAPAN HAVE BEEN USED IN POLITICAL BACKROOM DEAL-INGS SINCE THE END OF THE CENTURY. THEY'VE ALL BEEN PASSED ON TO FOREIGN COUNTRIES.
LISTEN, JUZO...
FOR ME TO BECOME THE ABSOLUTE RULER OF ALL OF ASIA, WE MUST MAKE USE OF NAZI POWER!!

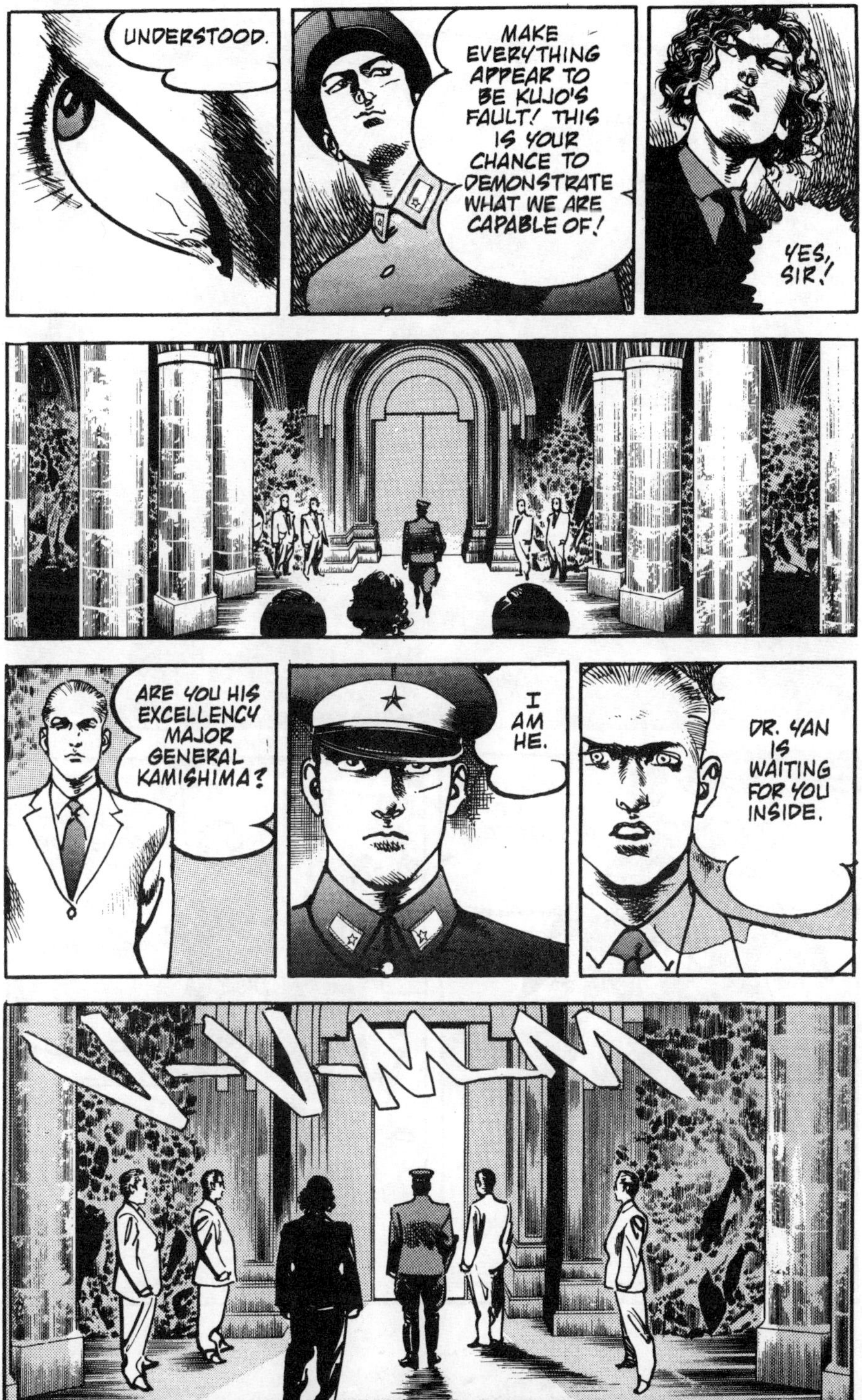
UNDERSTOOD.
MAKE EVERYTHING APPEAR TO BE KUJO'S FAULT! THIS IS YOUR CHANCE TO DEMONSTRATE WHAT WE ARE CAPABLE OF!
YES, SIR!
ARE YOU HIS EXCELLENCY MAJOR GENERAL KAMISHIMA?
I AM HE.
DR. YAN IS WAITING FOR YOU INSIDE.
V-V-M-M

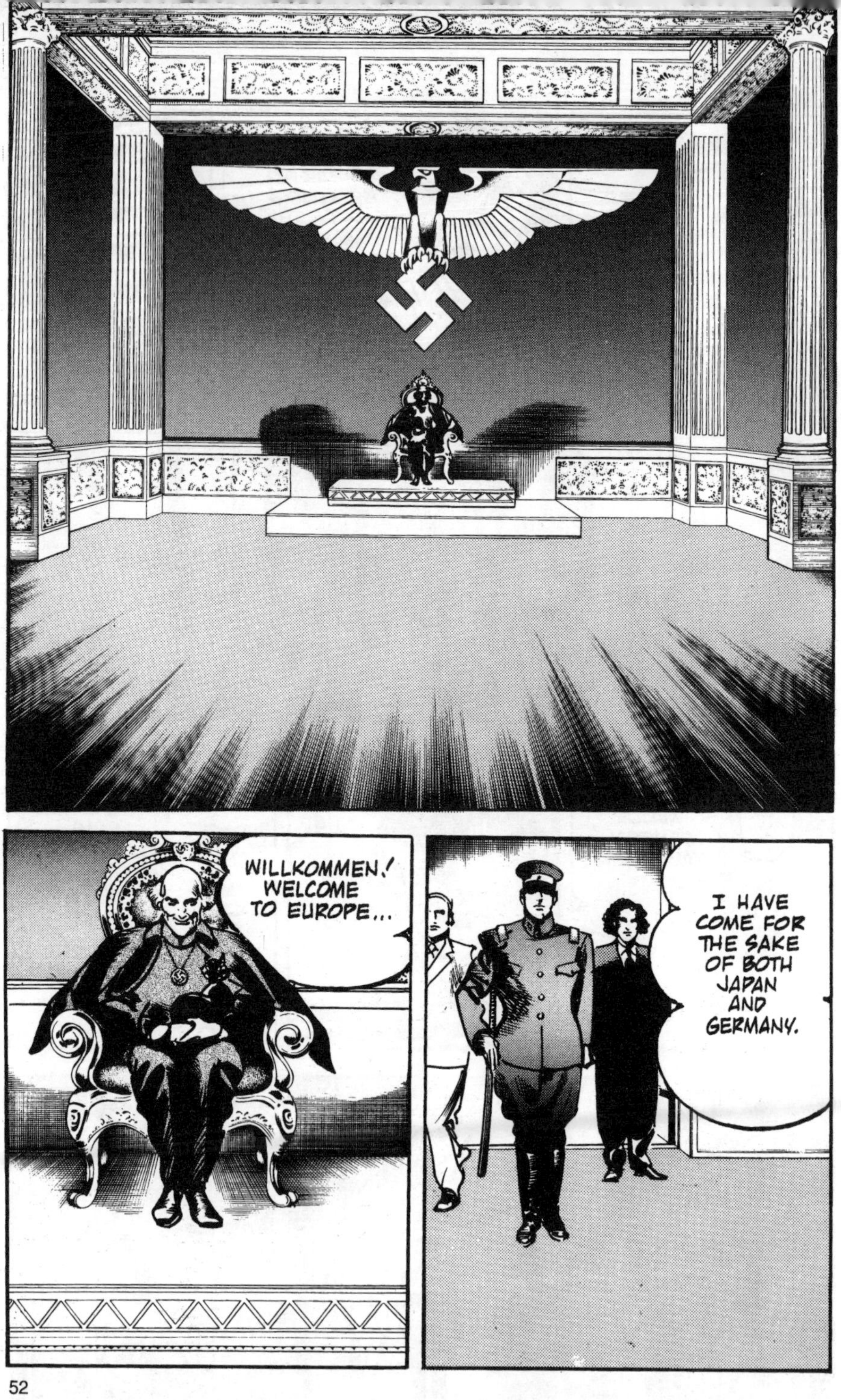
WILLKOMMEN! WELCOME TO EUROPE...
I HAVE COME FOR THE SAKE OF BOTH JAPAN AND GERMANY.

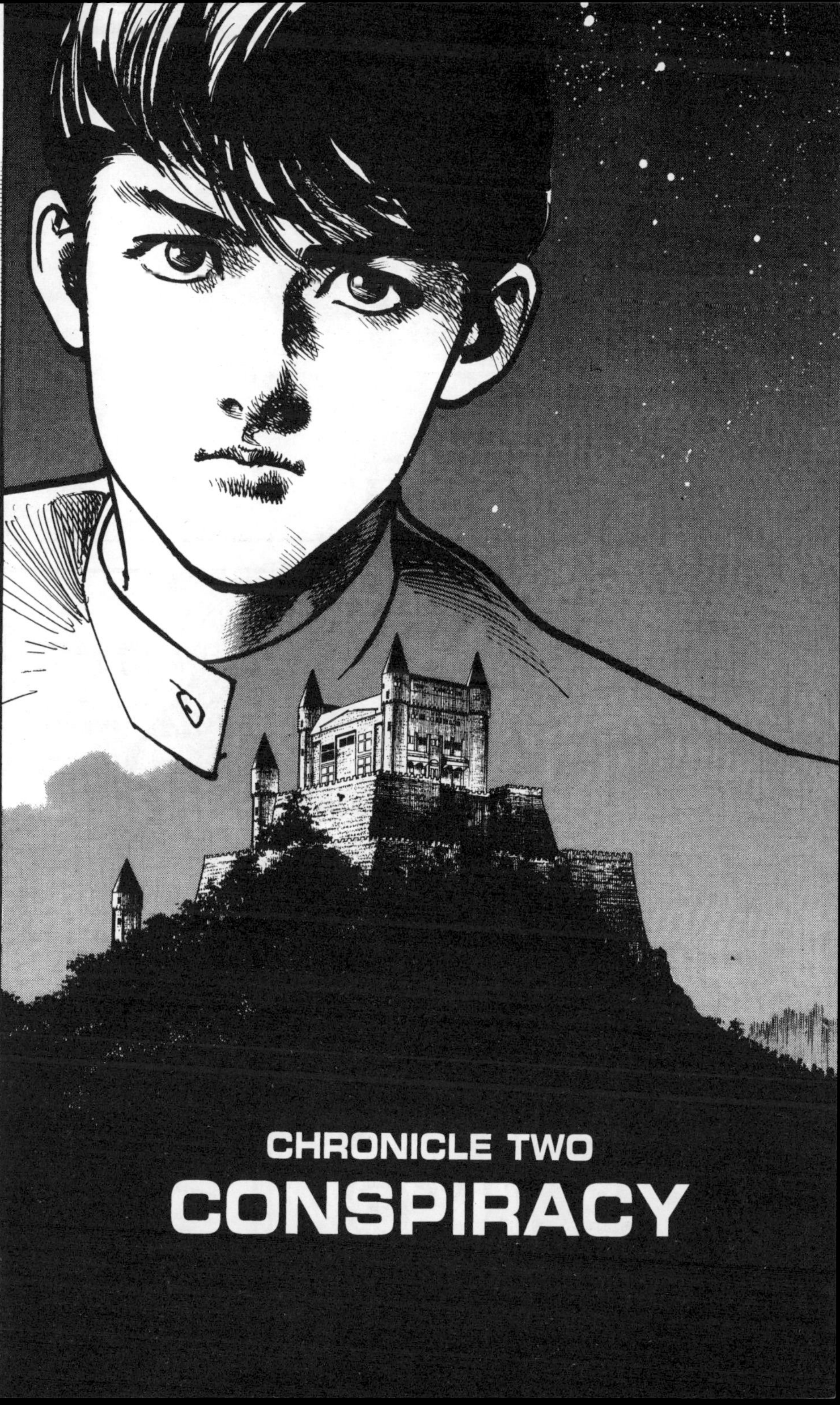

CHRONICLE TWO
CONSPIRACY

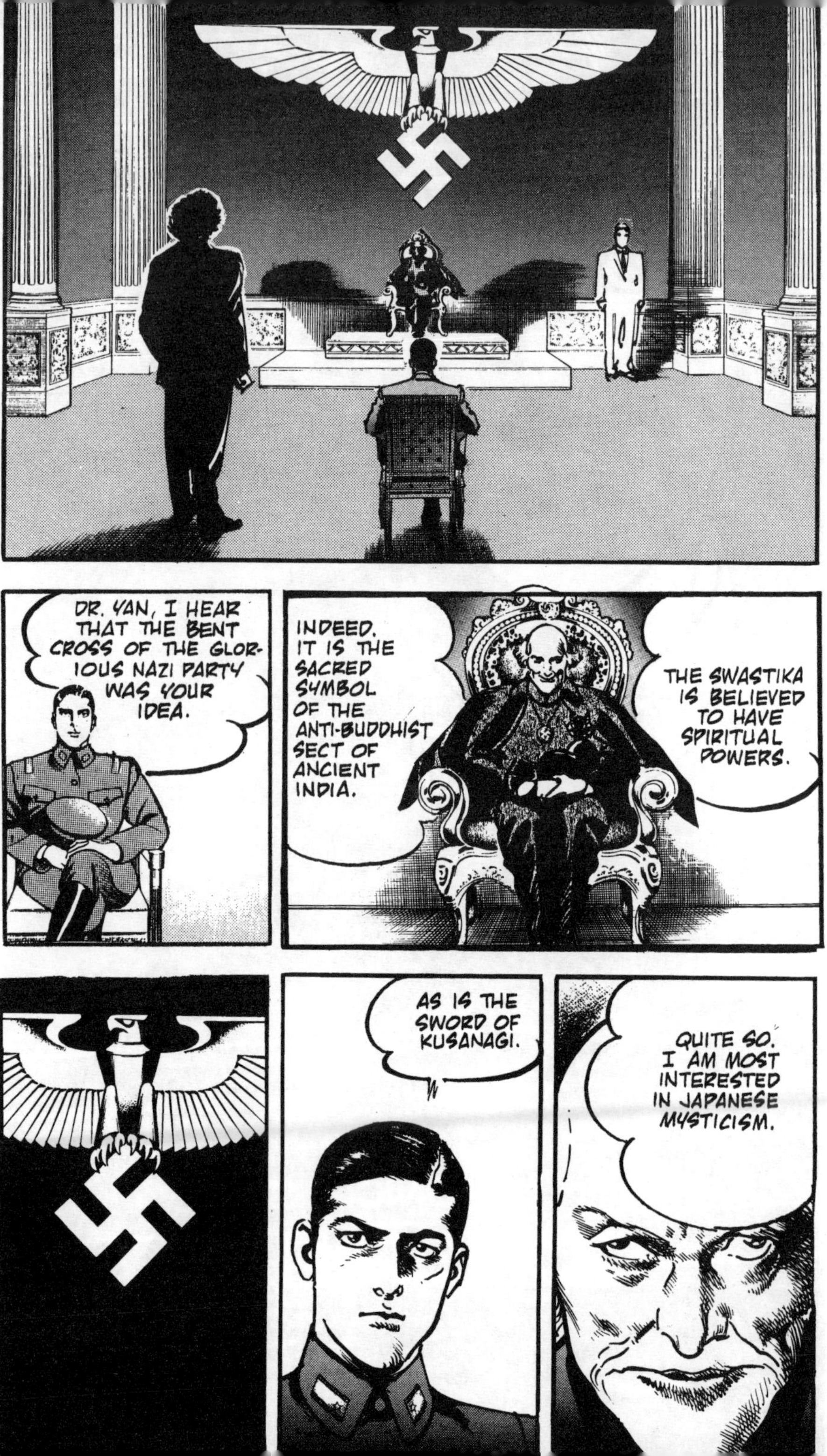
DR. YAN, I HEAR THAT THE BENT CROSS OF THE GLORIOUS NAZI PARTY WAS YOUR IDEA.
INDEED. IT IS THE SACRED SYMBOL OF THE ANTI-BUDDHIST SECT OF ANCIENT INDIA.
THE SWASTIKA IS BELIEVED TO HAVE SPIRITUAL POWERS.
AS IS THE SWORD OF KUSANAGI.
QUITE SO. I AM MOST INTERESTED IN JAPANESE MYSTICISM.

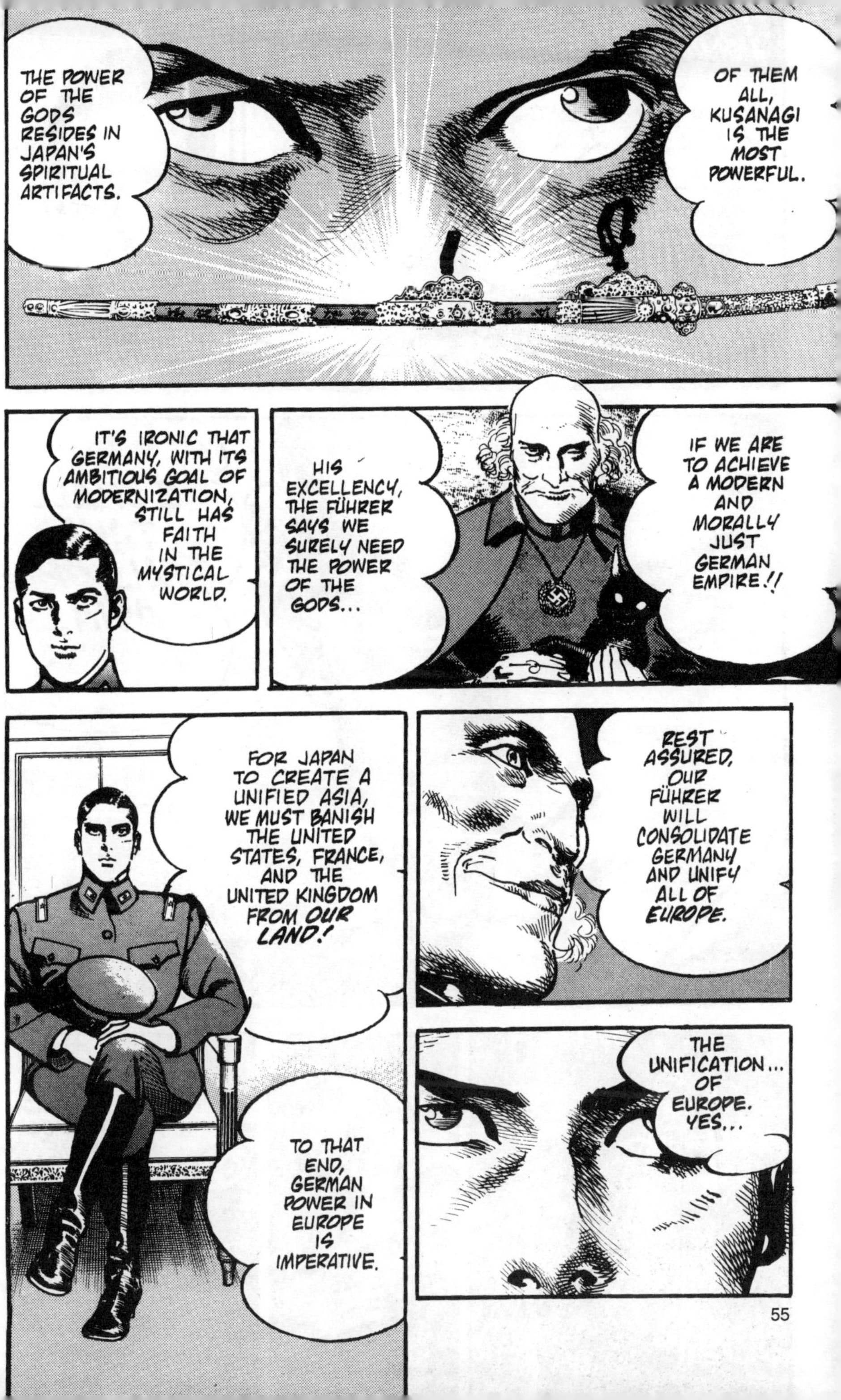

THE POWER OF THE GODS RESIDES IN JAPAN'S SPIRITUAL ARTIFACTS.
OF THEM ALL, KUSANAGI IS THE MOST POWERFUL.
IT'S IRONIC THAT GERMANY, WITH ITS AMBITIOUS GOAL OF MODERNIZATION, STILL HAS FAITH IN THE MYSTICAL WORLD.
HIS EXCELLENCY, THE FÜHRER SAYS WE SURELY NEED THE POWER OF THE GODS...
IF WE ARE TO ACHIEVE A MODERN AND MORALLY JUST GERMAN EMPIRE!!
FOR JAPAN TO CREATE A UNIFIED ASIA, WE MUST BANISH THE UNITED STATES, FRANCE, AND THE UNITED KINGDOM FROM OUR LAND!
TO THAT END, GERMAN POWER IN EUROPE IS IMPERATIVE.
REST ASSURED, OUR FÜHRER WILL CONSOLIDATE GERMANY AND UNIFY ALL OF EUROPE.
THE UNIFICATION... OF EUROPE. YES...

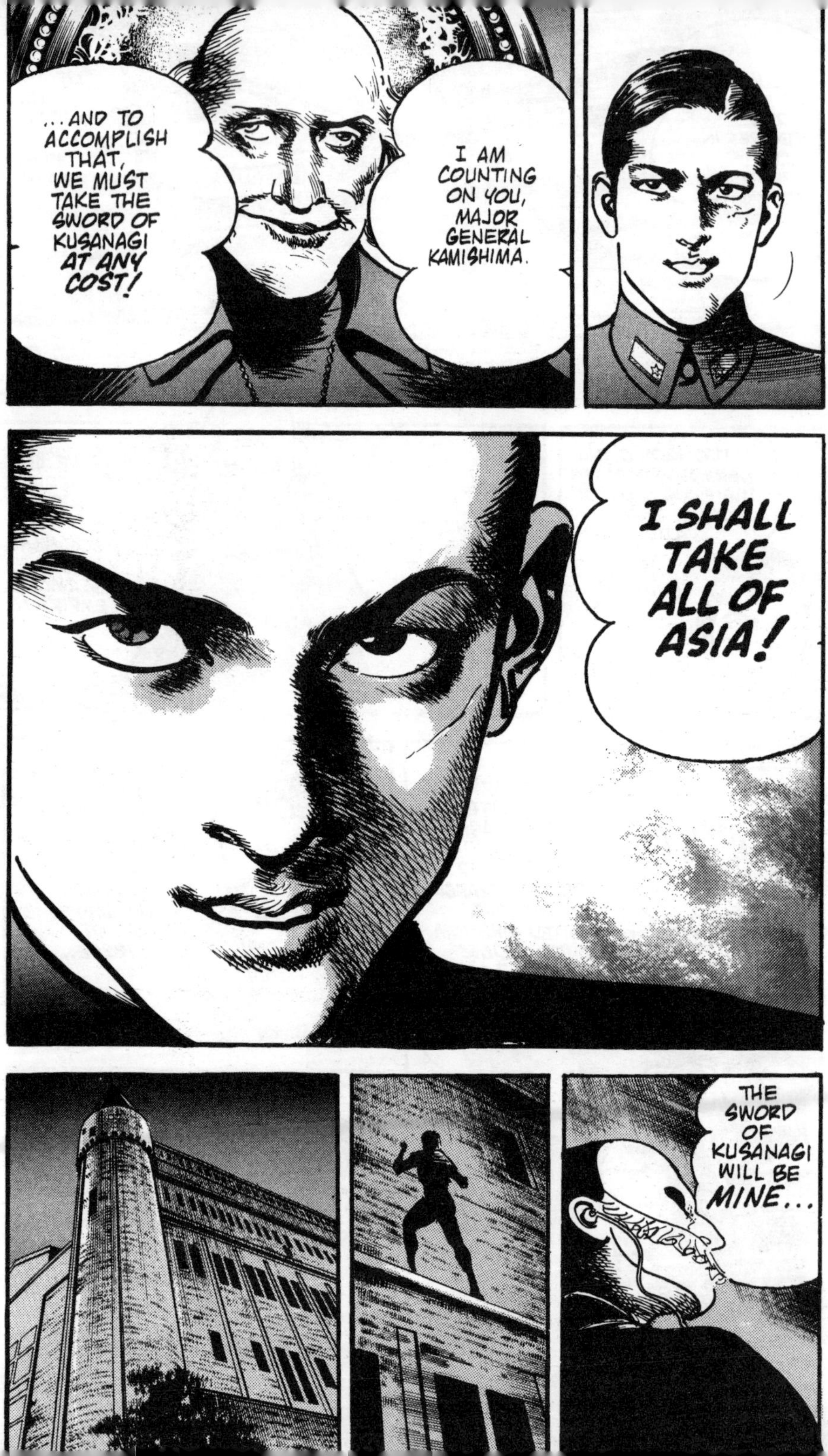
...AND TO ACCOMPLISH THAT, WE MUST TAKE THE SWORD OF KUSANAGI AT ANY COST!
I AM COUNTING ON YOU, MAJOR GENERAL KAMISHIMA.
I SHALL TAKE ALL OF ASIA!
THE SWORD OF KUSANAGI WILL BE MINE...

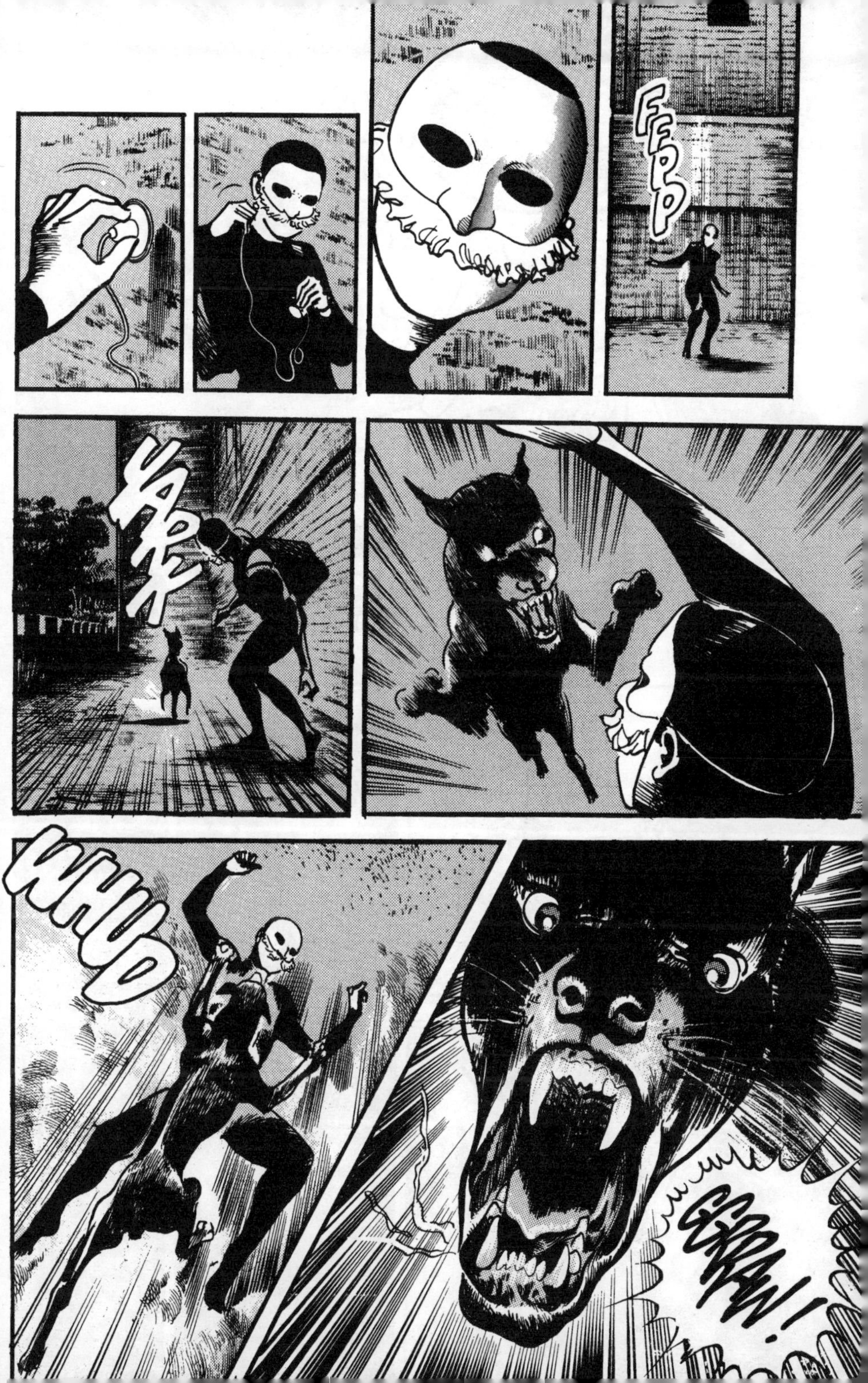
FFPP
YARK
WHUD
GGRAW!

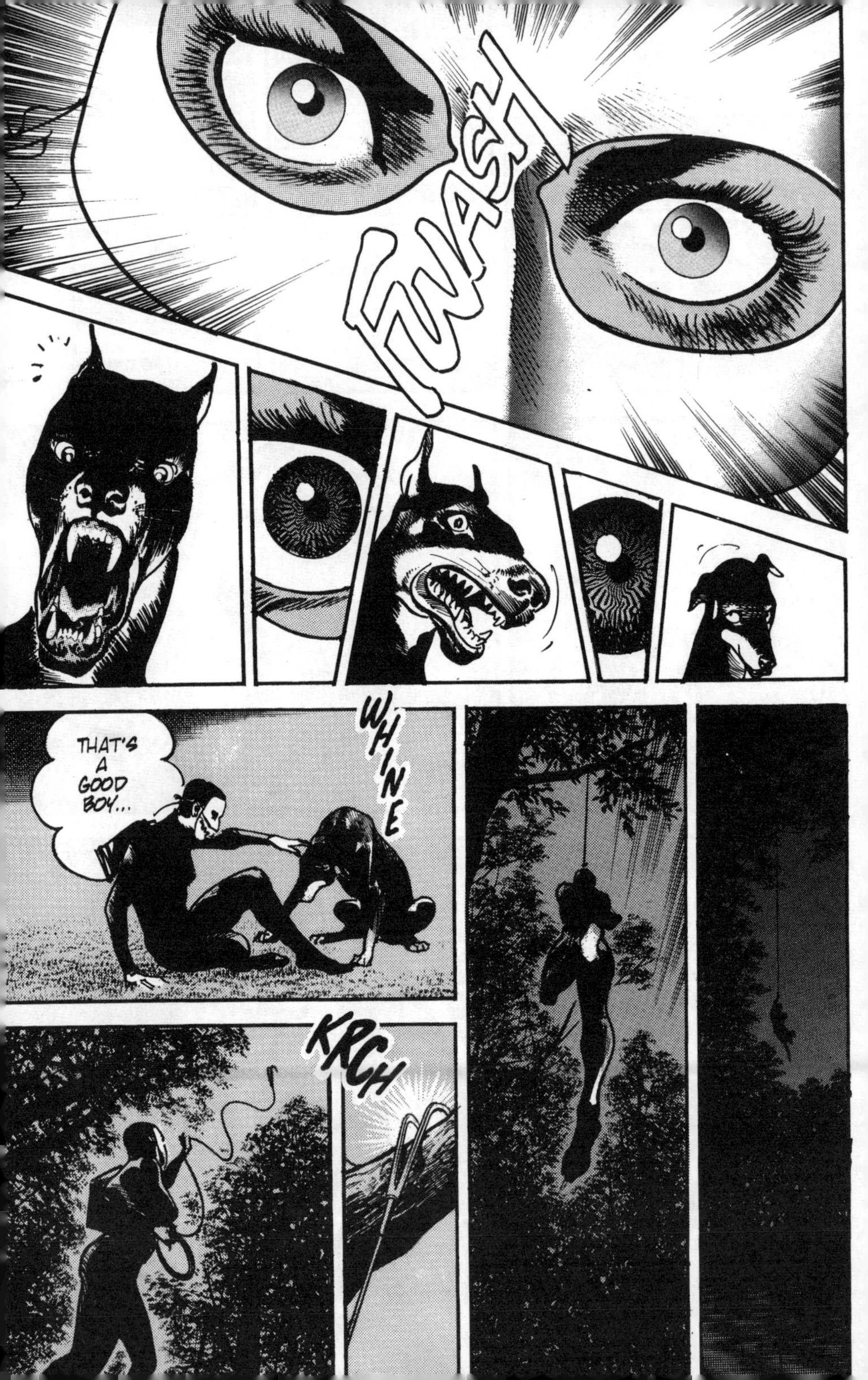
FWASH
THAT'S A GOOD BOY...
WHINE
KRCH

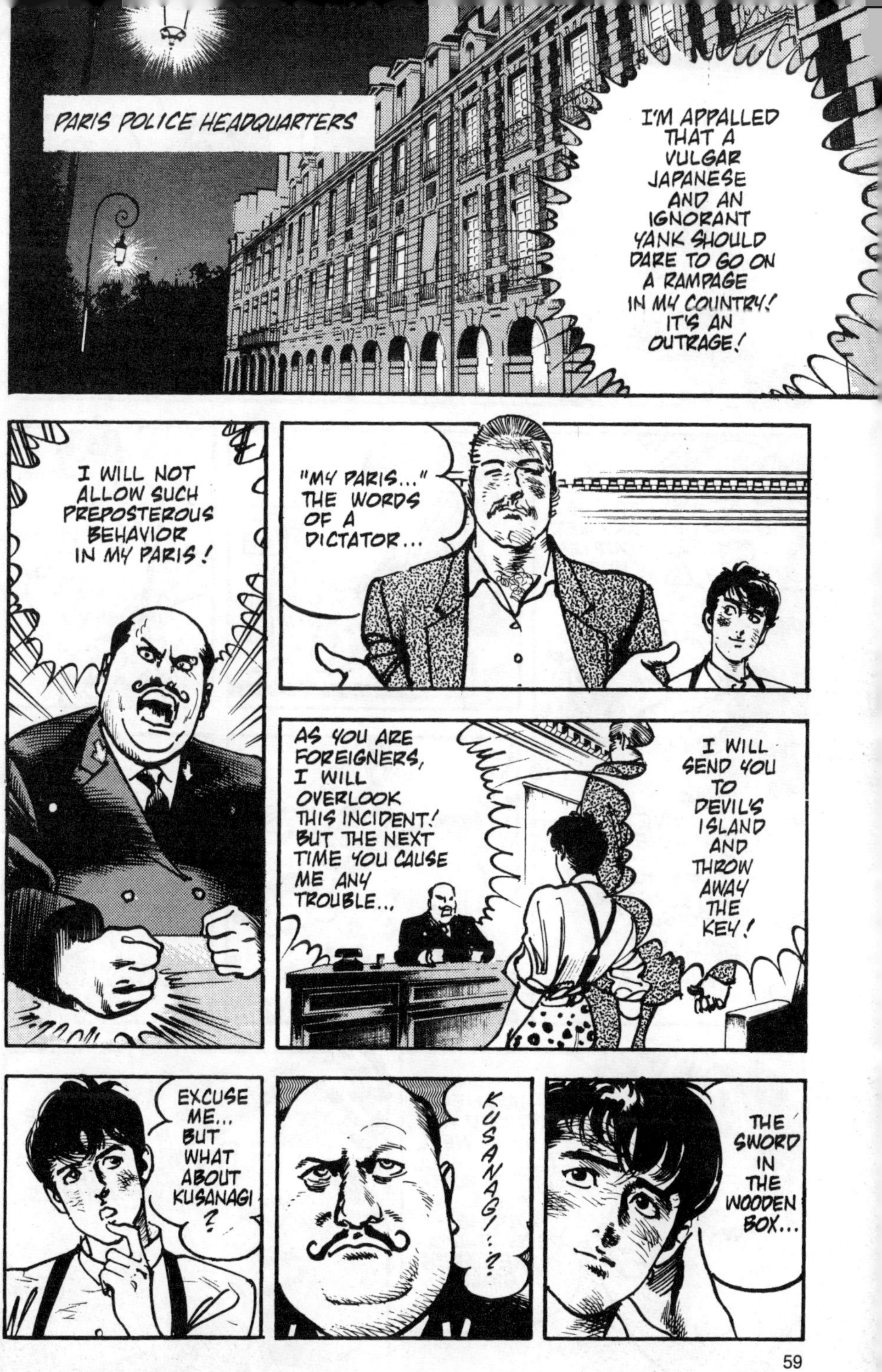
PARIS POLICE HEADQUARTERS
I'M APPALLED THAT A VULGAR JAPANESE AND AN IGNORANT YANK SHOULD DARE TO GO ON A RAMPAGE IN MY COUNTRY! IT'S AN OUTRAGE!
I WILL NOT ALLOW SUCH PREPOSTEROUS BEHAVIOR IN MY PARIS!
"MY PARIS..." THE WORDS OF A DICTATOR...
AS YOU ARE FOREIGNERS, I WILL OVERLOOK THIS INCIDENT! BUT THE NEXT TIME YOU CAUSE ME ANY TROUBLE...
I WILL SEND YOU TO DEVIL'S ISLAND AND THROW AWAY THE KEY!
EXCUSE ME... BUT WHAT ABOUT KUSANAGI?
KUSANAGI...?
THE SWORD IN THE WOODEN BOX...

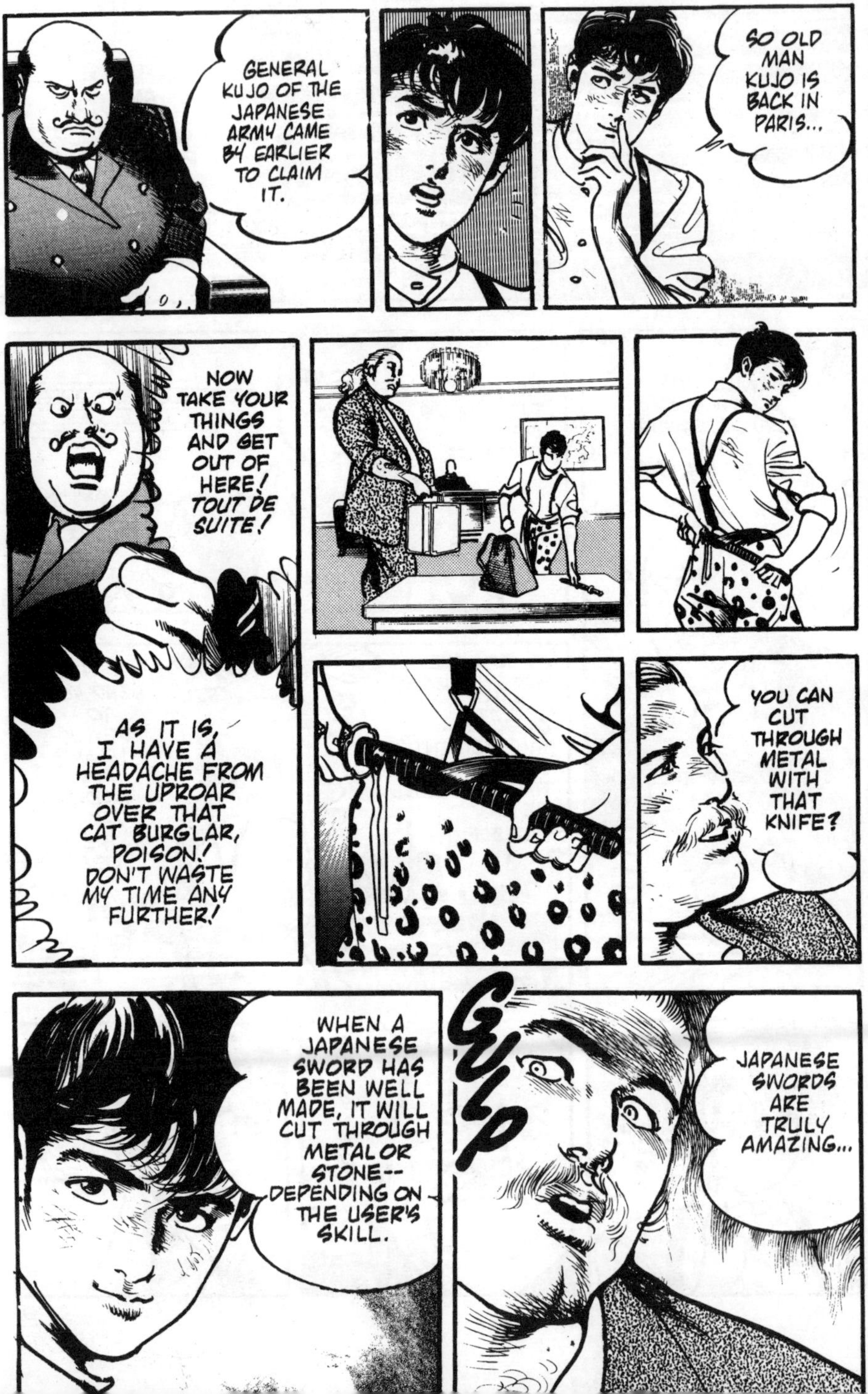
GENERAL KUJO OF THE JAPANESE ARMY CAME BY EARLIER TO CLAIM IT.
SO OLD MAN KUJO IS BACK IN PARIS...
NOW TAKE YOUR THINGS AND GET OUT OF HERE! TOUT DE SUITE!
AS IT IS, I HAVE A HEADACHE FROM THE UPROAR OVER THAT CAT BURGLAR, POISON! DON'T WASTE MY TIME ANY FURTHER!
YOU CAN CUT THROUGH METAL WITH THAT KNIFE?
WHEN A JAPANESE SWORD HAS BEEN WELL MADE, IT WILL CUT THROUGH METAL OR STONE-- DEPENDING ON THE USER'S SKILL.
GULP
JAPANESE SWORDS ARE TRULY AMAZING...

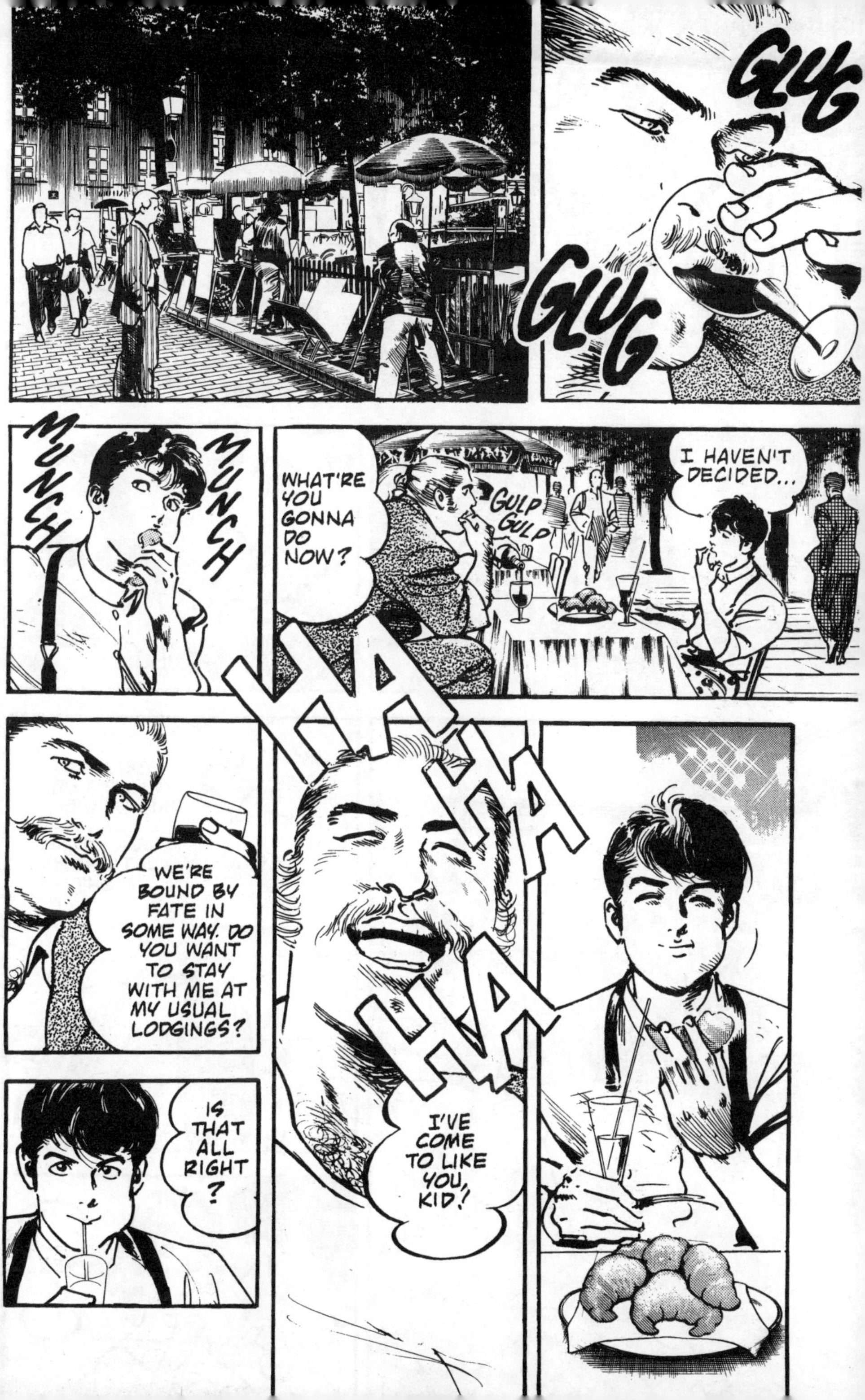
GLUG
GLUG
MUNCH
MUNCH
WHAT'RE YOU GONNA DO NOW?
GULP GULP
I HAVEN'T DECIDED...
WE'RE BOUND BY FATE IN SOME WAY. DO YOU WANT TO STAY WITH ME AT MY USUAL LODGINGS?
IS THAT ALL RIGHT?
HA HA HA
I'VE COME TO LIKE YOU, KID!

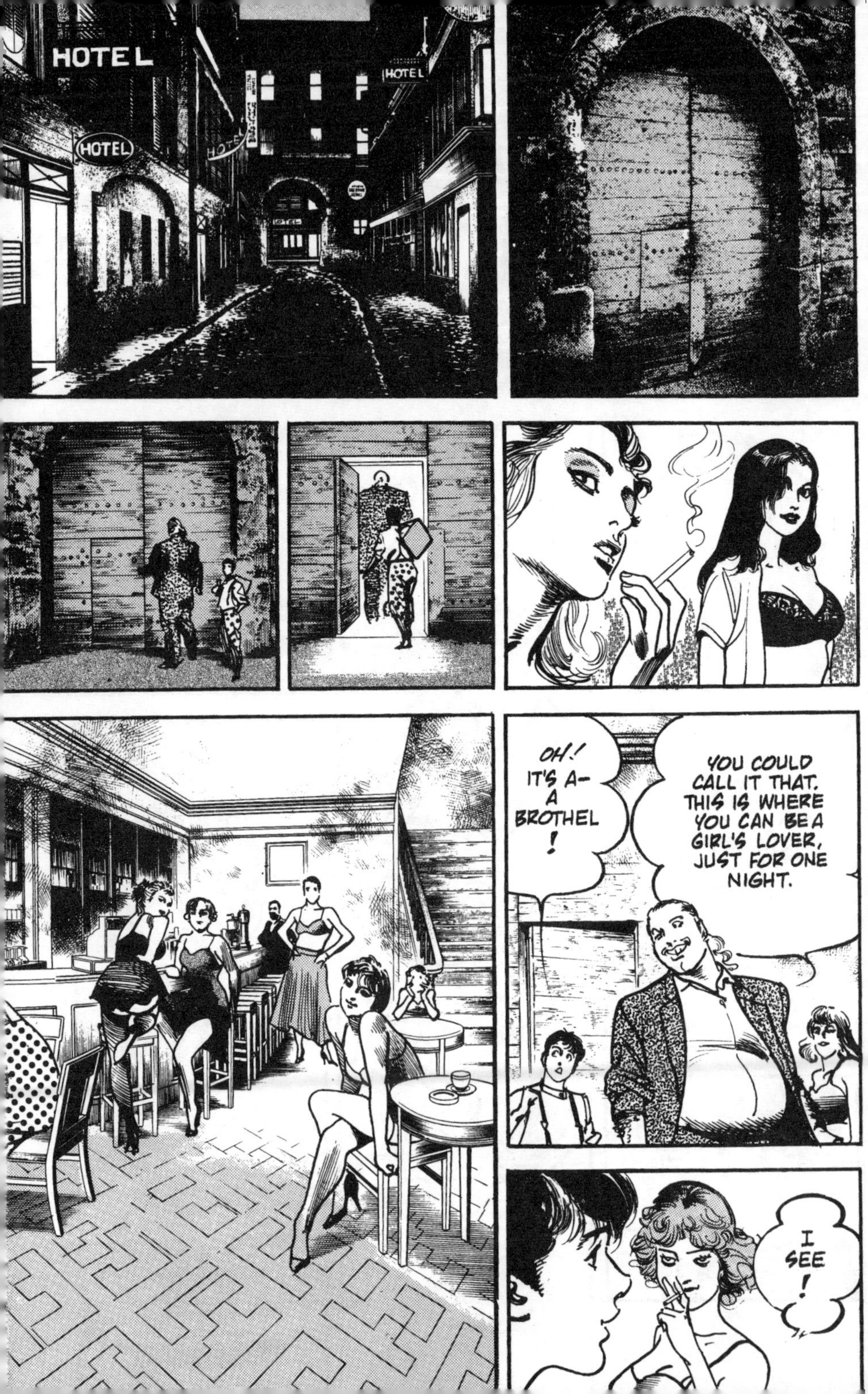
HOTEL
HOTEL
HOTEL
HOTEL
OH! IT'S A-- A BROTHEL!
YOU COULD CALL IT THAT. THIS IS WHERE YOU CAN BE A GIRL'S LOVER, JUST FOR ONE NIGHT.
I SEE!

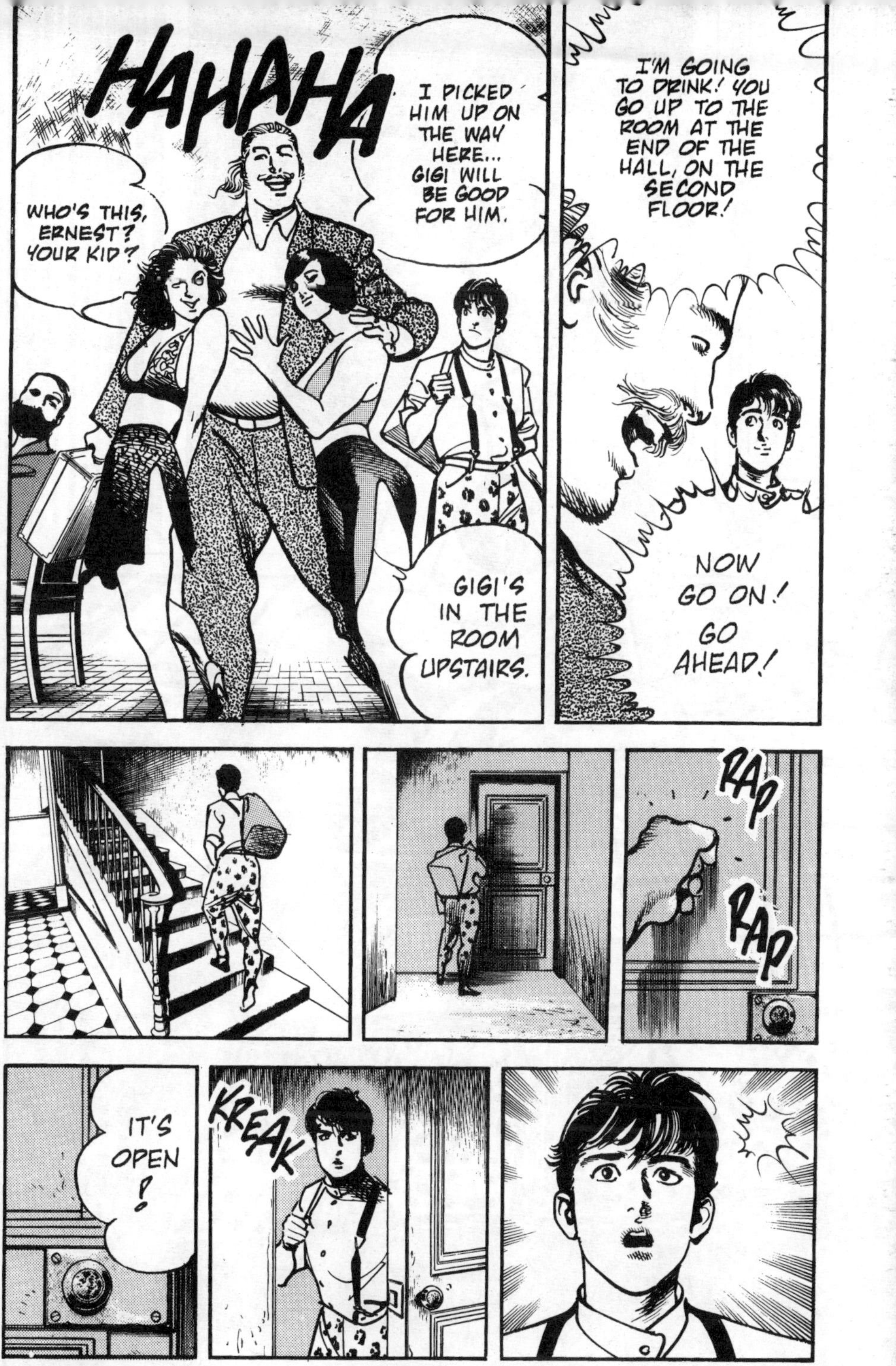
HAHAHA
WHO'S THIS, ERNEST? YOUR KID?
I PICKED HIM UP ON THE WAY HERE... GIGI WILL BE GOOD FOR HIM.
GIGI'S IN THE ROOM UPSTAIRS.
I'M GOING TO DRINK! YOU GO UP TO THE ROOM AT THE END OF THE HALL, ON THE SECOND FLOOR!
NOW GO ON!
GO AHEAD!
RAP
RAP
IT'S OPEN !
KREAK

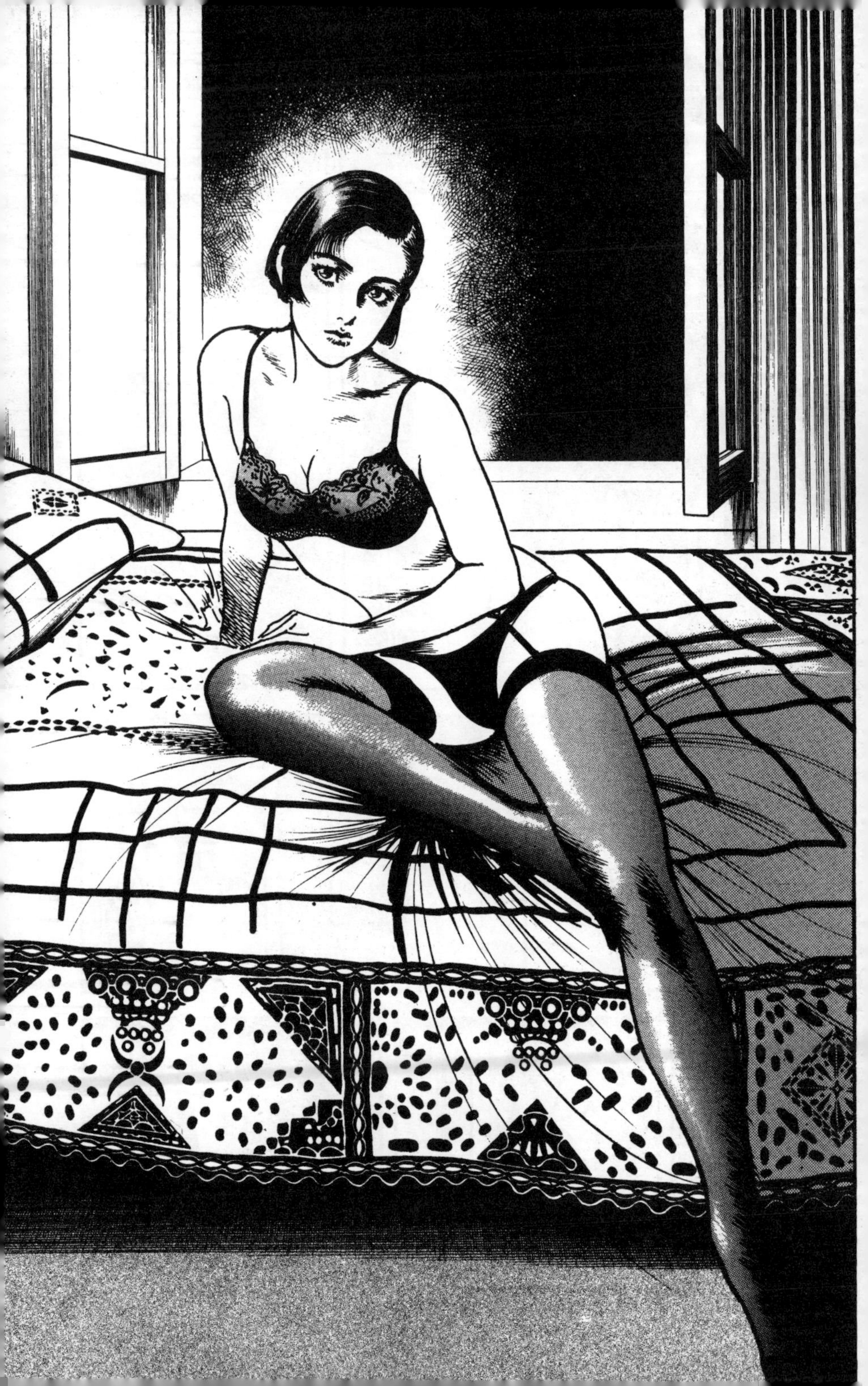

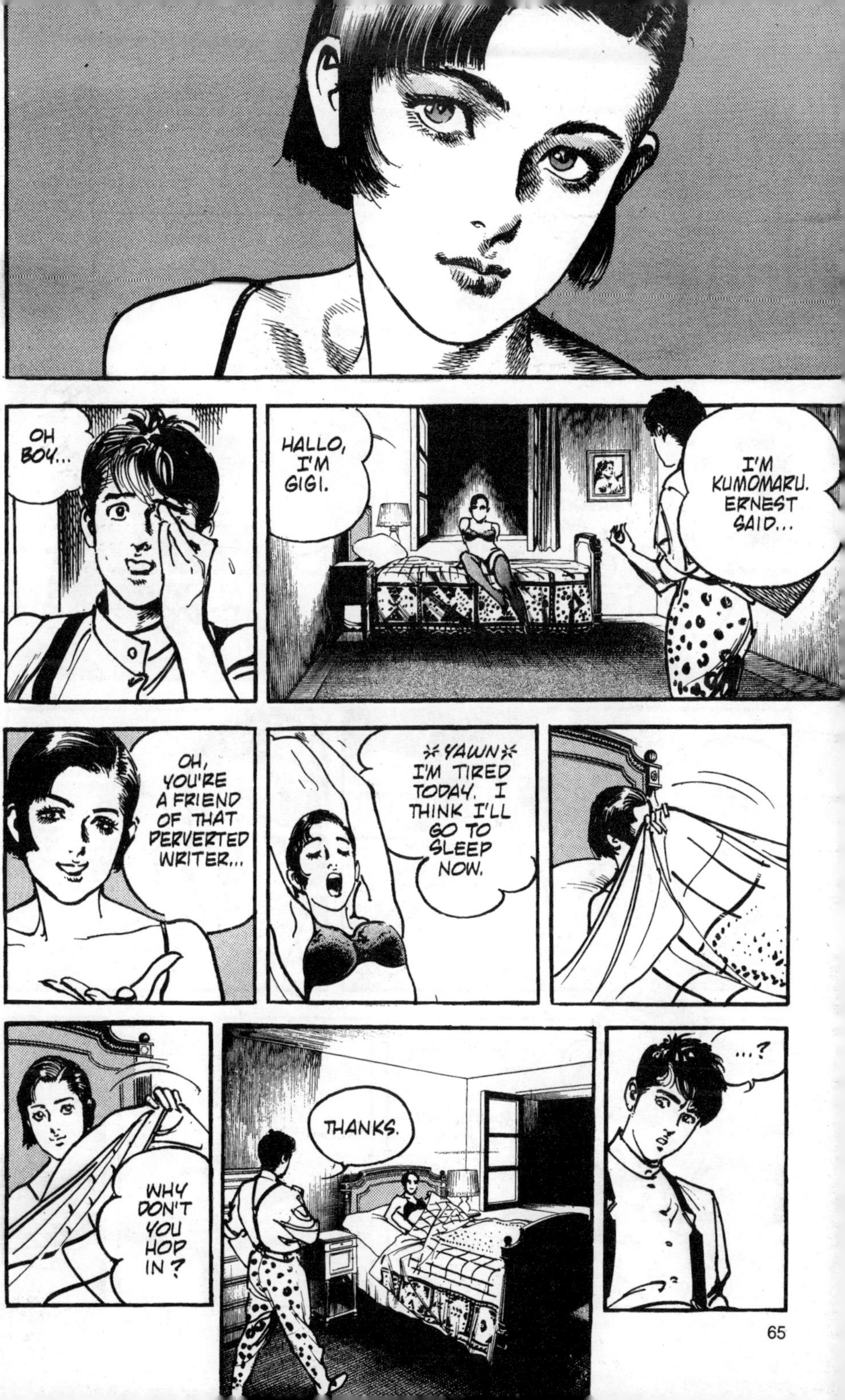

OH BOY...
HALLO, I'M GIGI.
I'M KUMOMARU. ERNEST SAID...
OH, YOU'RE A FRIEND OF THAT PERVERTED WRITER...
YAWN
I'M TIRED TODAY. I THINK I'LL GO TO SLEEP NOW.
WHY DON'T YOU HOP IN?
THANKS.
...?

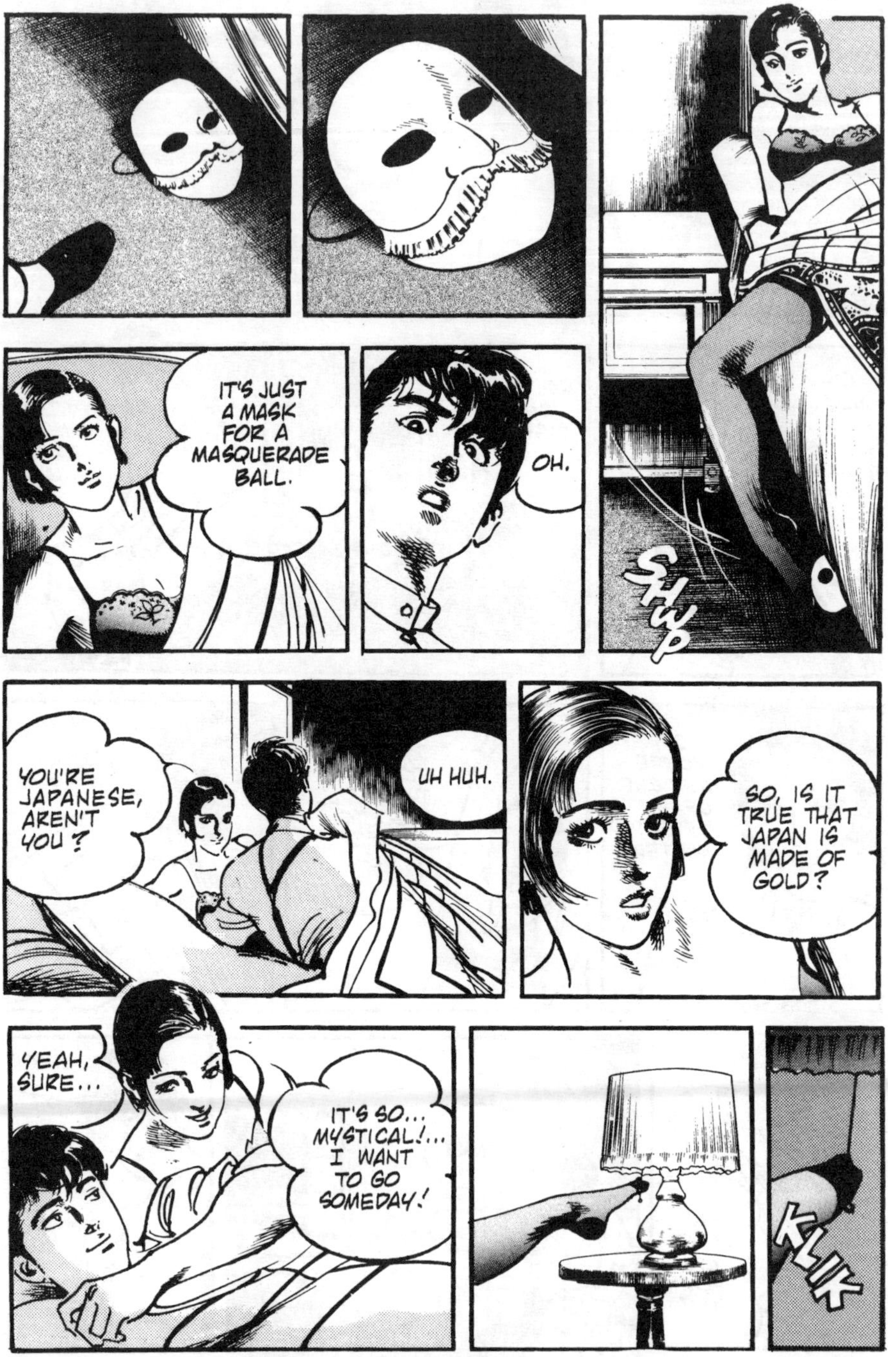
IT'S JUST A MASK FOR A MASQUERADE BALL.
OH.
SHUP
YOU'RE JAPANESE, AREN'T YOU?
UH HUH.
SO, IS IT TRUE THAT JAPAN IS MADE OF GOLD?
YEAH, SURE...
IT'S SO... MYSTICAL!... I WANT TO GO SOMEDAY!
KLIK

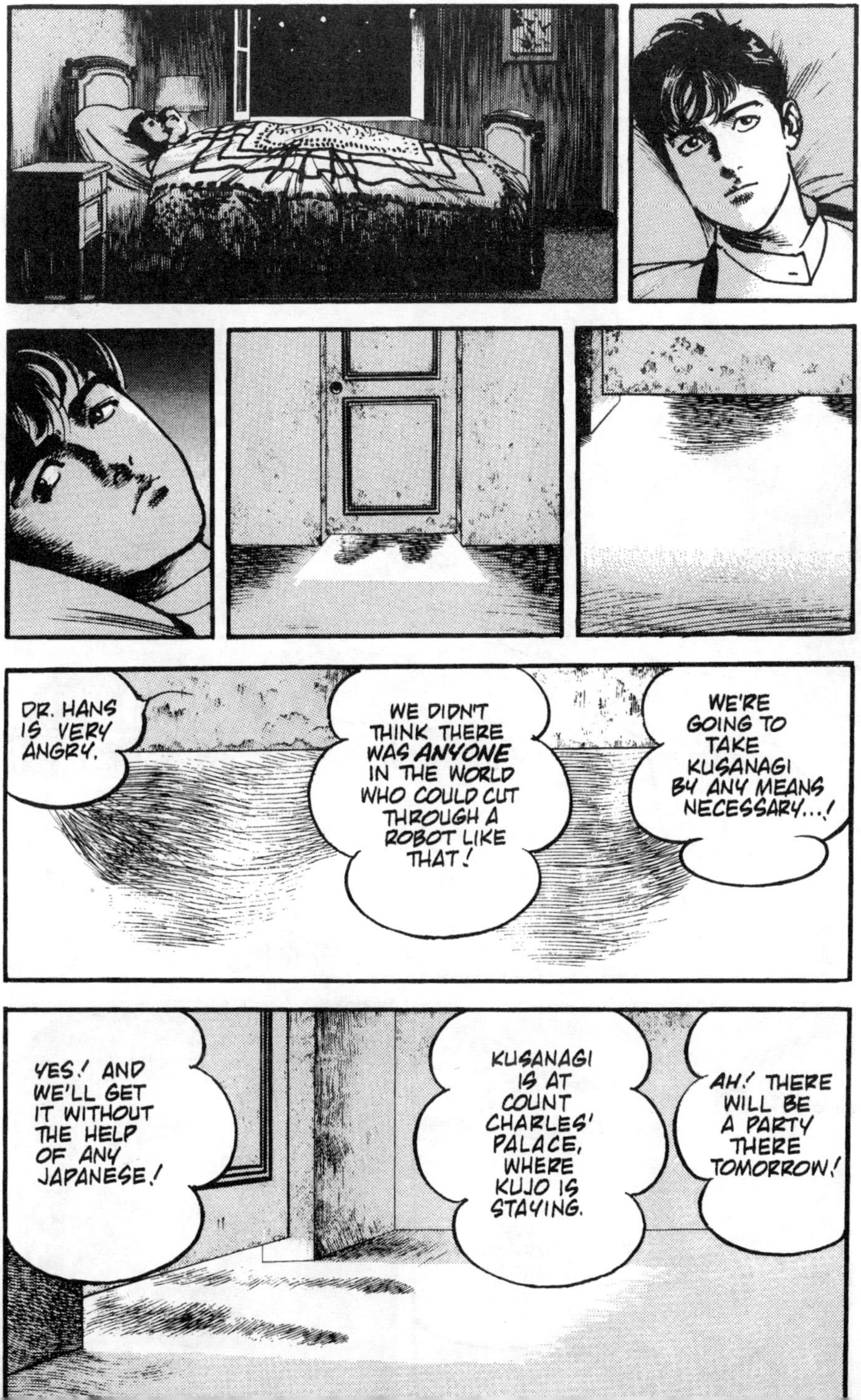
DR. HANS IS VERY ANGRY.
WE DIDN'T THINK THERE WAS ANYONE IN THE WORLD WHO COULD CUT THROUGH A ROBOT LIKE THAT!
WE'RE GOING TO TAKE KUSANAGI BY ANY MEANS NECESSARY...!
YES! AND WE'LL GET IT WITHOUT THE HELP OF ANY JAPANESE!
KUSANAGI IS AT COUNT CHARLES' PALACE, WHERE KUJO IS STAYING.
AH! THERE WILL BE A PARTY THERE TOMORROW!

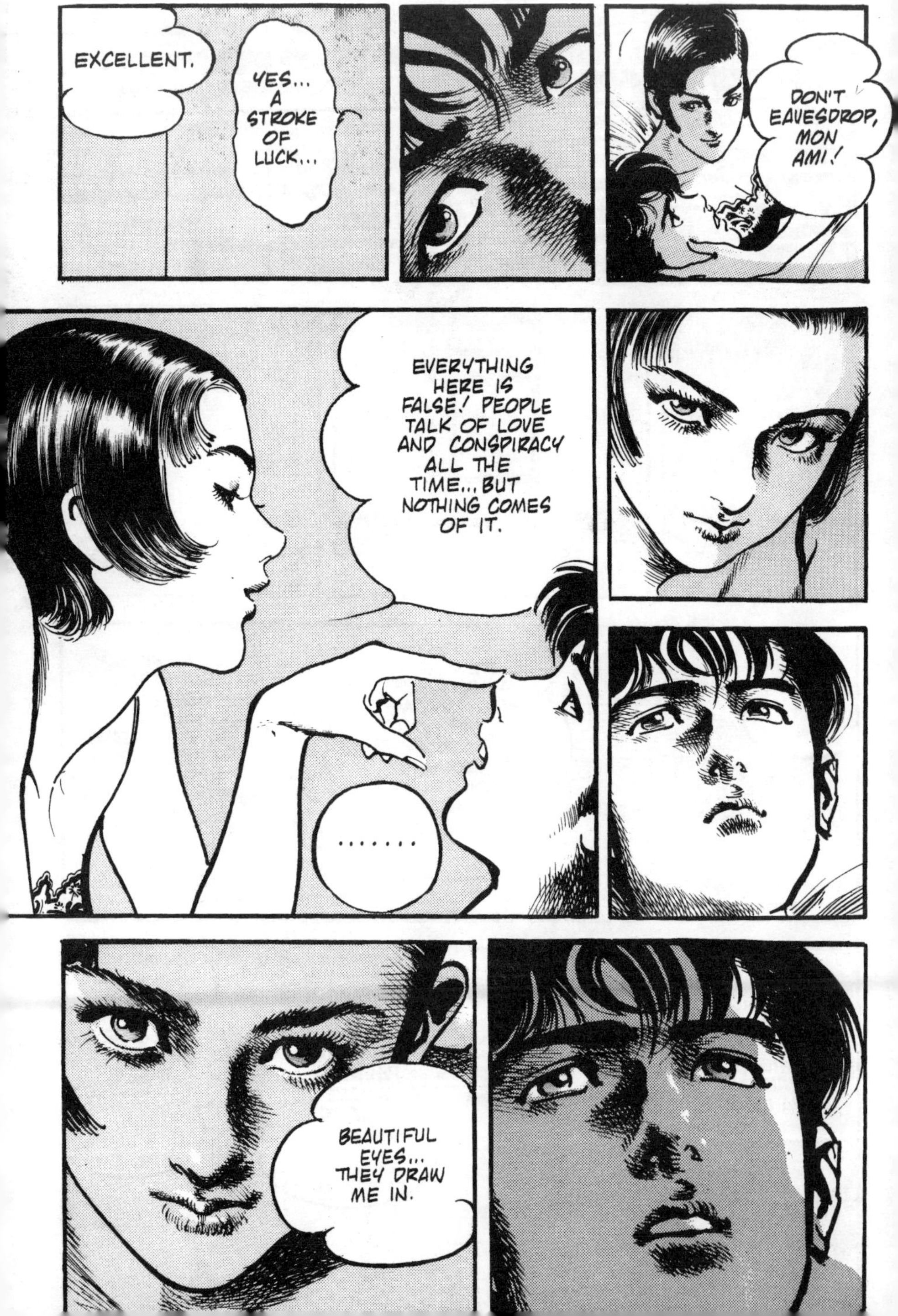
EXCELLENT.
YES... A STROKE OF LUCK...
DON'T EAVESDROP, MON AMI!
EVERYTHING HERE IS FALSE! PEOPLE TALK OF LOVE AND CONSPIRACY ALL THE TIME... BUT NOTHING COMES OF IT.
....
BEAUTIFUL EYES... THEY DRAW ME IN.

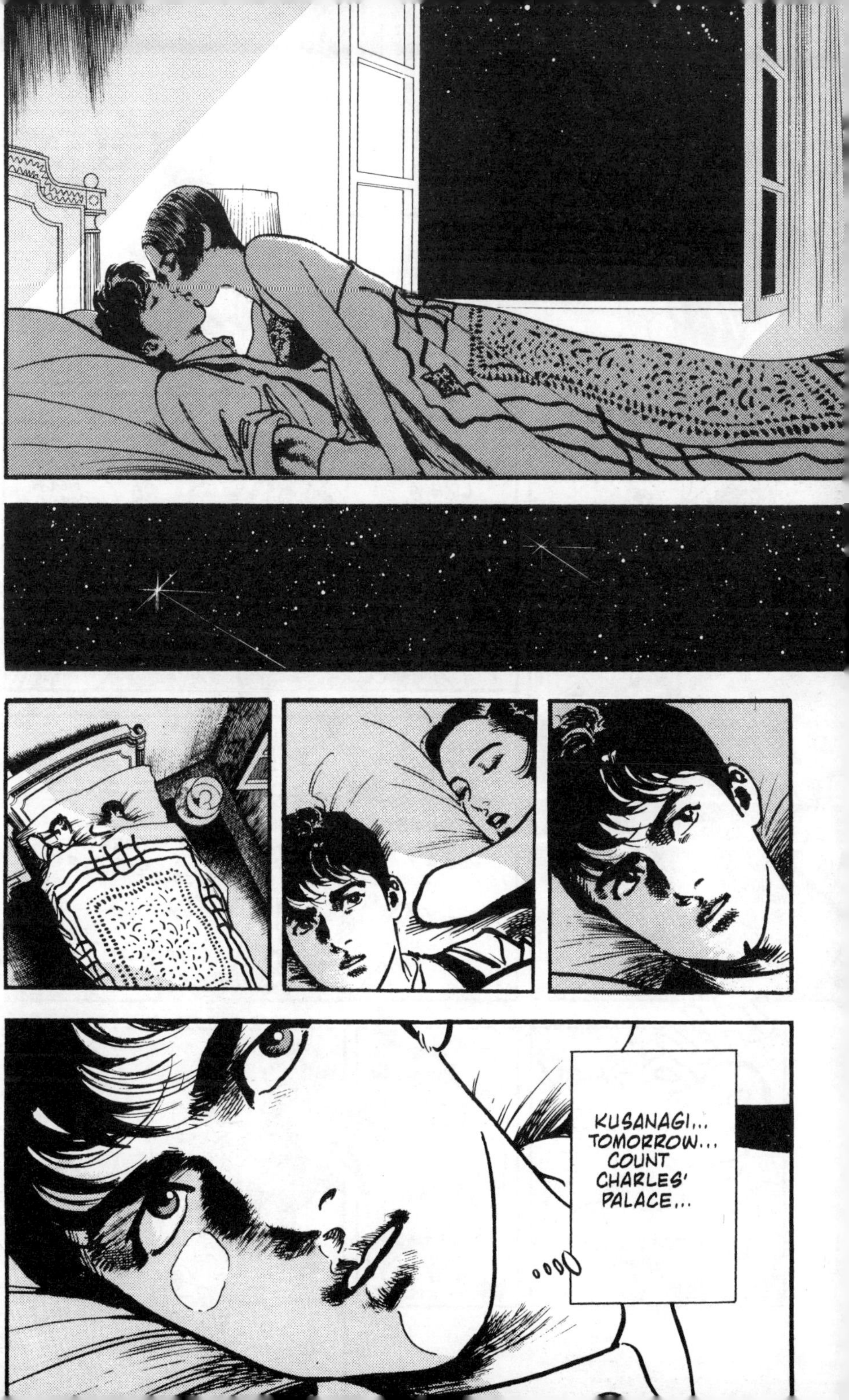
KUSANAGI... TOMORROW... COUNT CHARLES' PALACE...

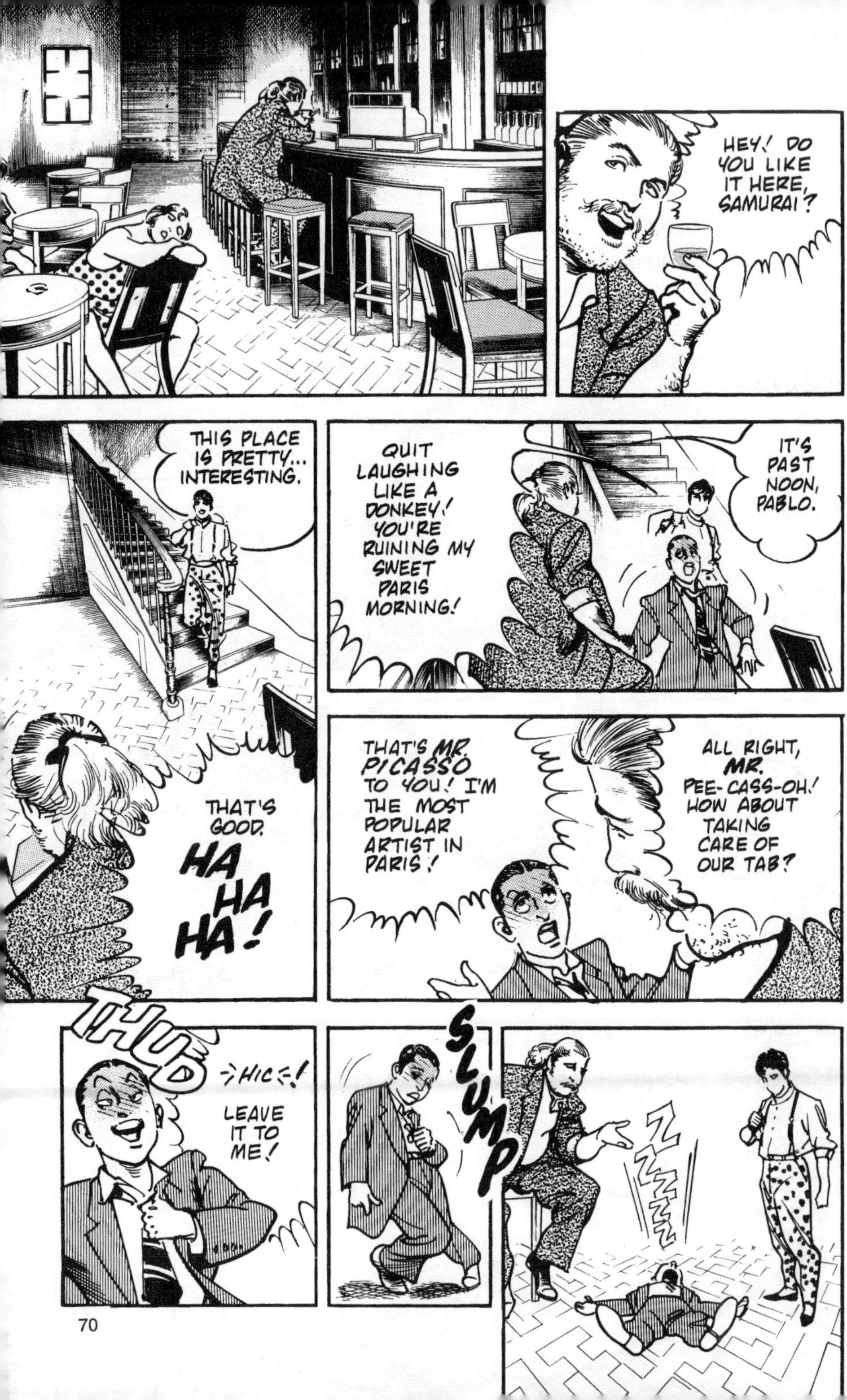
HEY! DO YOU LIKE IT HERE, SAMURAI?
THIS PLACE IS PRETTY... INTERESTING.
QUIT LAUGHING LIKE A DONKEY! YOU'RE RUINING MY SWEET PARIS MORNING!
IT'S PAST NOON, PABLO.
THAT'S GOOD.
HA HA HA!
THAT'S MR. PICASSO TO YOU! I'M THE MOST POPULAR ARTIST IN PARIS!
ALL RIGHT, MR. PEE-CASS-OH! HOW ABOUT TAKING CARE OF OUR TAB?
THUD
HIC
LEAVE IT TO ME!
SLUMP
Z Z Z Z Z

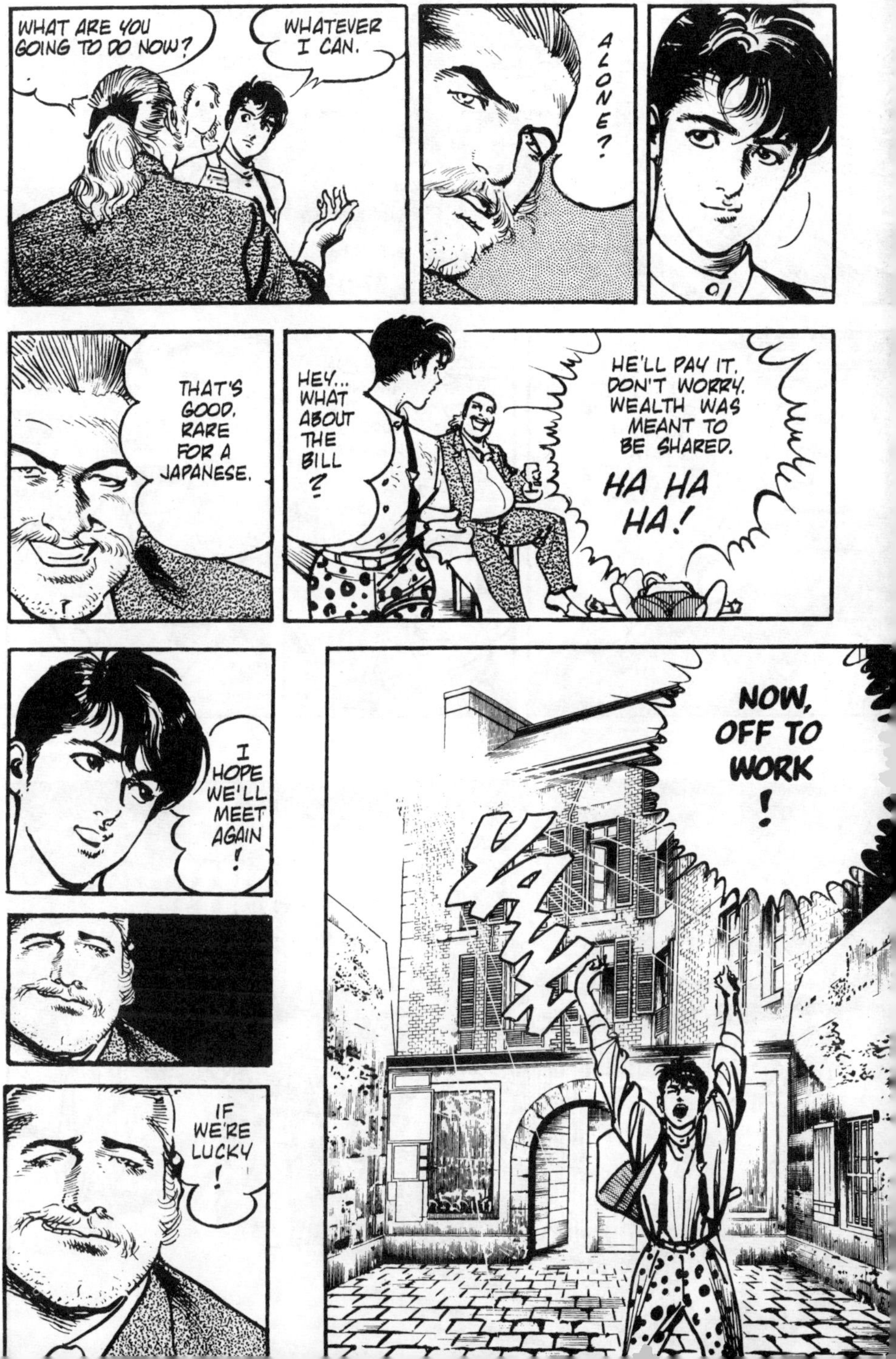

WHAT ARE YOU GOING TO DO NOW?
WHATEVER I CAN.
ALONE?
THAT'S GOOD. RARE FOR A JAPANESE.
HEY... WHAT ABOUT THE BILL?
HE'LL PAY IT. DON'T WORRY. WEALTH WAS MEANT TO BE SHARED.
HA HA HA!
I HOPE WE'LL MEET AGAIN!
IF WE'RE LUCKY!
NOW, OFF TO WORK!

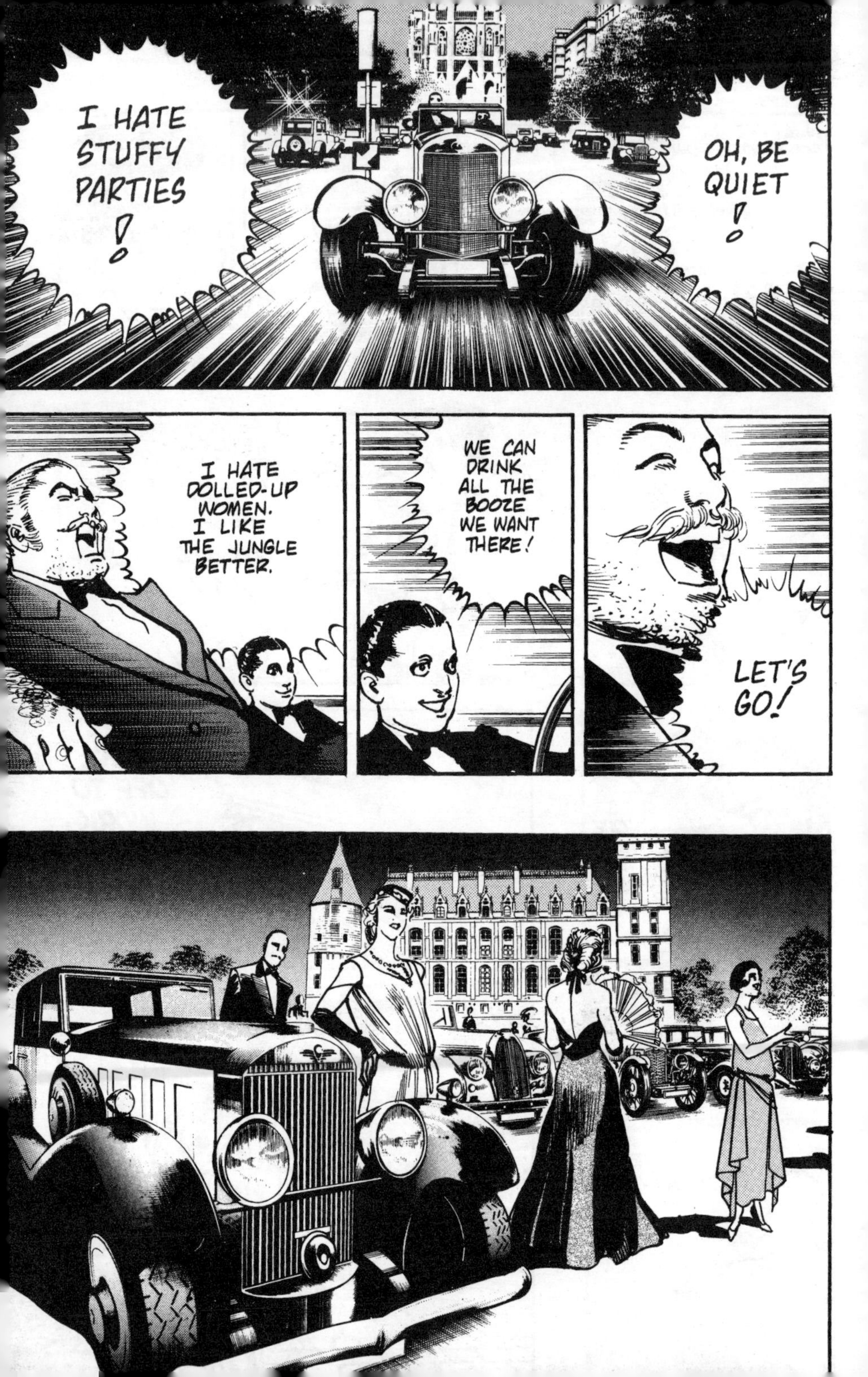
I HATE STUFFY PARTIES!
OH, BE QUIET!
I HATE DOLLED-UP WOMEN. I LIKE THE JUNGLE BETTER.
WE CAN DRINK ALL THE BOOZE WE WANT THERE!
LET'S GO!

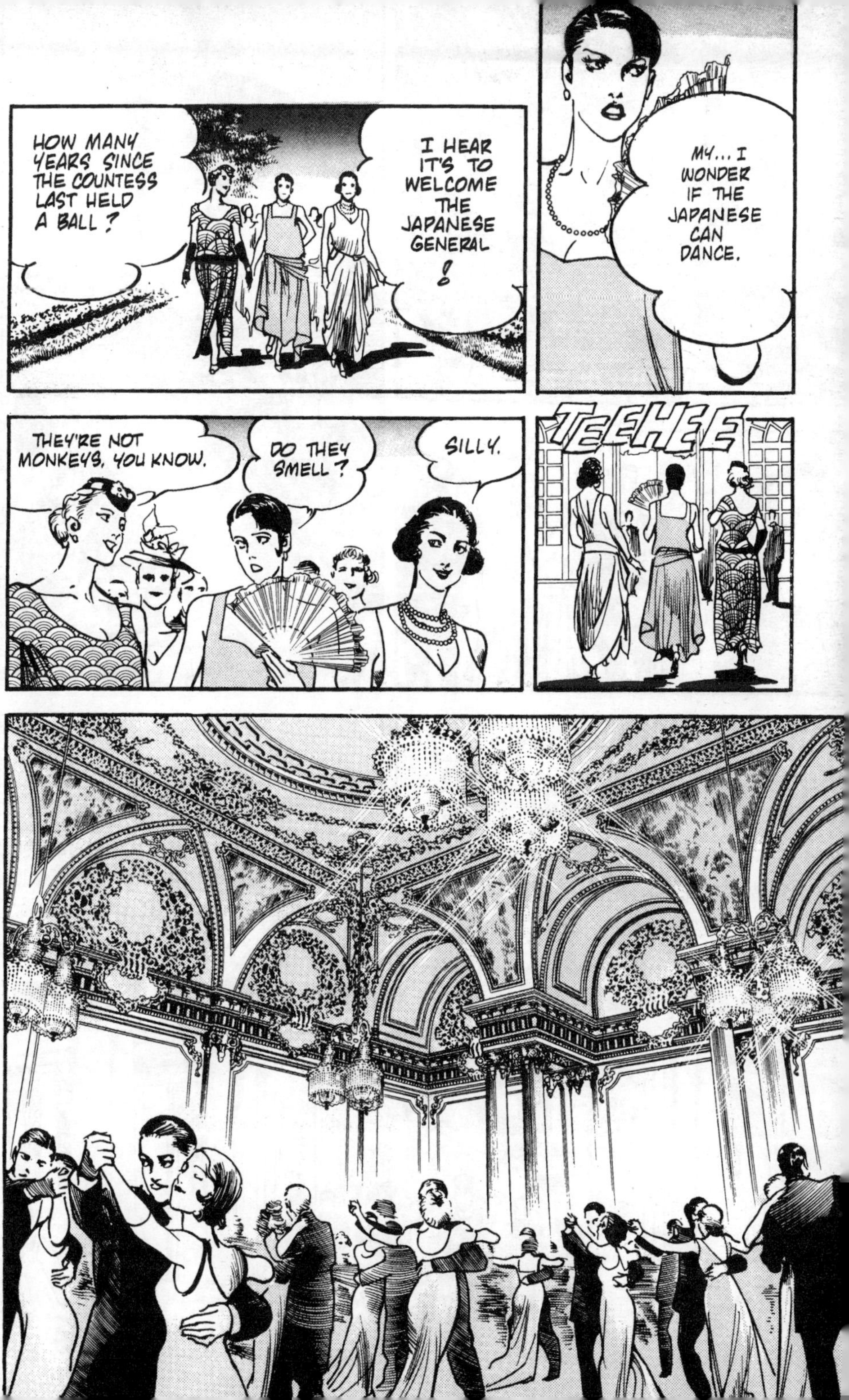
HOW MANY YEARS SINCE THE COUNTESS LAST HELD A BALL?
I HEAR IT'S TO WELCOME THE JAPANESE GENERAL!
MY... I WONDER IF THE JAPANESE CAN DANCE.
THEY'RE NOT MONKEYS, YOU KNOW.
DO THEY SMELL?
SILLY.
TEEHEE

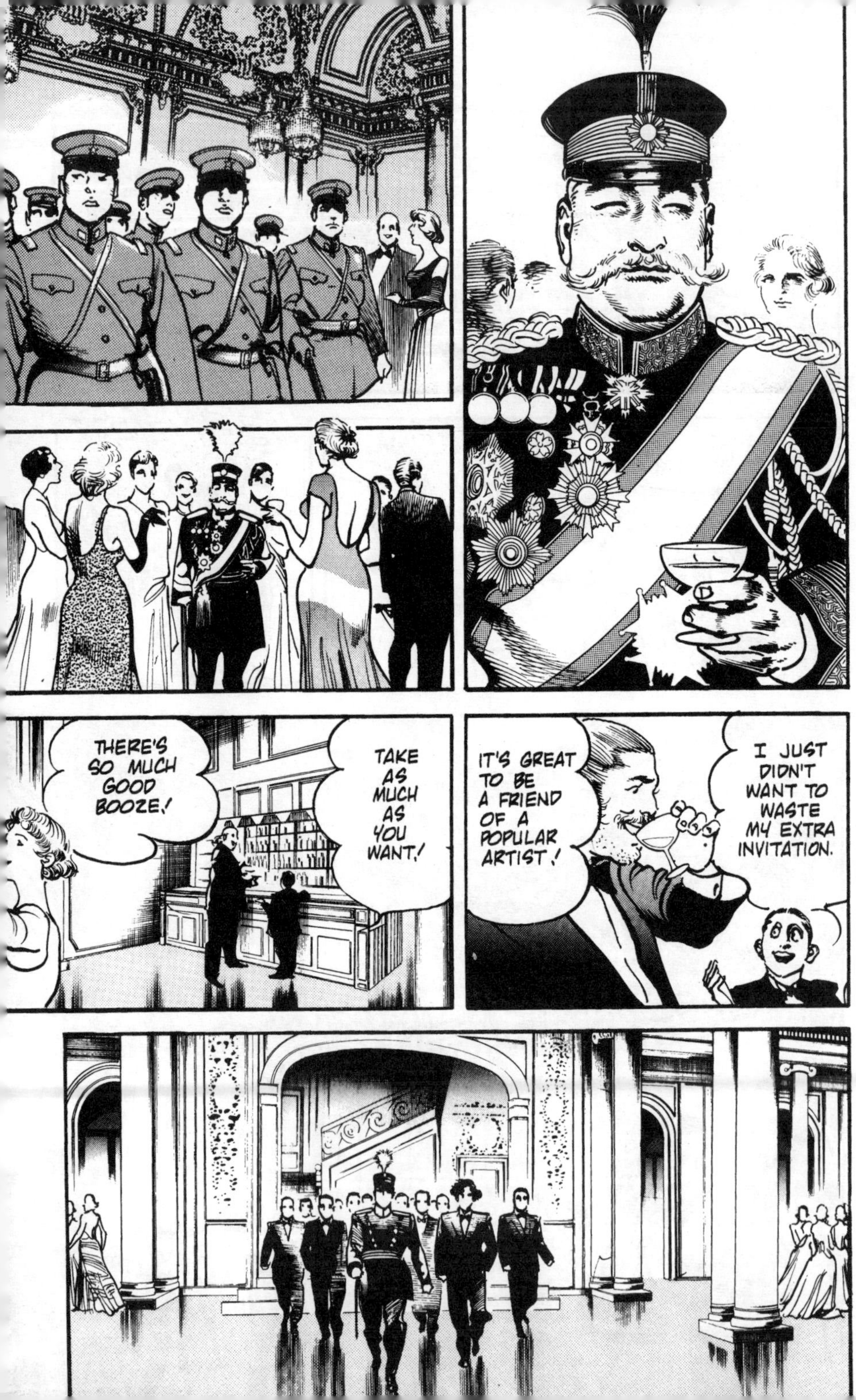
THERE'S SO MUCH GOOD BOOZE!
TAKE AS MUCH AS YOU WANT!
IT'S GREAT TO BE A FRIEND OF A POPULAR ARTIST!
I JUST DIDN'T WANT TO WASTE MY EXTRA INVITATION.

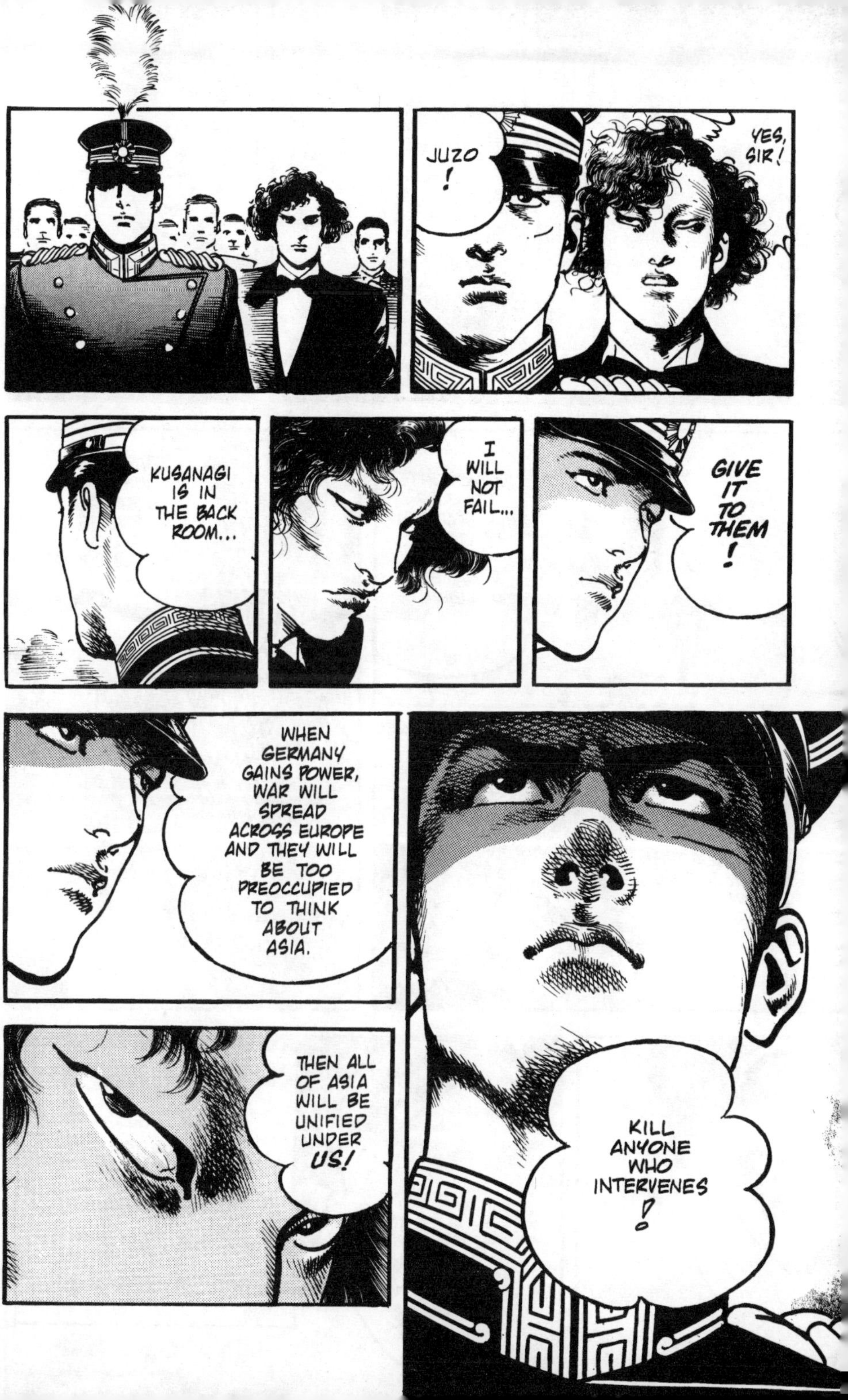
JUZO!
YES, SIR!
KUSANAGI IS IN THE BACK ROOM...
I WILL NOT FAIL...
GIVE IT TO THEM!
WHEN GERMANY GAINS POWER, WAR WILL SPREAD ACROSS EUROPE AND THEY WILL BE TOO PREOCCUPIED TO THINK ABOUT ASIA.
THEN ALL OF ASIA WILL BE UNIFIED UNDER US!
KILL ANYONE WHO INTERVENES!

OH, KAMISHIMA! WHEN DID YOU ARRIVE IN PARIS?

YESTERDAY, SIR...

YOU CAME TO OBSERVE EUROPE?

I THOUGHT IT WOULD HELP BROADEN MY VIEWS, SIR! I CAME TO...LEARN.

THAT IS VERY PRUDENT OF YOU. WELL, WE CAN RELAX AND DROP THE FORMALITIES NOW.

YES, SIR!

BIENVENUE! WELCOME, EVERYONE! PLEASE ENJOY YOURSELVES!

HMPF-- ENJOY IT WHILE YOU CAN. THE AGE OF THE ARISTOCRATIC CLASS IS ABOUT TO END!

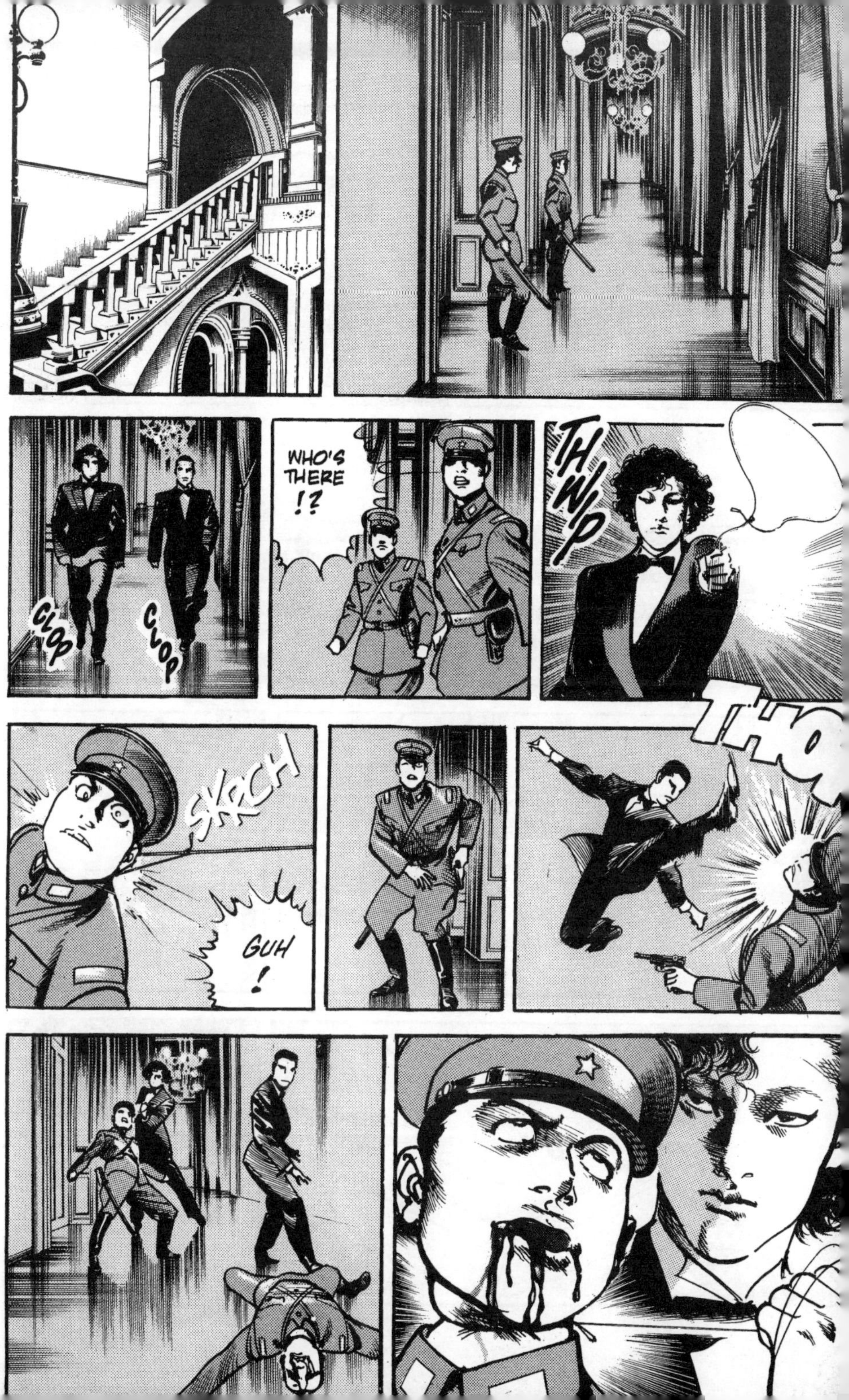
CLOP
CLOP
WHO'S THERE !?
THWIP
THO
SKRCH
GUH !

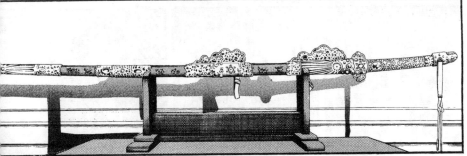

CHAK!

78

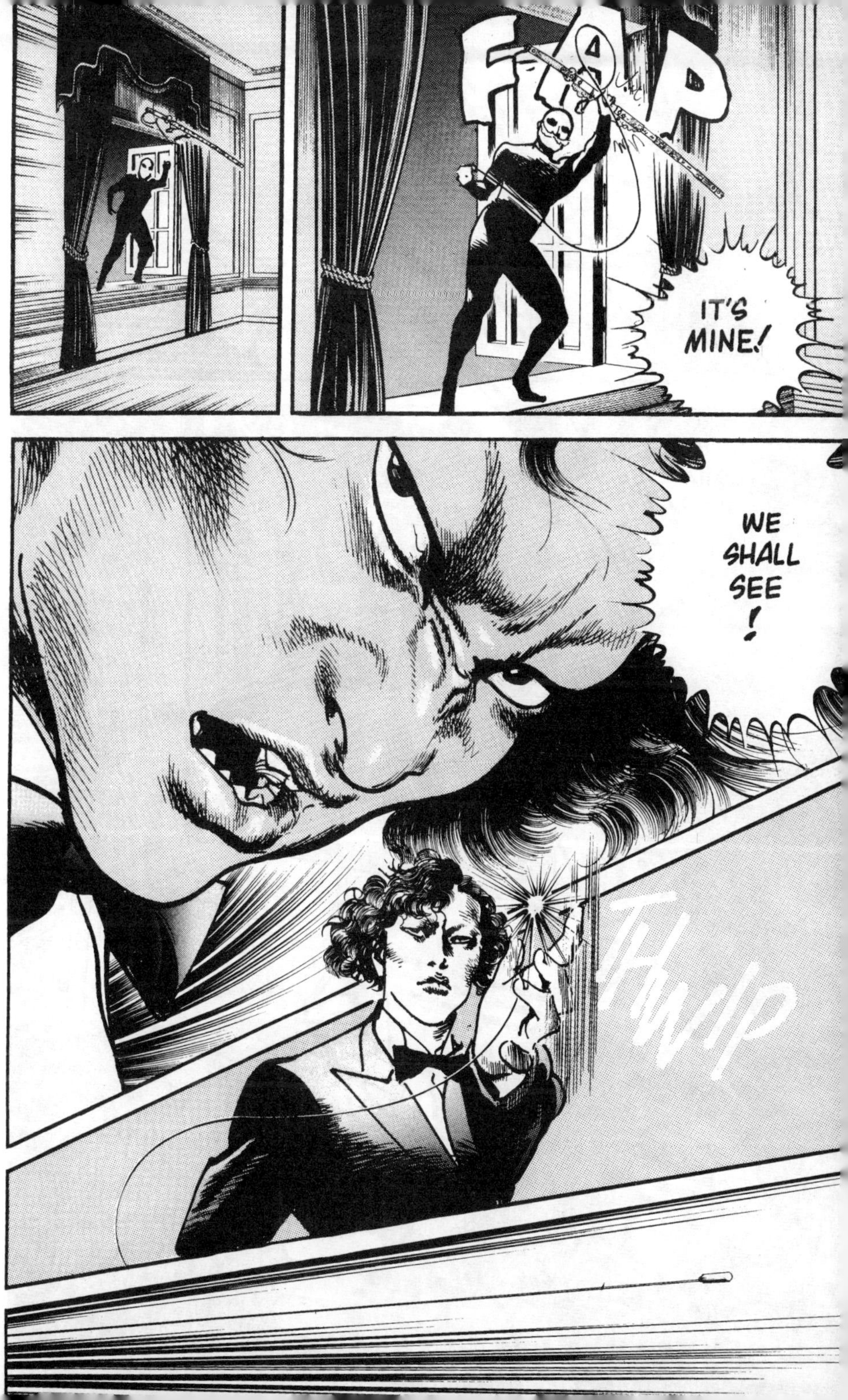
FLAP
IT'S MINE!
WE SHALL SEE!
THWIP

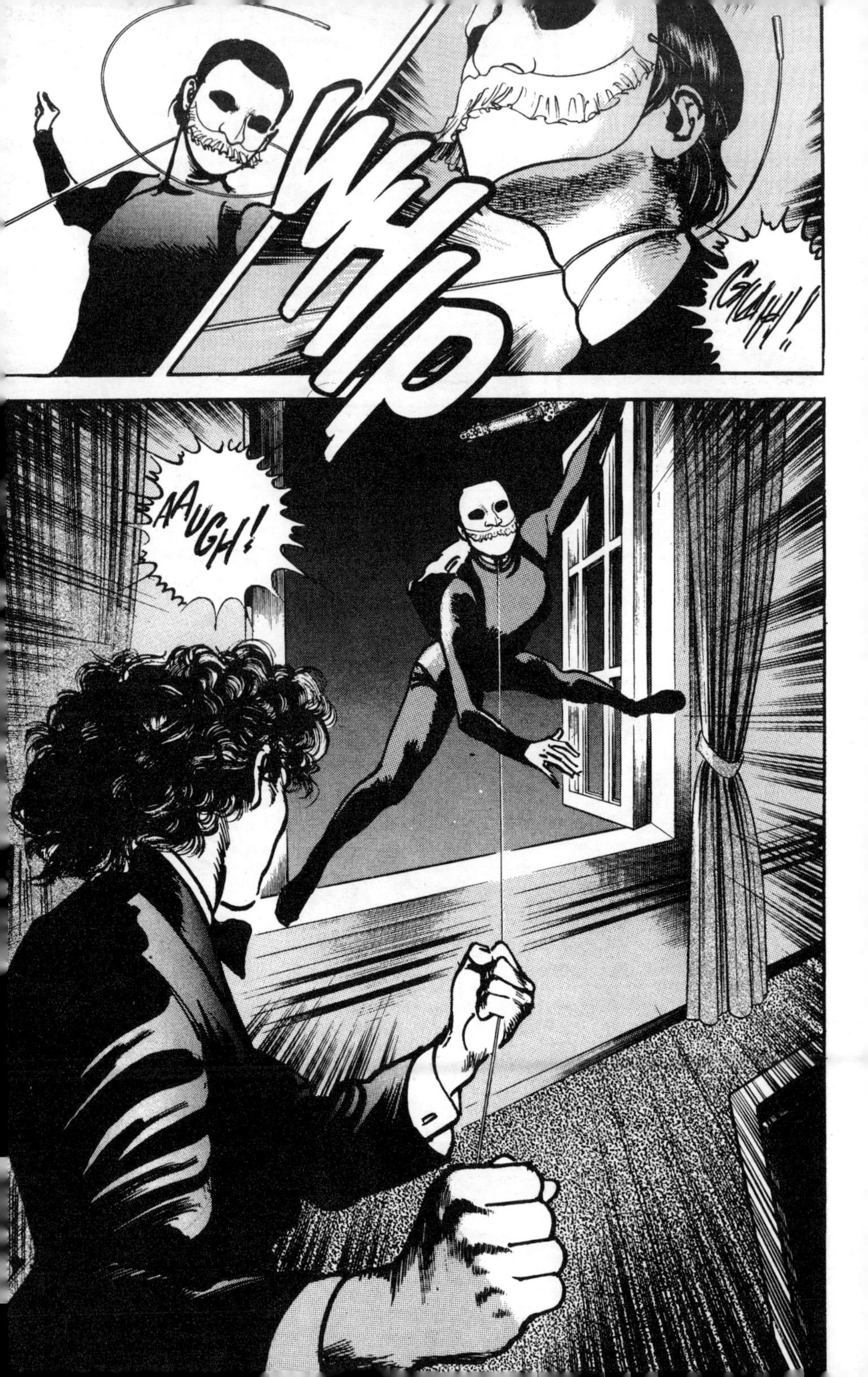
WHIP
GLAHH!!
AAUGH!

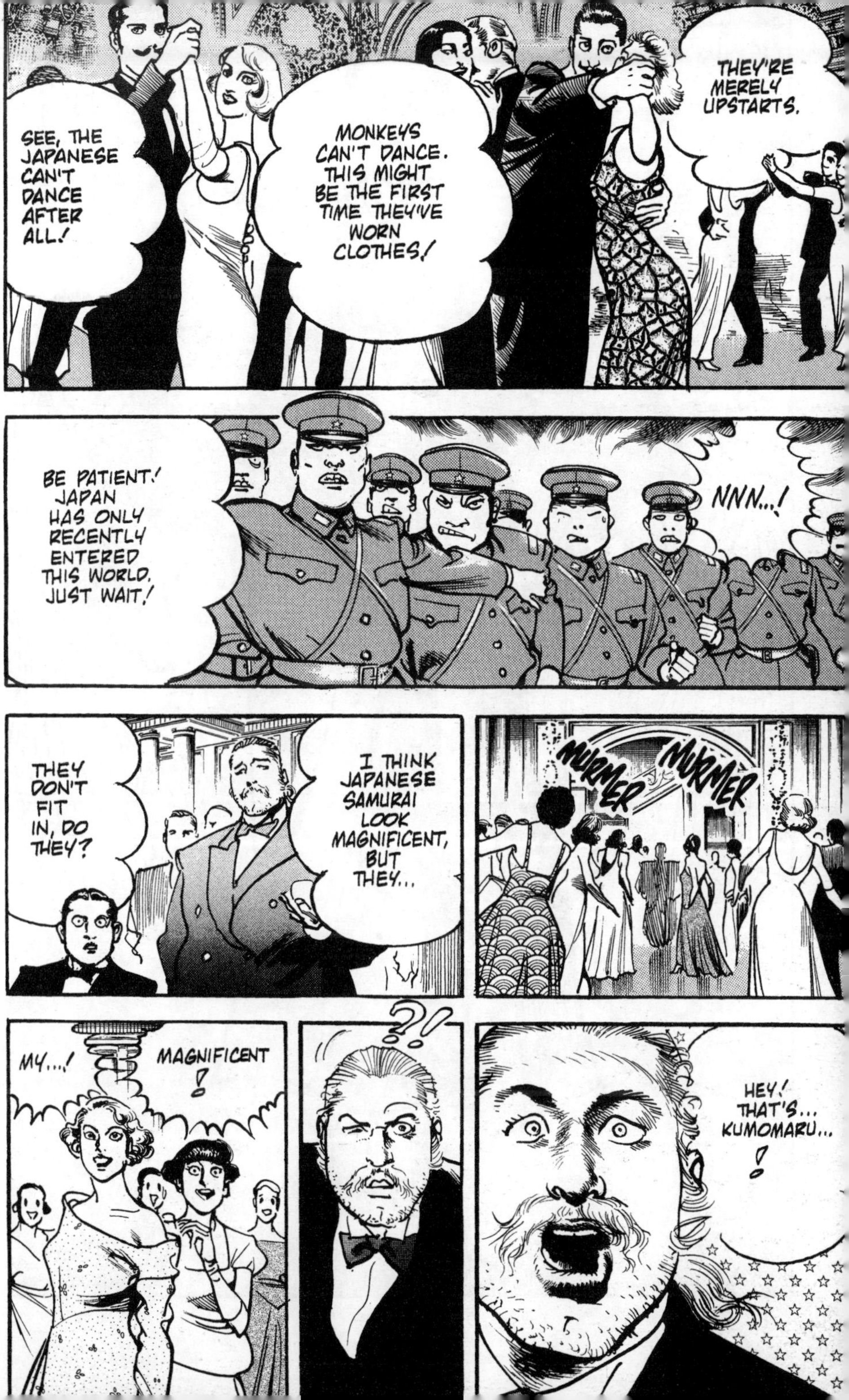
SEE, THE JAPANESE CAN'T DANCE AFTER ALL!
MONKEYS CAN'T DANCE. THIS MIGHT BE THE FIRST TIME THEY'VE WORN CLOTHES!
THEY'RE MERELY UPSTARTS.
BE PATIENT! JAPAN HAS ONLY RECENTLY ENTERED THIS WORLD. JUST WAIT!
NNN...!
THEY DON'T FIT IN, DO THEY?
I THINK JAPANESE SAMURAI LOOK MAGNIFICENT, BUT THEY...
MURMER
MURMER
MY...!
MAGNIFICENT!
?!
HEY! THAT'S... KUMOMARU...!

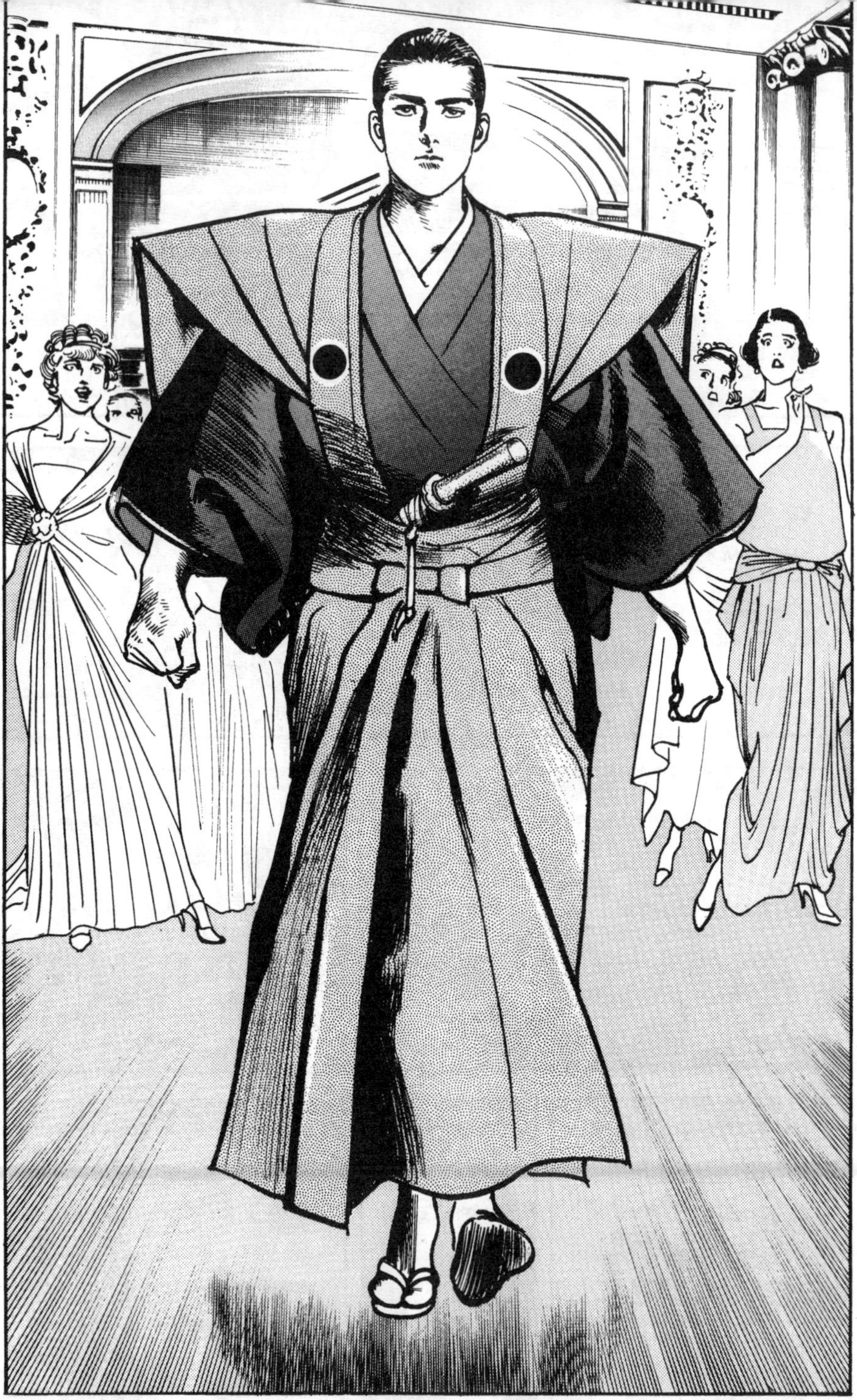

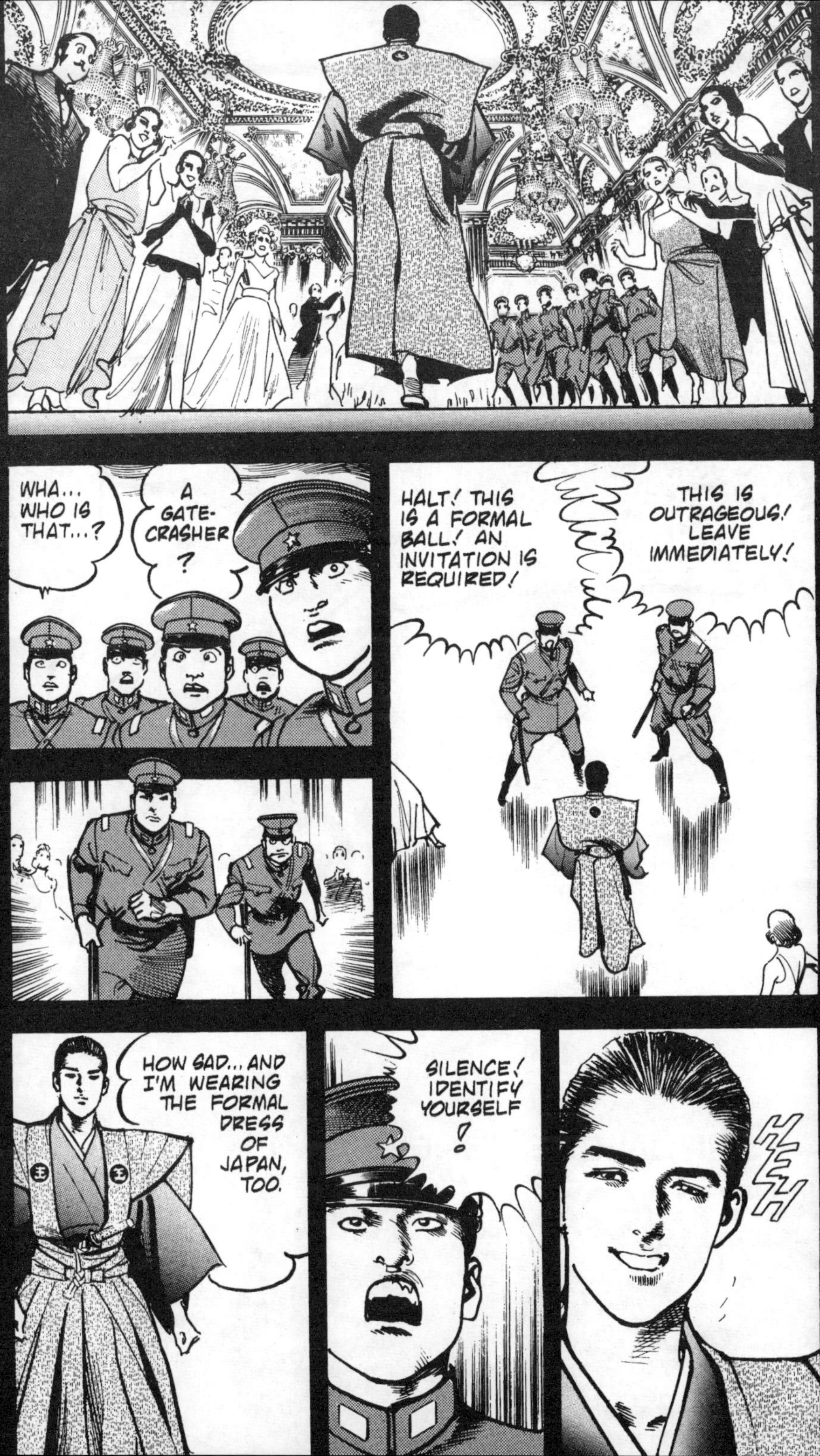
WHA... WHO IS THAT...?
A GATE-CRASHER?
HALT! THIS IS A FORMAL BALL! AN INVITATION IS REQUIRED!
THIS IS OUTRAGEOUS! LEAVE IMMEDIATELY!
HOW SAD... AND I'M WEARING THE FORMAL DRESS OF JAPAN, TOO.
SILENCE! IDENTIFY YOURSELF!
HEH

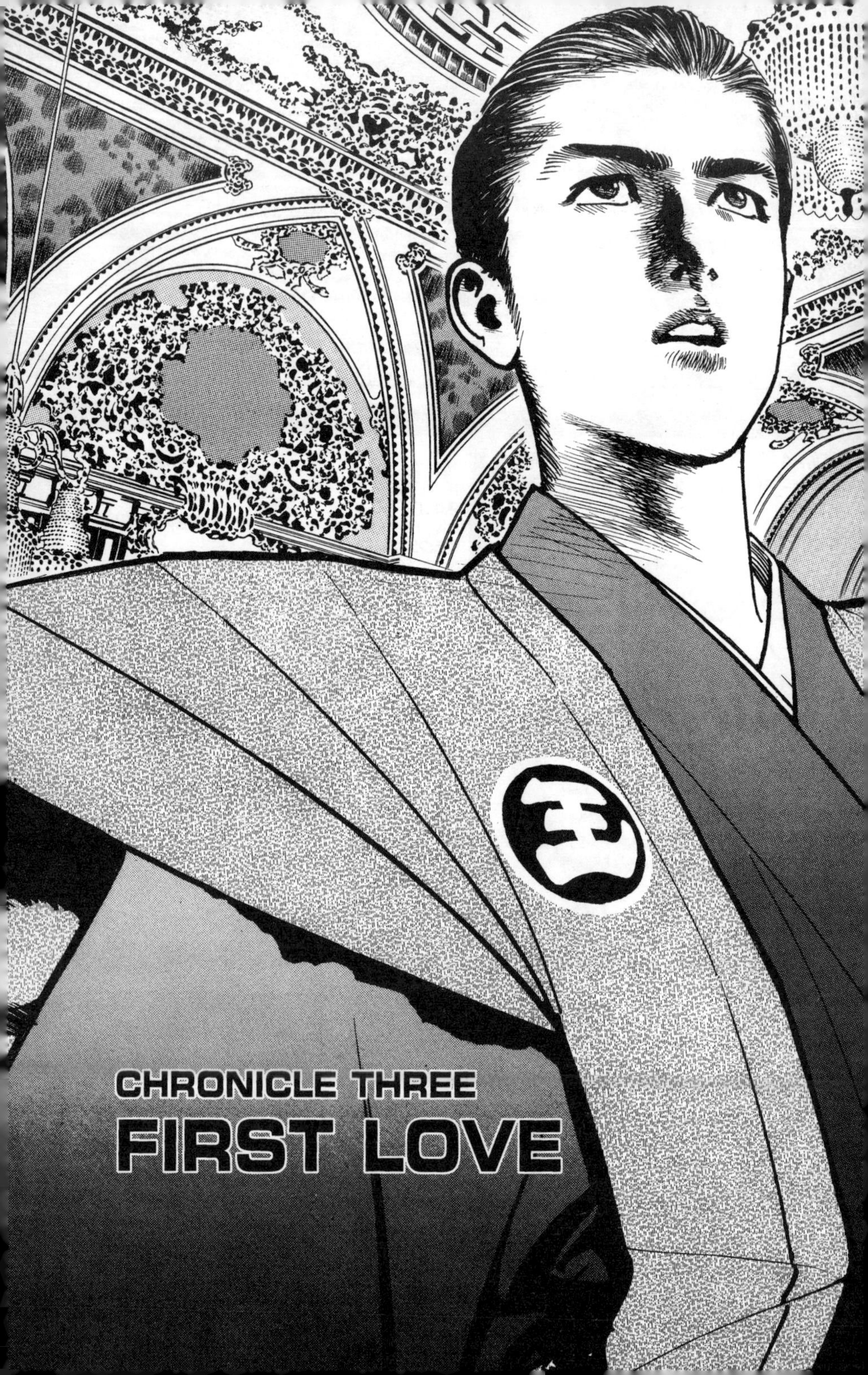
CHRONICLE THREE
FIRST LOVE

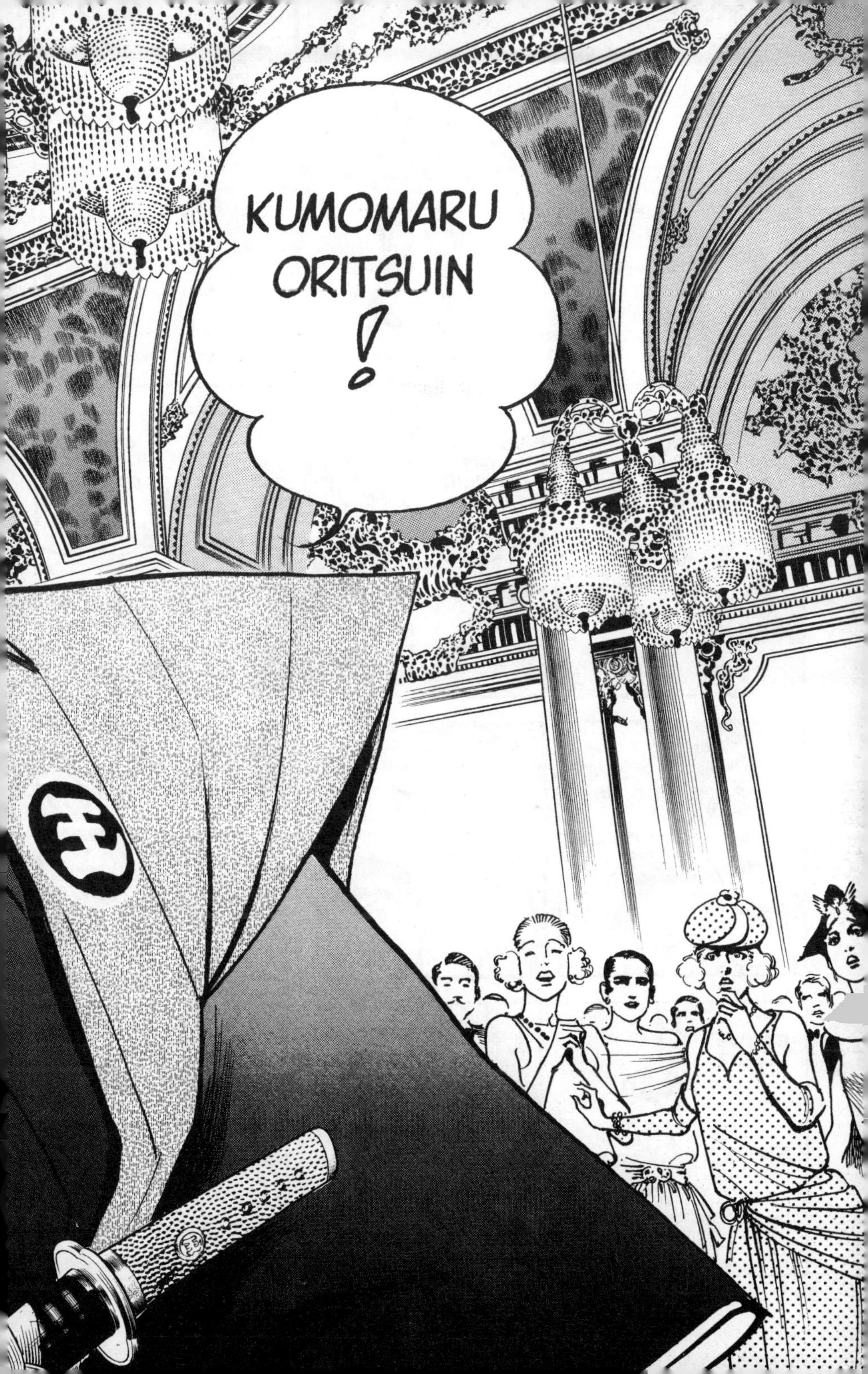
KUMOMARU ORITSUIN !

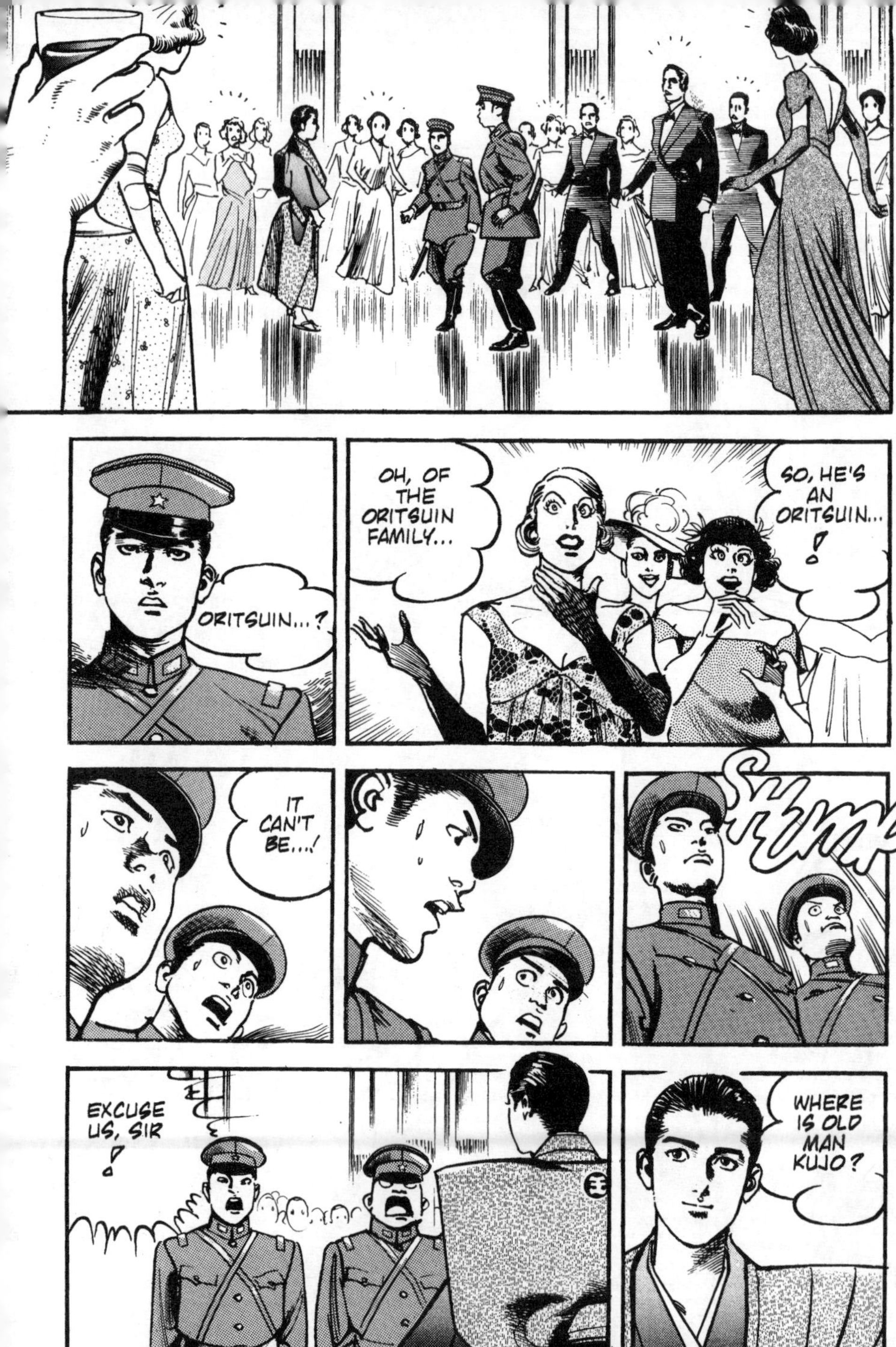
ORITSUIN...?
OH, OF THE ORITSUIN FAMILY...
SO, HE'S AN ORITSUIN...!
IT CAN'T BE...!
SHUNK
EXCUSE US, SIR!
WHERE IS OLD MAN KUJO?

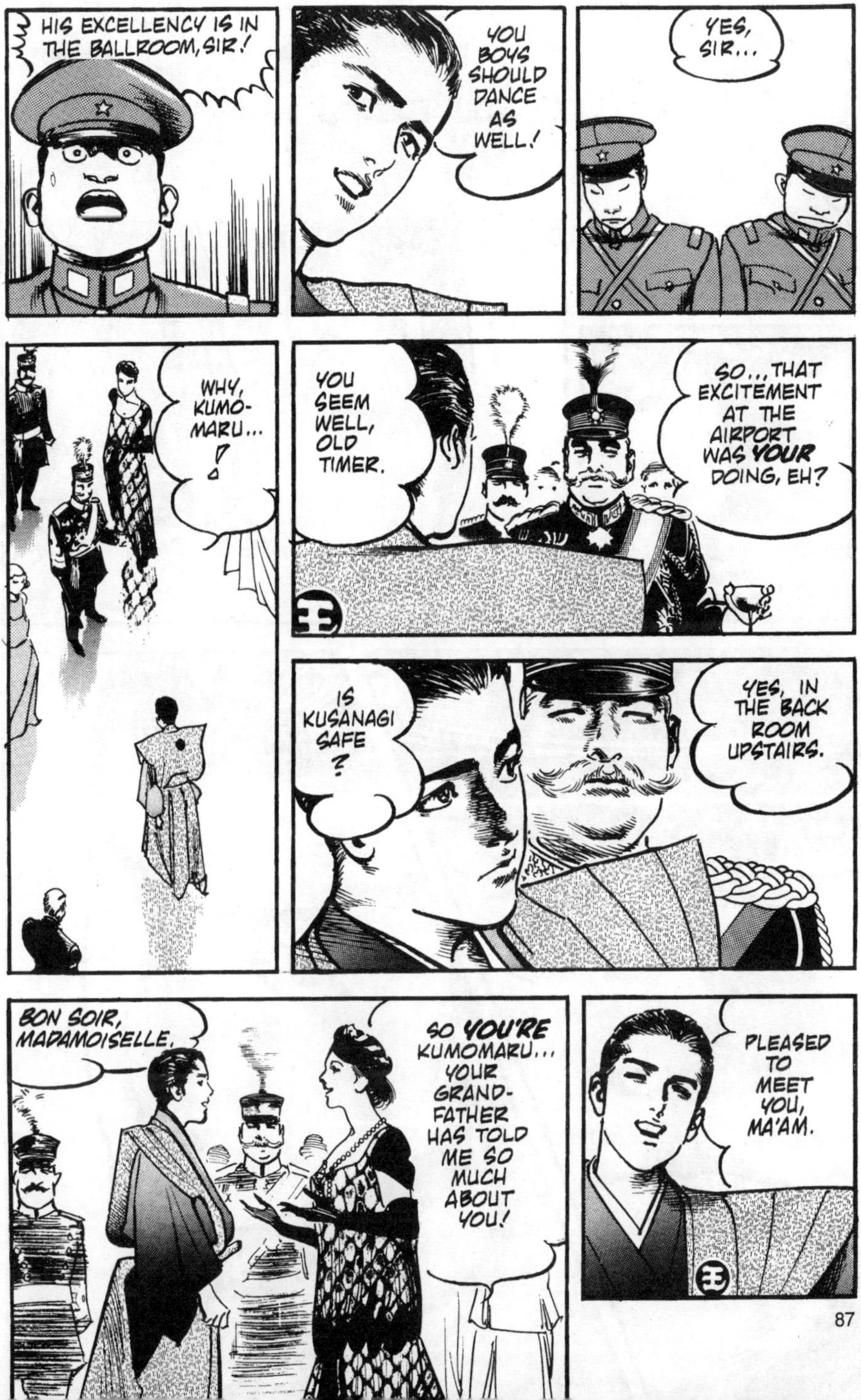
HIS EXCELLENCY IS IN THE BALLROOM, SIR!
YOU BOYS SHOULD DANCE AS WELL!
YES, SIR...
WHY, KUMO-MARU...!
YOU SEEM WELL, OLD TIMER.
SO.., THAT EXCITEMENT AT THE AIRPORT WAS YOUR DOING, EH?
IS KUSANAGI SAFE?
YES, IN THE BACK ROOM UPSTAIRS.
BON SOIR, MADAMOISELLE.
SO YOU'RE KUMOMARU... YOUR GRAND-FATHER HAS TOLD ME SO MUCH ABOUT YOU!
PLEASED TO MEET YOU, MA'AM.

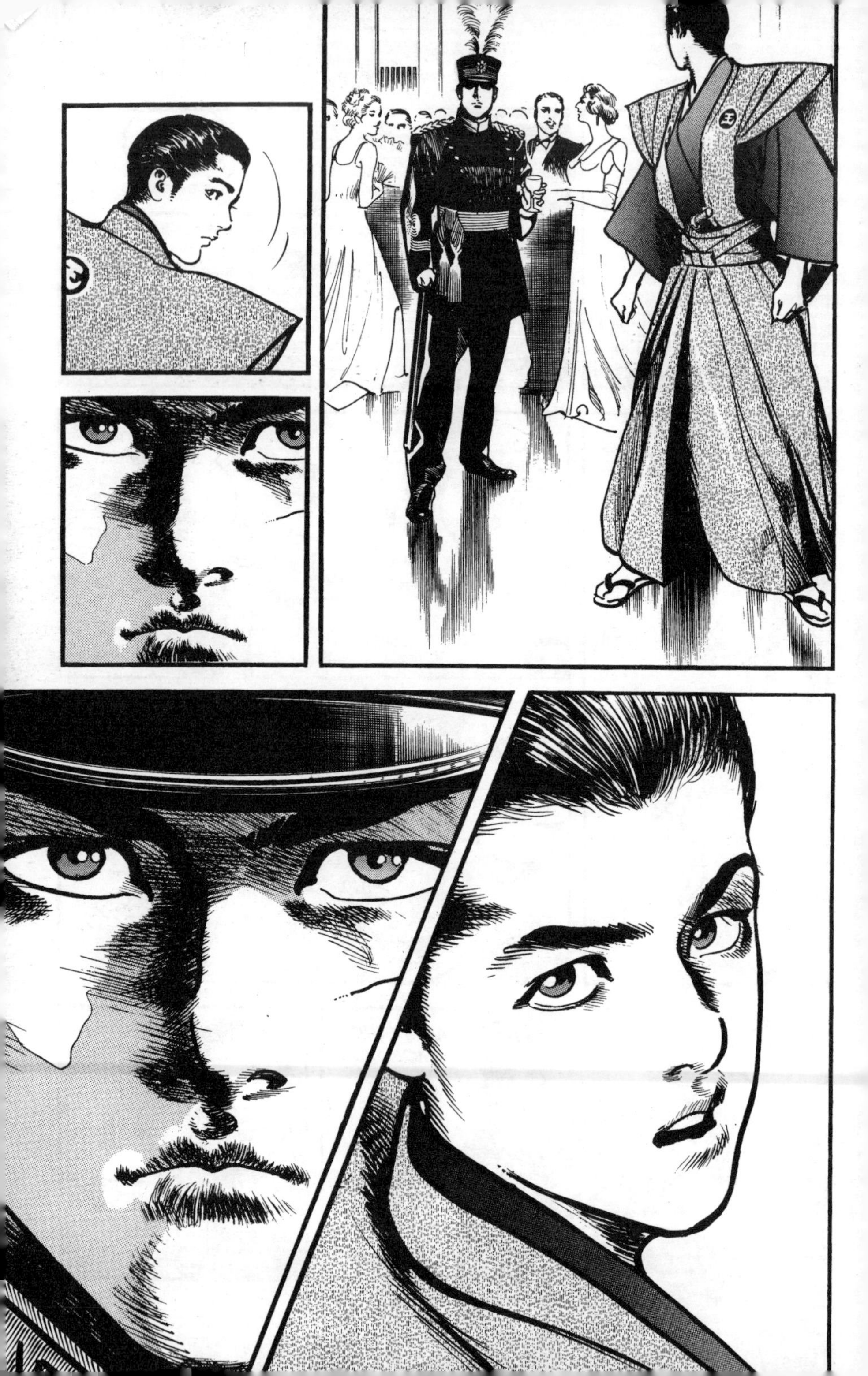

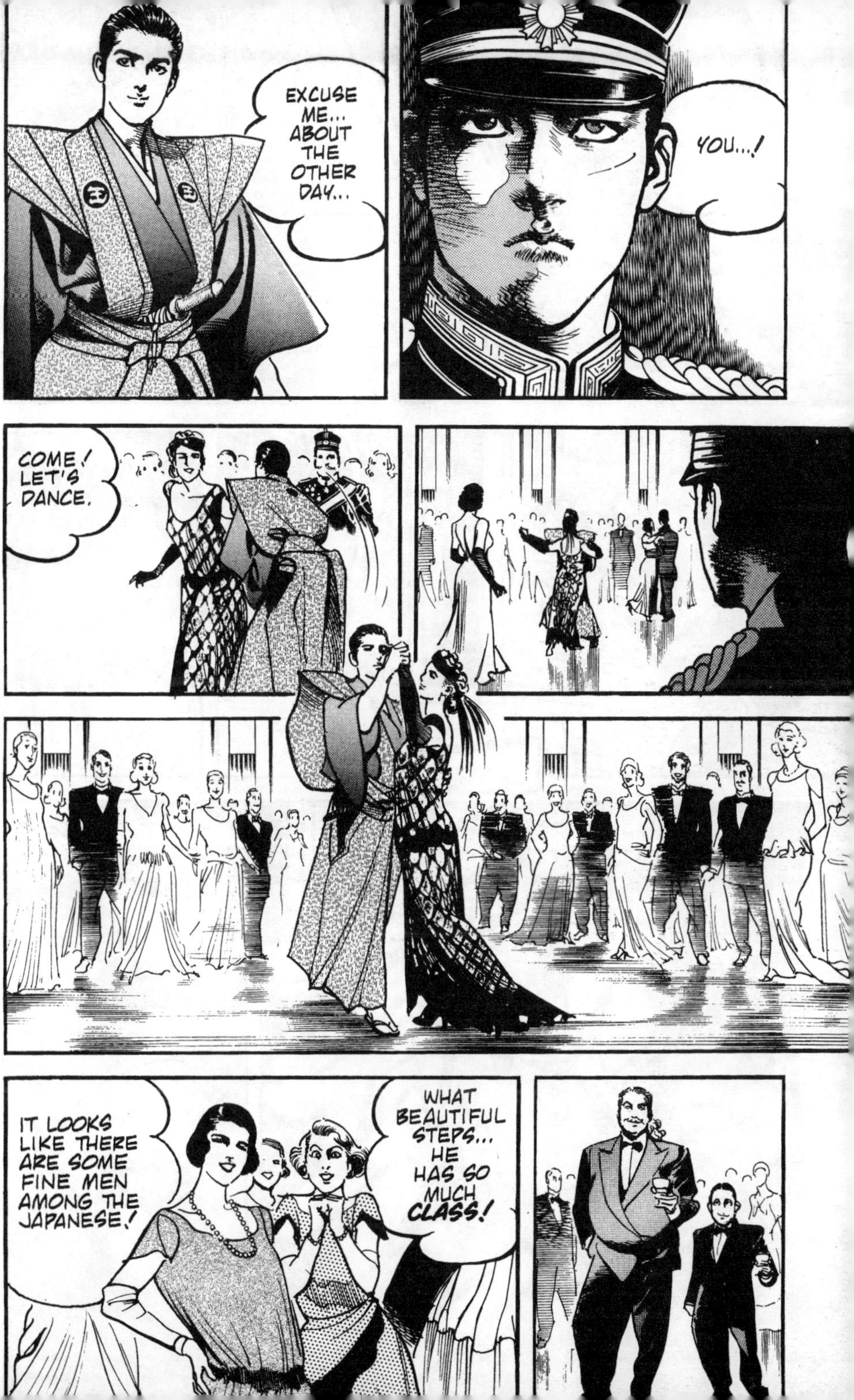
EXCUSE ME... ABOUT THE OTHER DAY...
YOU...!
COME! LET'S DANCE.
IT LOOKS LIKE THERE ARE SOME FINE MEN AMONG THE JAPANESE!
WHAT BEAUTIFUL STEPS... HE HAS SO MUCH CLASS!

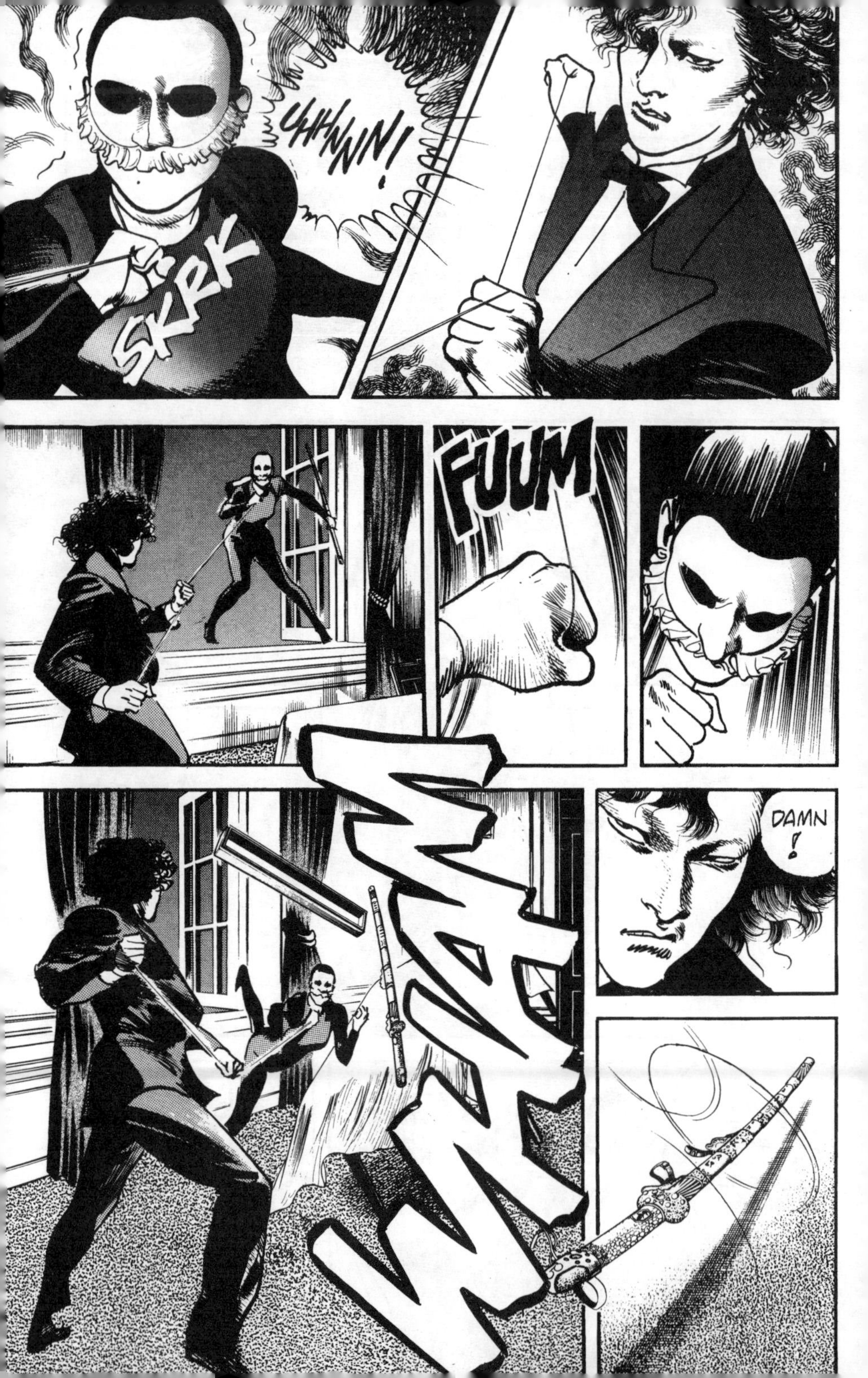

UHHNNN!
SKRK
FUUM
DAMN!

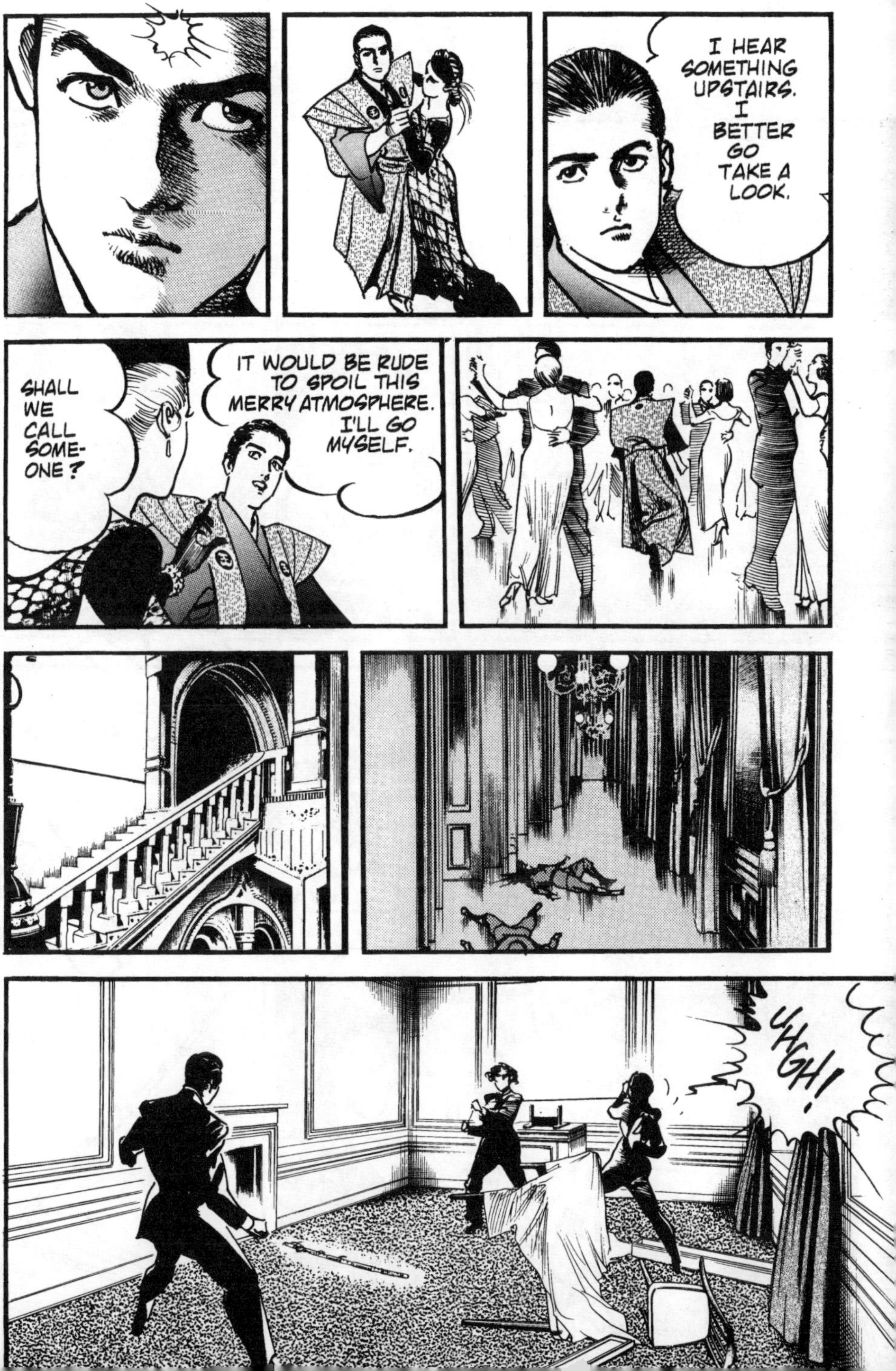
I HEAR SOMETHING UPSTAIRS. I BETTER GO TAKE A LOOK.
SHALL WE CALL SOME-ONE?
IT WOULD BE RUDE TO SPOIL THIS MERRY ATMOSPHERE. I'LL GO MYSELF.
UHGH!

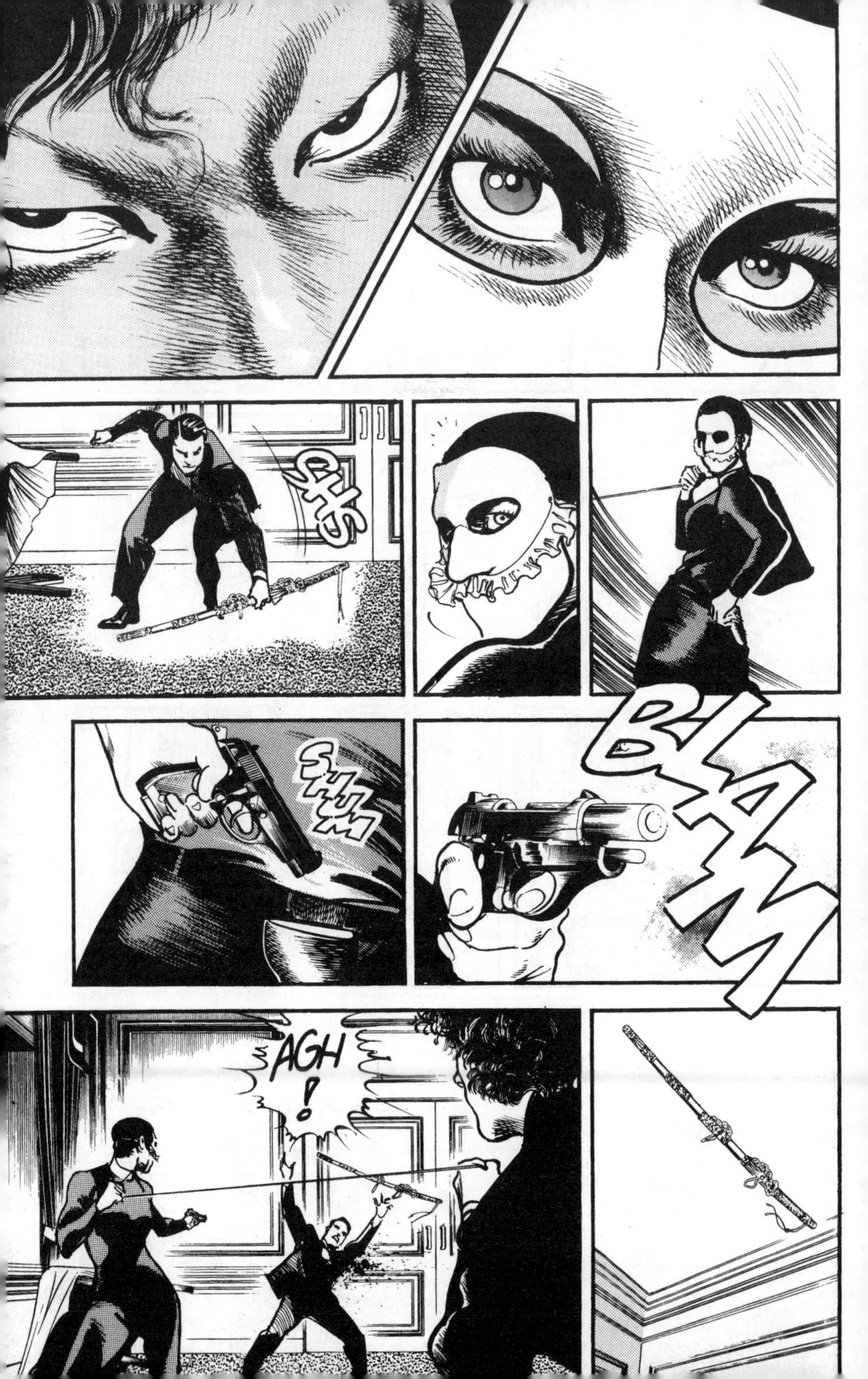
SHS
SHUM
BLAM
AGH!

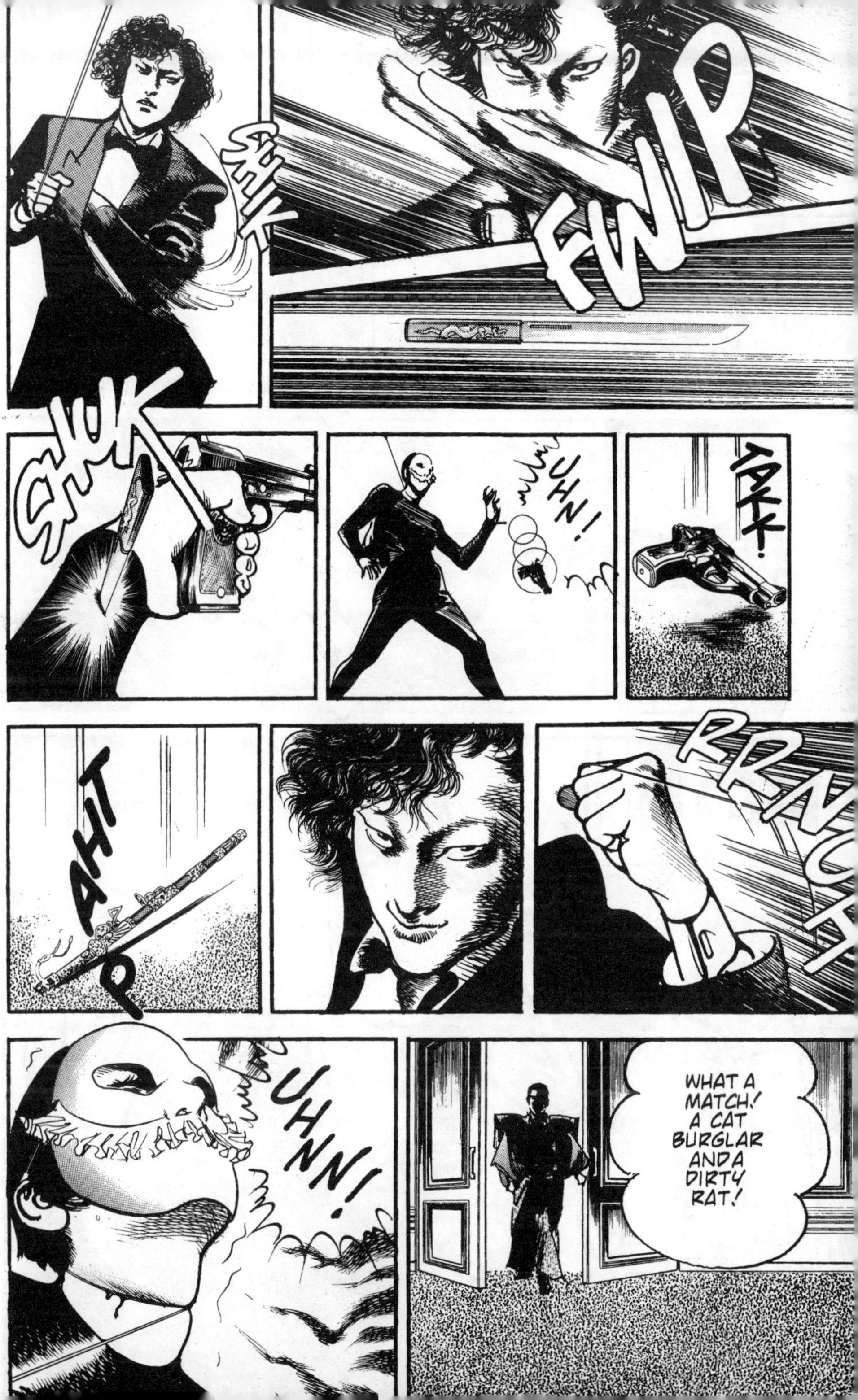
SHIK
FWIP
SHUK
UHN!
TAKK!
AHT
RRNGH
UHNN!
WHAT A MATCH! A CAT BURGLAR AND A DIRTY RAT!

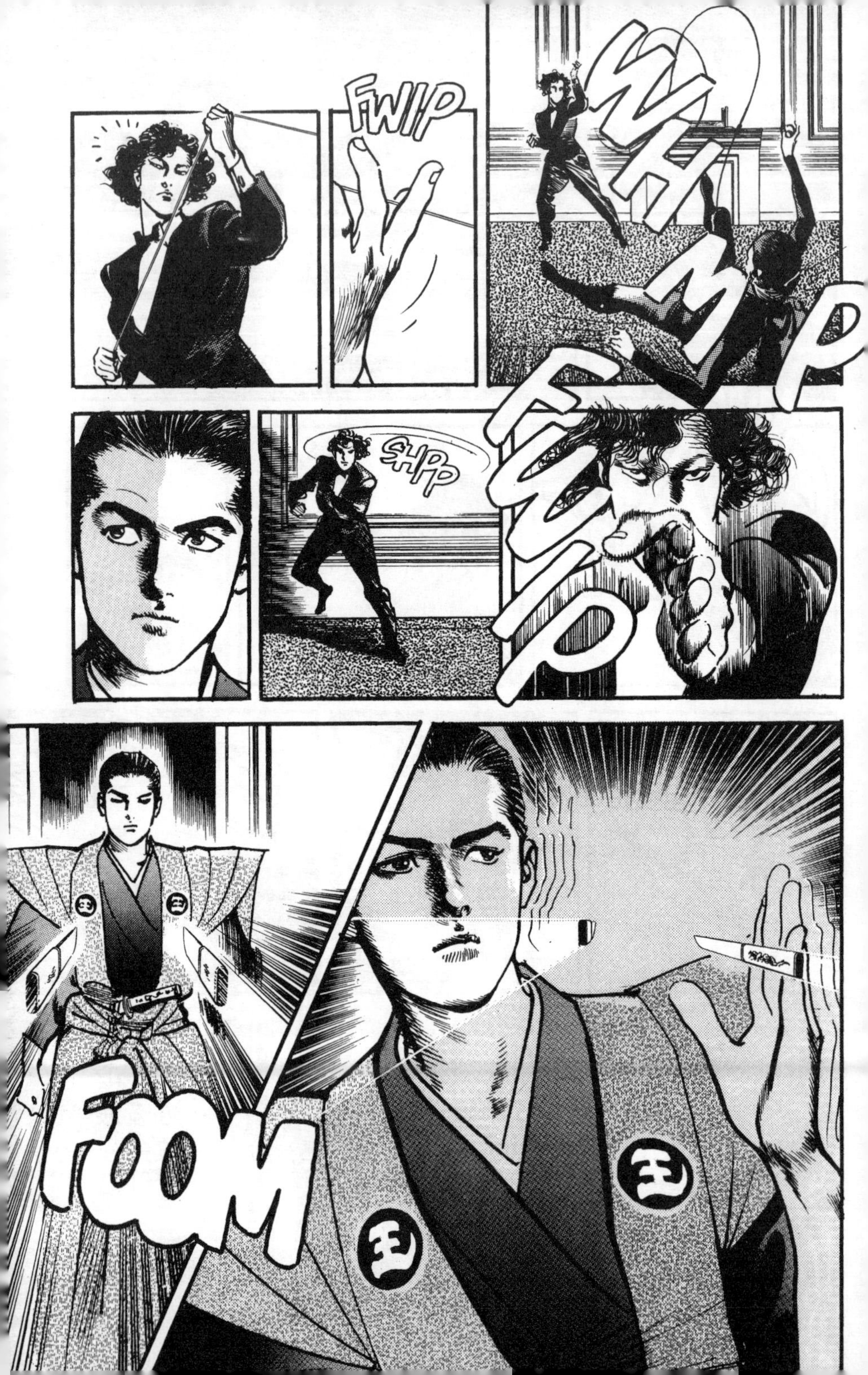
FWIP
WHMP
SHPP
FWIP
FOOM

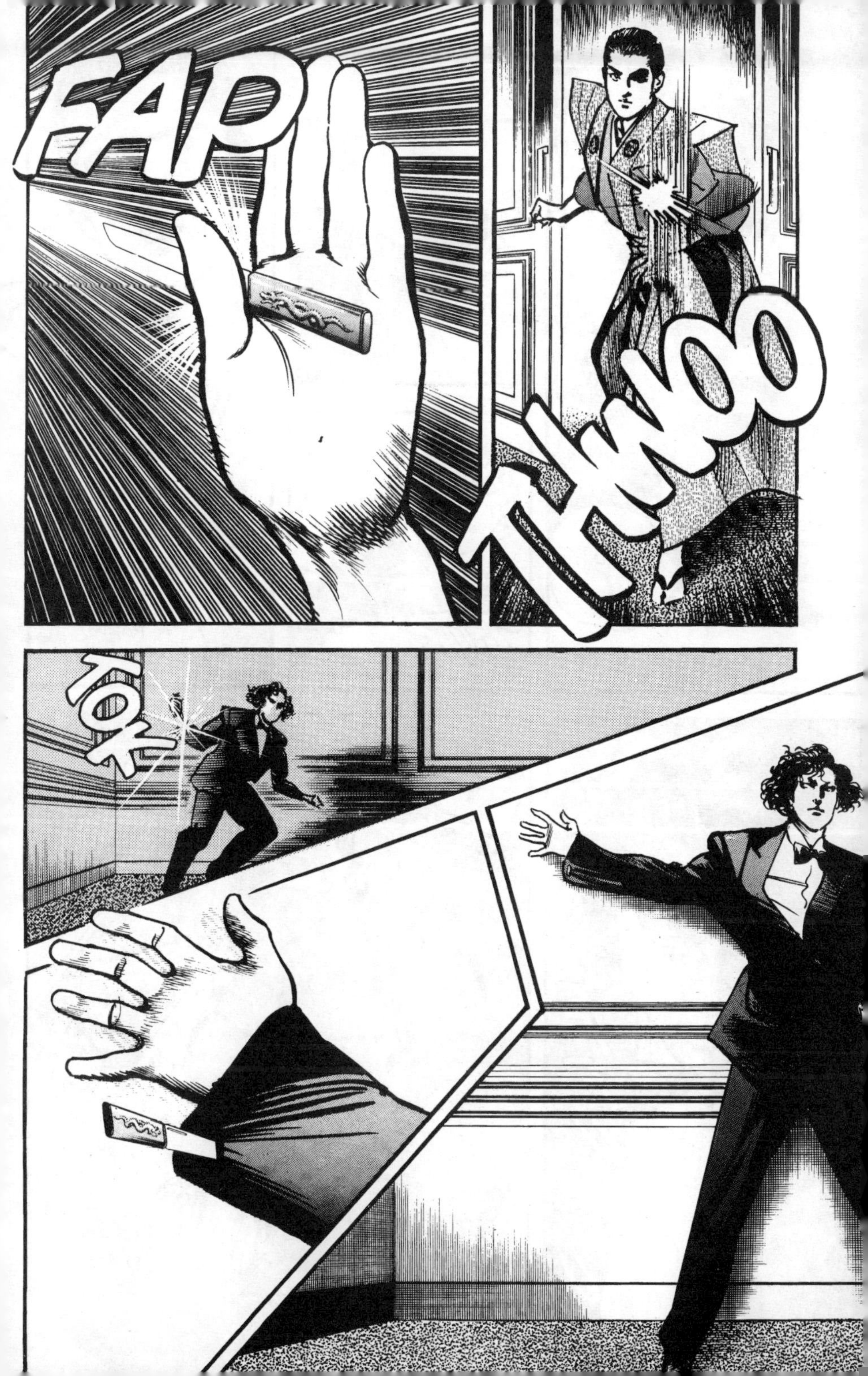
FAP
THWOO
TOK

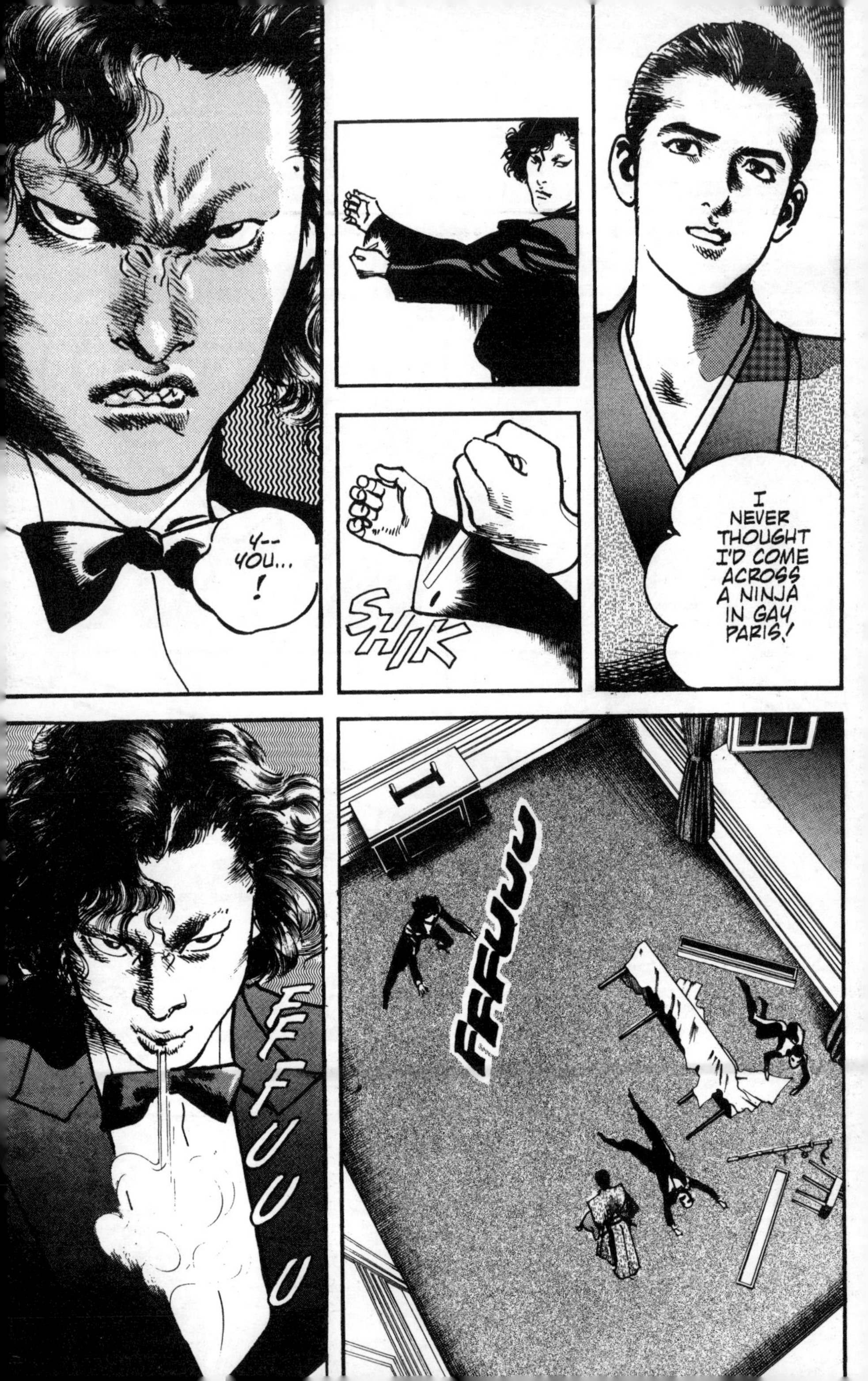
Y-- YOU... !
SHIK
I NEVER THOUGHT I'D COME ACROSS A NINJA IN GAY PARIS!
FFFUUUU
FFFUUU

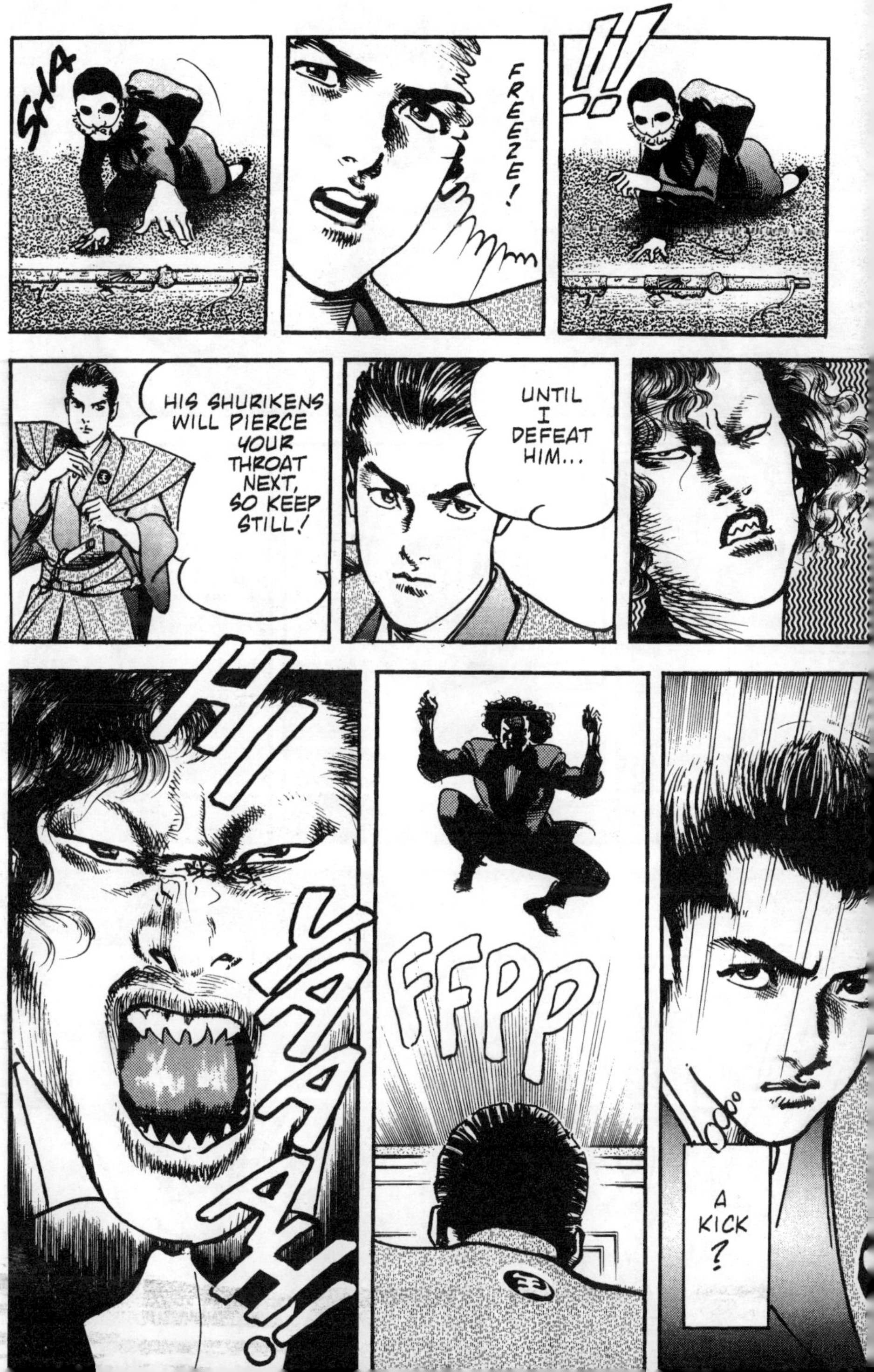
SHA
FREEZE!
!!
HIS SHURIKENS WILL PIERCE YOUR THROAT NEXT, SO KEEP STILL!
UNTIL I DEFEAT HIM...
HIYAAAAH!!
FFPP
A KICK?

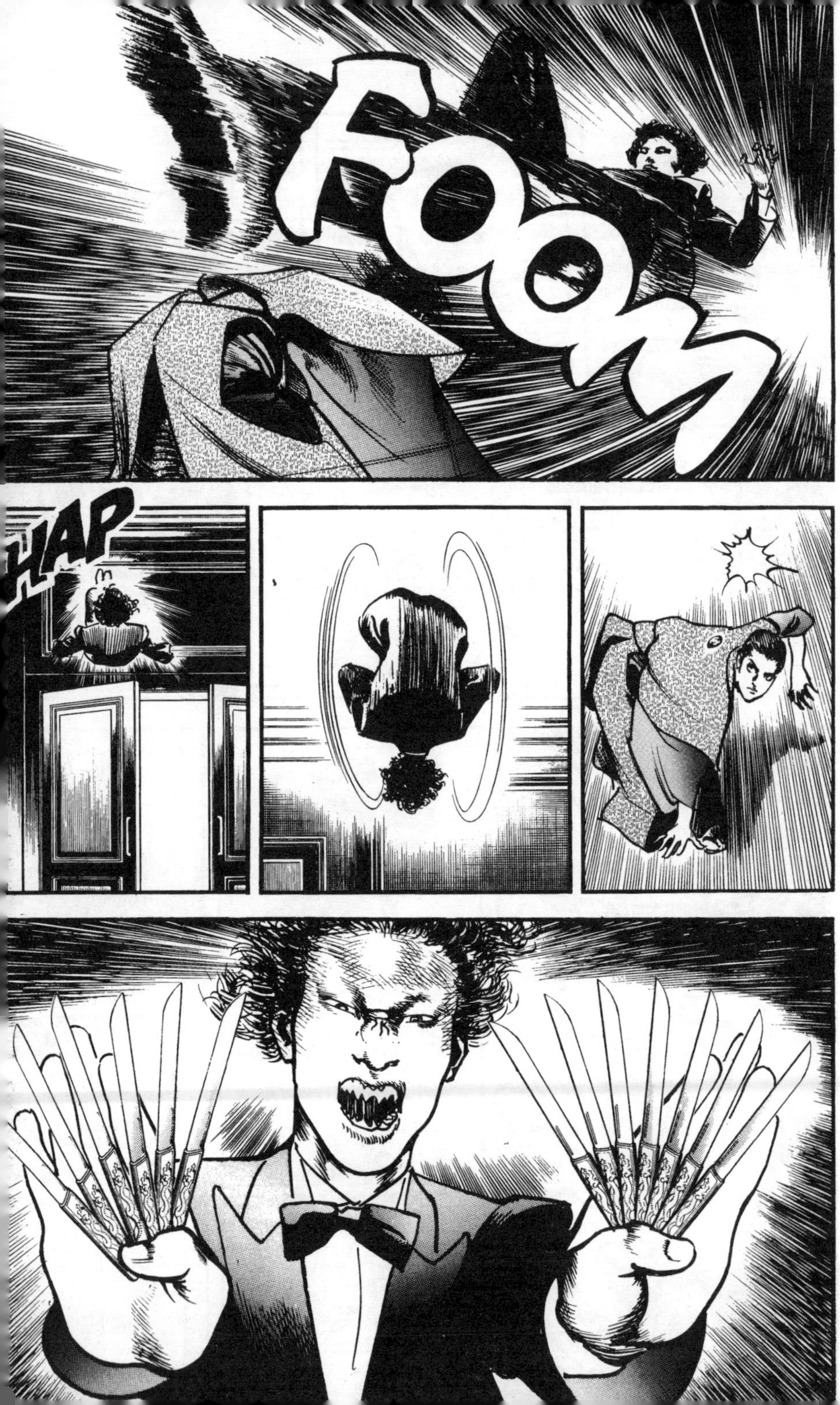
FOOOM
HAP

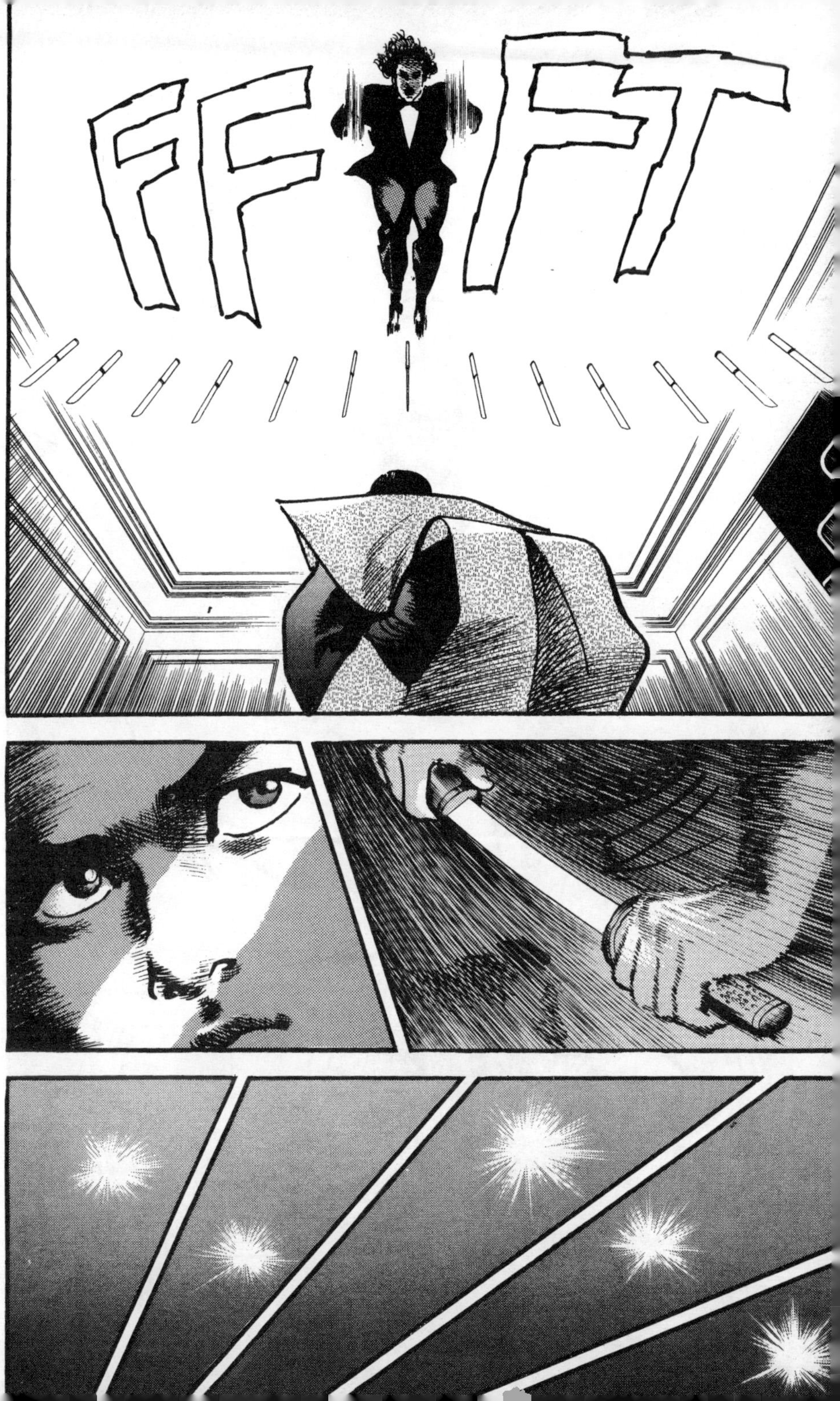
FFFT

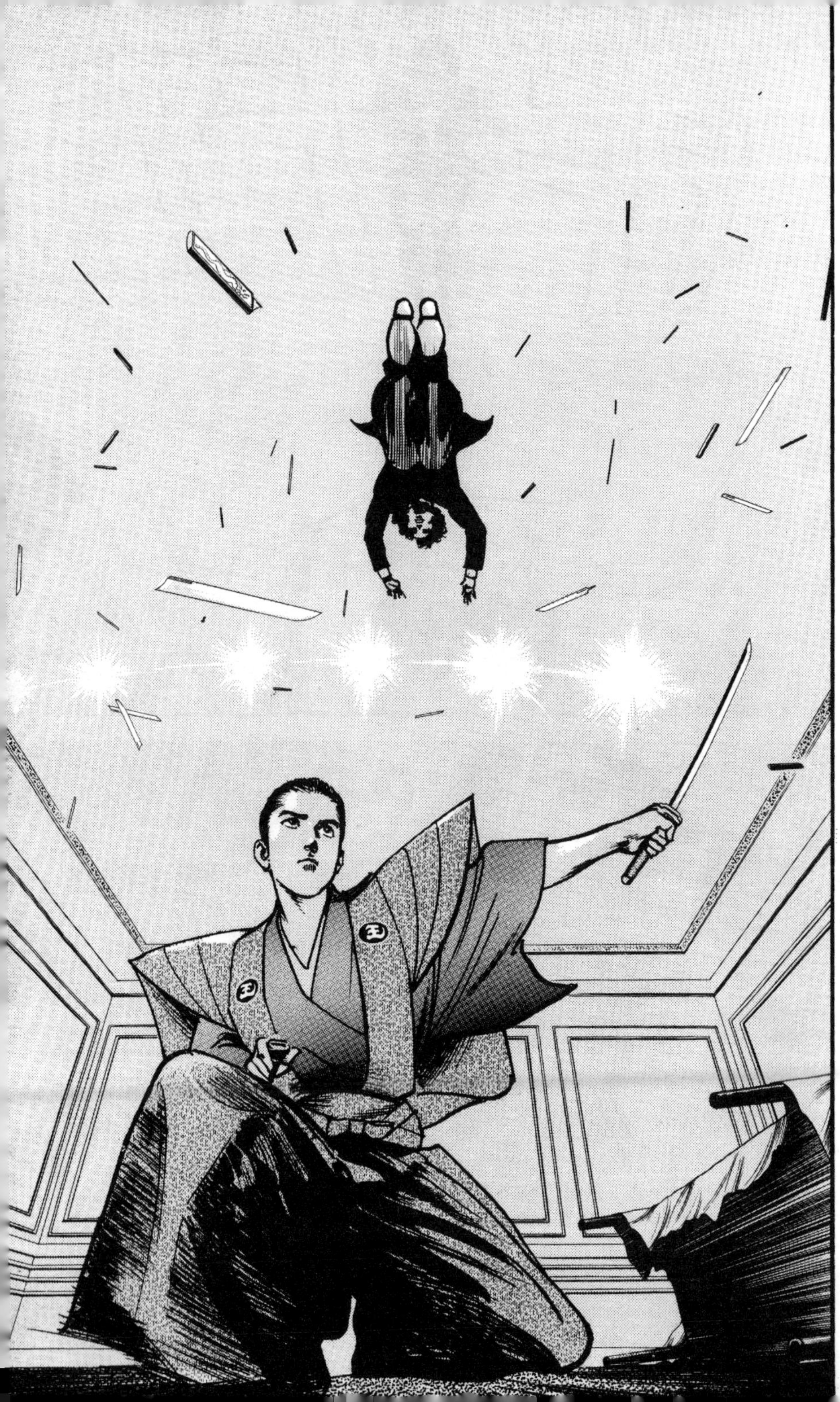

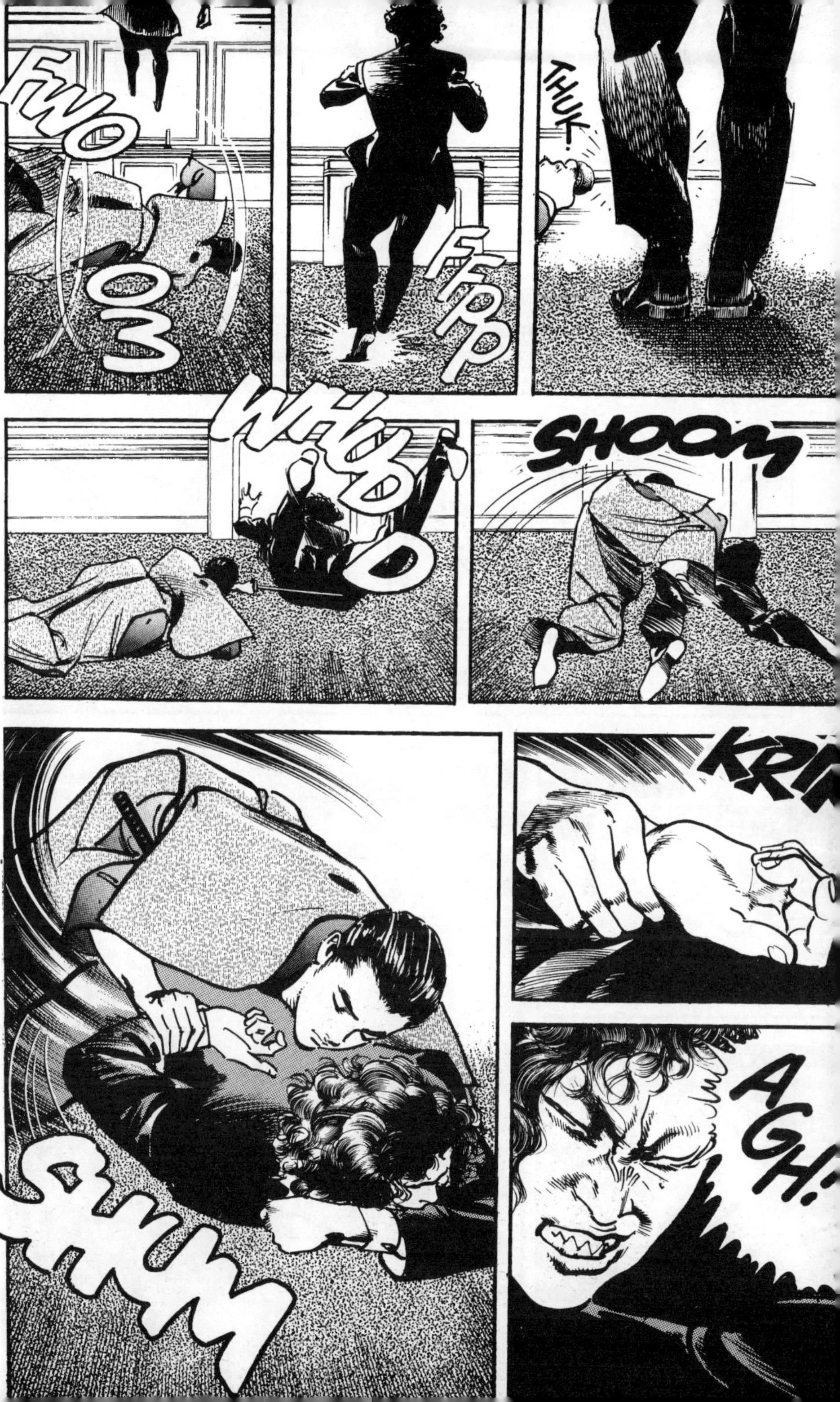
FWOOM
FFRP
THUK!
WHUD
SHOOM
GHM
KRIK
AGH!!

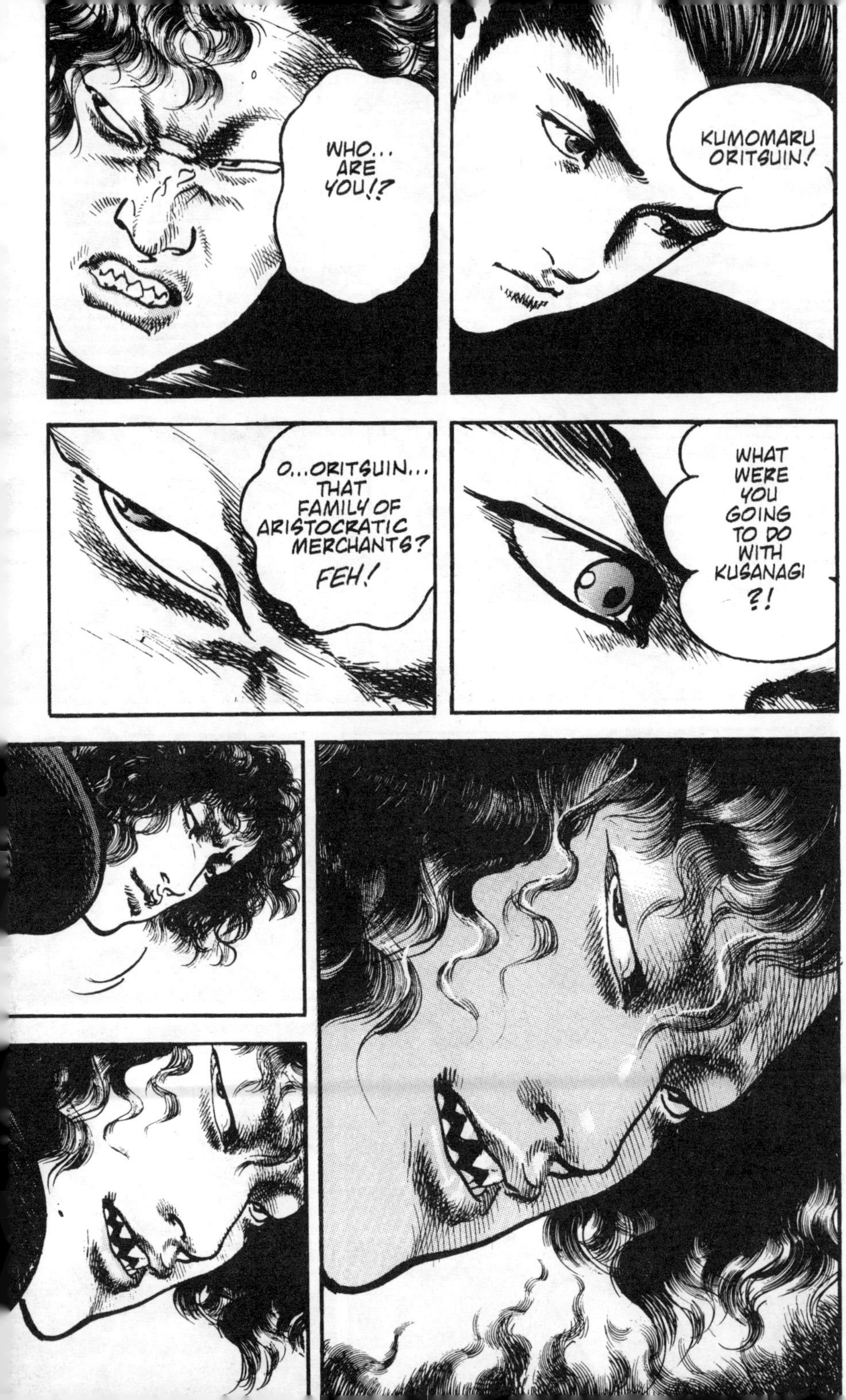
WHO... ARE YOU!?
KUMOMARU ORITSUIN!
O...ORITSUIN... THAT FAMILY OF ARISTOCRATIC MERCHANTS? FEH!
WHAT WERE YOU GOING TO DO WITH KUSANAGI ?!

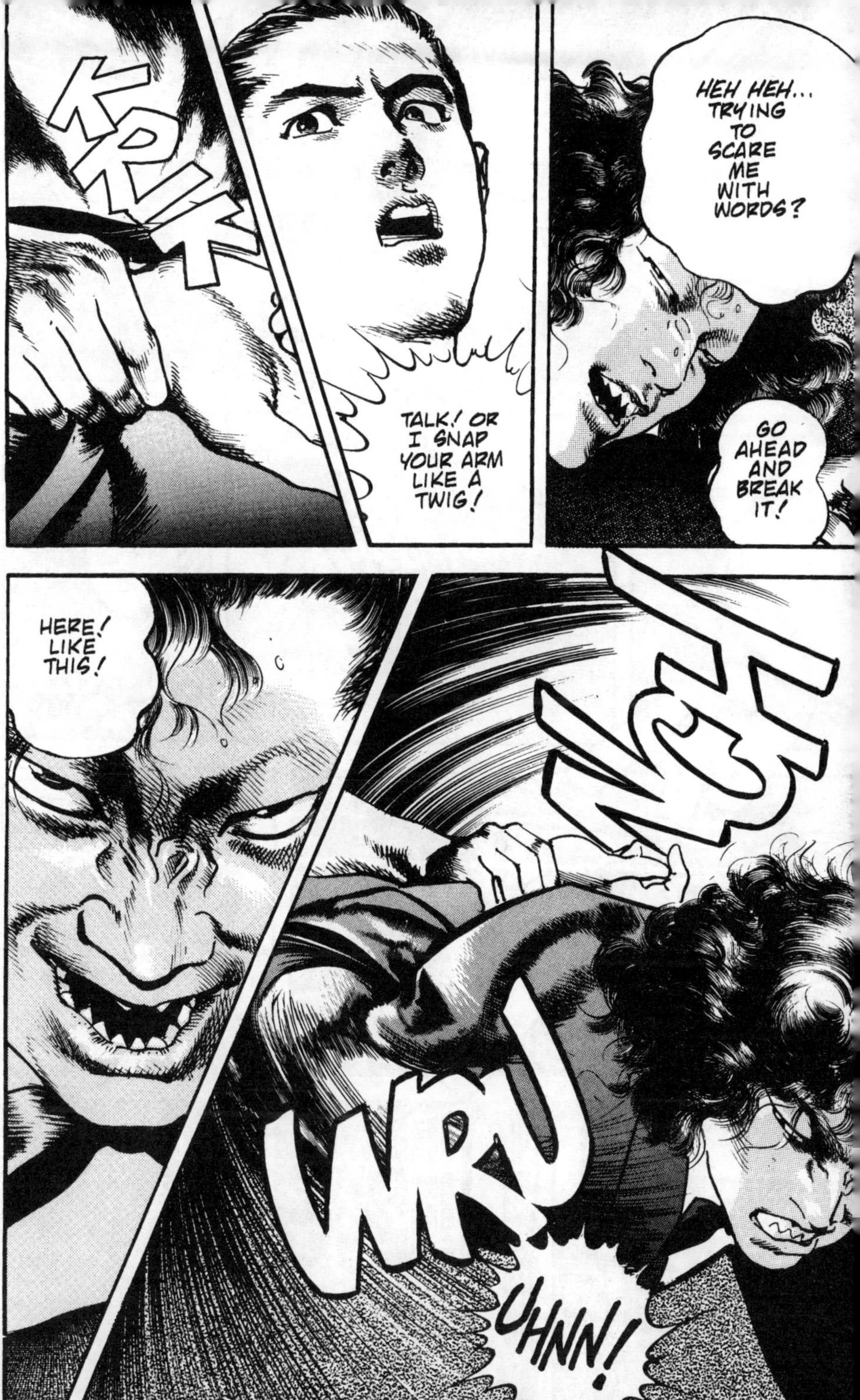
KRIK
TALK! OR I SNAP YOUR ARM LIKE A TWIG!
HEH HEH... TRYING TO SCARE ME WITH WORDS?
GO AHEAD AND BREAK IT!
HERE! LIKE THIS!
NCH
WRU
UHNN!

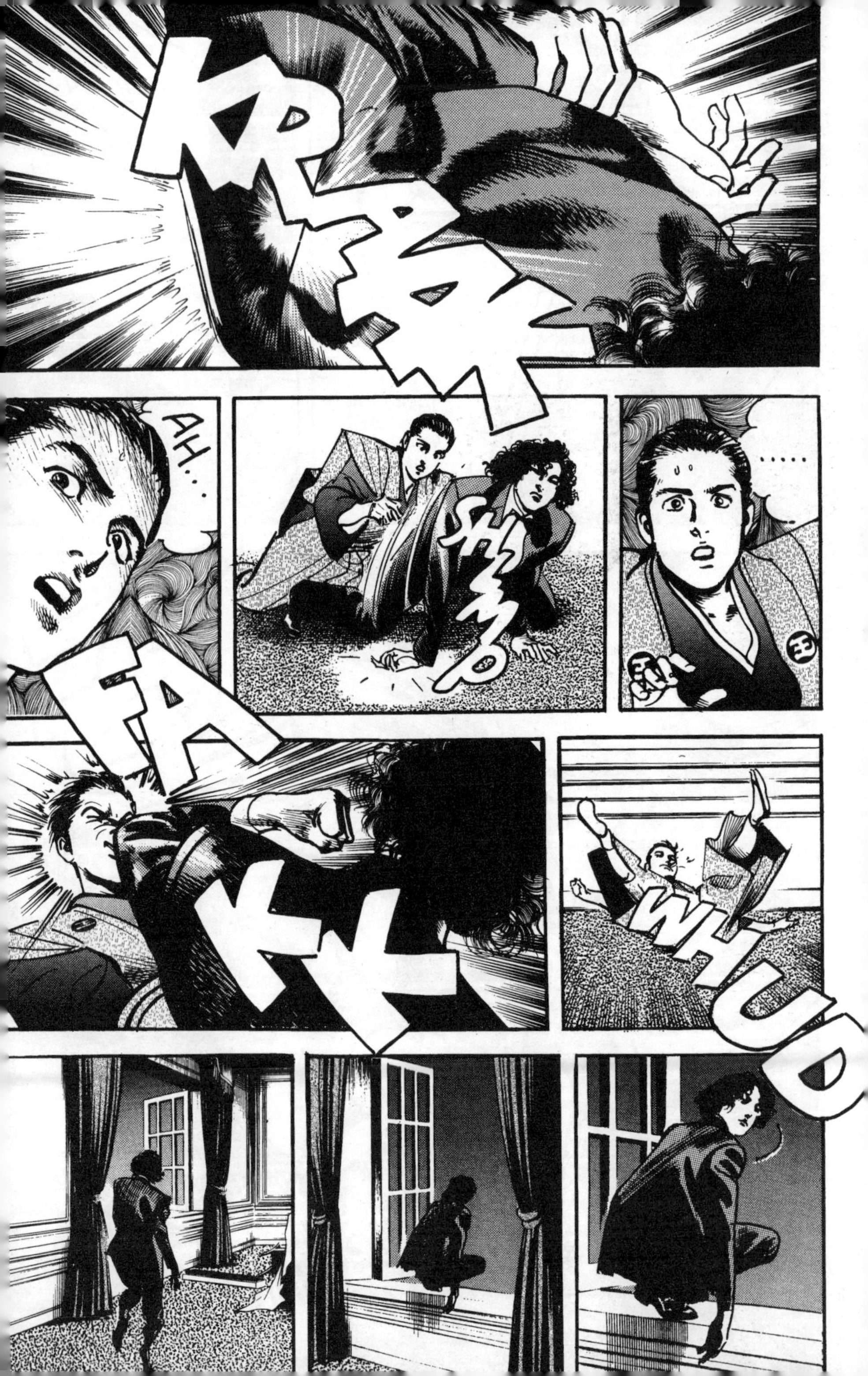
AH...
......
WHUD

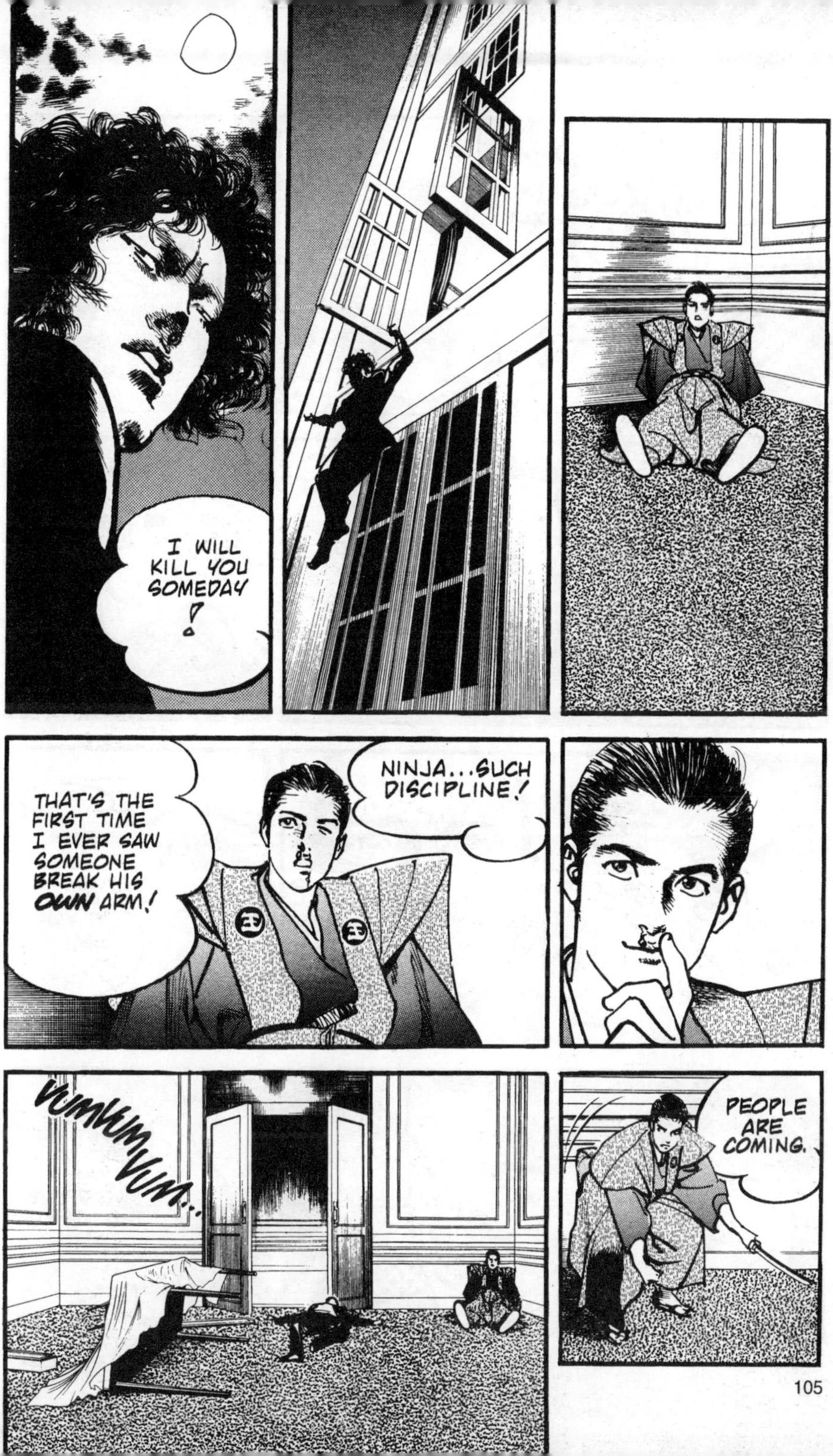
I WILL KILL YOU SOMEDAY!
THAT'S THE FIRST TIME I EVER SAW SOMEONE BREAK HIS OWN ARM!
NINJA...SUCH DISCIPLINE!
VUMVUMVUM...
PEOPLE ARE COMING.

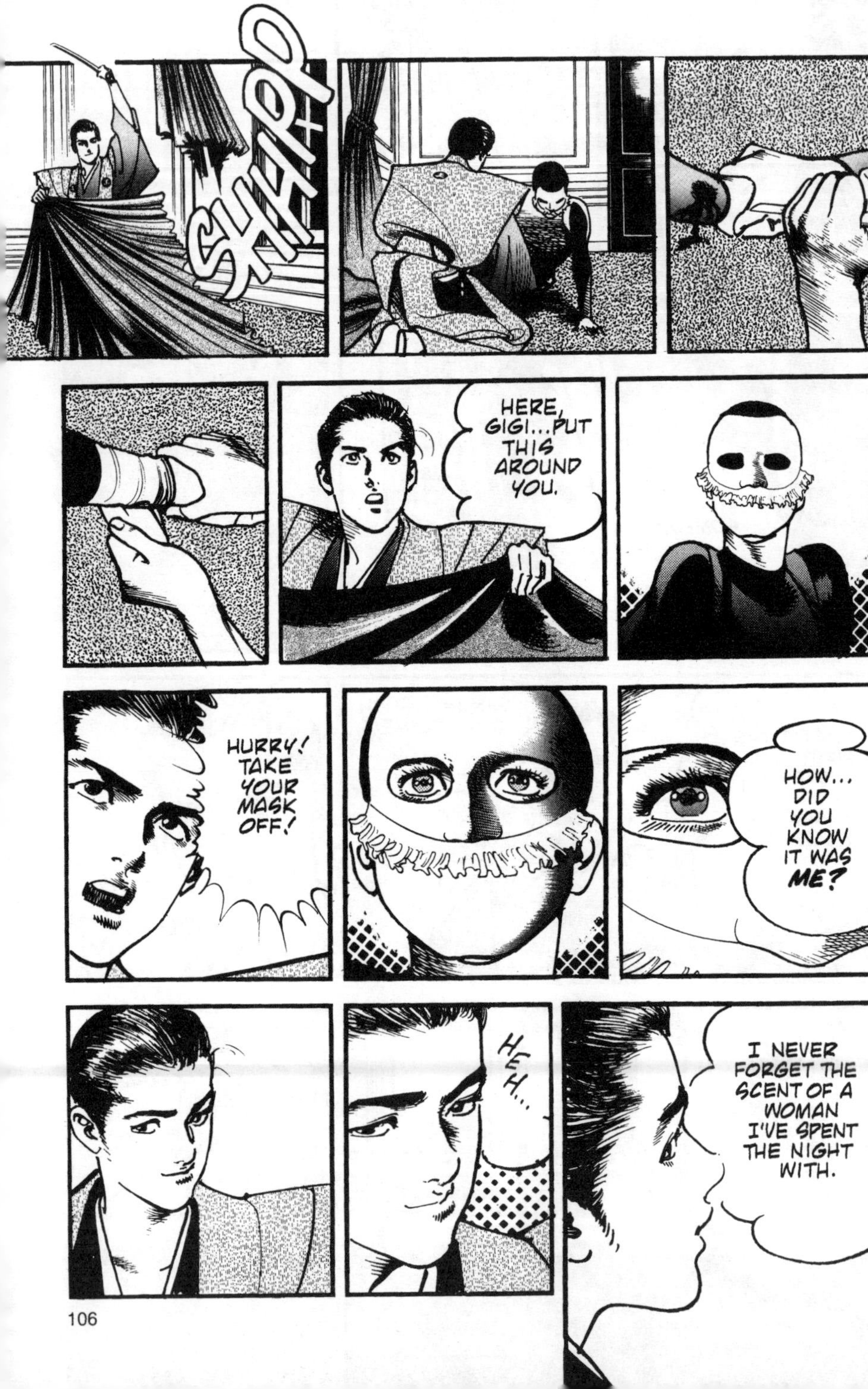
SHHPP
HERE, GIGI...PUT THIS AROUND YOU.
HURRY! TAKE YOUR MASK OFF!
HOW... DID YOU KNOW IT WAS **ME?**
HEH...
I NEVER FORGET THE SCENT OF A WOMAN I'VE SPENT THE NIGHT WITH.

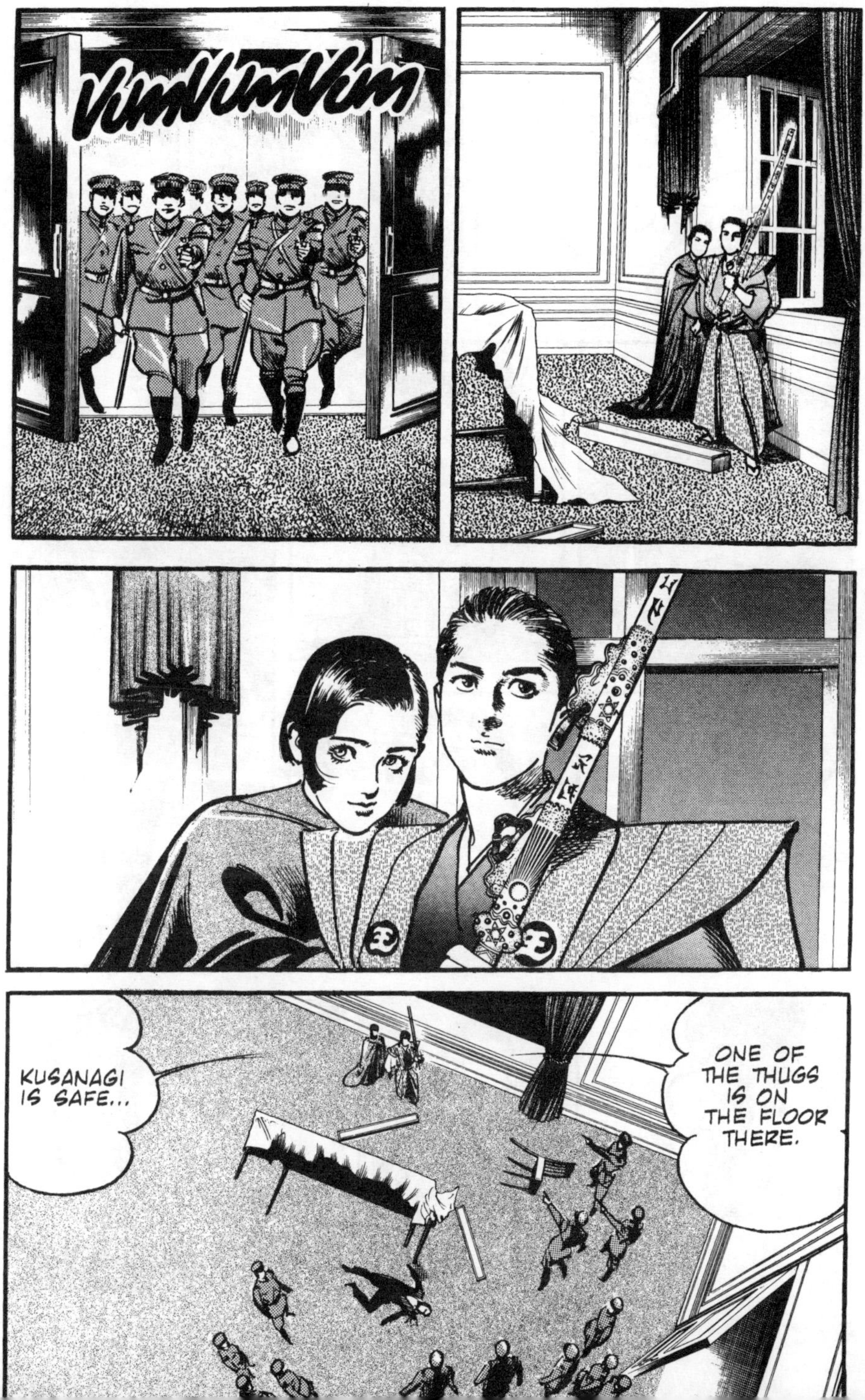
KUSANAGI IS SAFE...
ONE OF THE THUGS IS ON THE FLOOR THERE.

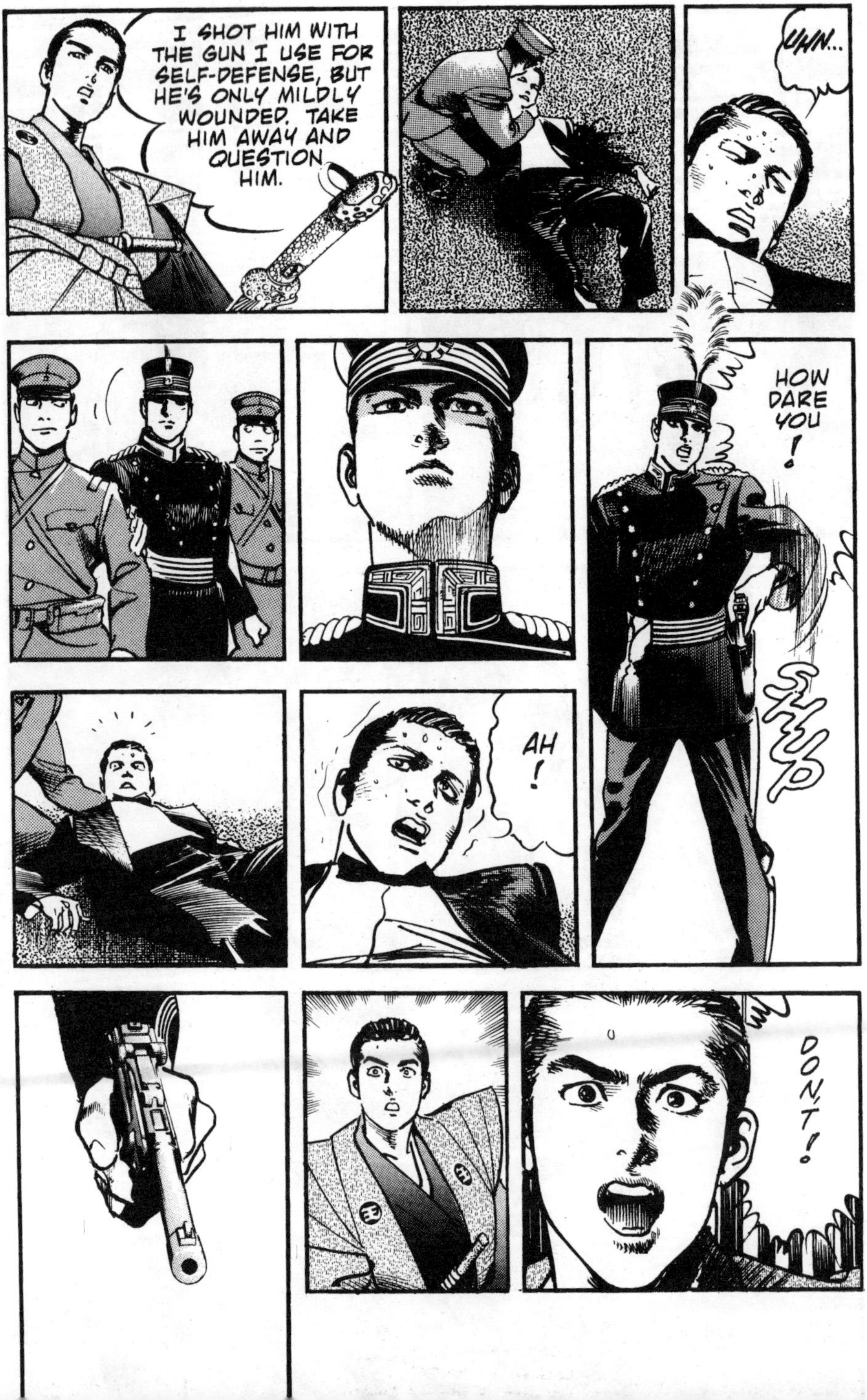
I SHOT HIM WITH THE GUN I USE FOR SELF-DEFENSE, BUT HE'S ONLY MILDLY WOUNDED. TAKE HIM AWAY AND QUESTION HIM.
UHN...
HOW DARE YOU!
SHHP
AH!
DON'T!

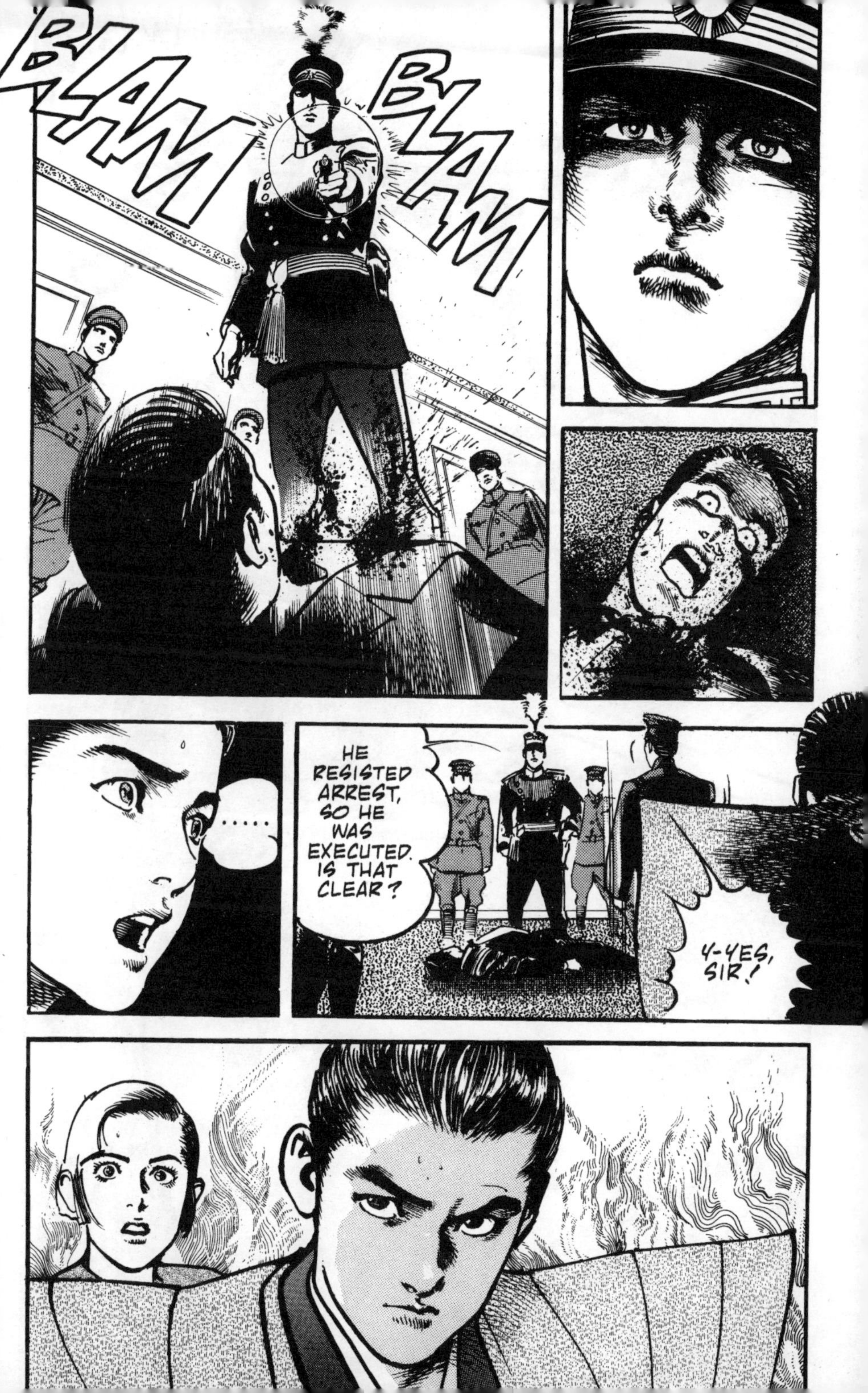
BLAM
BLAM
......
HE RESISTED ARREST, SO HE WAS EXECUTED. IS THAT CLEAR?
Y-YES, SIR!

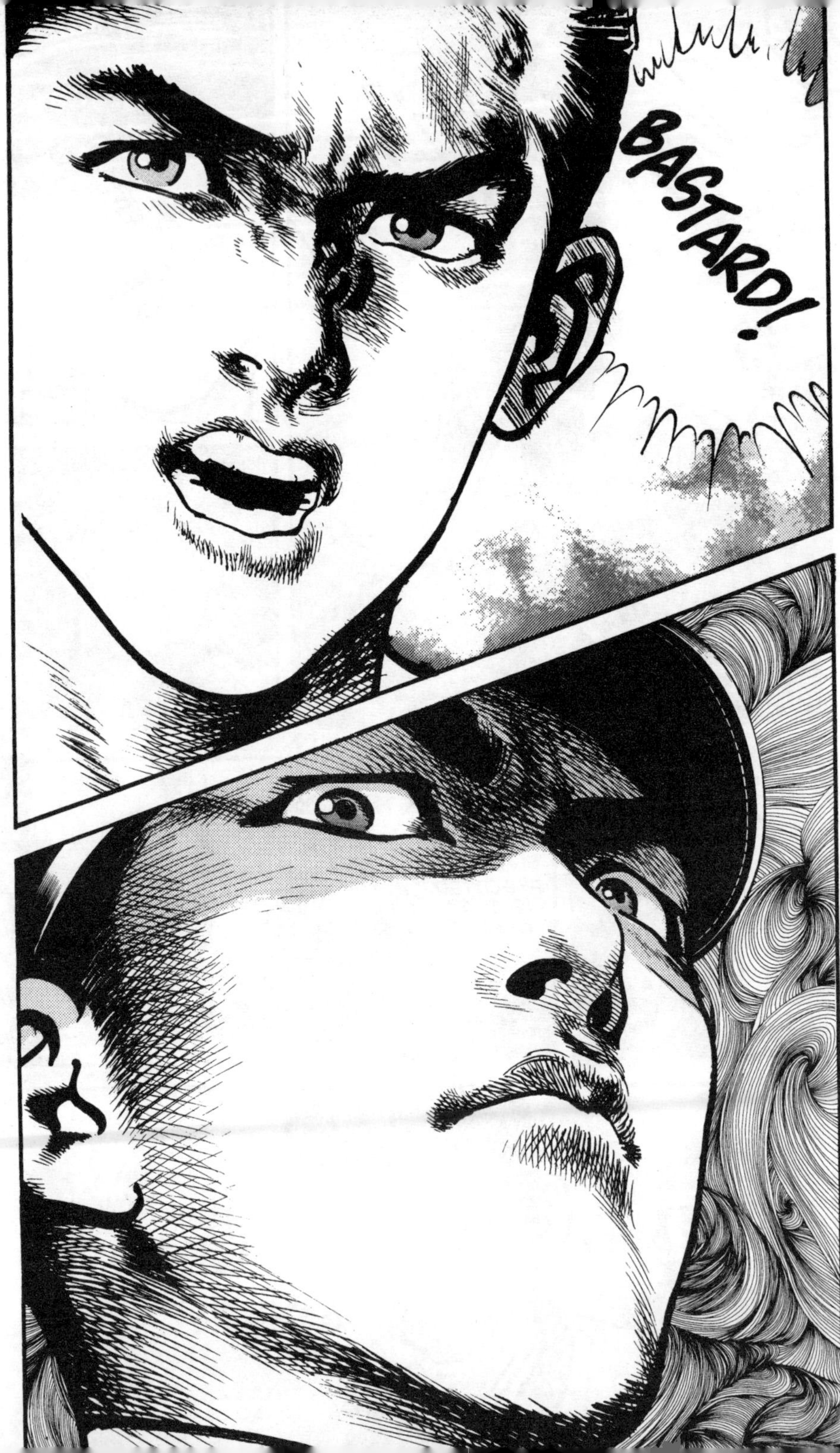
BASTARD!

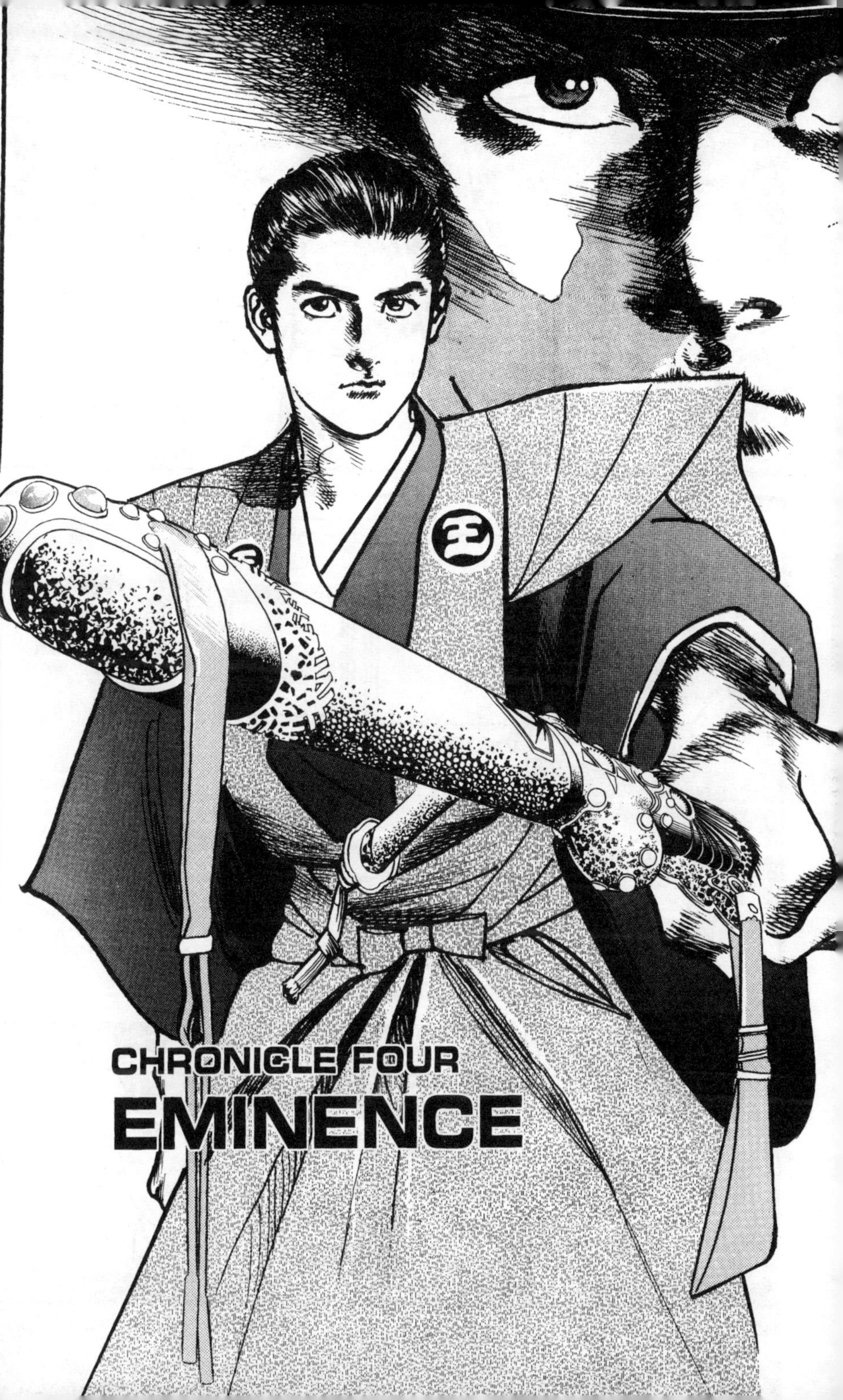

CHRONICLE FOUR
EMINENCE

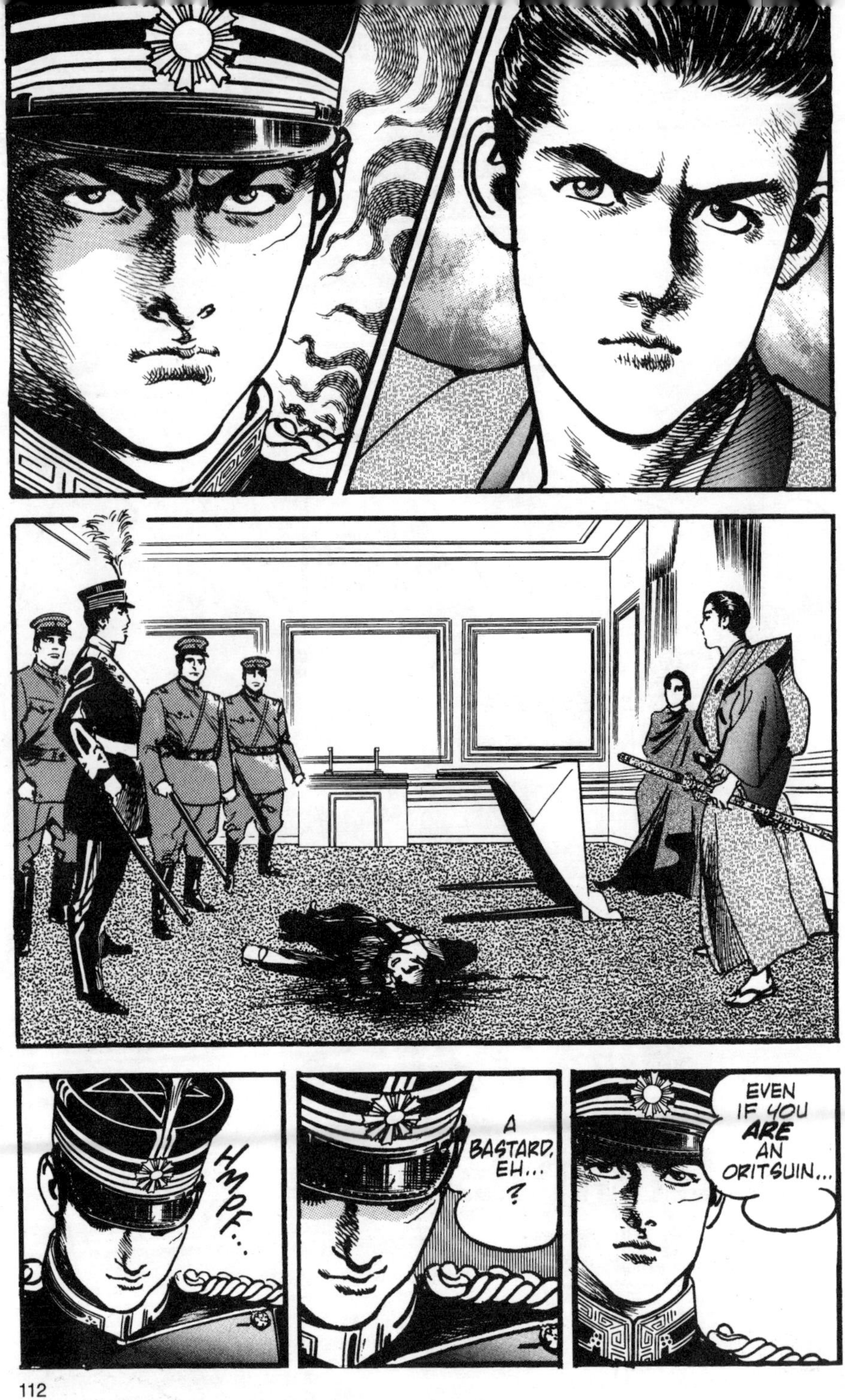
HMPF...
A BASTARD, EH...?
EVEN IF YOU **ARE** AN ORITSUIN...

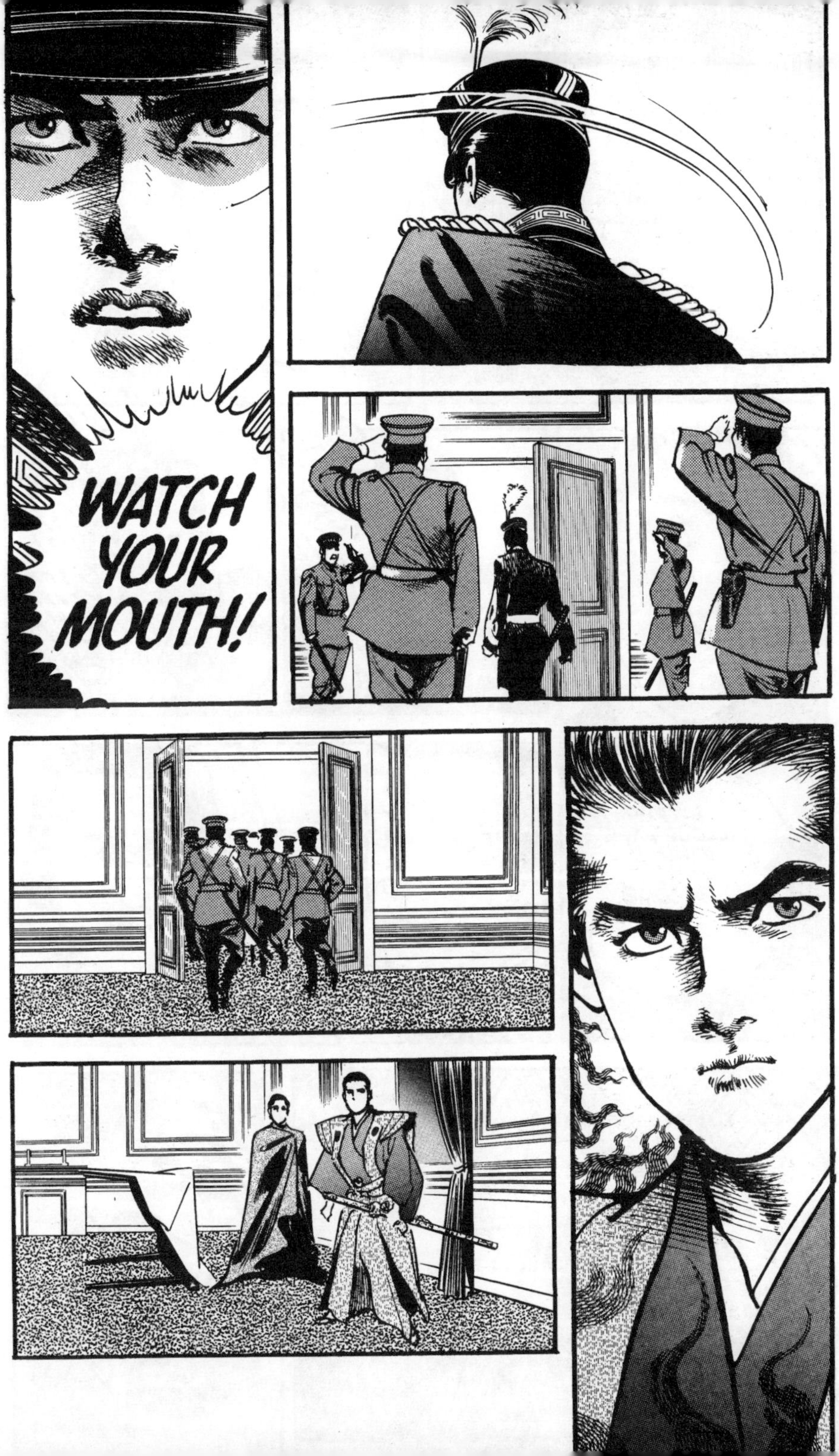
WATCH YOUR MOUTH!

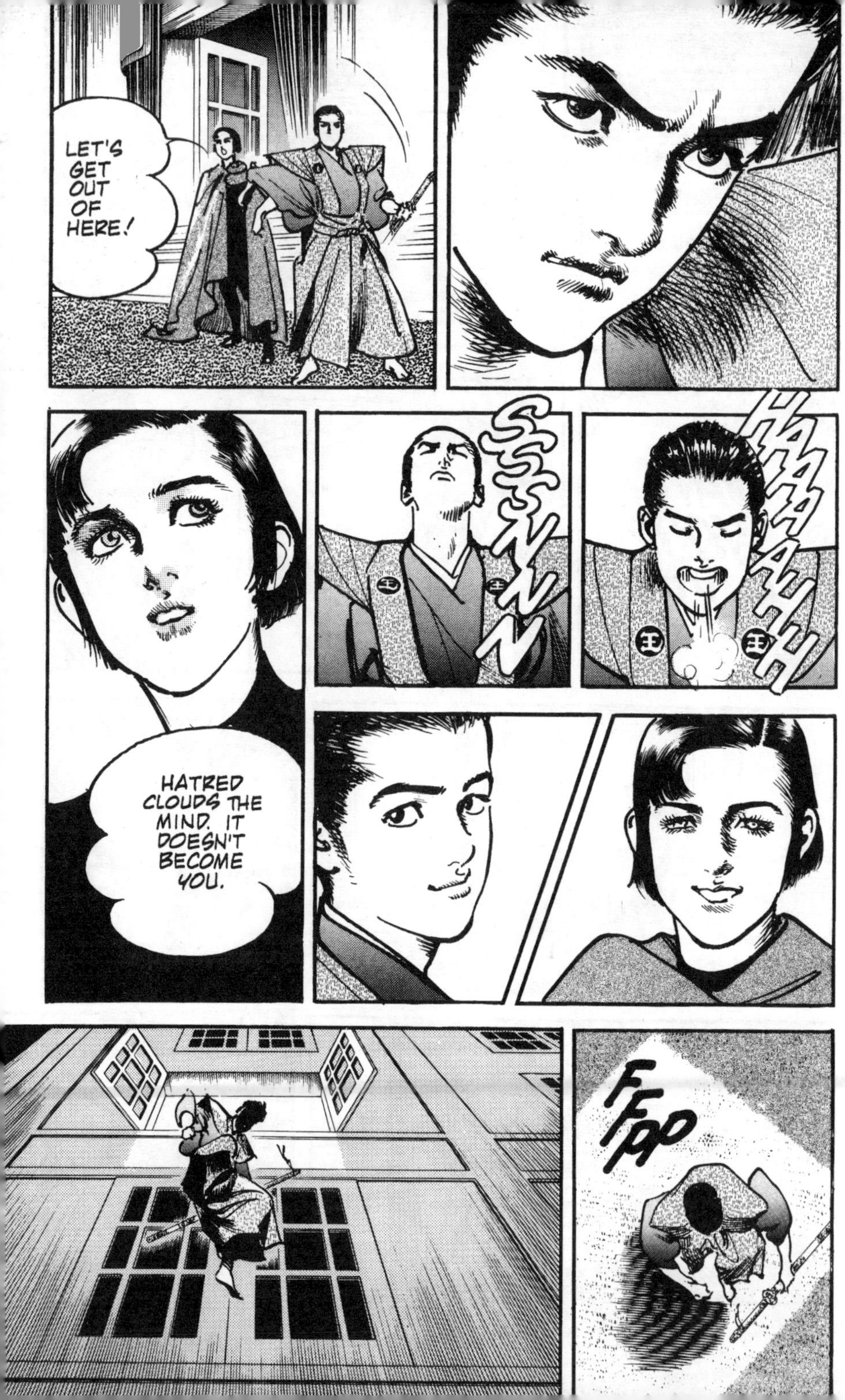
LET'S GET OUT OF HERE!
SSSNNN
HAHAHAHHH
HATRED CLOUDS THE MIND. IT DOESN'T BECOME YOU.
FFOP

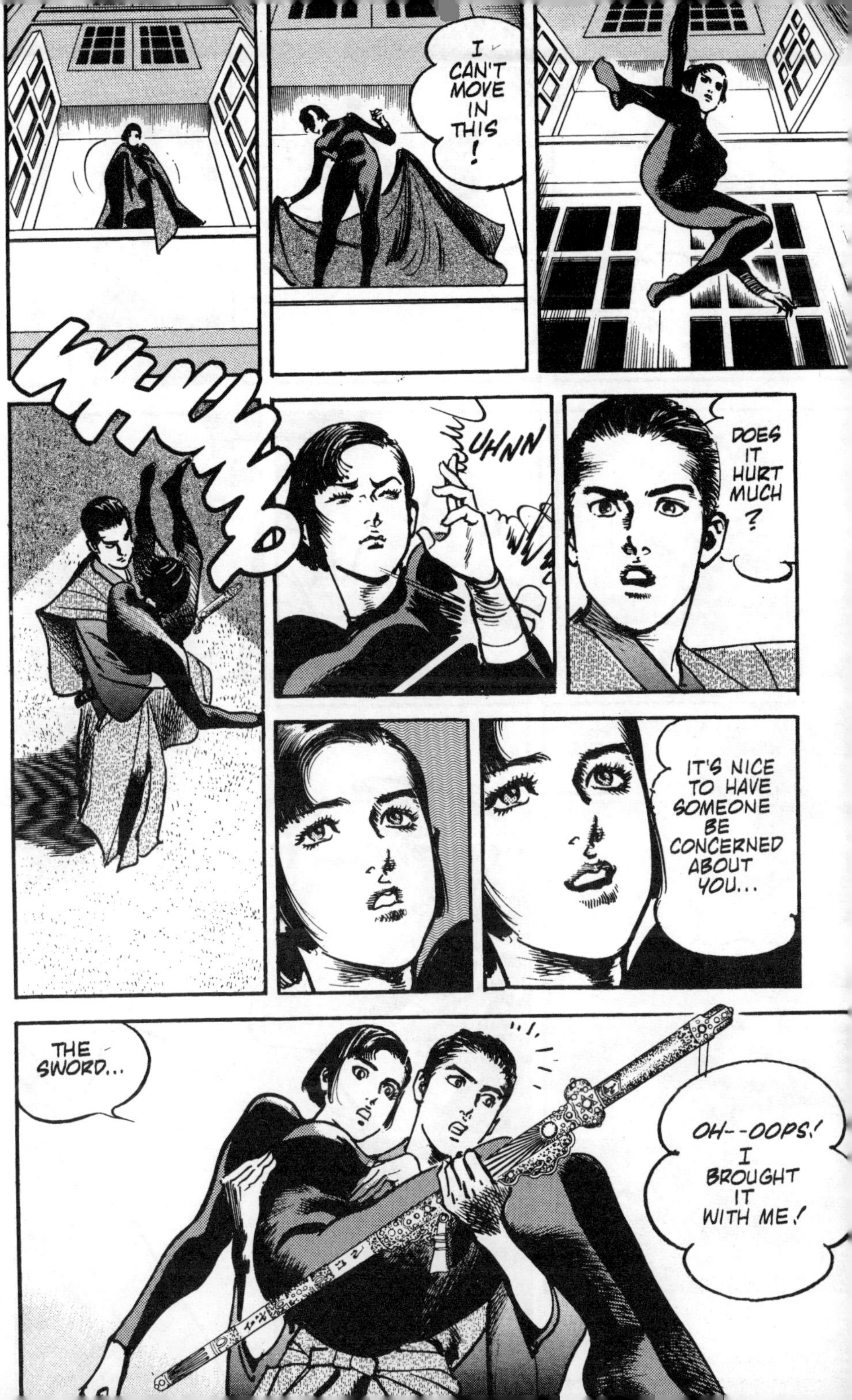
I CAN'T MOVE IN THIS!
WHUMP
UHNN
DOES IT HURT MUCH?
IT'S NICE TO HAVE SOMEONE BE CONCERNED ABOUT YOU...
THE SWORD...
OH--OOPS! I BROUGHT IT WITH ME!

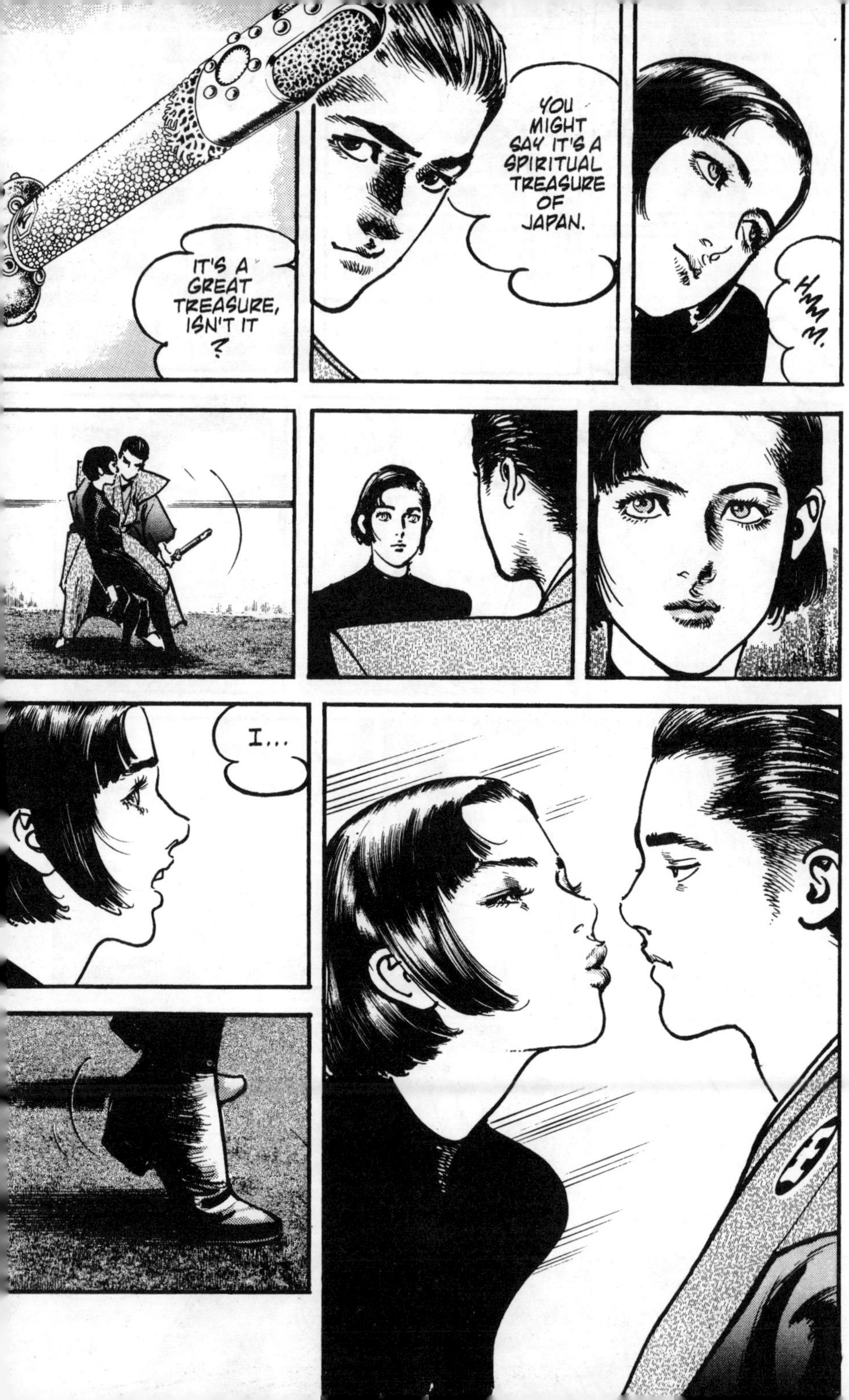
IT'S A GREAT TREASURE, ISN'T IT ?
YOU MIGHT SAY IT'S A SPIRITUAL TREASURE OF JAPAN.
HMMM.
I...

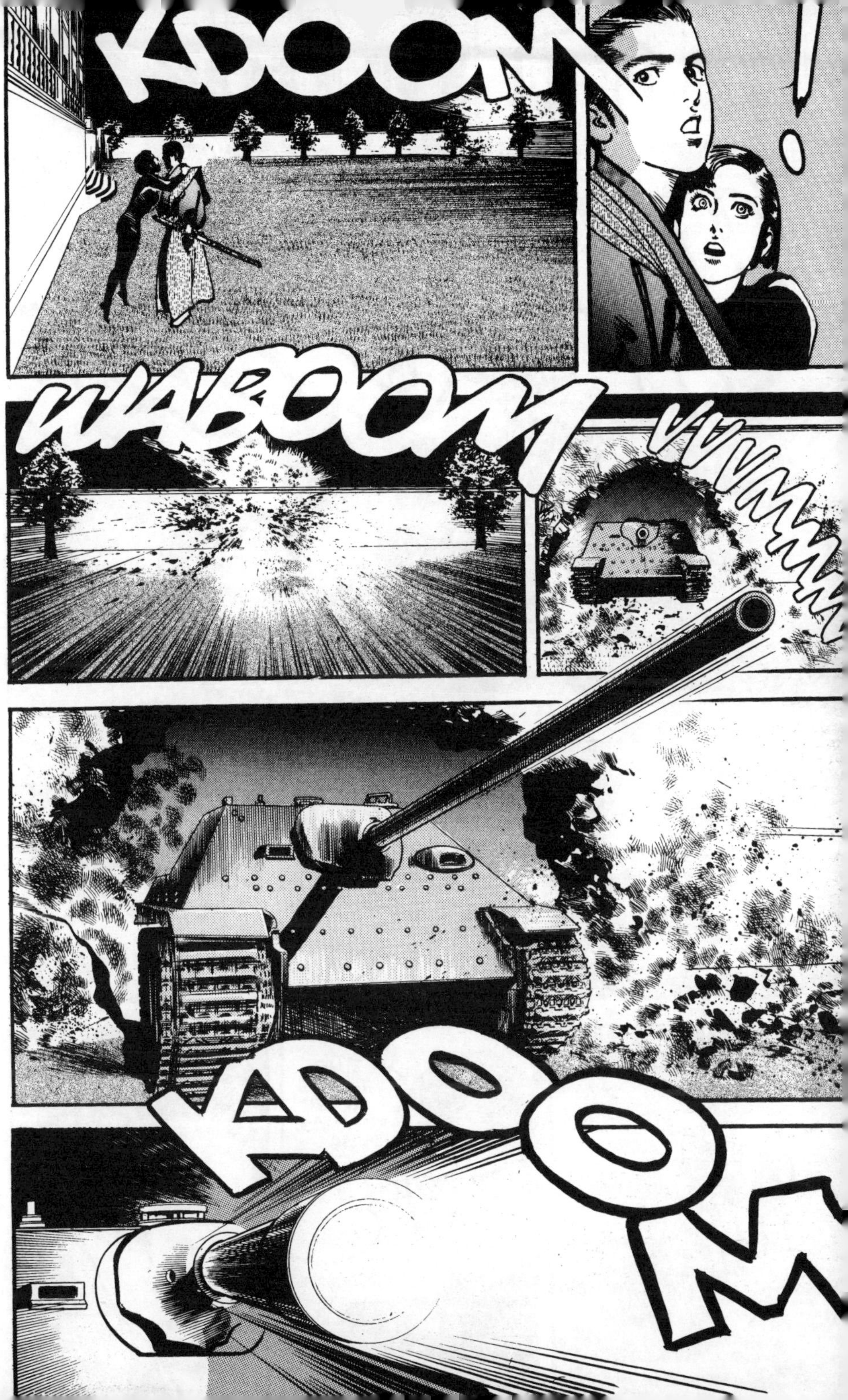
KDOOM
!
WABOOM
VVVMMM
KDOOOM

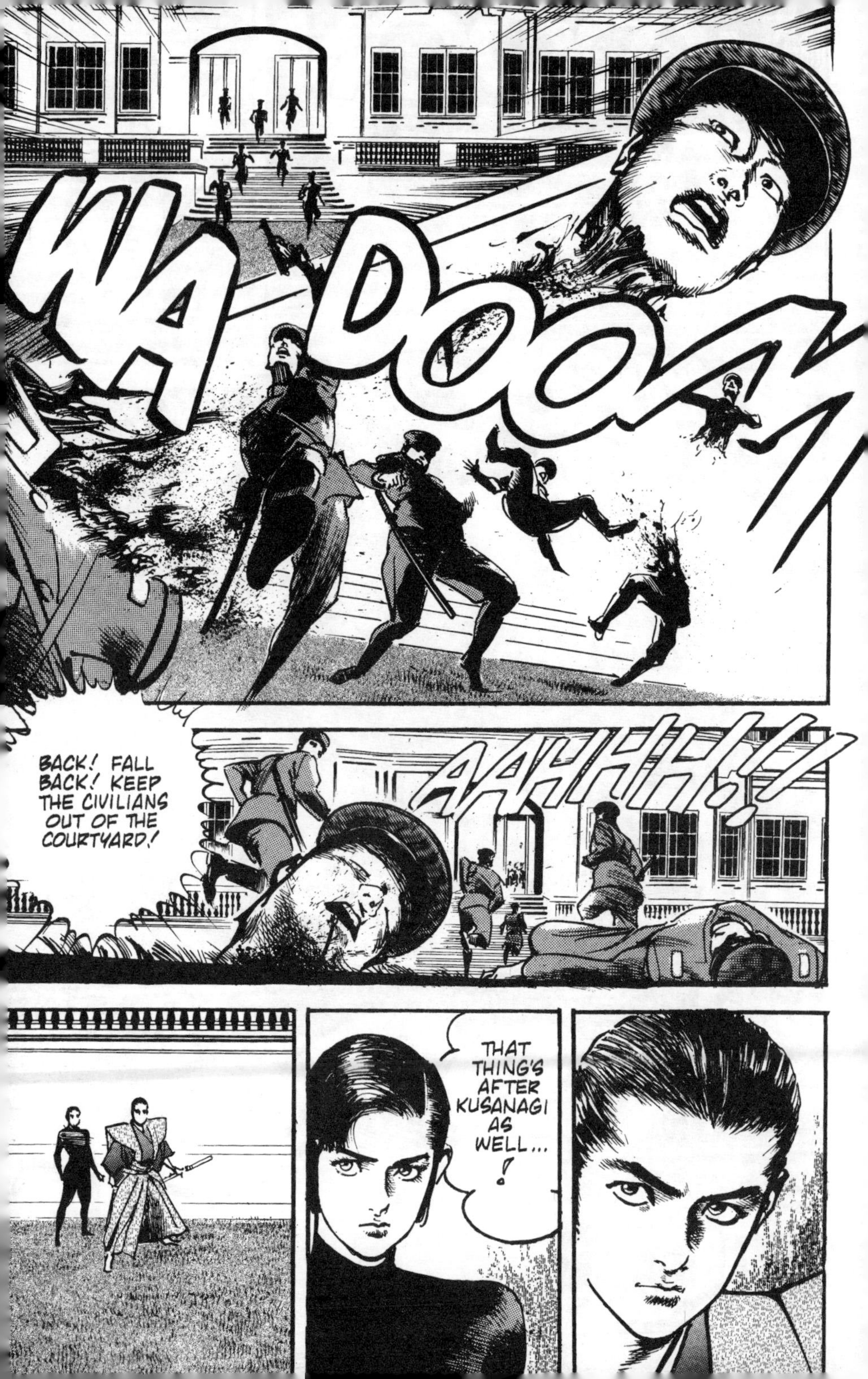
WA-DOOM
BACK! FALL BACK! KEEP THE CIVILIANS OUT OF THE COURTYARD!
AAHHH!!!
THAT THING'S AFTER KUSANAGI AS WELL... !

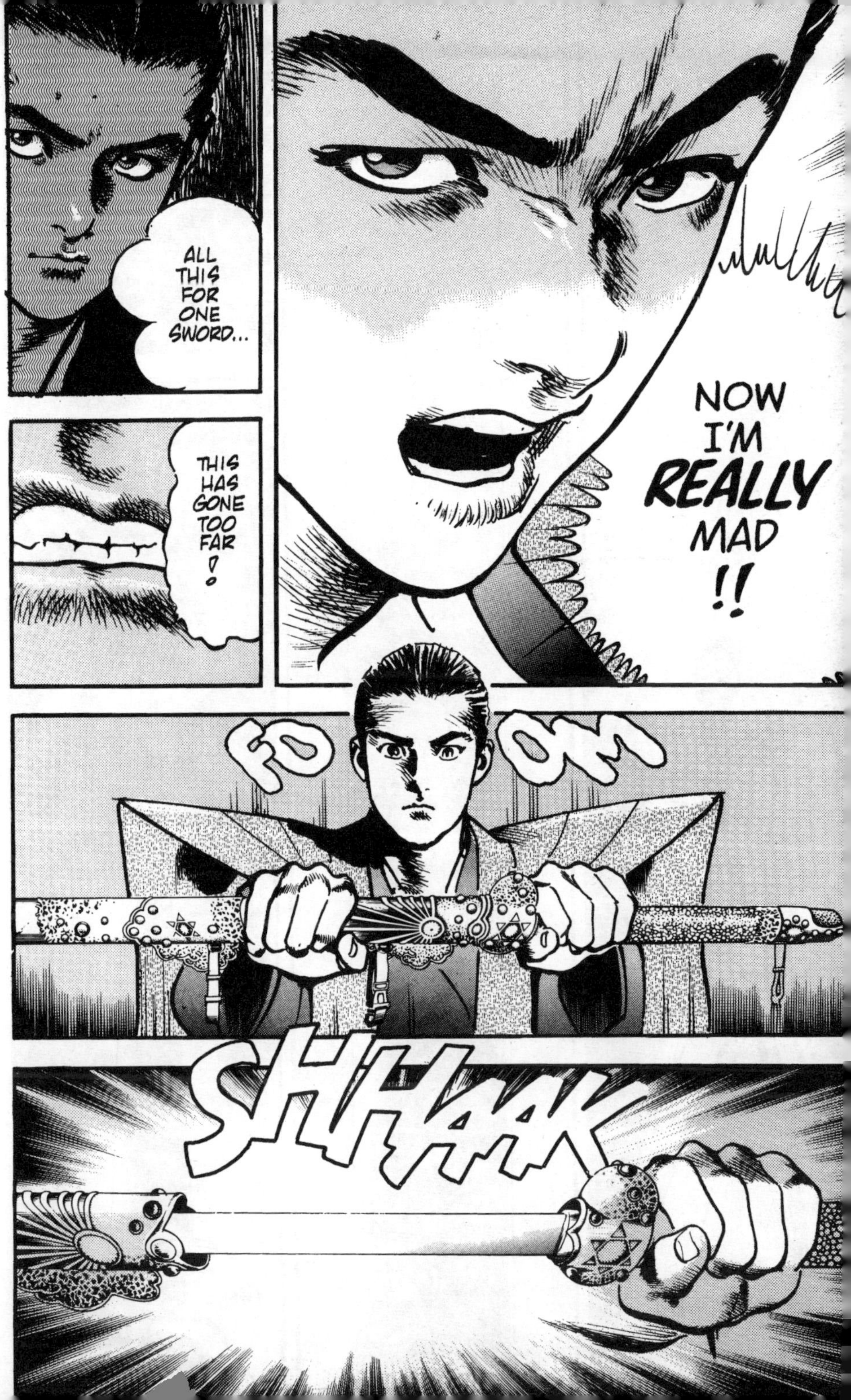
ALL THIS FOR ONE SWORD...
NOW I'M REALLY MAD!!
THIS HAS GONE TOO FAR!
FOOM
SHHAAK

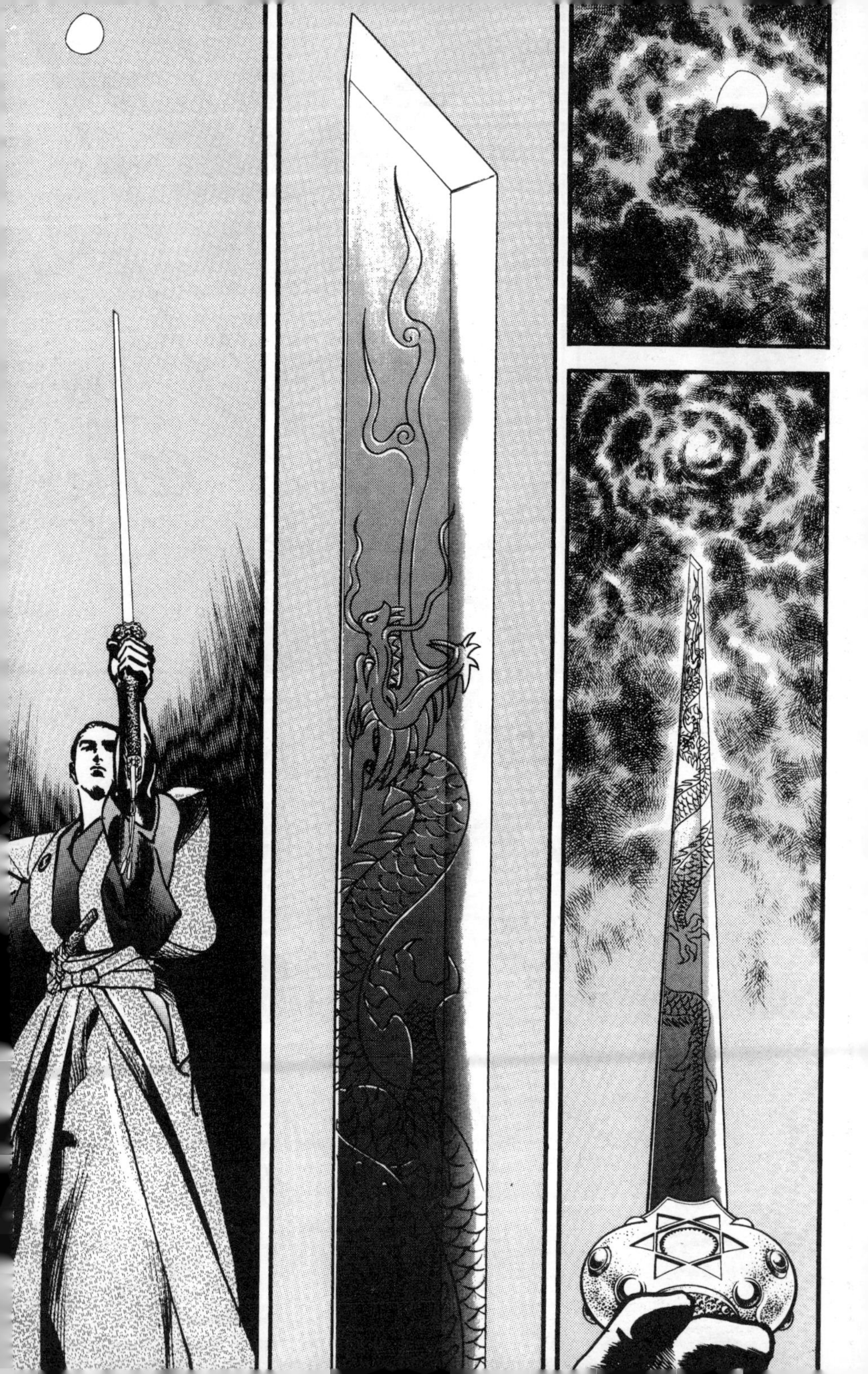

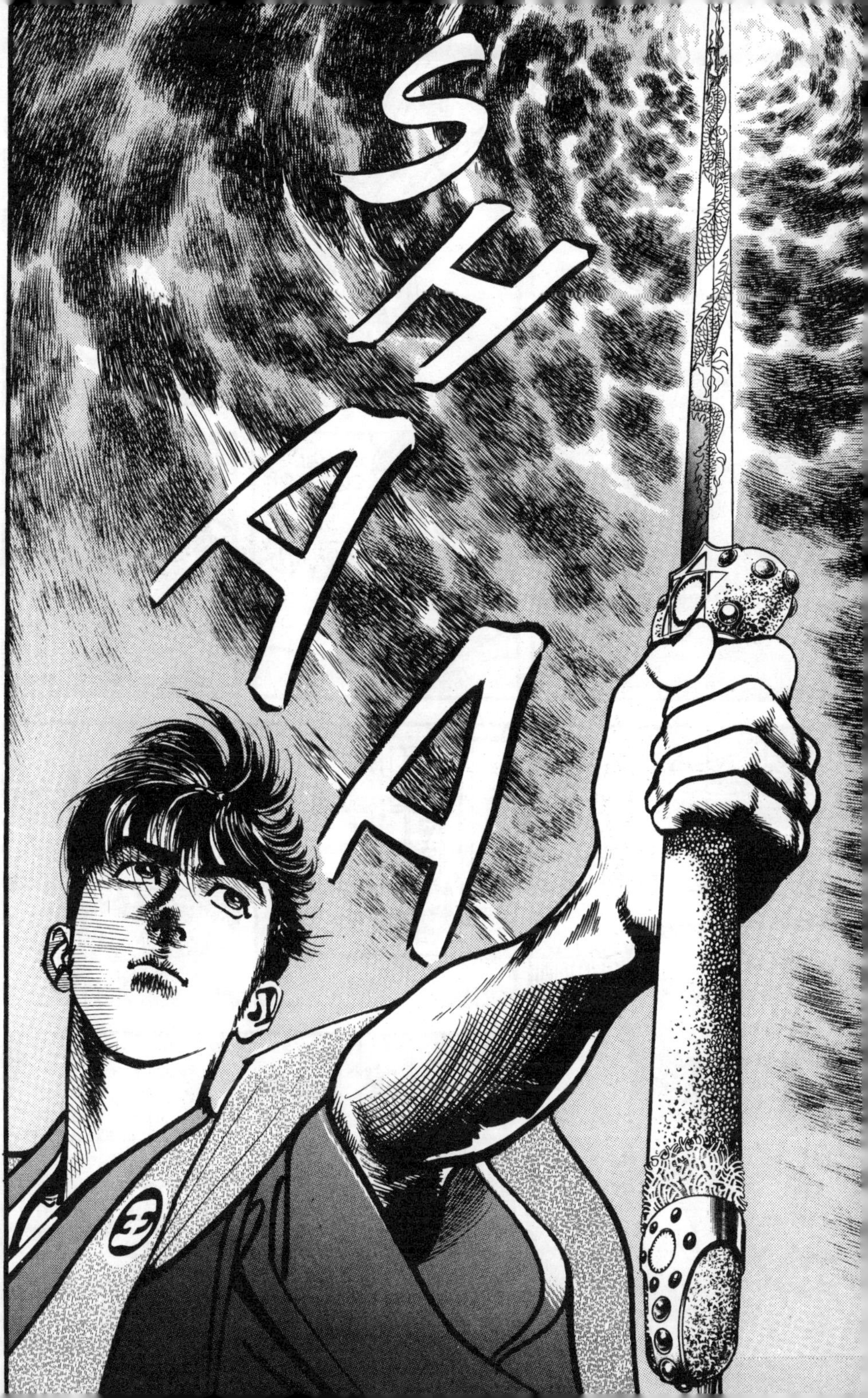
SHAAA

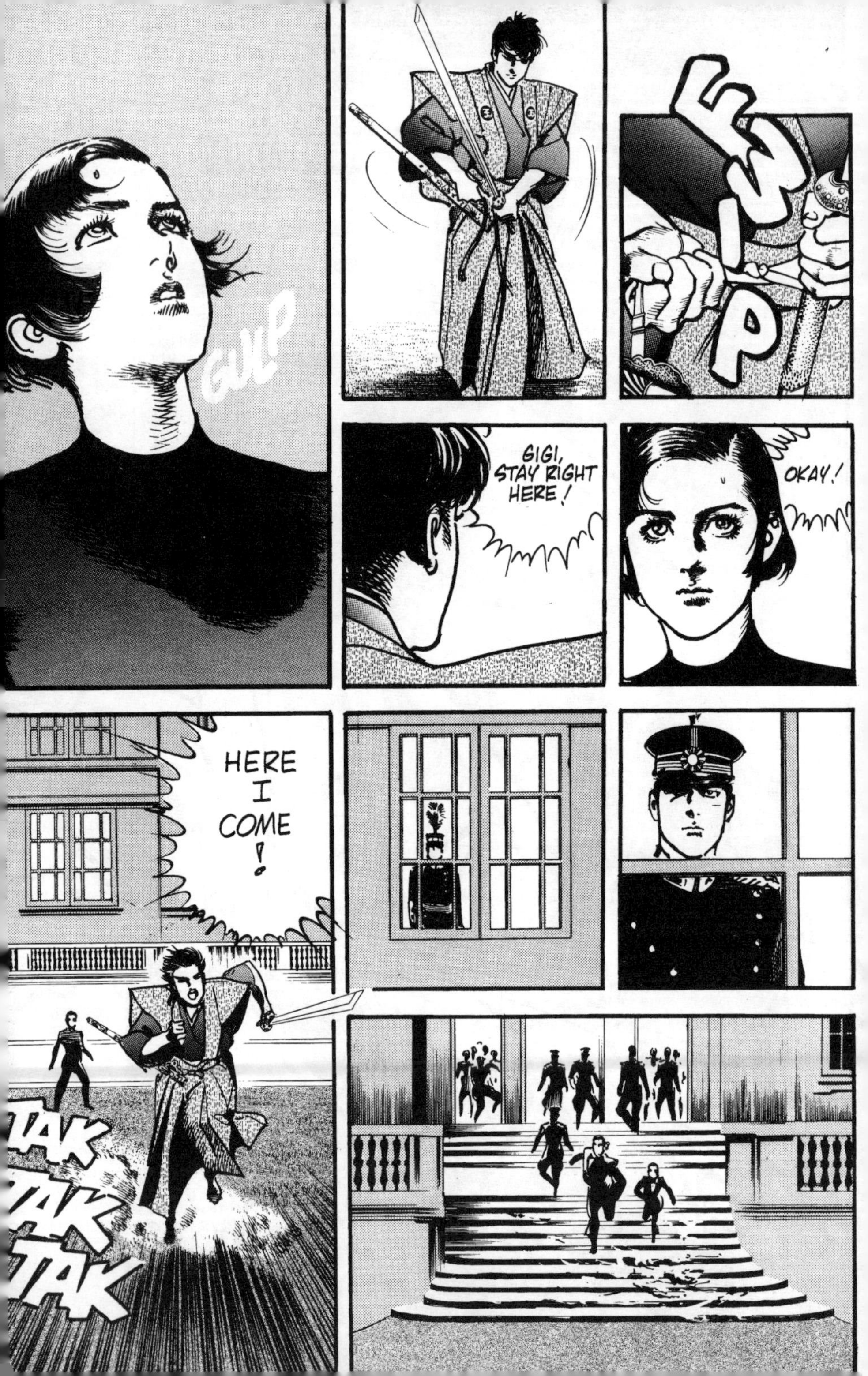
GULP
ZWIP
GIGI, STAY RIGHT HERE!
OKAY!
HERE I COME!
TAK TAK TAK

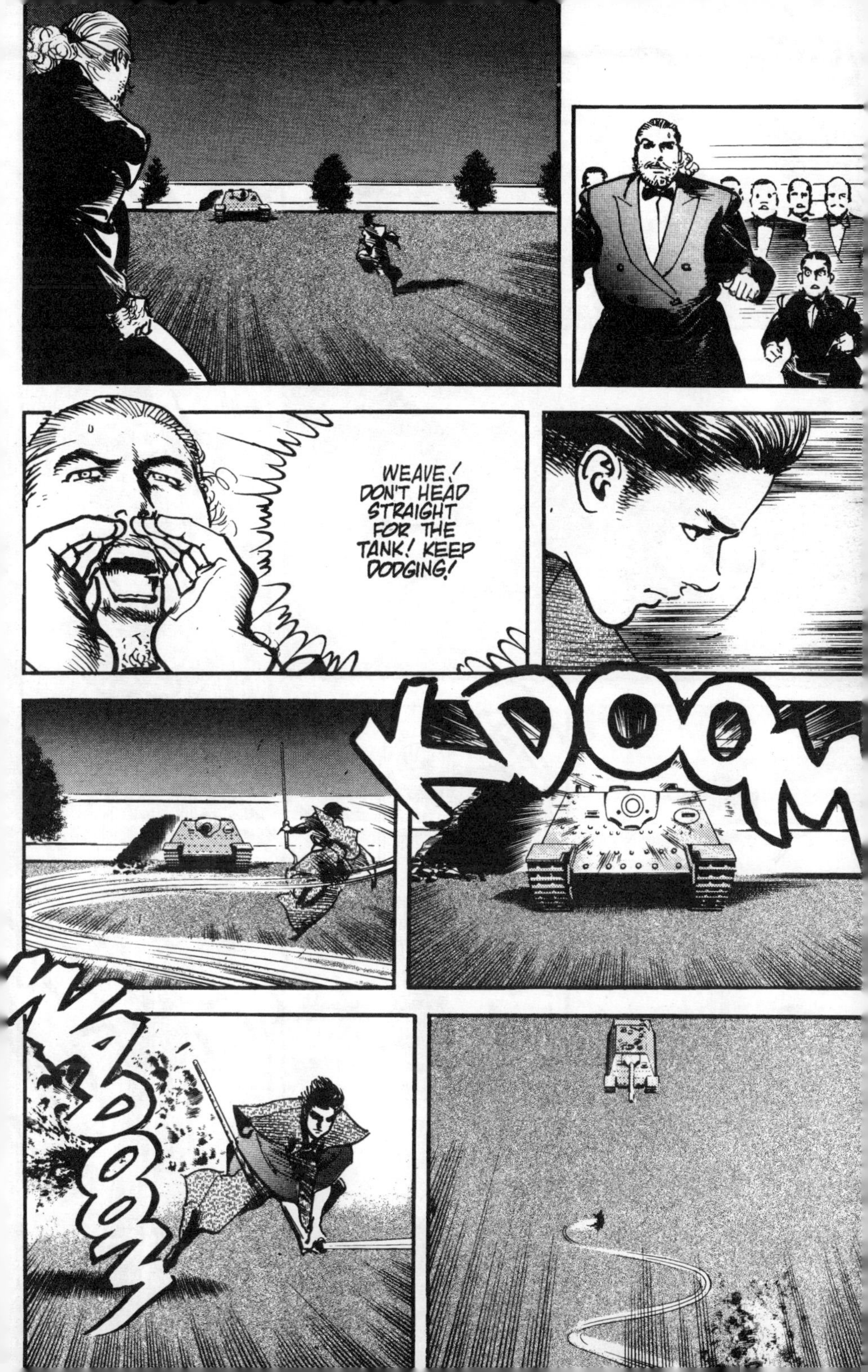
WEAVE! DON'T HEAD STRAIGHT FOR THE TANK! KEEP DODGING!
KDOOM
KADOOM

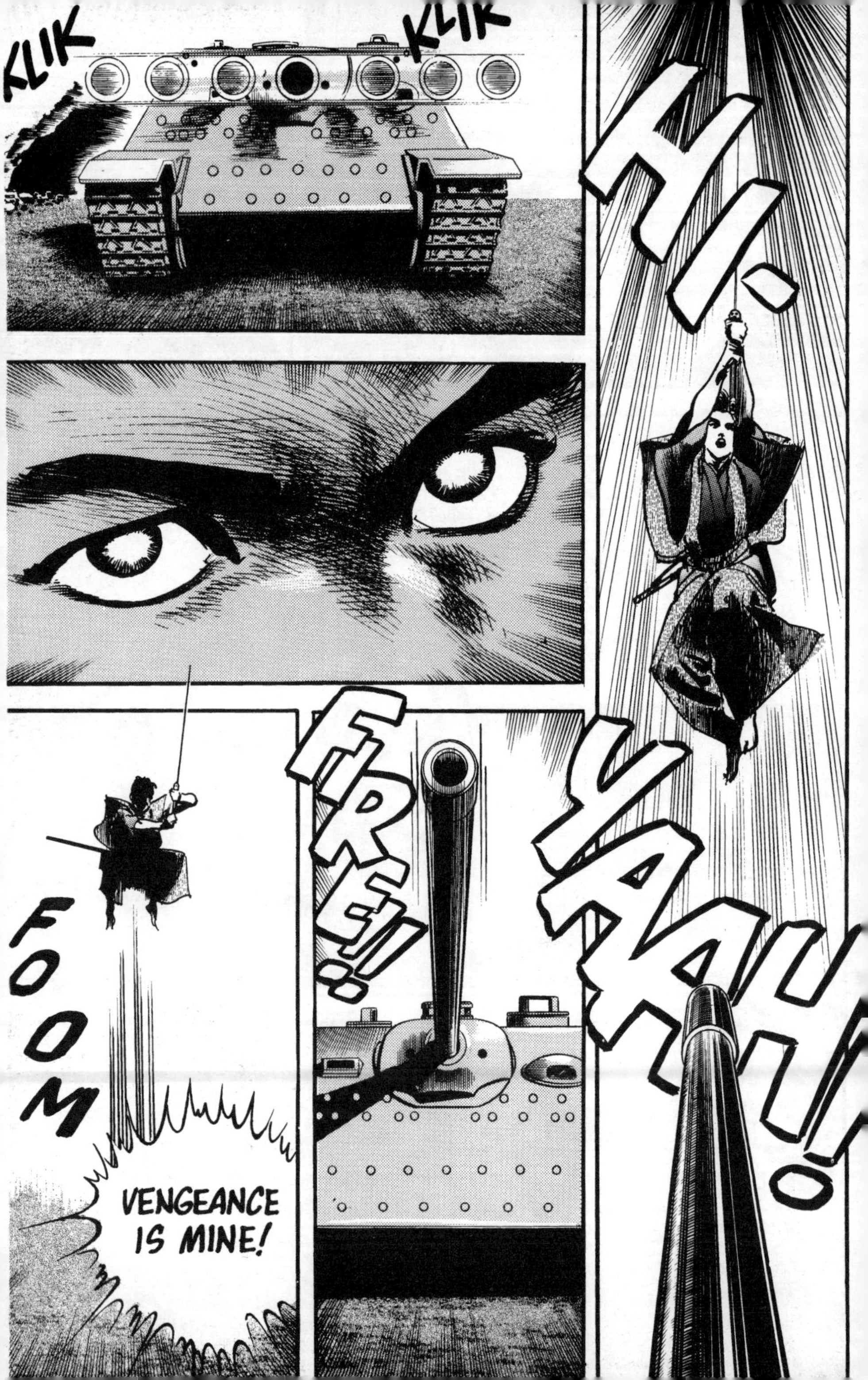
KLIK
KLIK
FOOM
VENGEANCE IS MINE!
FIRE!!
HI-YAAH!!

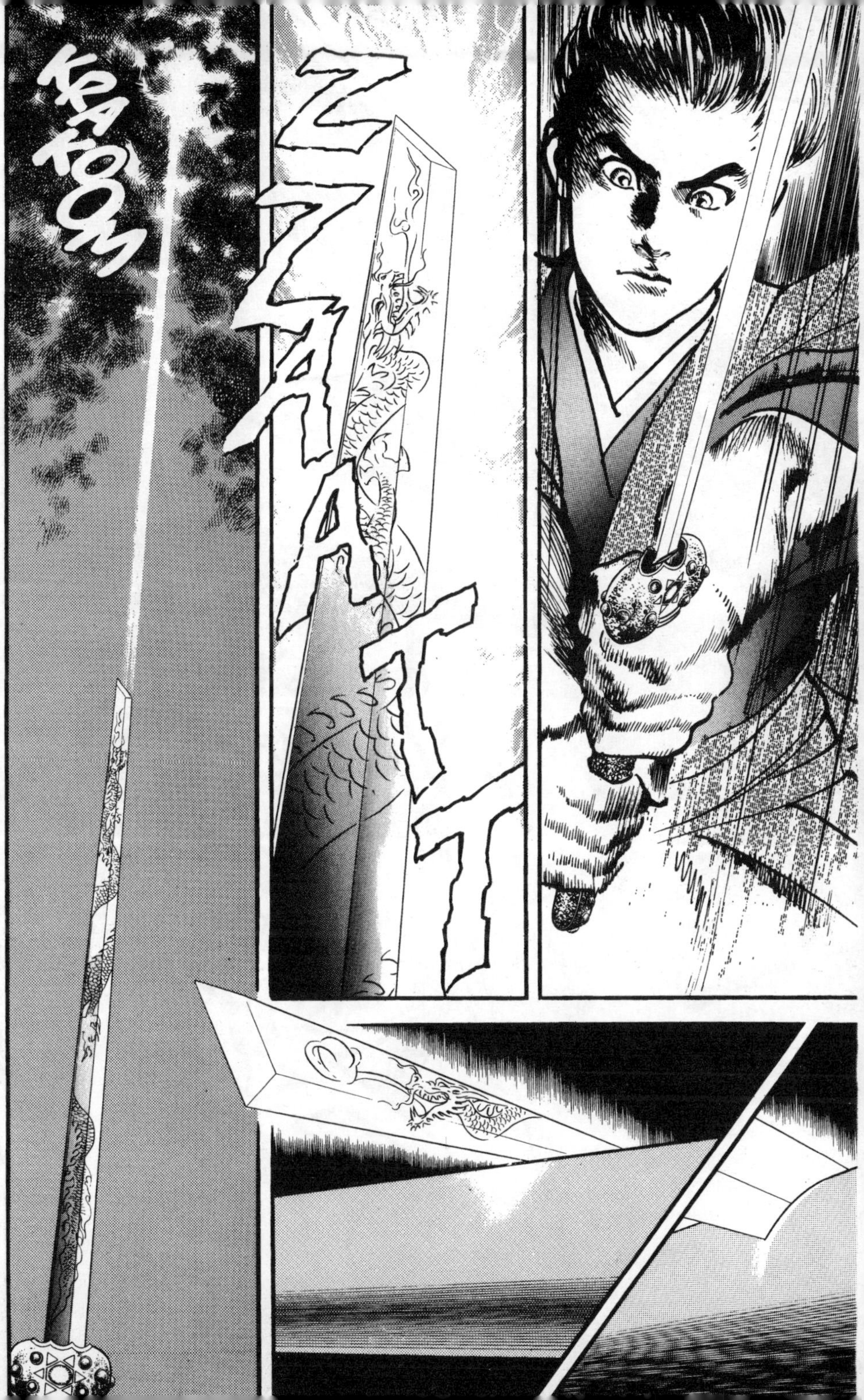
KRAKOOM
ZZAATT

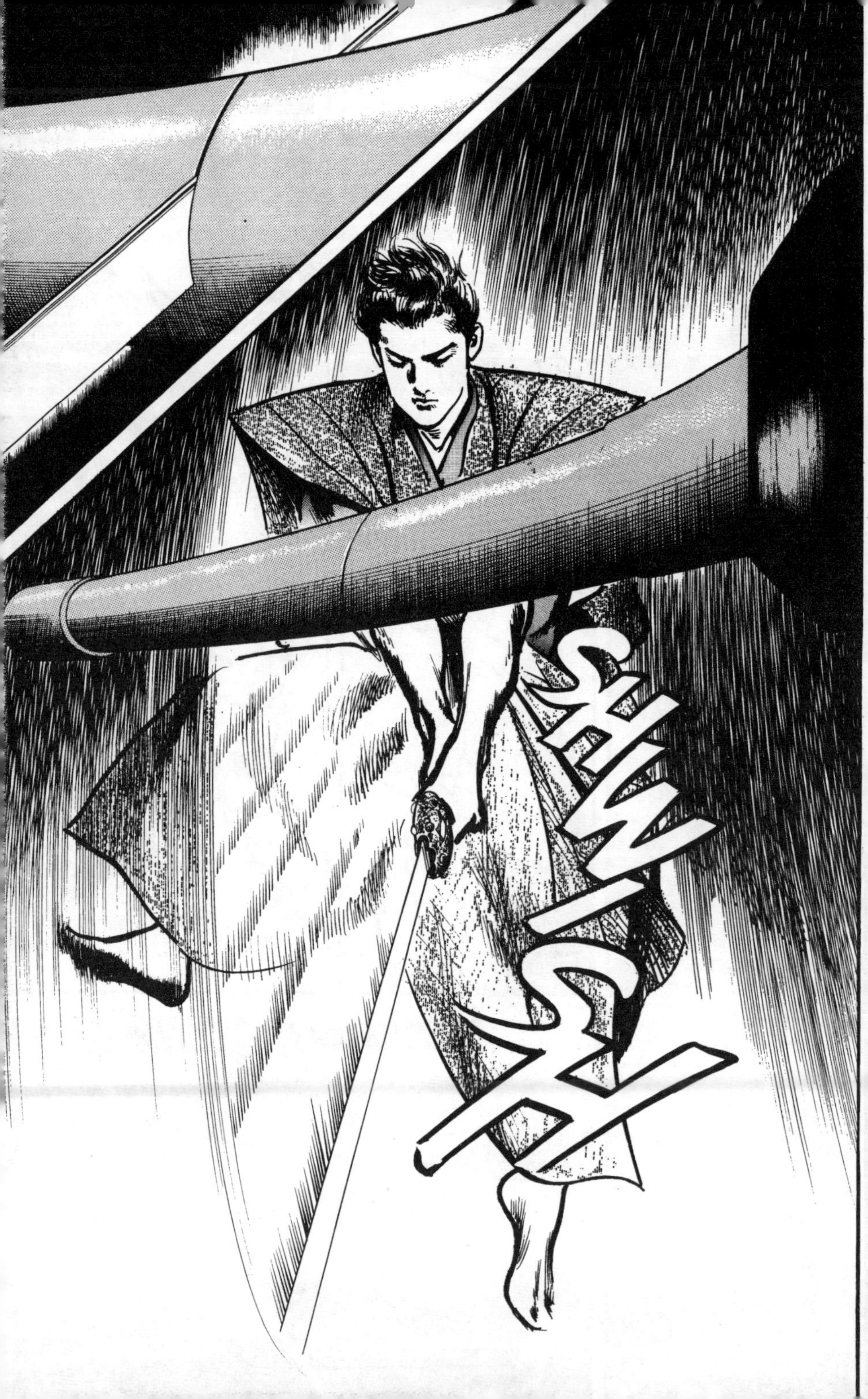
SHEWISH

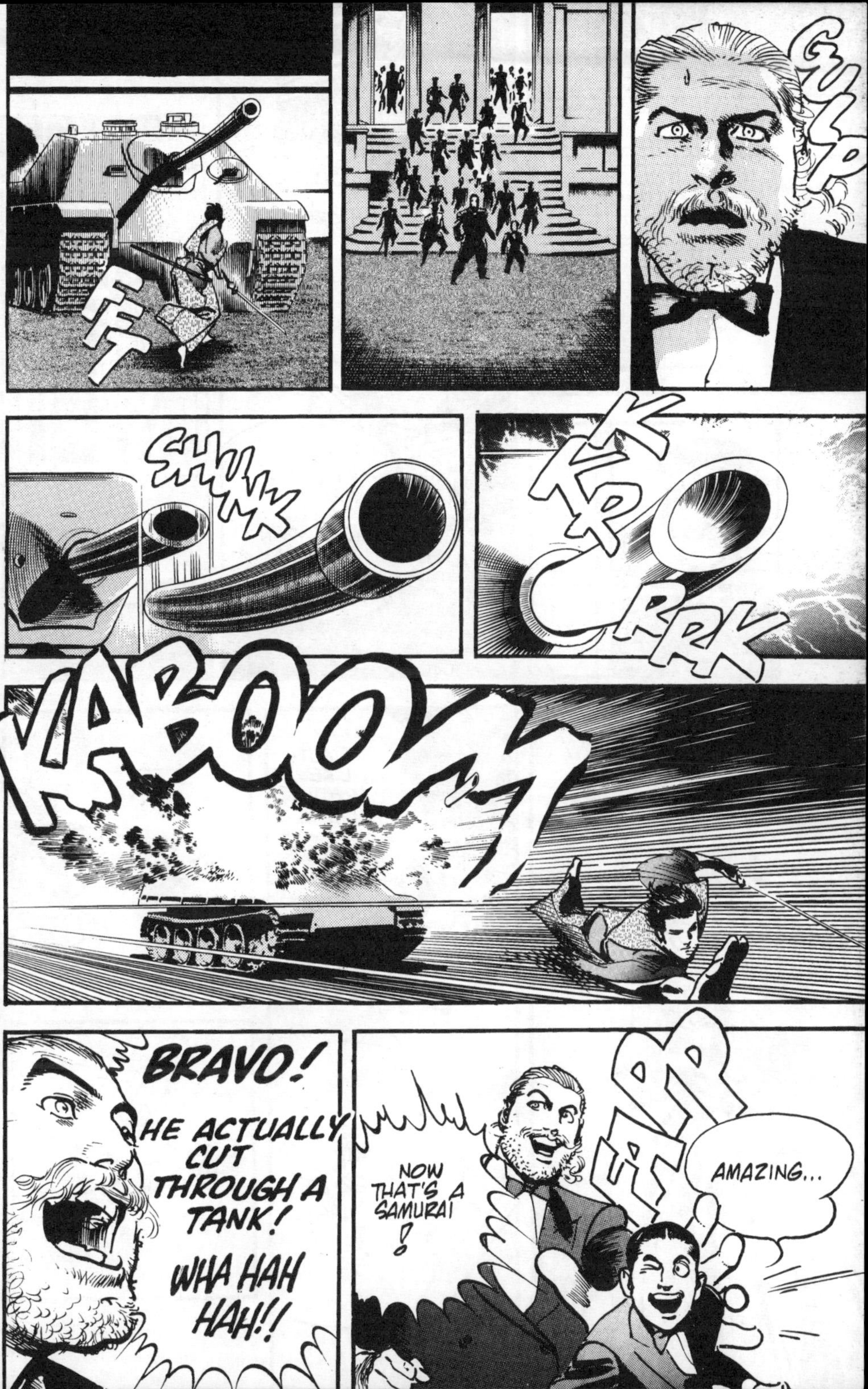
FFFT
GULP
SHUNK
KKRRRK
KABOOM
BRAVO!
HE ACTUALLY CUT THROUGH A TANK!
WHA HAH HAH!!
NOW THAT'S A SAMURAI!
AMAZING...

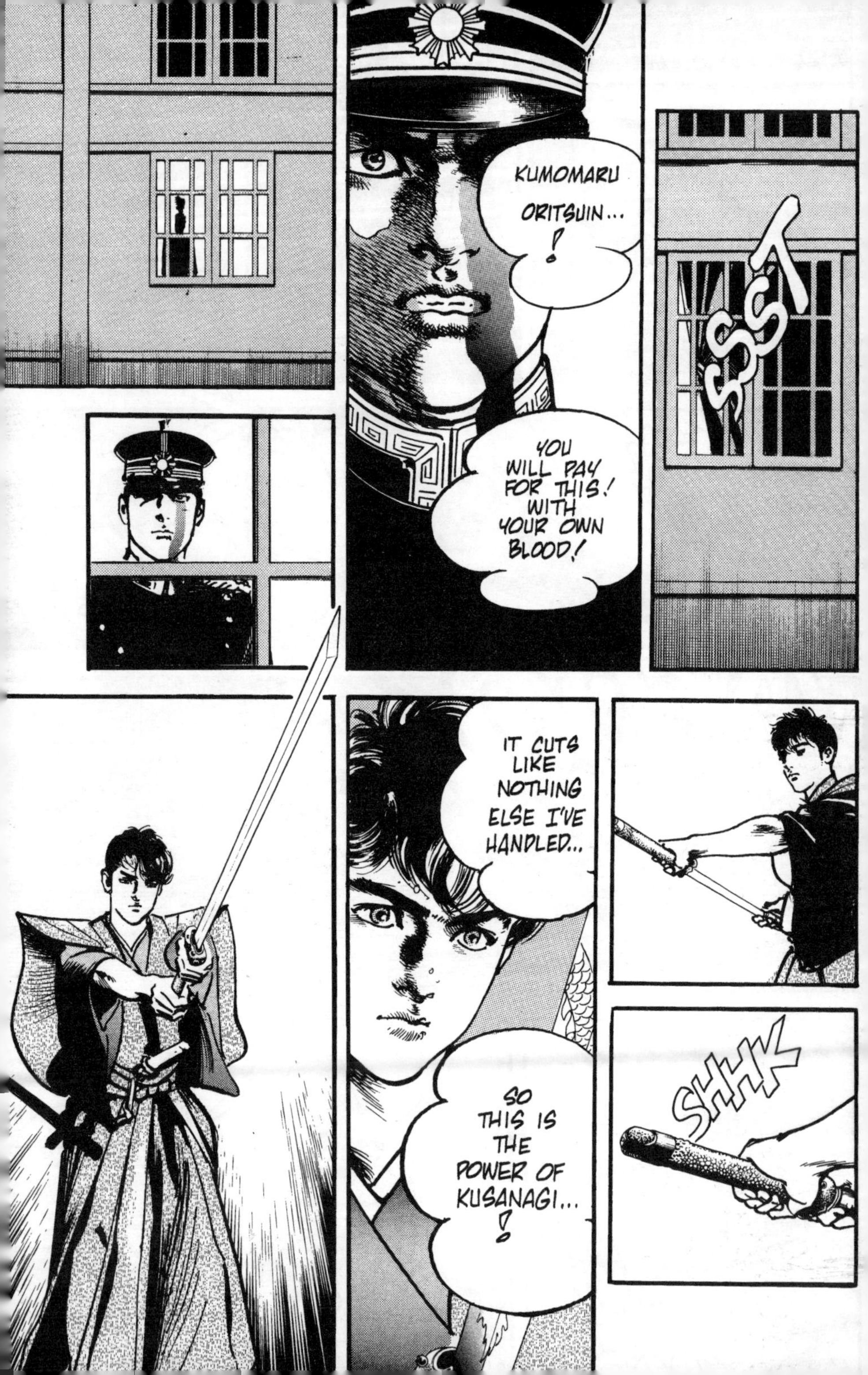
KUMOMARU ORITSUIN...!
YOU WILL PAY FOR THIS! WITH YOUR OWN BLOOD!
SST
IT CUTS LIKE NOTHING ELSE I'VE HANDLED...
SO THIS IS THE POWER OF KUSANAGI...!
SHHK

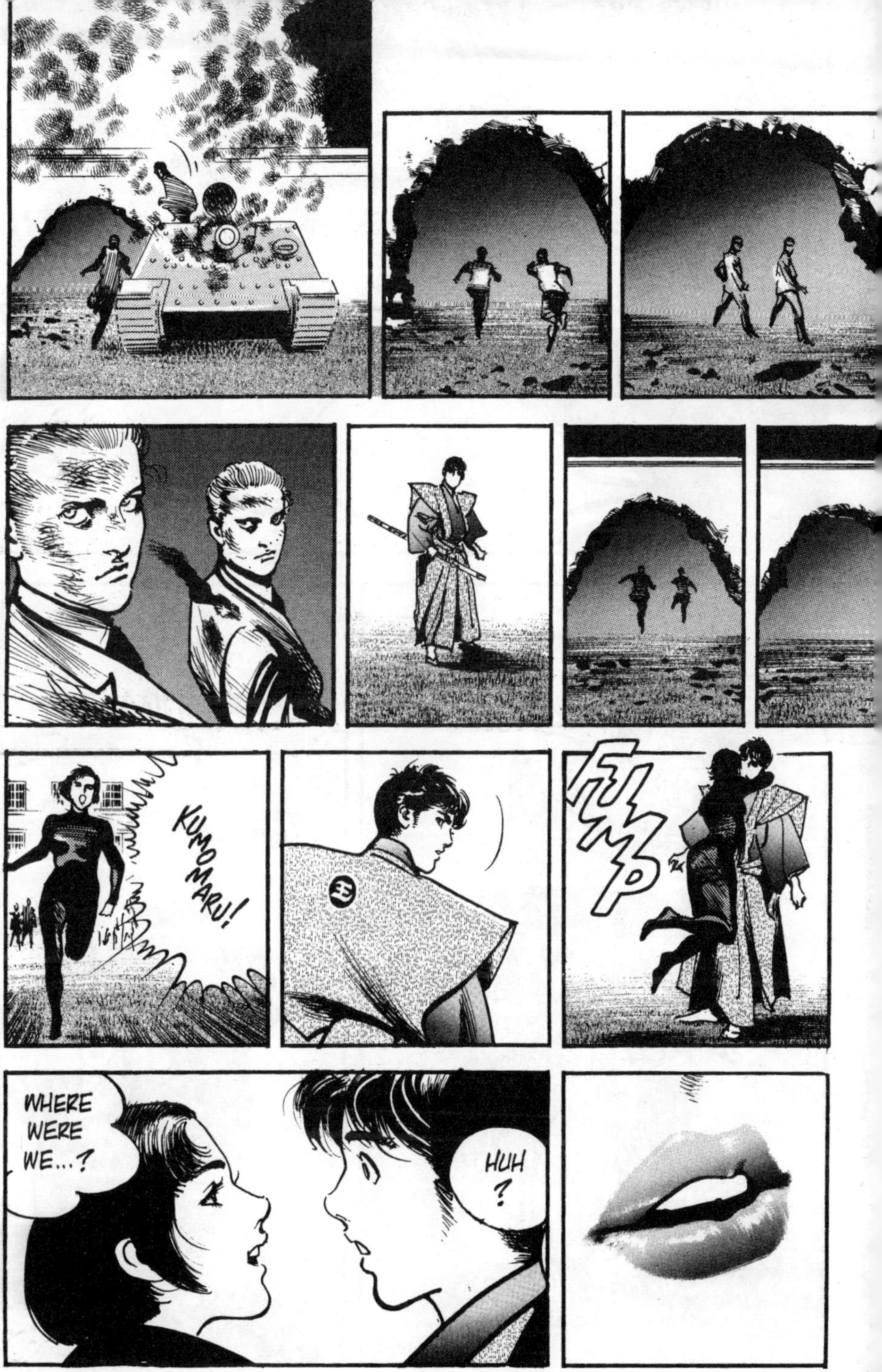
KUMOMARU!
FUMP
WHERE WERE WE...?
HUH ?

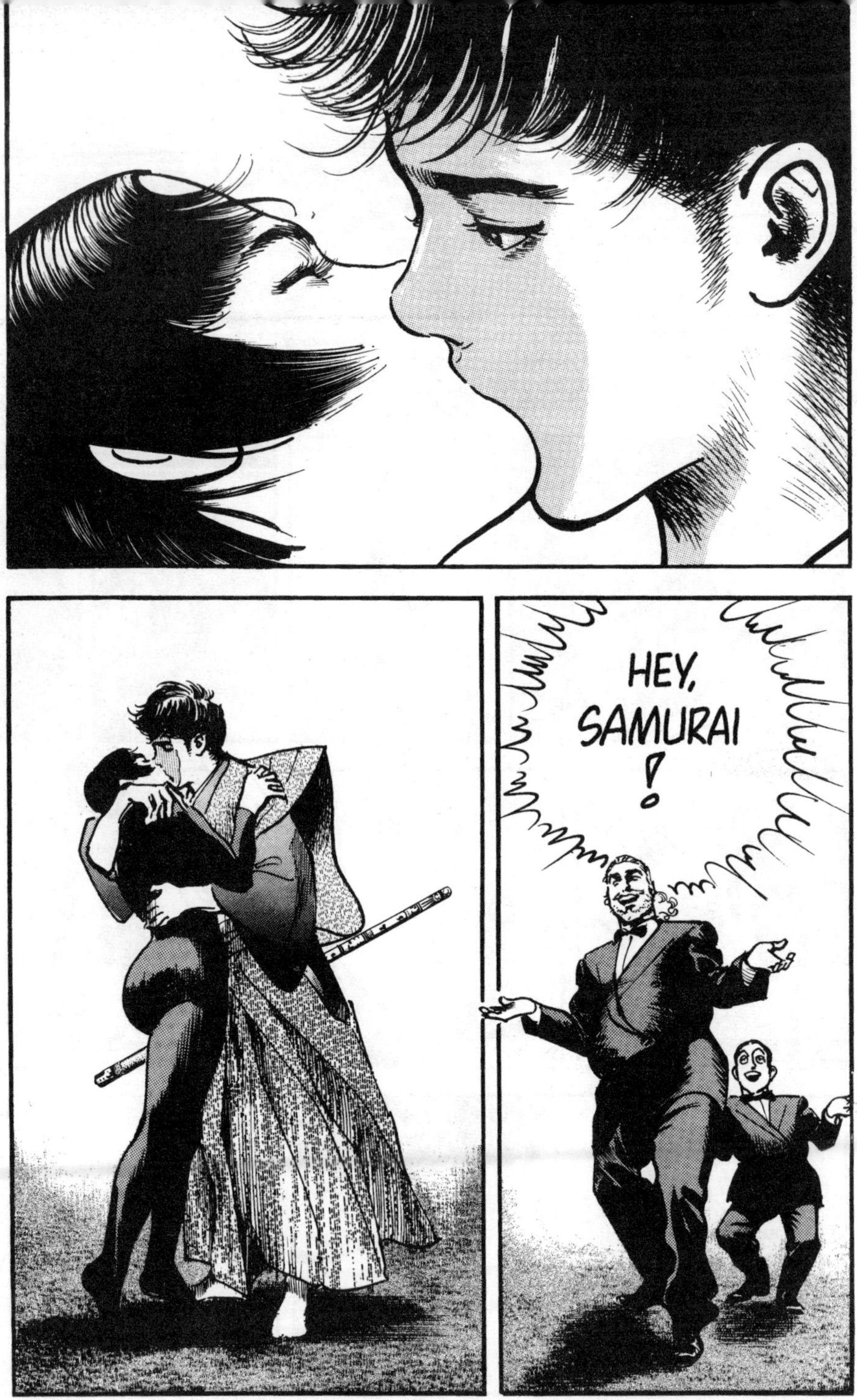
HEY, SAMURAI!

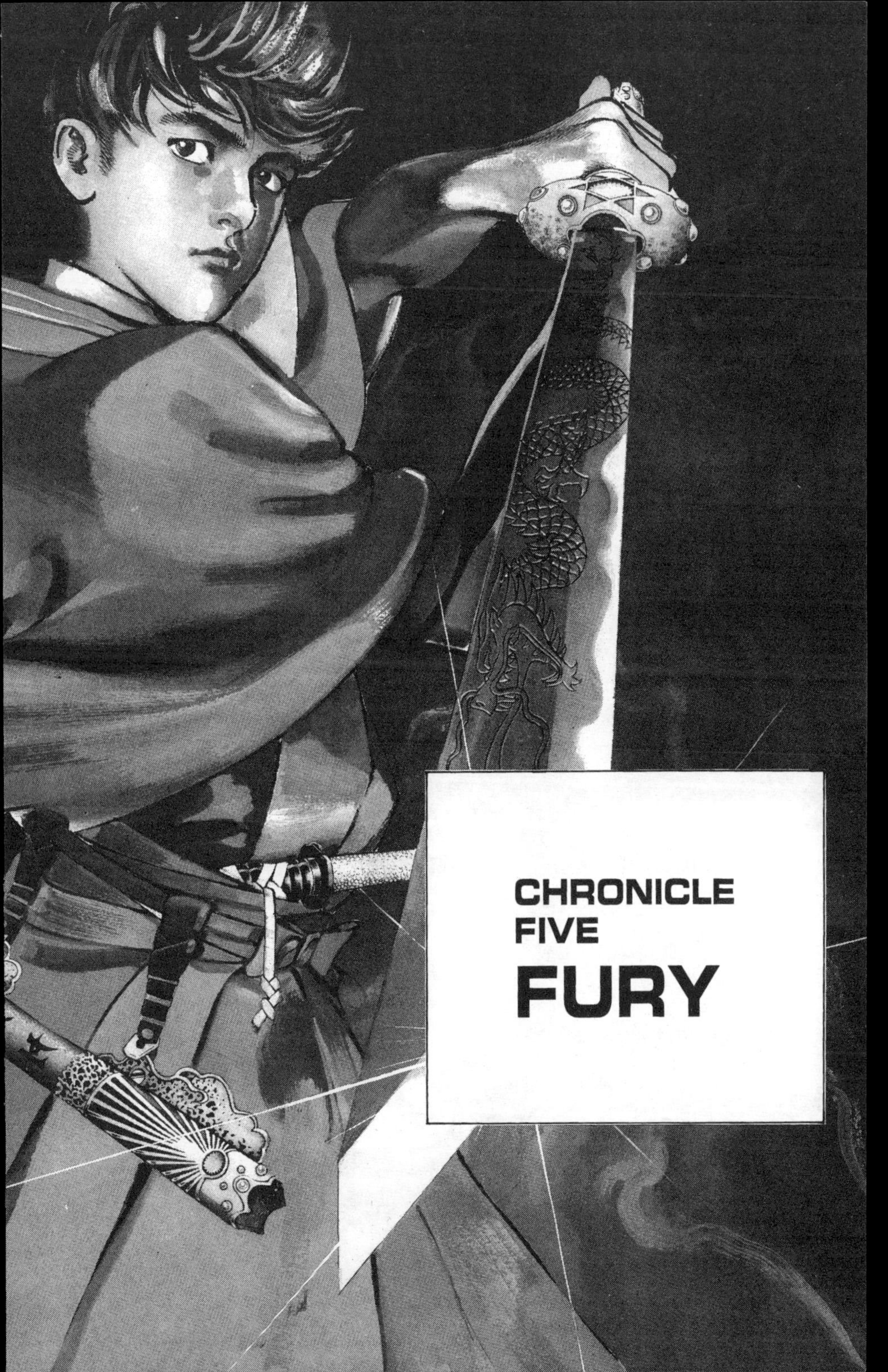

CHRONICLE FIVE
FURY

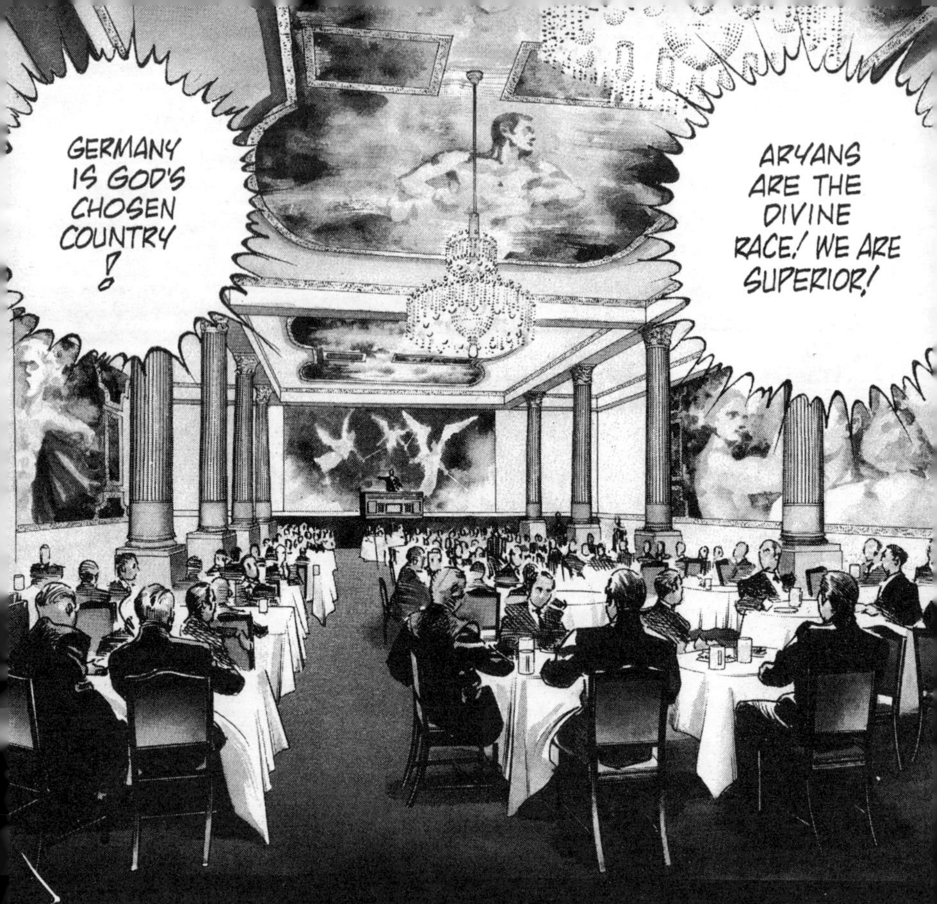
GERMANY IS GOD'S CHOSEN COUNTRY!
ARYANS ARE THE DIVINE RACE! WE ARE SUPERIOR!
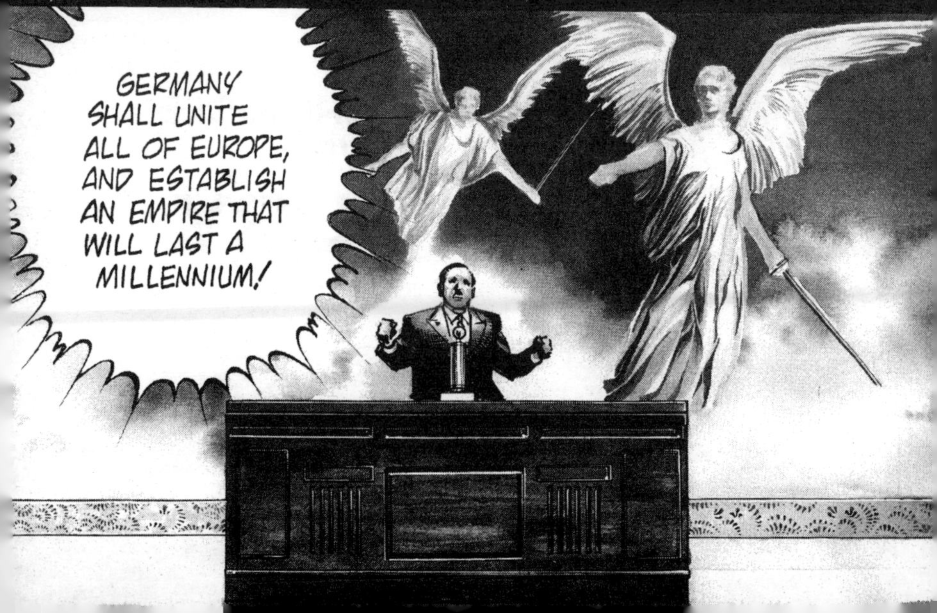
GERMANY SHALL UNITE ALL OF EUROPE, AND ESTABLISH AN EMPIRE THAT WILL LAST A MILLENNIUM!

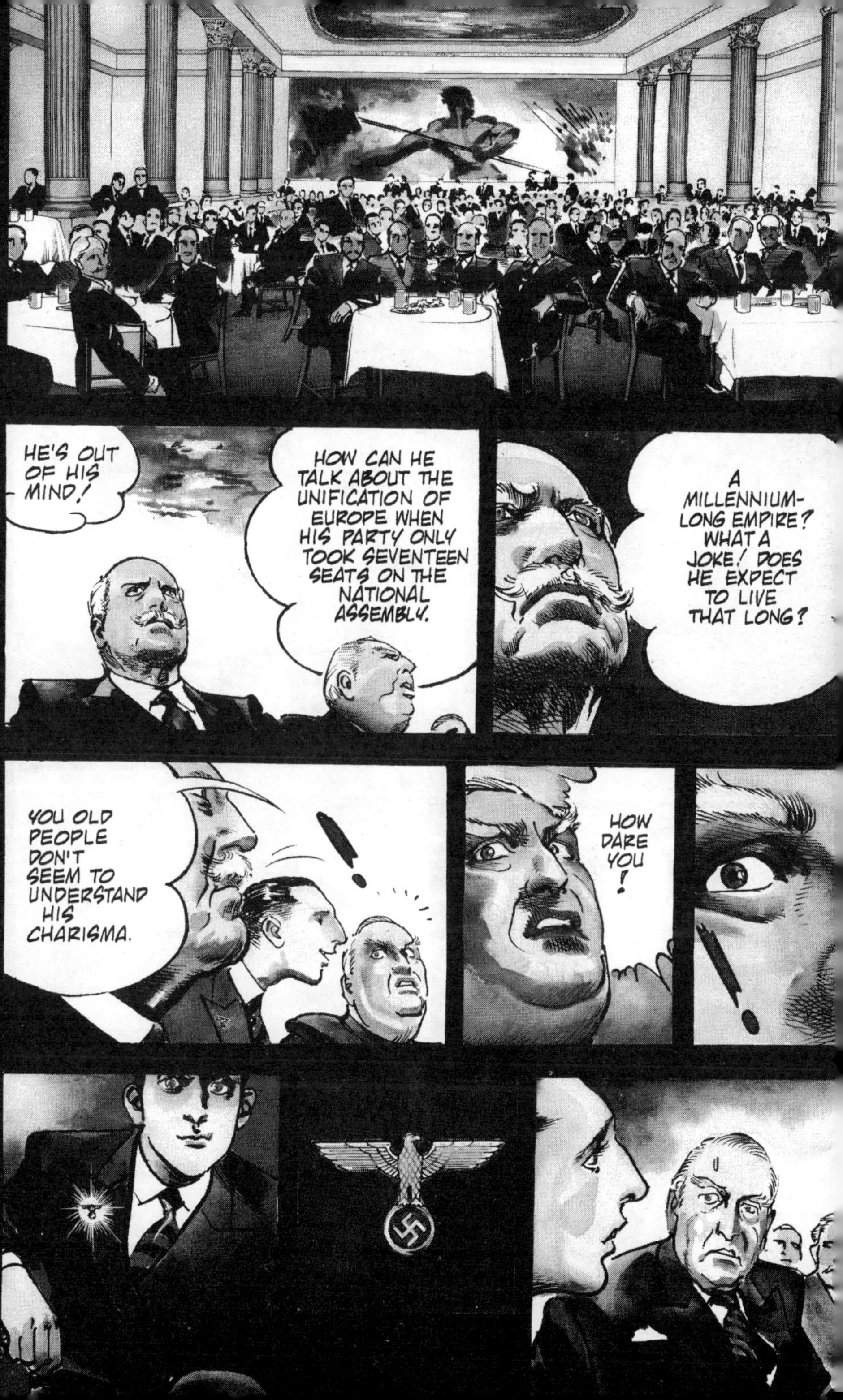
HE'S OUT OF HIS MIND!
HOW CAN HE TALK ABOUT THE UNIFICATION OF EUROPE WHEN HIS PARTY ONLY TOOK SEVENTEEN SEATS ON THE NATIONAL ASSEMBLY.
A MILLENNIUM-LONG EMPIRE? WHAT A JOKE! DOES HE EXPECT TO LIVE THAT LONG?
YOU OLD PEOPLE DON'T SEEM TO UNDERSTAND HIS CHARISMA.
!
HOW DARE YOU!
!

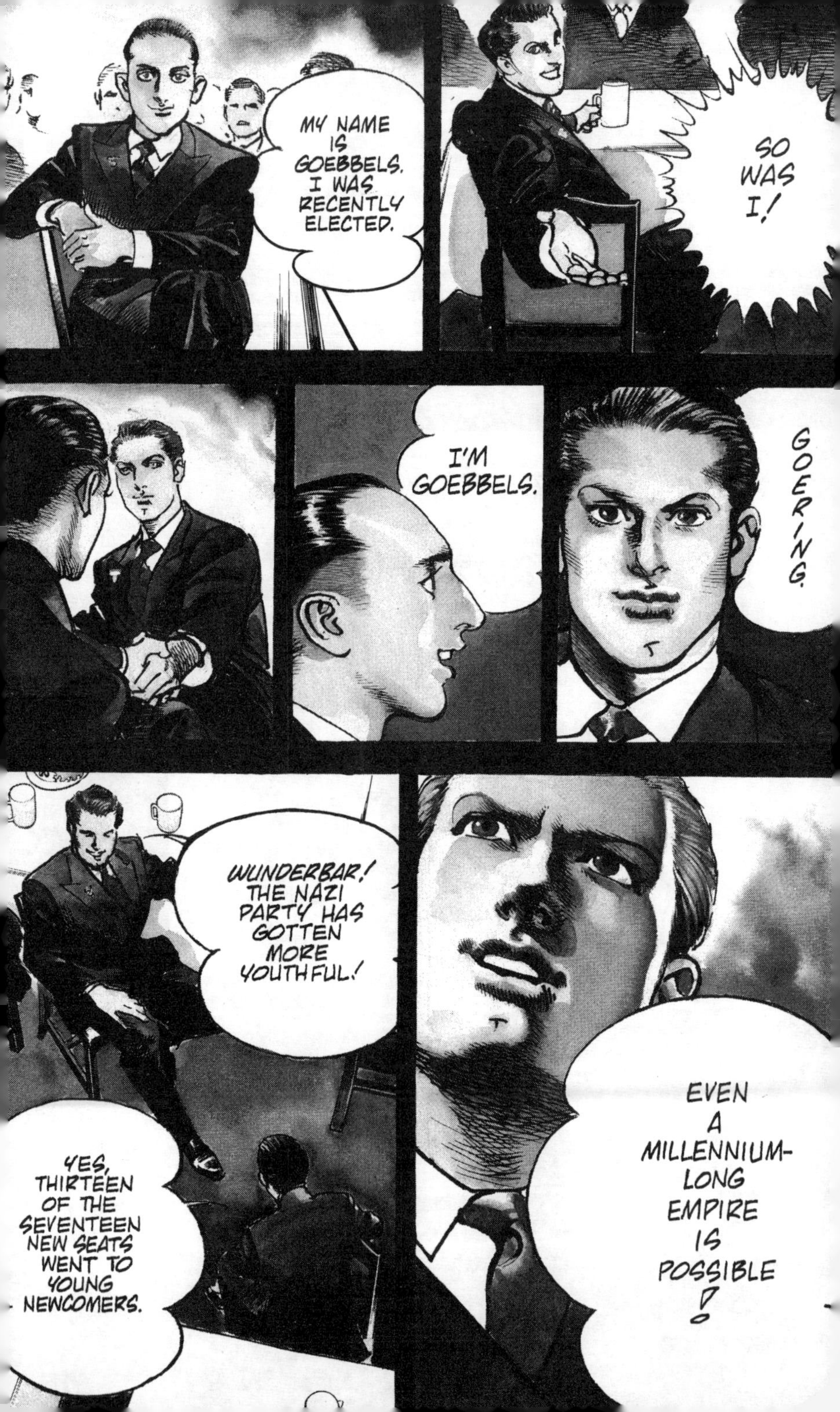

MY NAME IS GOEBBELS. I WAS RECENTLY ELECTED.
SO WAS I!
I'M GOEBBELS.
GOERING.
WUNDERBAR! THE NAZI PARTY HAS GOTTEN MORE YOUTHFUL!
YES, THIRTEEN OF THE SEVENTEEN NEW SEATS WENT TO YOUNG NEWCOMERS.
EVEN A MILLENNIUM-LONG EMPIRE IS POSSIBLE!

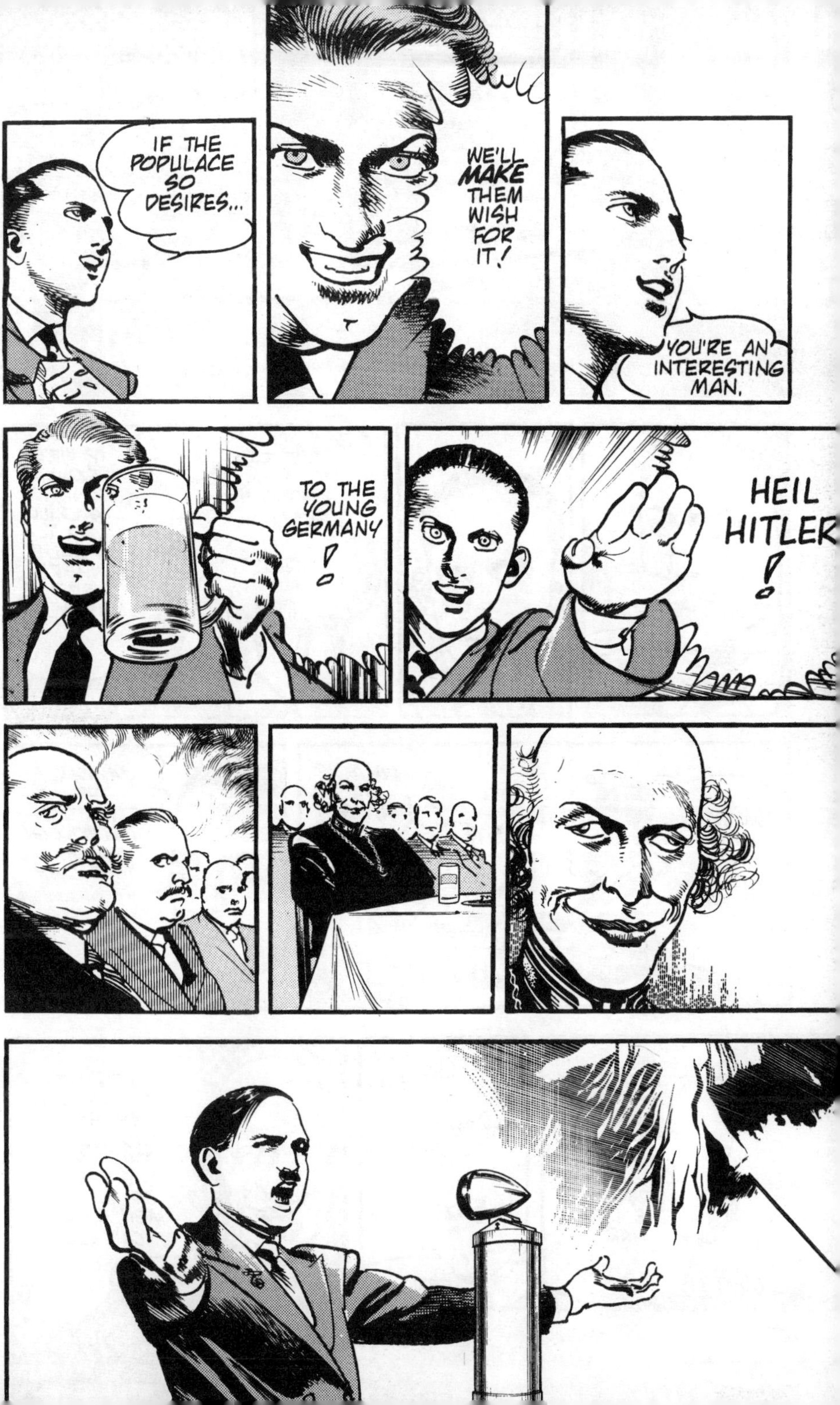
IF THE POPULACE SO DESIRES...
WE'LL MAKE THEM WISH FOR IT!
YOU'RE AN INTERESTING MAN.
TO THE YOUNG GERMANY!
HEIL HITLER!

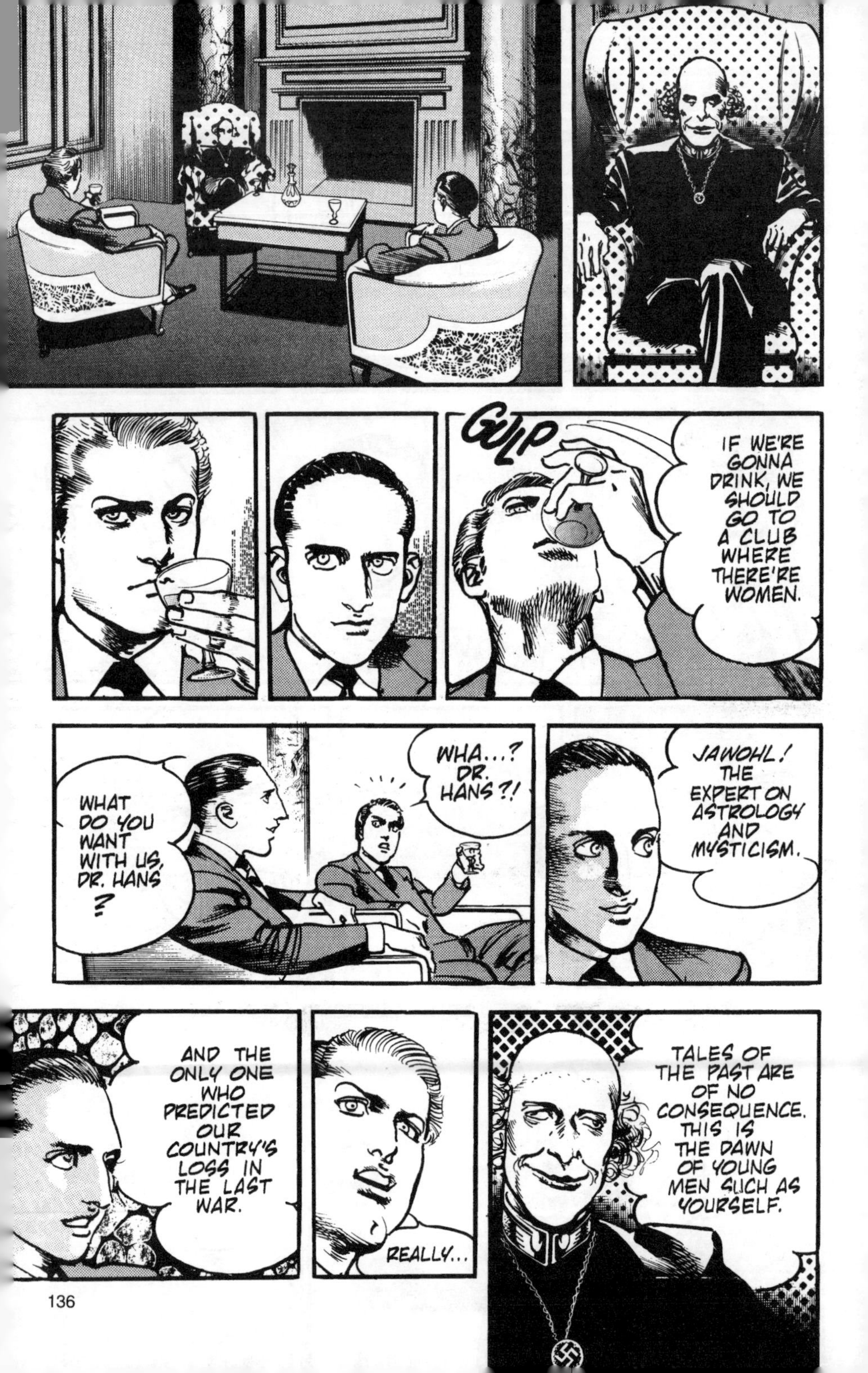
GULP
IF WE'RE GONNA DRINK, WE SHOULD GO TO A CLUB WHERE THERE'RE WOMEN.
WHAT DO YOU WANT WITH US, DR. HANS ?
WHA...? DR. HANS ?!
JAWOHL! THE EXPERT ON ASTROLOGY AND MYSTICISM.
AND THE ONLY ONE WHO PREDICTED OUR COUNTRY'S LOSS IN THE LAST WAR.
REALLY...
TALES OF THE PAST ARE OF NO CONSEQUENCE. THIS IS THE DAWN OF YOUNG MEN SUCH AS YOURSELF.

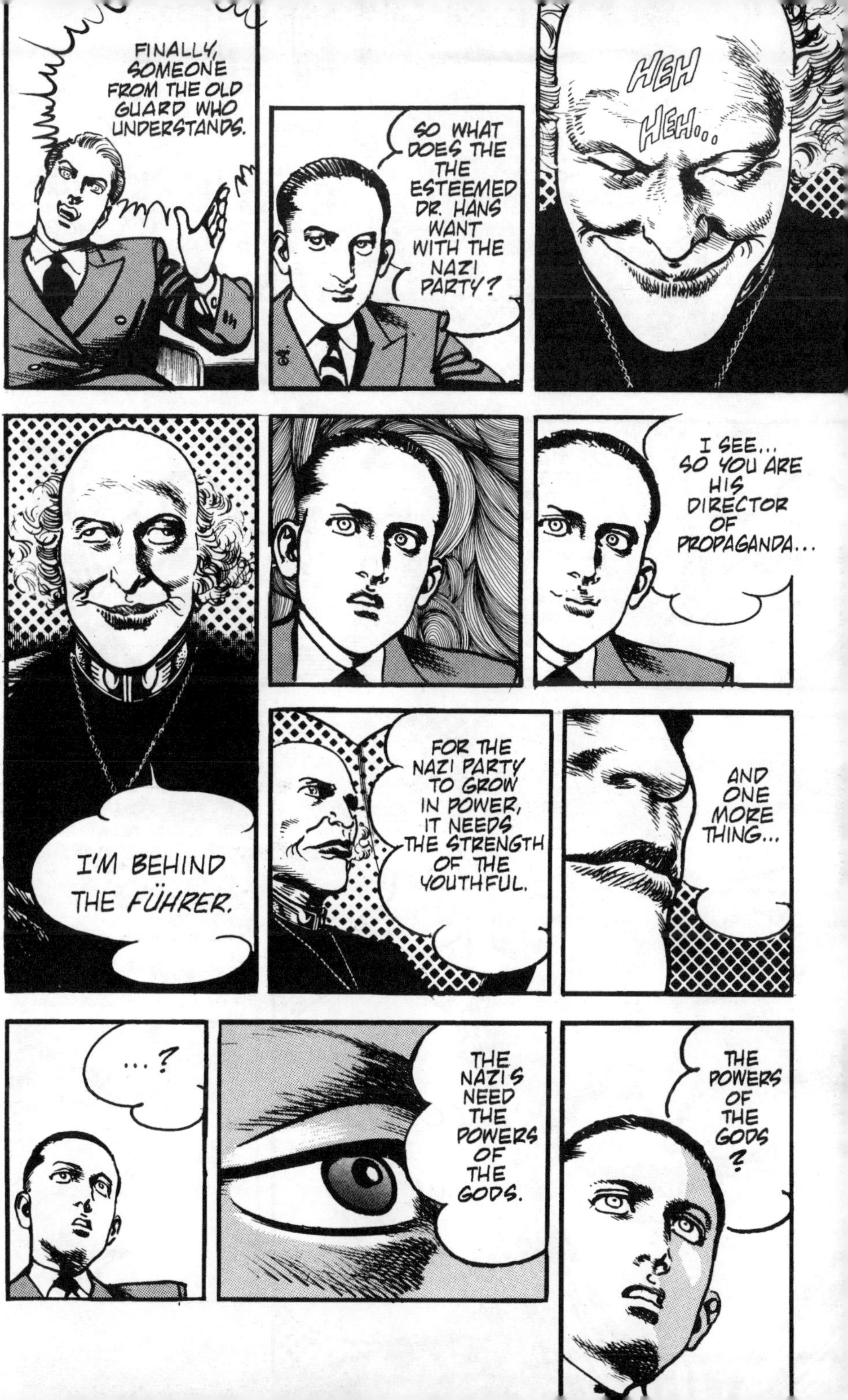
FINALLY, SOMEONE FROM THE OLD GUARD WHO UNDERSTANDS.
SO WHAT DOES THE THE ESTEEMED DR. HANS WANT WITH THE NAZI PARTY?
HEH HEH...
I'M BEHIND THE FÜHRER.
I SEE... SO YOU ARE HIS DIRECTOR OF PROPAGANDA...
FOR THE NAZI PARTY TO GROW IN POWER, IT NEEDS THE STRENGTH OF THE YOUTHFUL.
AND ONE MORE THING...
...?
THE NAZIS NEED THE POWERS OF THE GODS.
THE POWERS OF THE GODS?

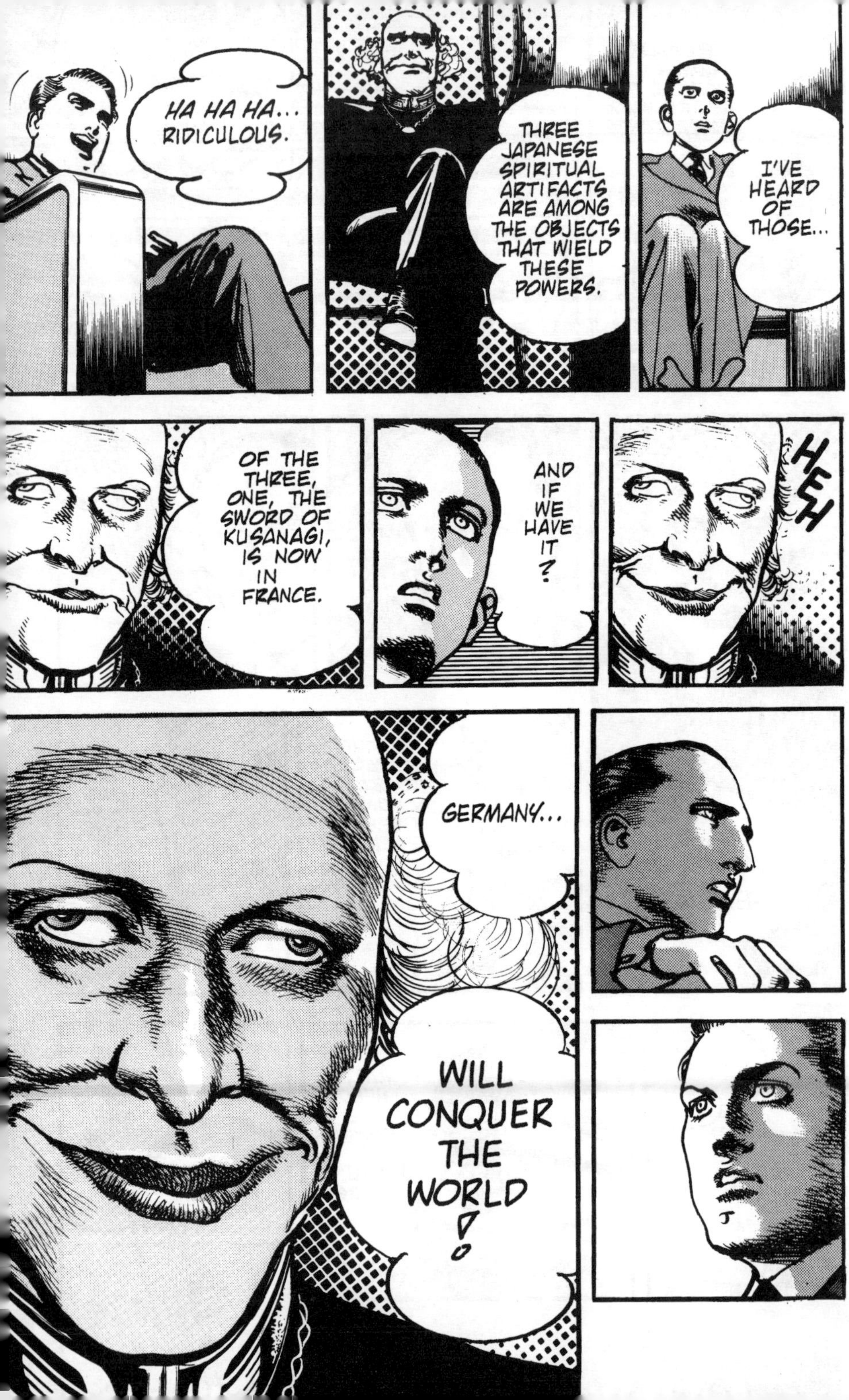
HA HA HA... RIDICULOUS.
THREE JAPANESE SPIRITUAL ARTIFACTS ARE AMONG THE OBJECTS THAT WIELD THESE POWERS.
I'VE HEARD OF THOSE...
OF THE THREE, ONE, THE SWORD OF KUSANAGI, IS NOW IN FRANCE.
AND IF WE HAVE IT?
HEH
GERMANY...
WILL CONQUER THE WORLD!!

PARIS--

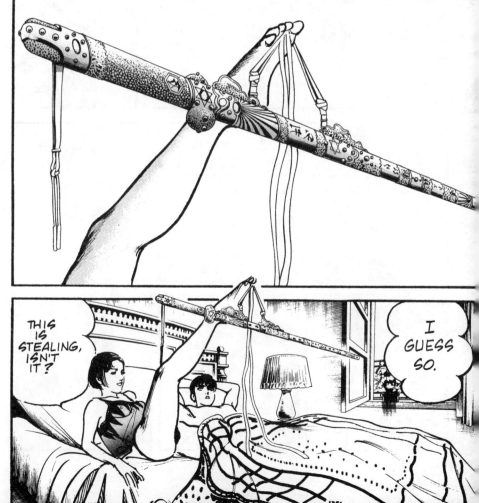

THIS
IS
STEALING,
ISN'T
IT?

I
GUESS
SO.

SAY...WHY DON'T WE SELL THIS KUSANAGI, AND TRAVEL AROUND THE WORLD TOGETHER!?

WE?

THAT'S RIGHT, JUST THE TWO OF US...

BECAUSE... I'VE TAKEN A FANCY TO YOU.

B-BUT...

THE CAT BURGLAR POISON ALWAYS GETS WHAT SHE SETS HER EYES ON.

SHA

I WANT TO GIVE IT TO YOU...

BUT OLD MAN KUJO WOULD BE RUINED. I... JUST CAN'T DO IT.

PLEASE, I'M BEGGING YOU TO GIVE THIS ONE UP!

YOU ARE UP-FRONT WITH A LADY, AREN'T YOU.

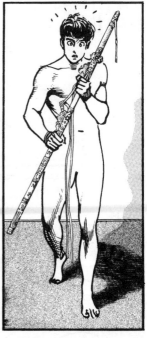

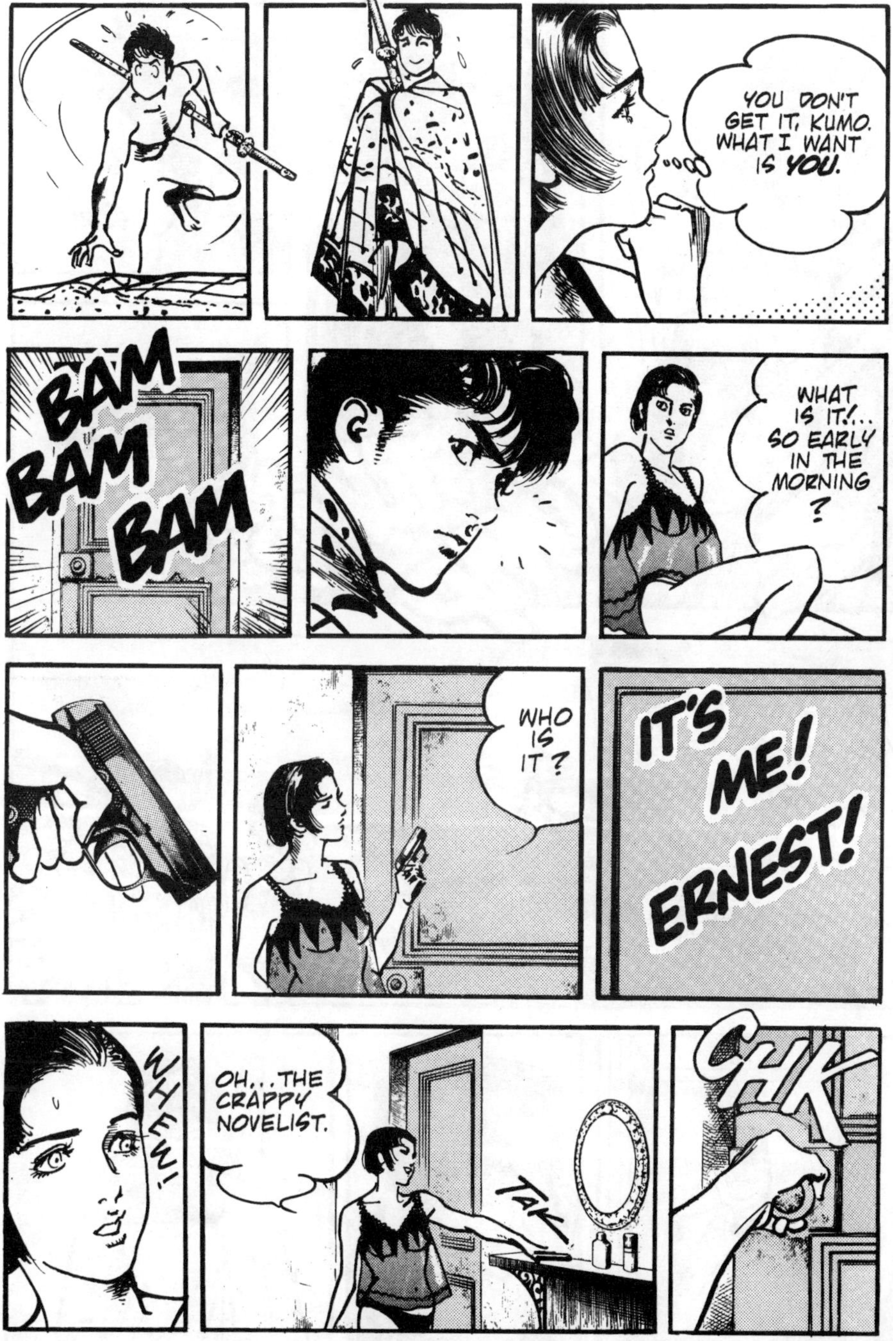
YOU DON'T GET IT, KUMO. WHAT I WANT IS **YOU**.
BAM BAM BAM
WHAT IS IT!... SO EARLY IN THE MORNING ?
WHO IS IT ?
IT'S ME! ERNEST!
WHEW!
OH,... THE CRAPPY NOVELIST.
TAK
CHK

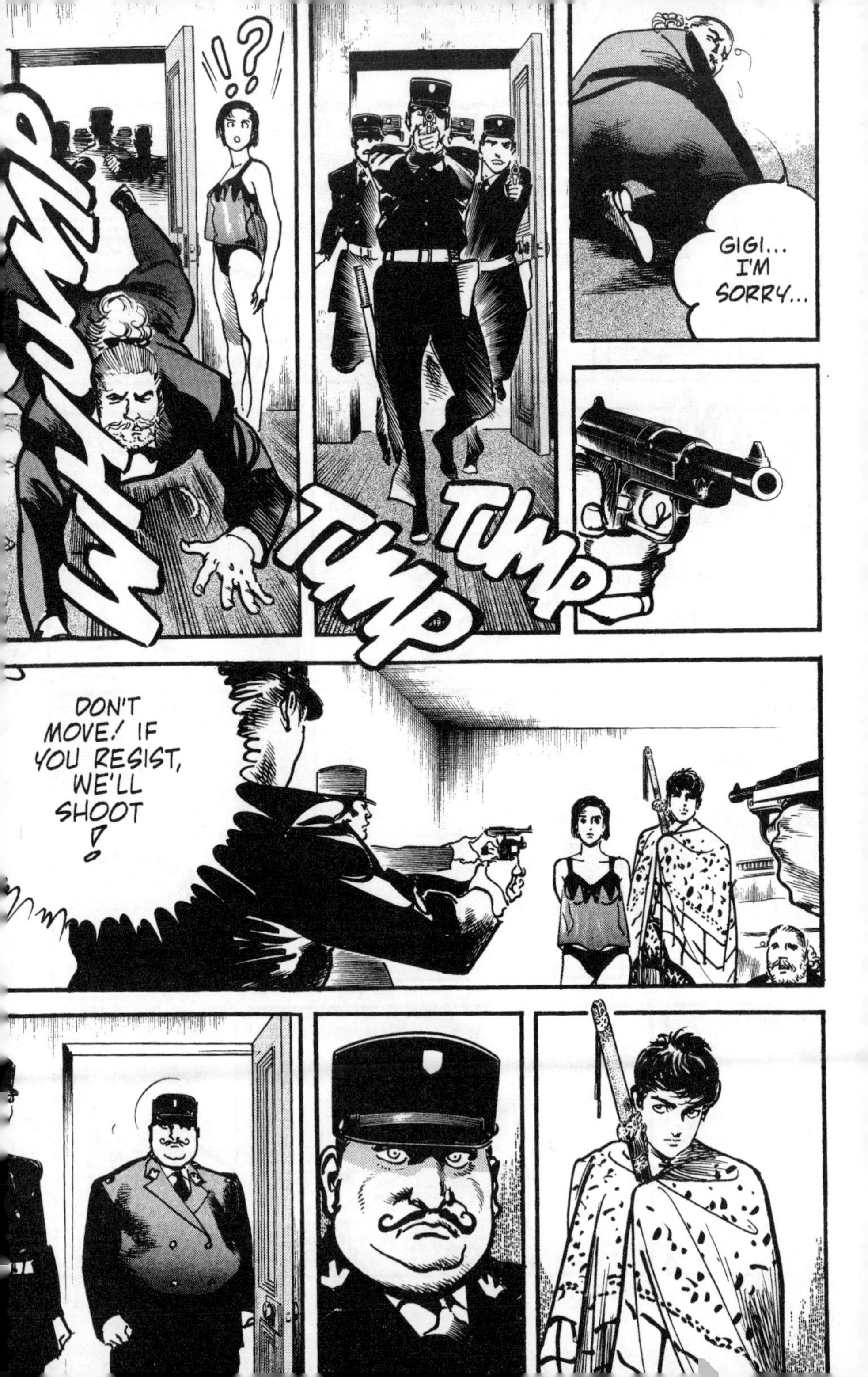
WHUMP
!?
TUMP
TUMP
GIGI... I'M SORRY...
DON'T MOVE! IF YOU RESIST, WE'LL SHOOT!

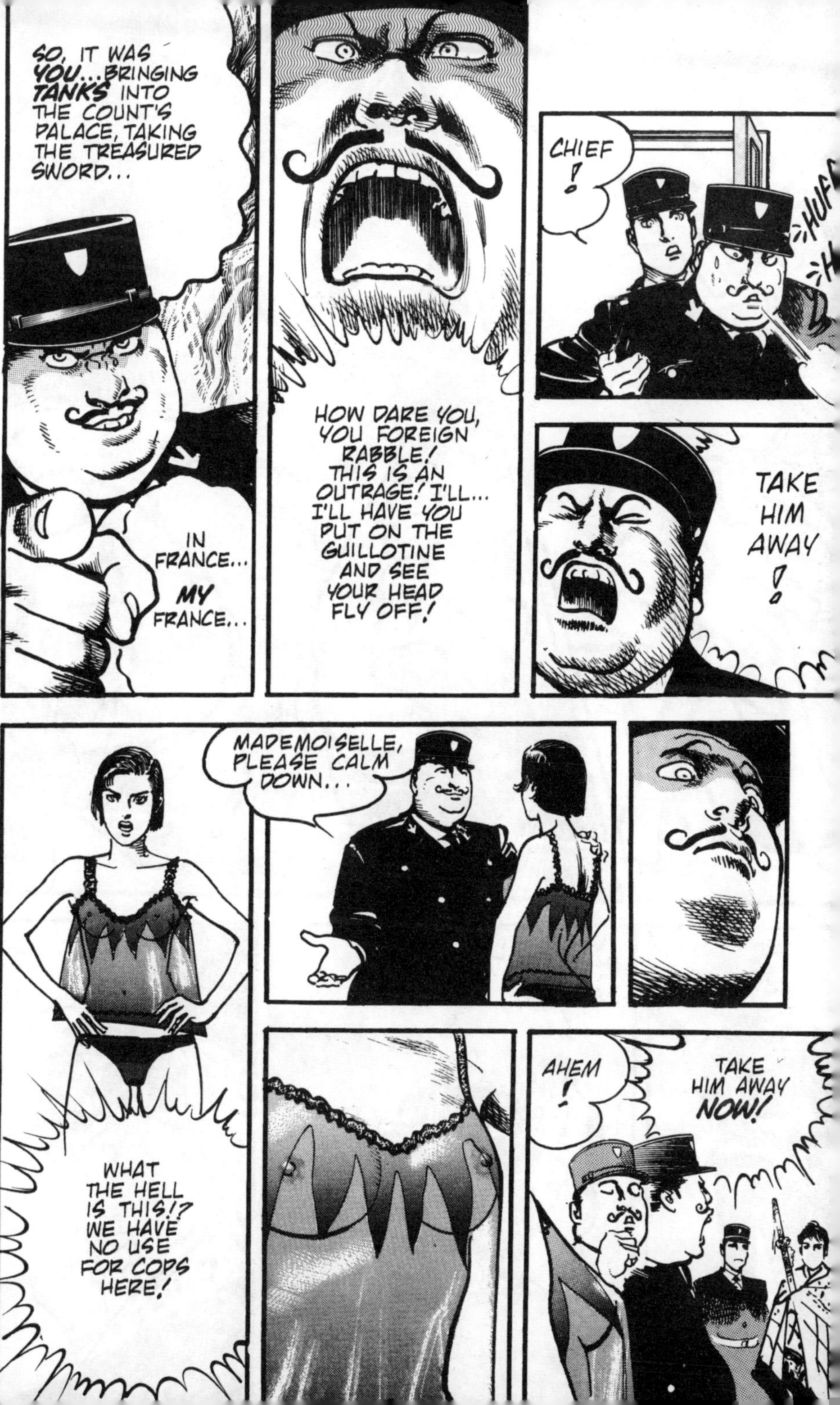
SO, IT WAS YOU...BRINGING TANKS INTO THE COUNT'S PALACE, TAKING THE TREASURED SWORD...
IN FRANCE...
MY FRANCE...
HOW DARE YOU, YOU FOREIGN RABBLE! THIS IS AN OUTRAGE! I'LL... I'LL HAVE YOU PUT ON THE GUILLOTINE AND SEE YOUR HEAD FLY OFF!
CHIEF!
TAKE HIM AWAY!
WHAT THE HELL IS THIS!? WE HAVE NO USE FOR COPS HERE!
MADEMOISELLE, PLEASE CALM DOWN...
AHEM!
TAKE HIM AWAY NOW!

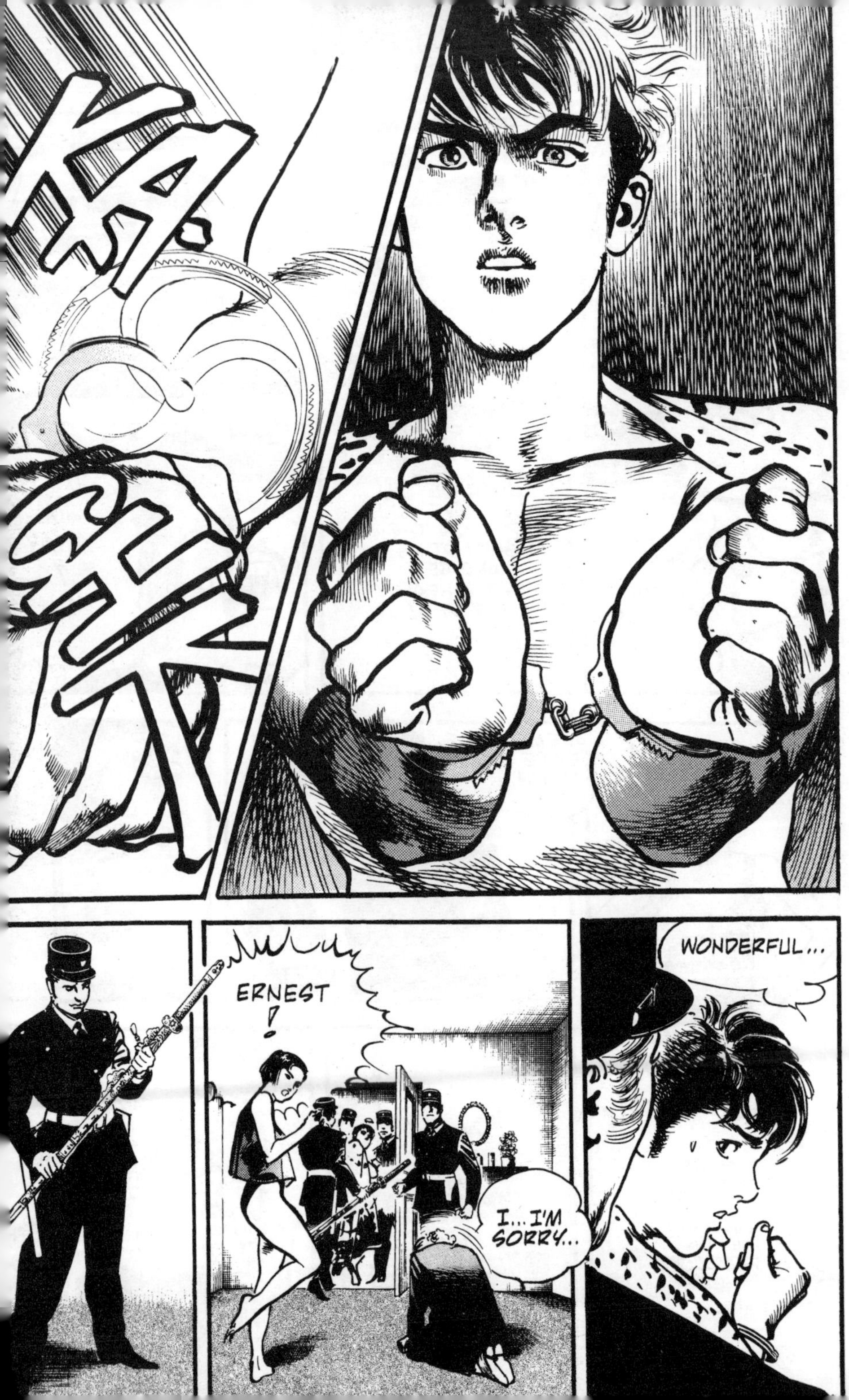
KA. CHA
ERNEST!
I... I'M SORRY...
WONDERFUL...

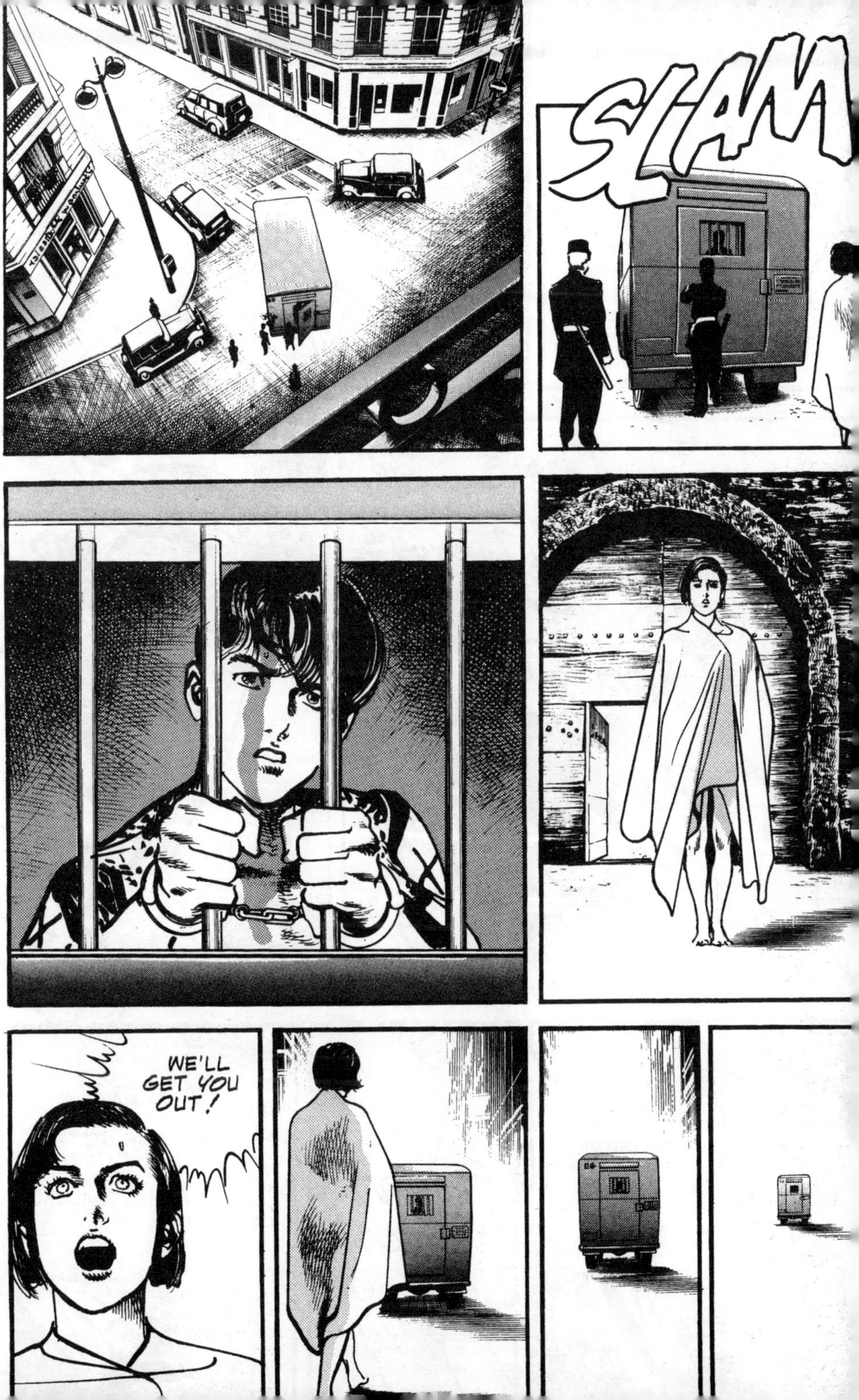
SLAM
WE'LL GET YOU OUT!

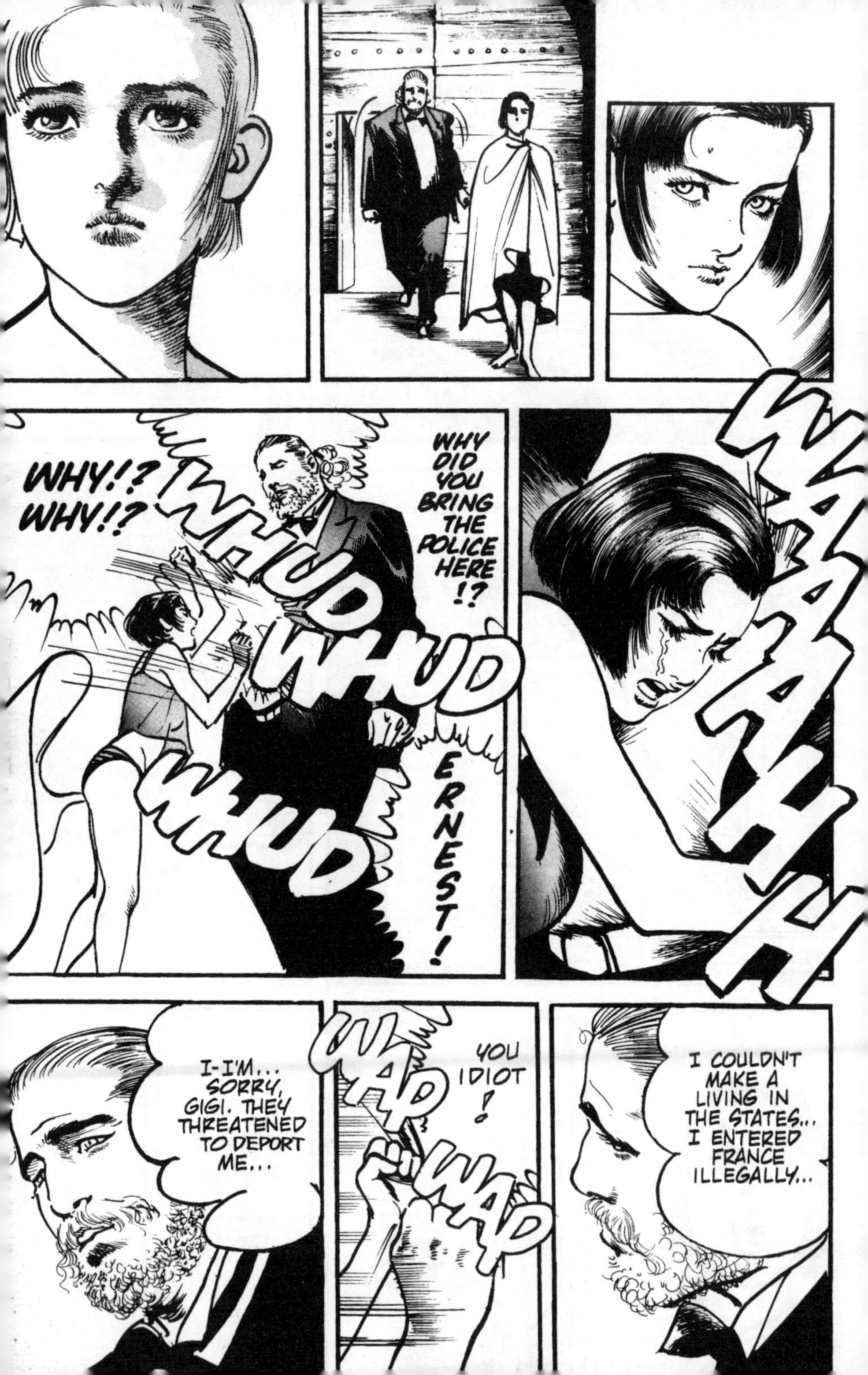
WHY!? WHY!?
WHUD
WHY DID YOU BRING THE POLICE HERE!?
WHUD
WHUD
ERNEST!
WAAAHHH
I-I'M... SORRY, GIGI. THEY THREATENED TO DEPORT ME...
WAP
YOU IDIOT!
WAP
I COULDN'T MAKE A LIVING IN THE STATES... I ENTERED FRANCE ILLEGALLY...

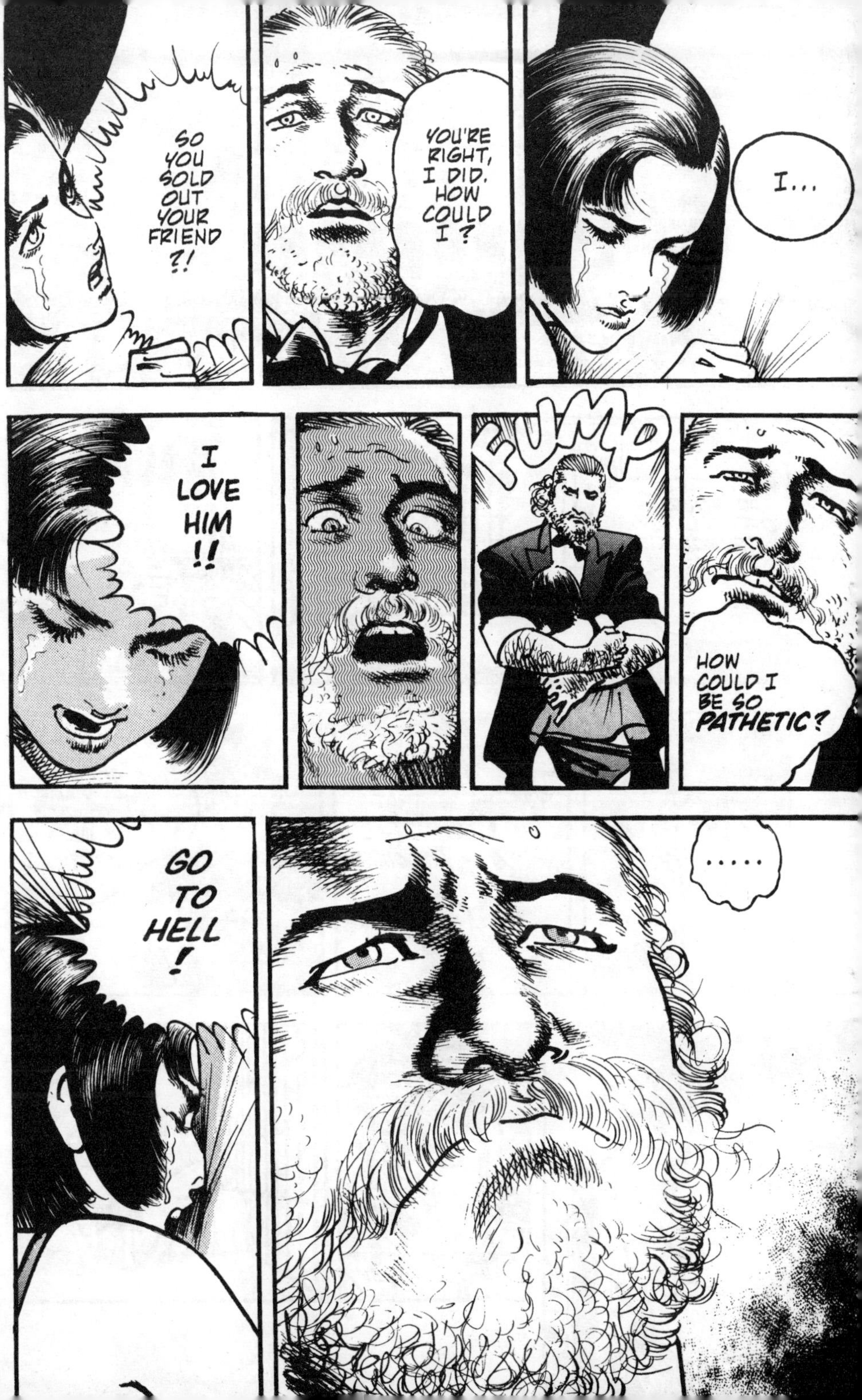
SO YOU SOLD OUT YOUR FRIEND ?!
YOU'RE RIGHT, I DID. HOW COULD I ?
I...
I LOVE HIM !!
FUMP
HOW COULD I BE SO PATHETIC?
GO TO HELL !
.....

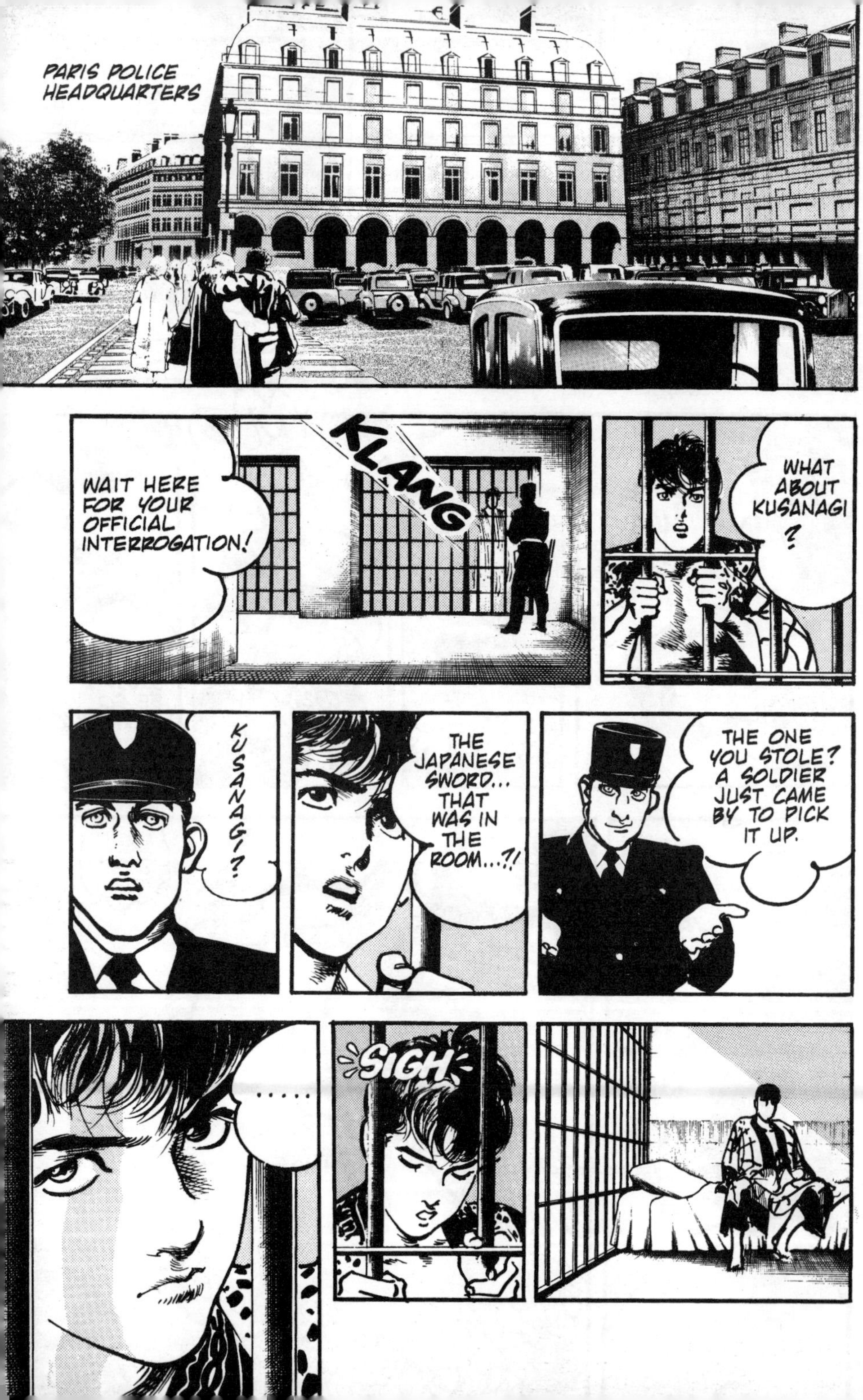
PARIS POLICE HEADQUARTERS
KLANG
WAIT HERE FOR YOUR OFFICIAL INTERROGATION!
WHAT ABOUT KUSANAGI ?
KUSANAGI?
THE JAPANESE SWORD... THAT WAS IN THE ROOM...?!
THE ONE YOU STOLE? A SOLDIER JUST CAME BY TO PICK IT UP.
.....
SIGH

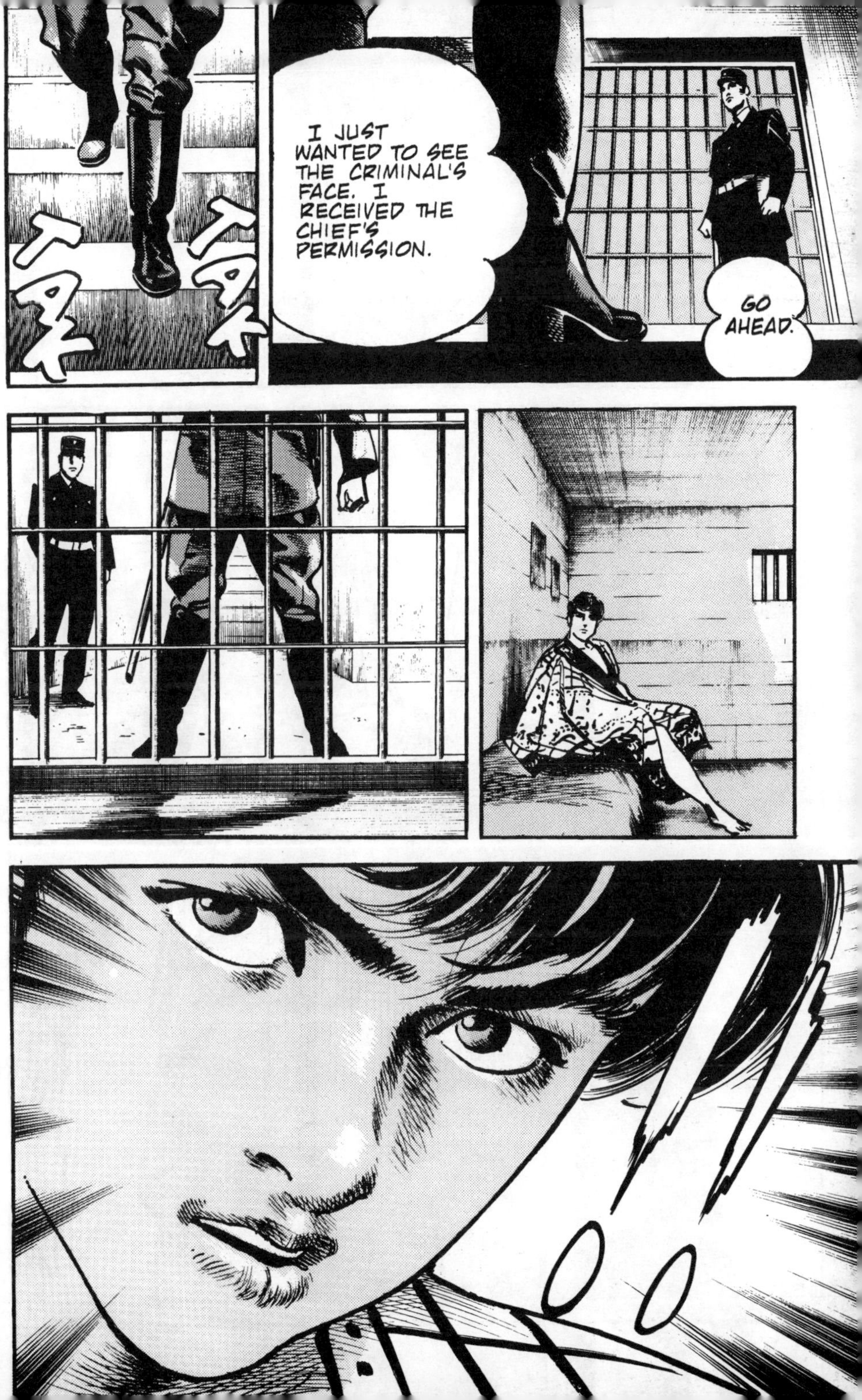
TAK TAK
I JUST WANTED TO SEE THE CRIMINAL'S FACE. I RECEIVED THE CHIEF'S PERMISSION.
GO AHEAD.

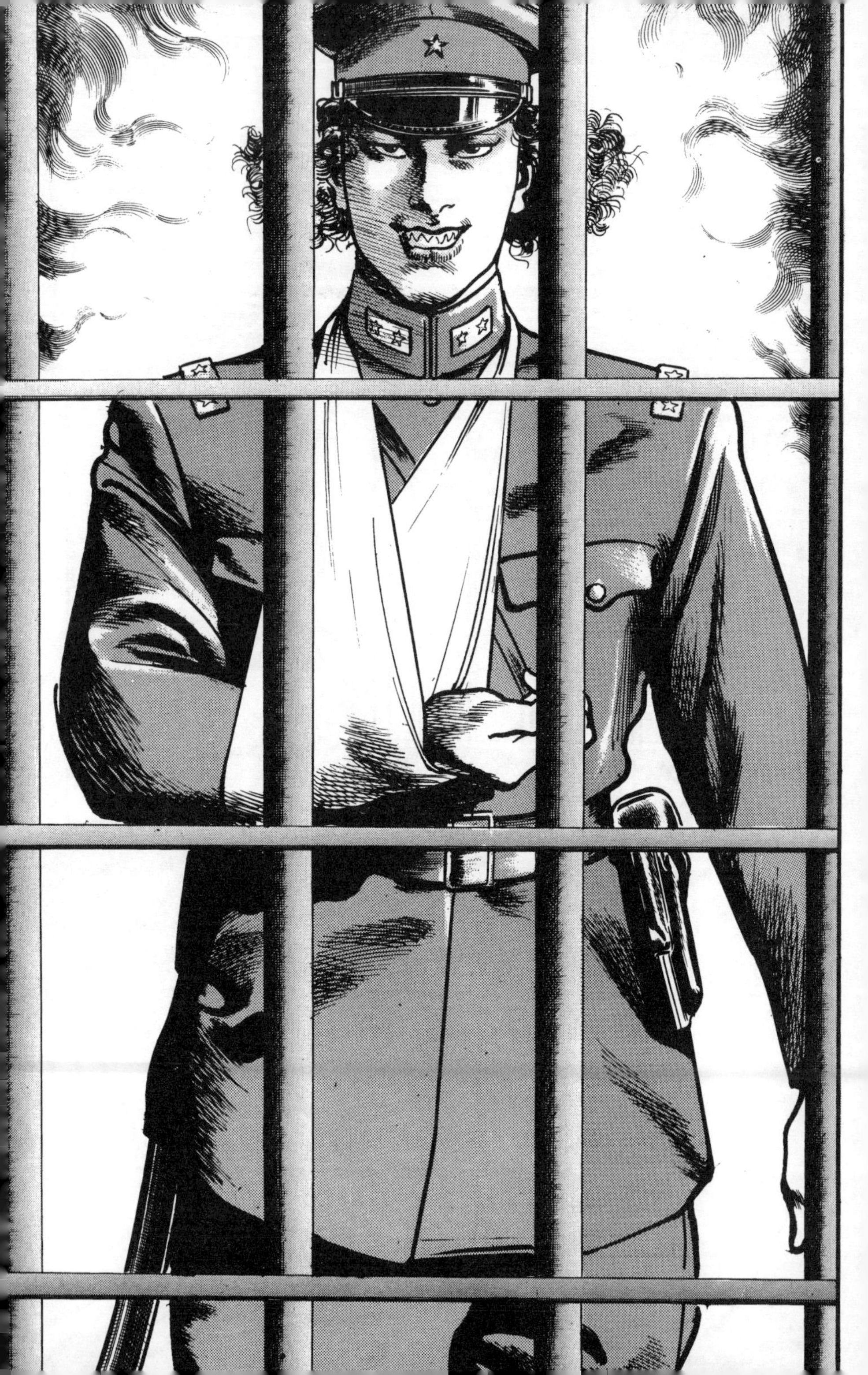

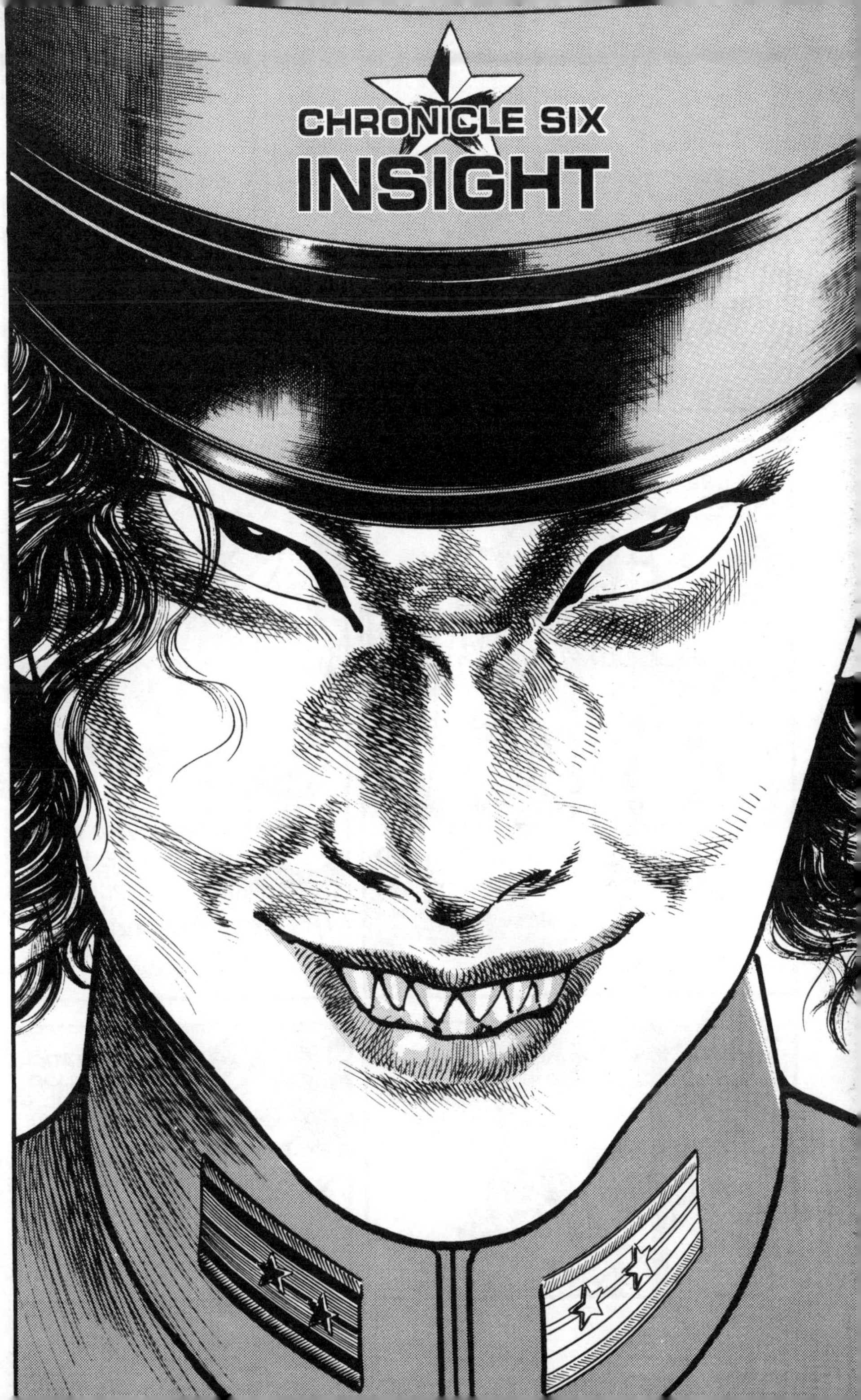
CHRONICLE SIX
INSIGHT

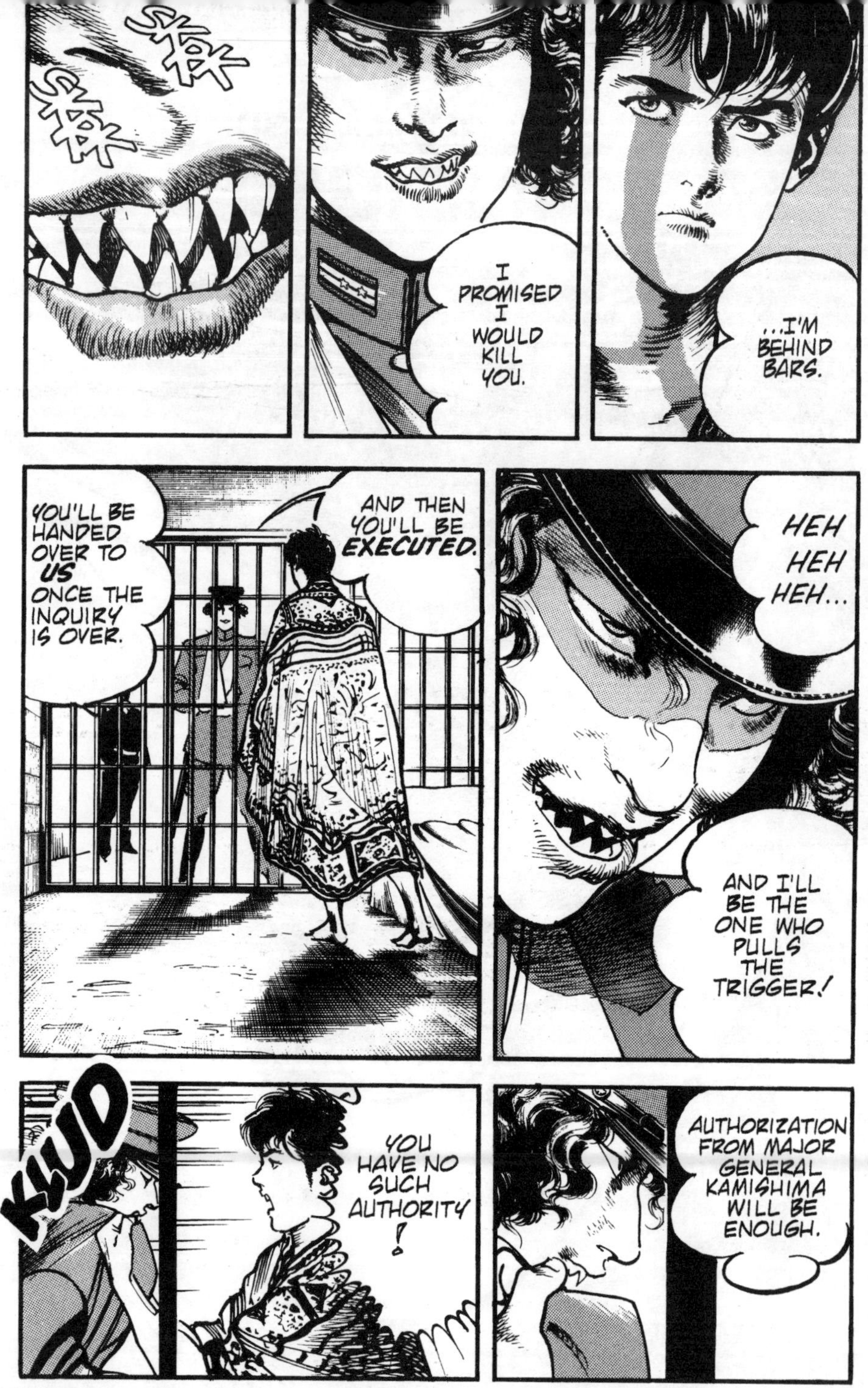
SKOK
SKOK
I PROMISED I WOULD KILL YOU.
...I'M BEHIND BARS.
YOU'LL BE HANDED OVER TO **US** ONCE THE INQUIRY IS OVER.
AND THEN YOU'LL BE ***EXECUTED.***
HEH HEH HEH...
AND I'LL BE THE ONE WHO PULLS THE TRIGGER!
KLUD
YOU HAVE NO SUCH AUTHORITY!
AUTHORIZATION FROM MAJOR GENERAL KAMISHIMA WILL BE ENOUGH.

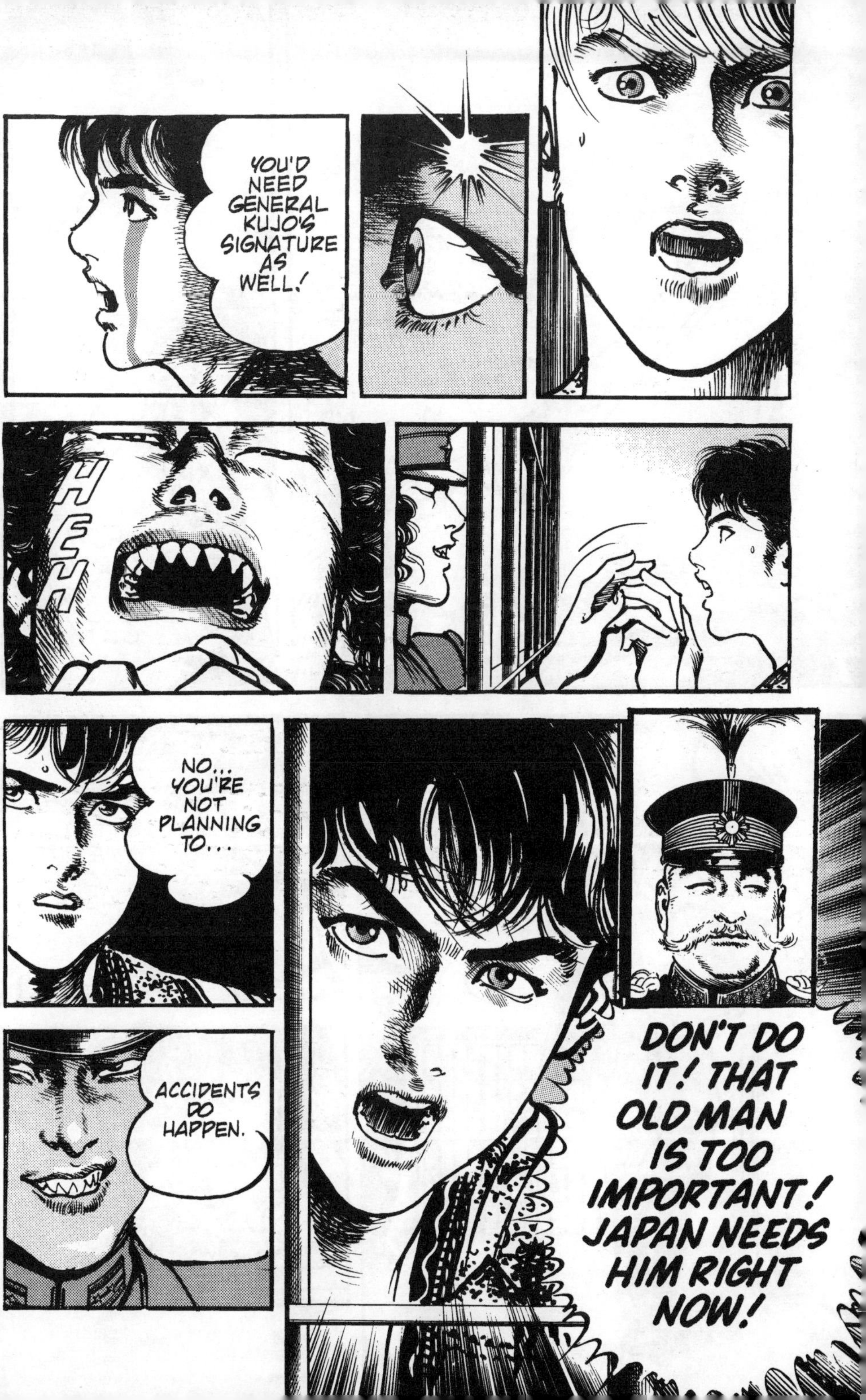

YOU'D NEED GENERAL KUJO'S SIGNATURE AS WELL!
HEH HEH
NO... YOU'RE NOT PLANNING TO...
ACCIDENTS DO HAPPEN.
DON'T DO IT! THAT OLD MAN IS TOO IMPORTANT! JAPAN NEEDS HIM RIGHT NOW!

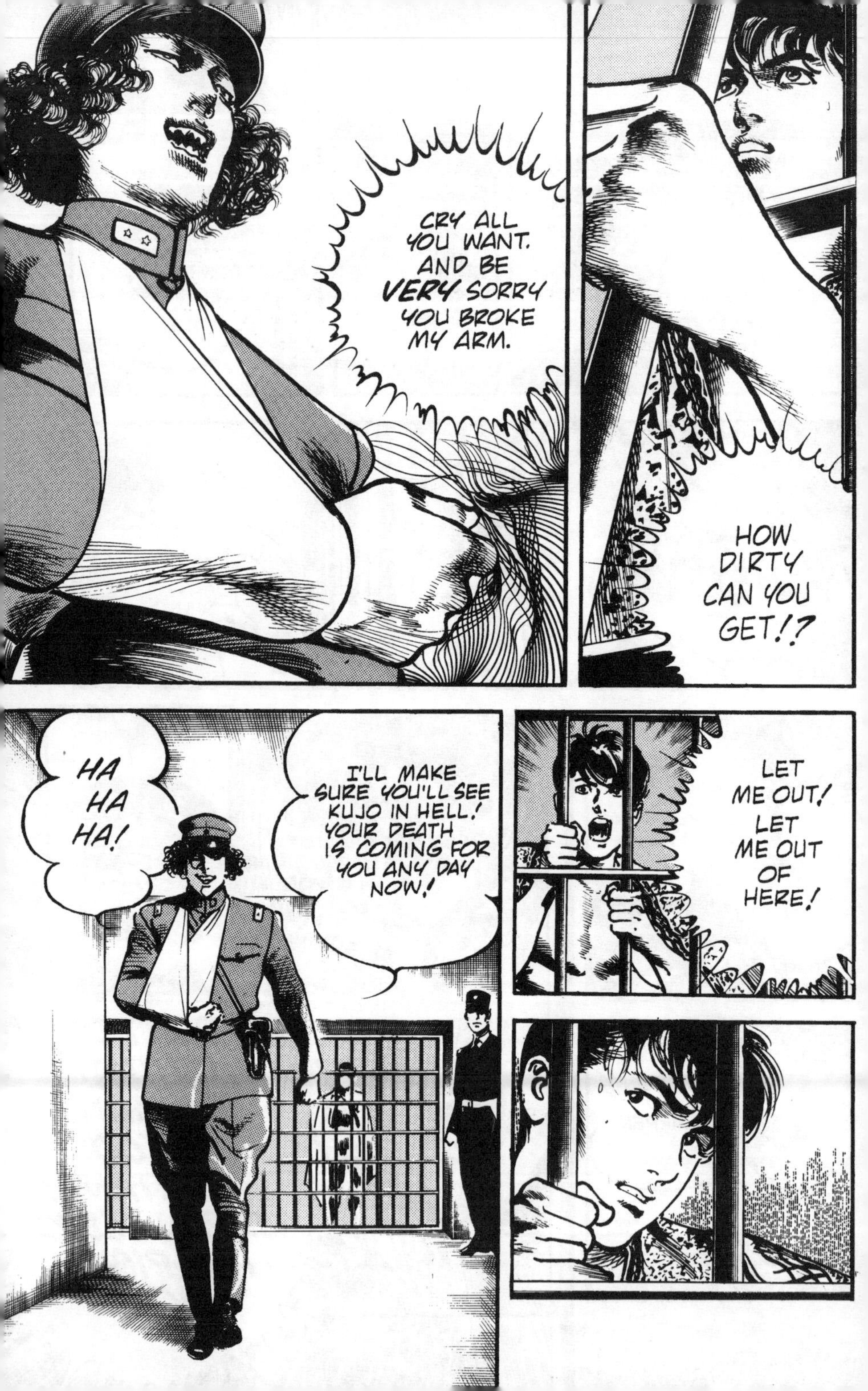
CRY ALL YOU WANT. AND BE VERY SORRY YOU BROKE MY ARM.
HOW DIRTY CAN YOU GET!?
HA HA HA!
I'LL MAKE SURE YOU'LL SEE KUJO IN HELL! YOUR DEATH IS COMING FOR YOU ANY DAY NOW!
LET ME OUT! LET ME OUT OF HERE!

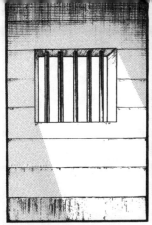
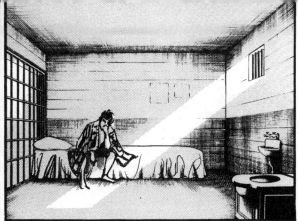

KUMO!
WHERE ARE YOU!?

ER... ERNEST...
IS THAT YOU?

YEAH!

KUMOMARU?

FWIP

ERNEST! I'M HERE!

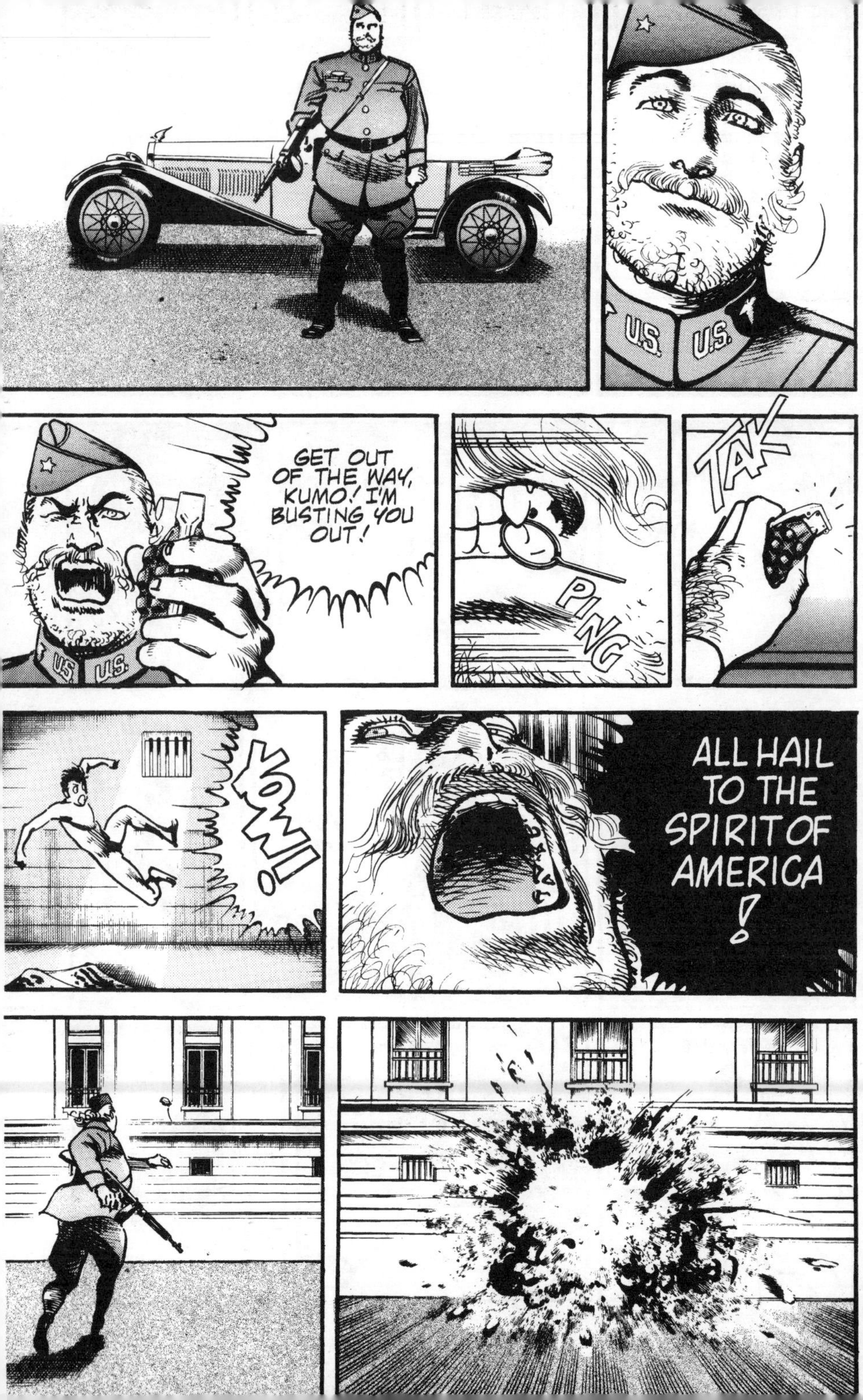
GET OUT OF THE WAY, KUMO! I'M BUSTING YOU OUT!
PING
TAK
YOW!!
ALL HAIL TO THE SPIRIT OF AMERICA!

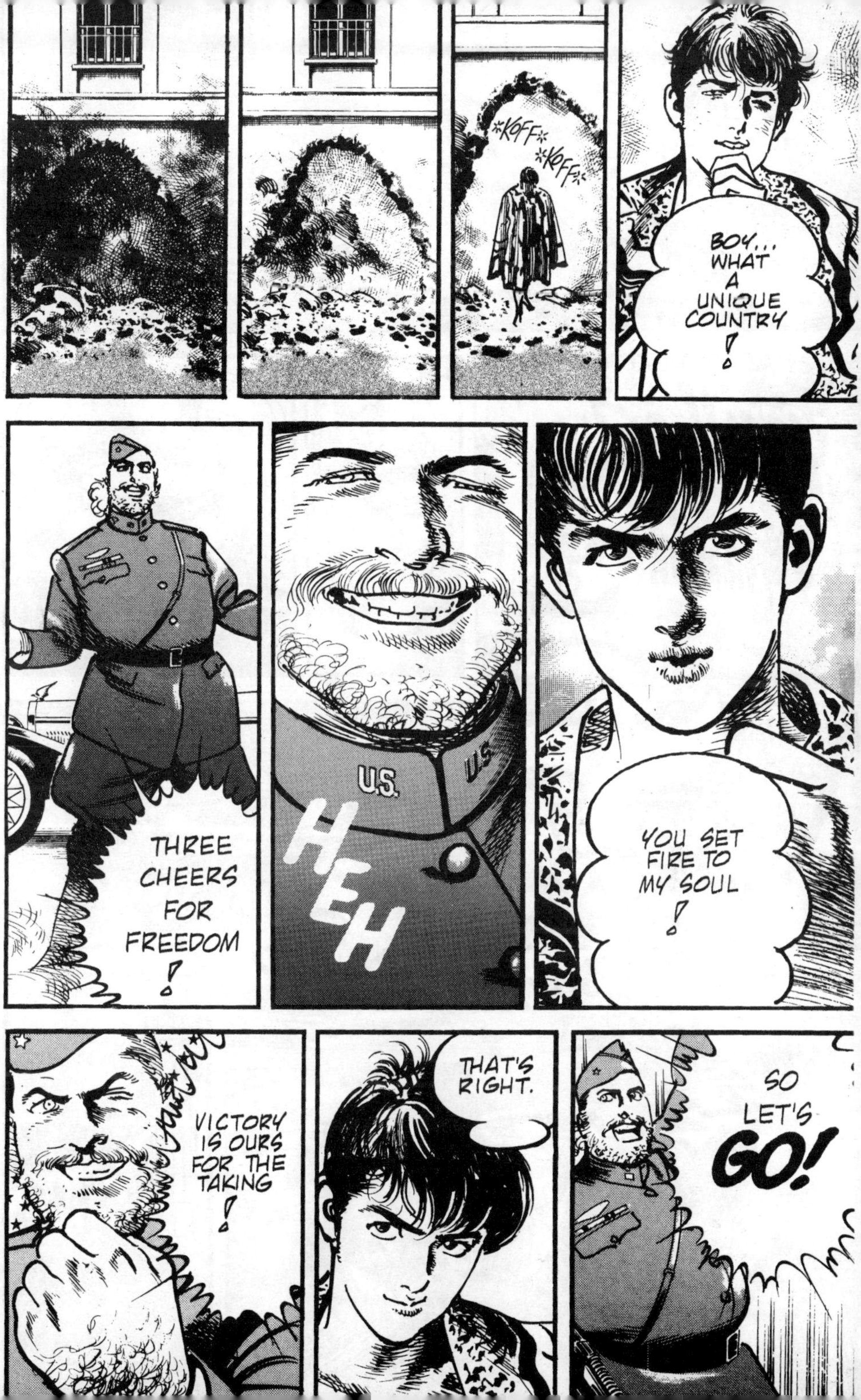
KOFF *KOFF*
BOY... WHAT A UNIQUE COUNTRY!
THREE CHEERS FOR FREEDOM!
U.S. U.S.
HEH
YOU SET FIRE TO MY SOUL!
VICTORY IS OURS FOR THE TAKING!
THAT'S RIGHT.
SO LET'S GO!

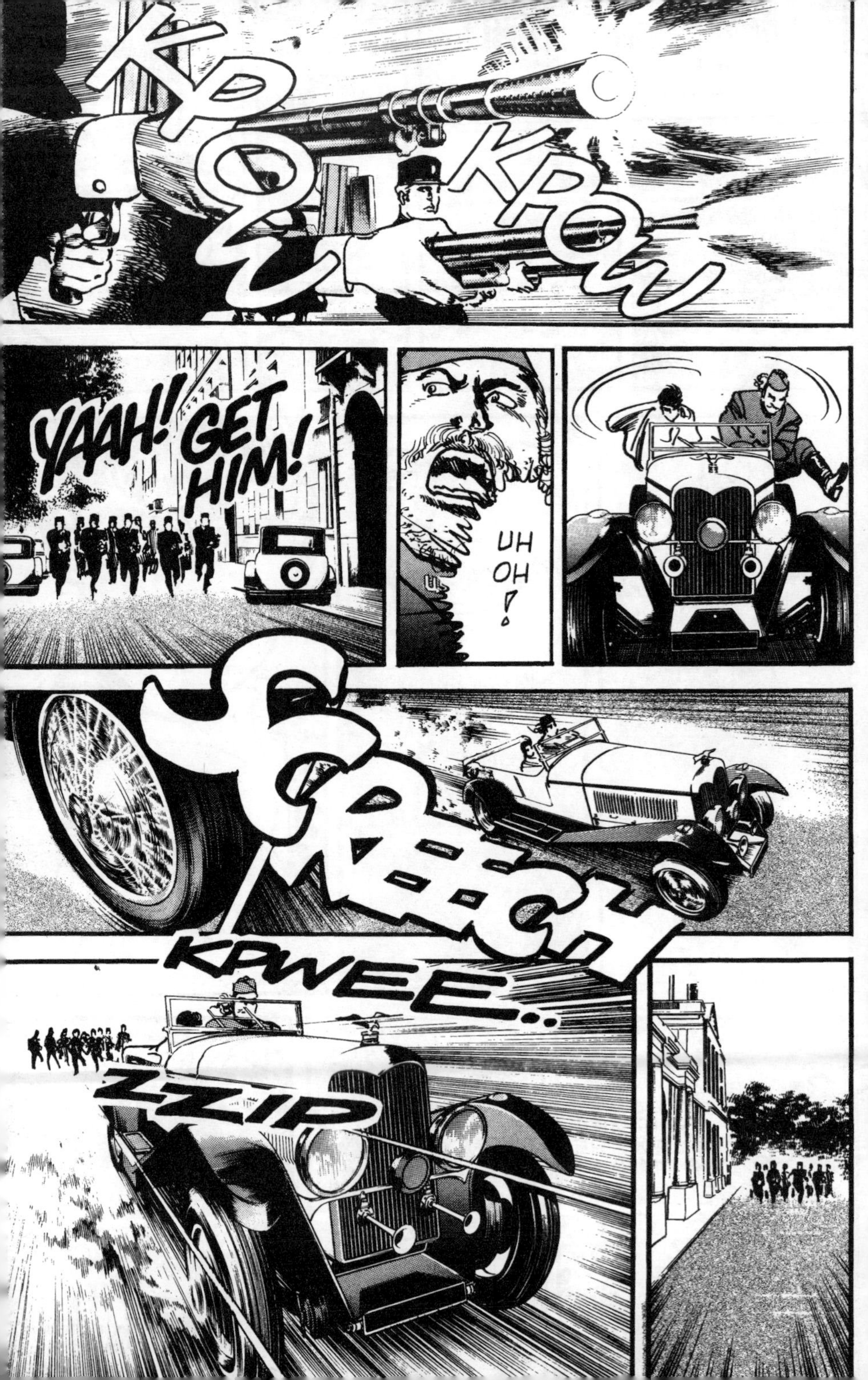
KROW
KROW
YAAH! GET HIM!
UH OH!
SCREECH
KRWEE..
ZZIP

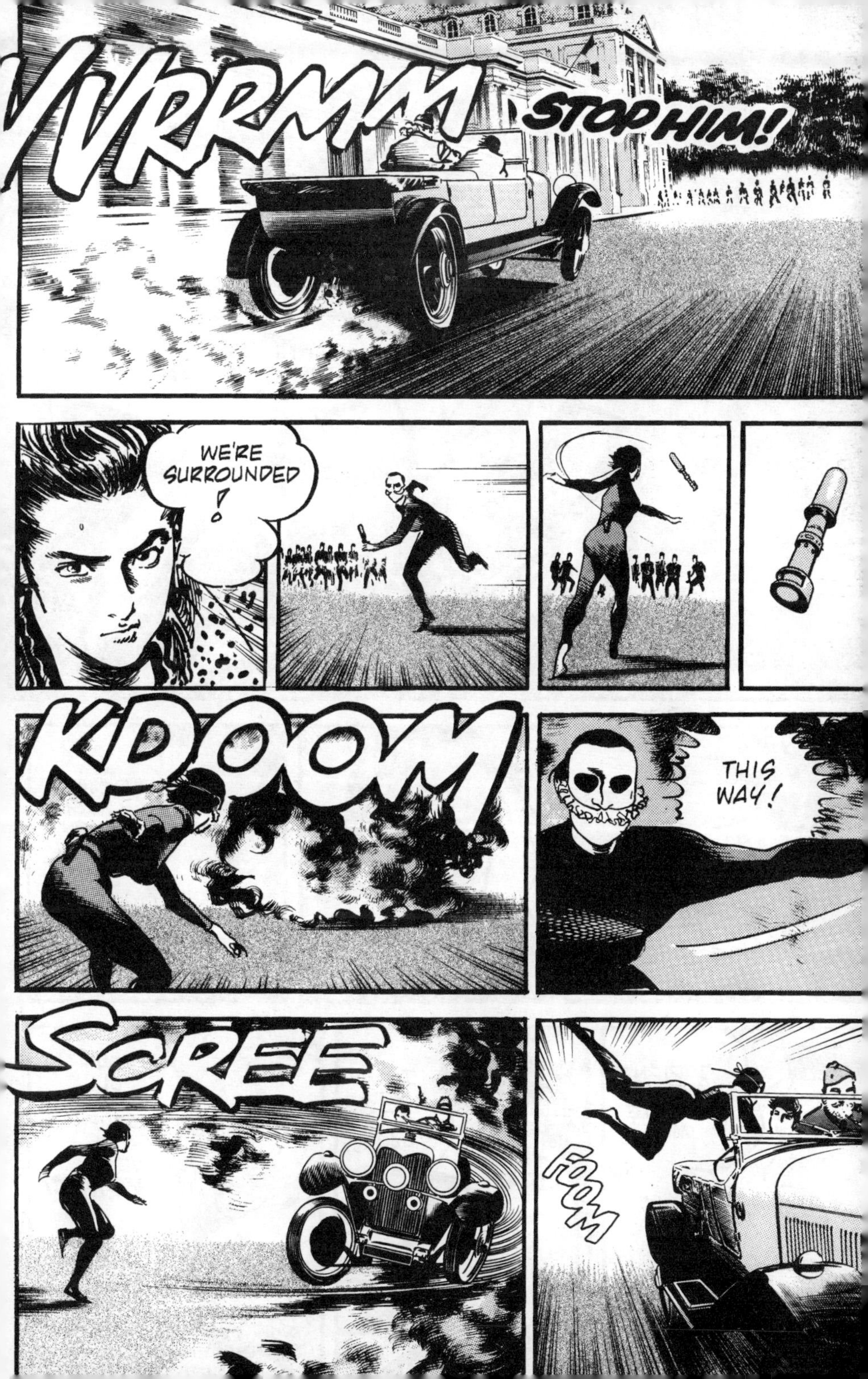
VVRRMM
STOP HIM!
WE'RE SURROUNDED !
KDOOM
THIS WAY!
SCREE
FOOM

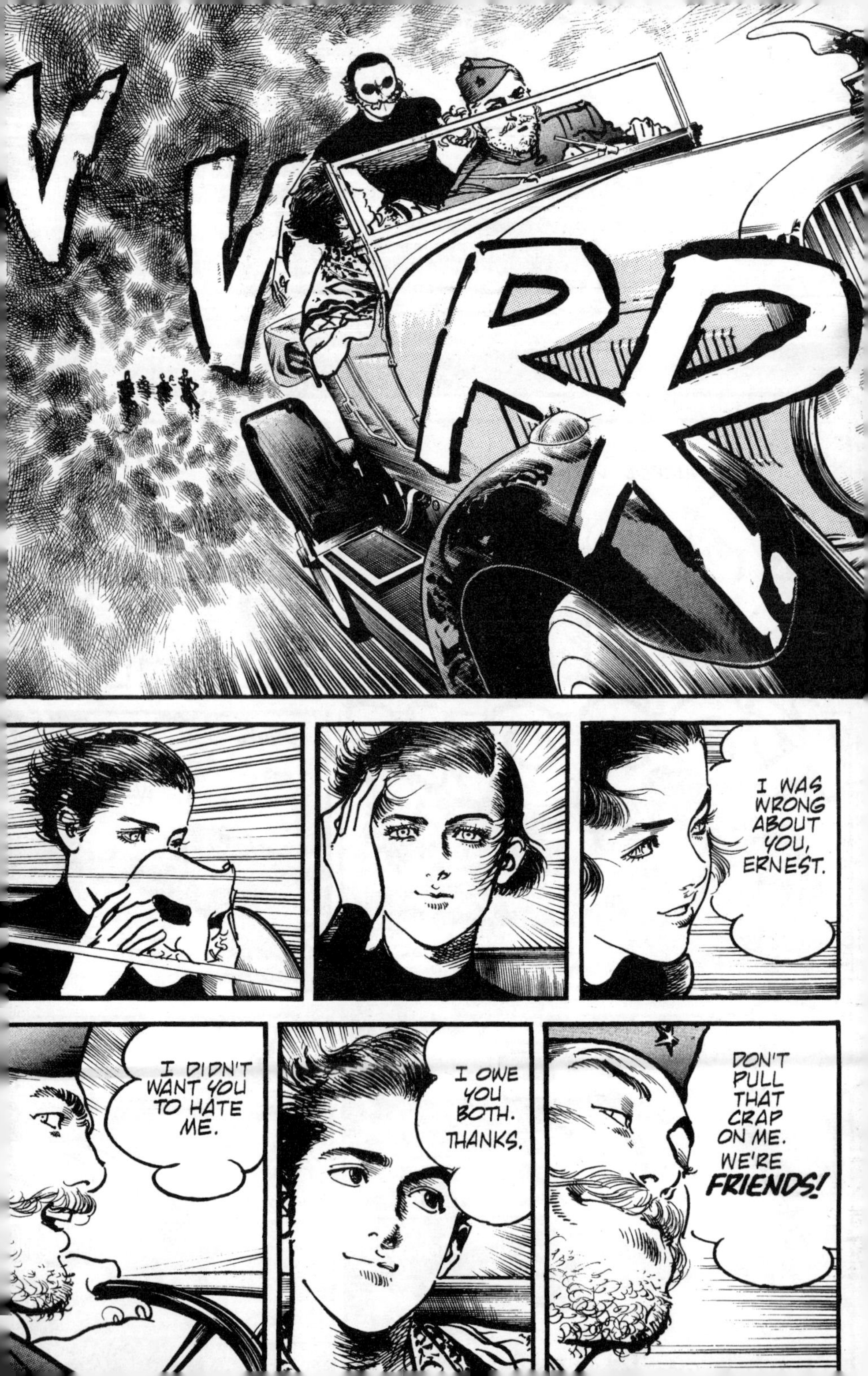
VVRR
I WAS WRONG ABOUT YOU, ERNEST.
I DIDN'T WANT YOU TO HATE ME.
I OWE YOU BOTH. THANKS.
DON'T PULL THAT CRAP ON ME. WE'RE FRIENDS!

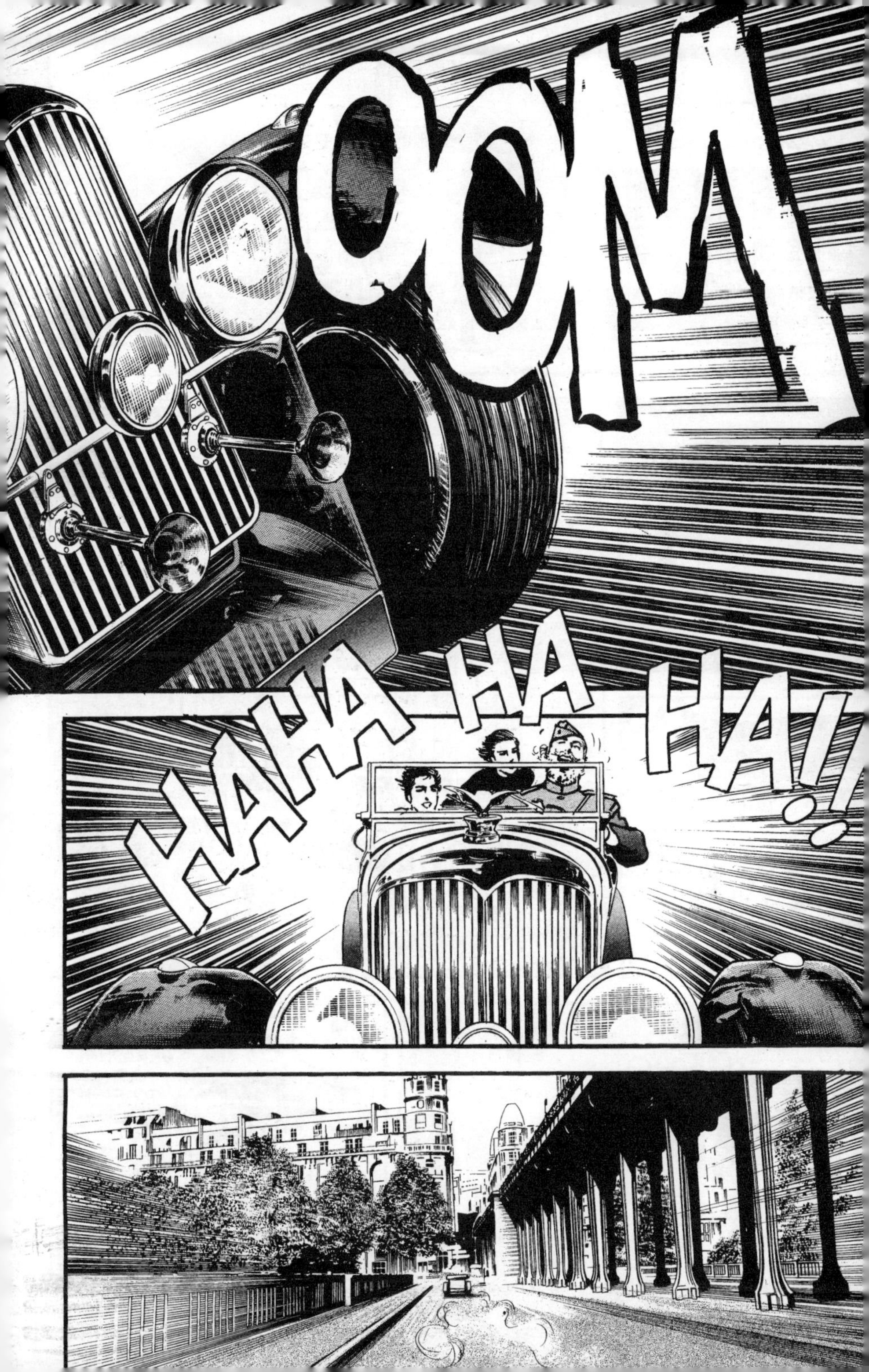
OOM
HAHA HA HA!!!

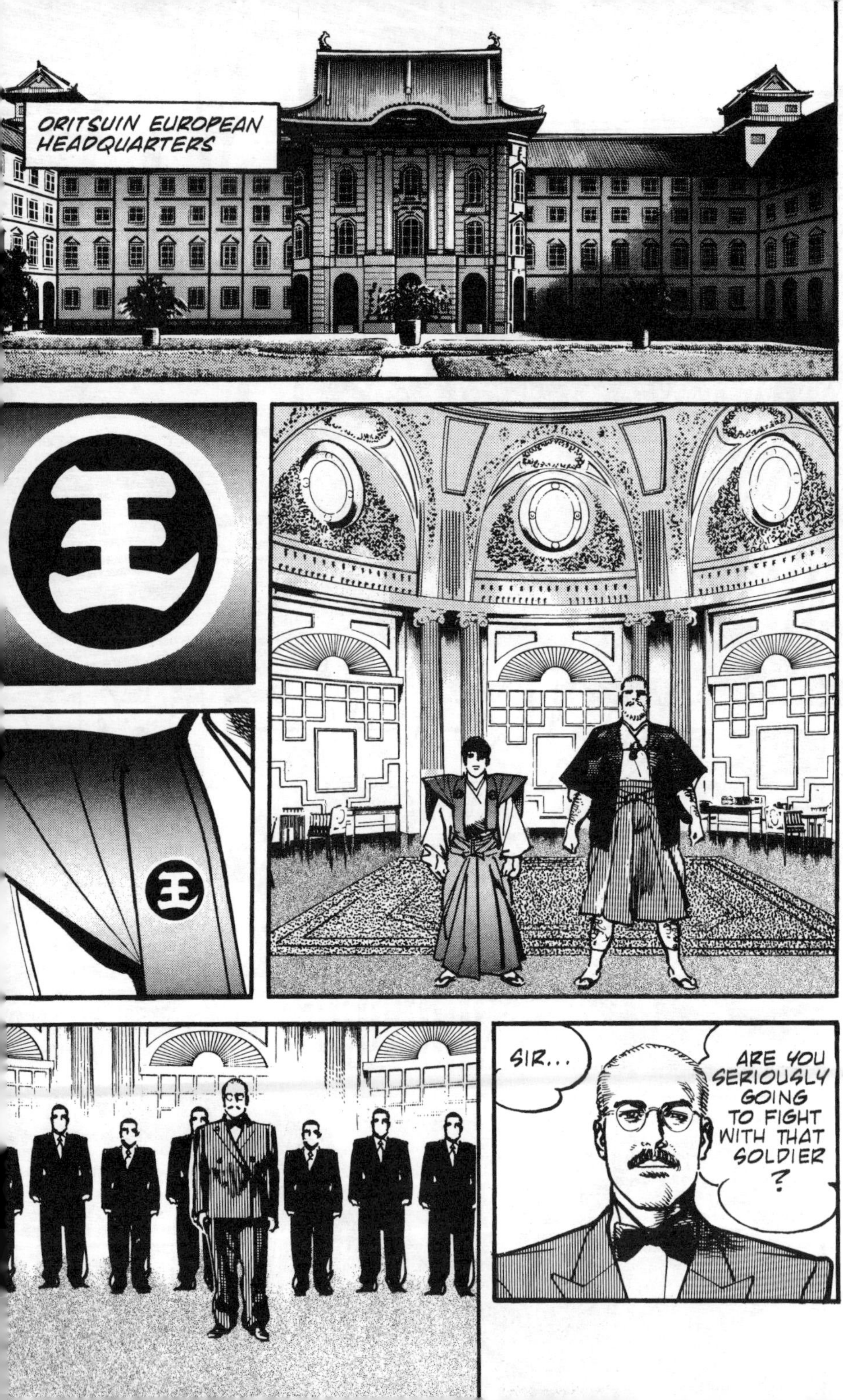
ORITSUIN EUROPEAN HEADQUARTERS
SIR...
ARE YOU SERIOUSLY GOING TO FIGHT WITH THAT SOLDIER ?

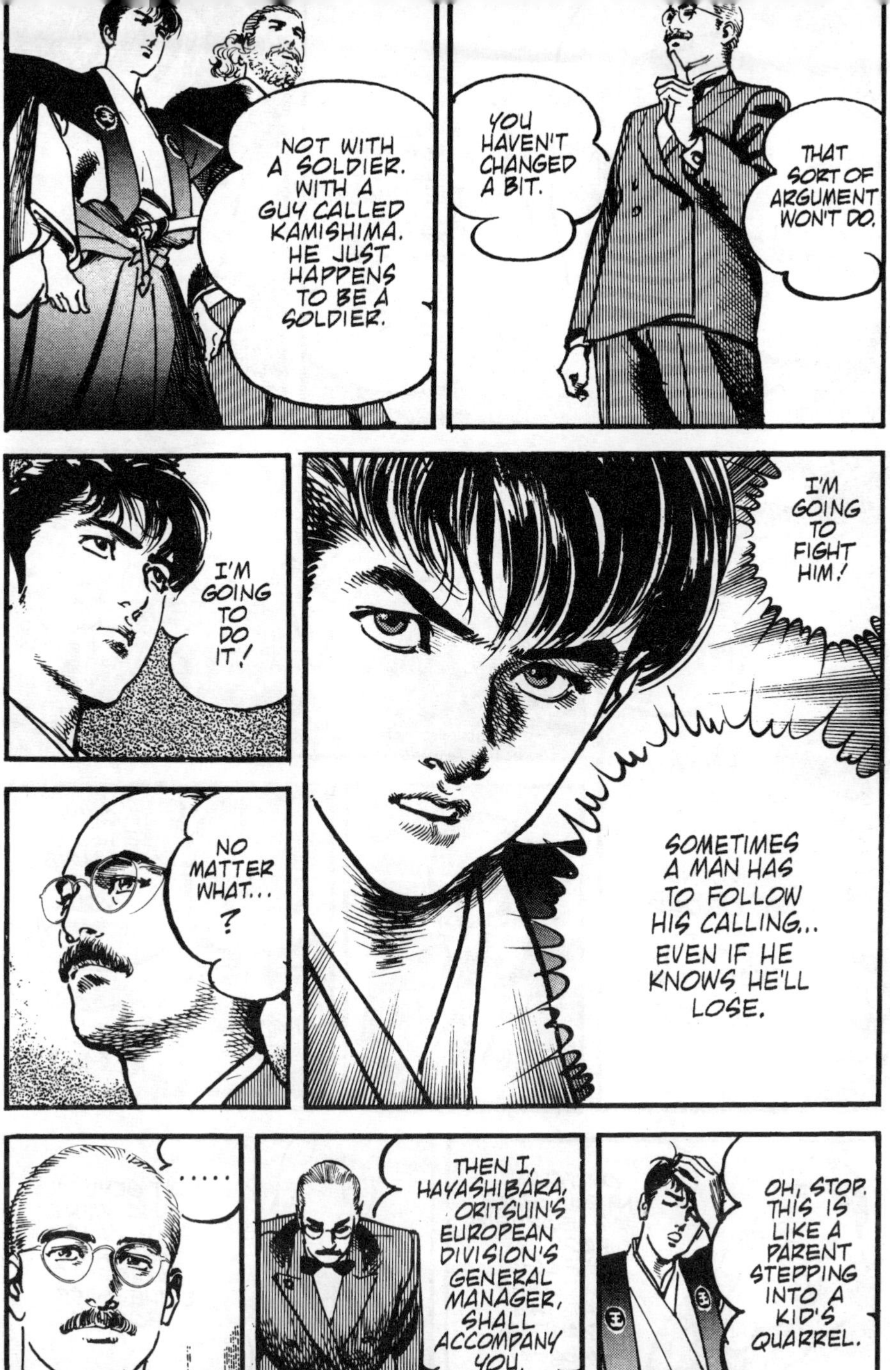
NOT WITH A SOLDIER. WITH A GUY CALLED KAMISHIMA. HE JUST HAPPENS TO BE A SOLDIER.
YOU HAVEN'T CHANGED A BIT.
THAT SORT OF ARGUMENT WON'T DO.
I'M GOING TO DO IT!
NO MATTER WHAT...?
I'M GOING TO FIGHT HIM!
SOMETIMES A MAN HAS TO FOLLOW HIS CALLING... EVEN IF HE KNOWS HE'LL LOSE.
.....
THEN I, HAYASHIBARA, ORITSUIN'S EUROPEAN DIVISION'S GENERAL MANAGER, SHALL ACCOMPANY YOU.
OH, STOP. THIS IS LIKE A PARENT STEPPING INTO A KID'S QUARREL.

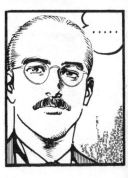

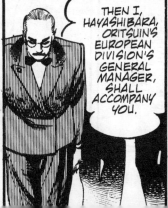

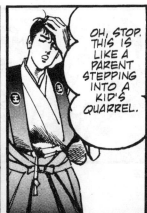

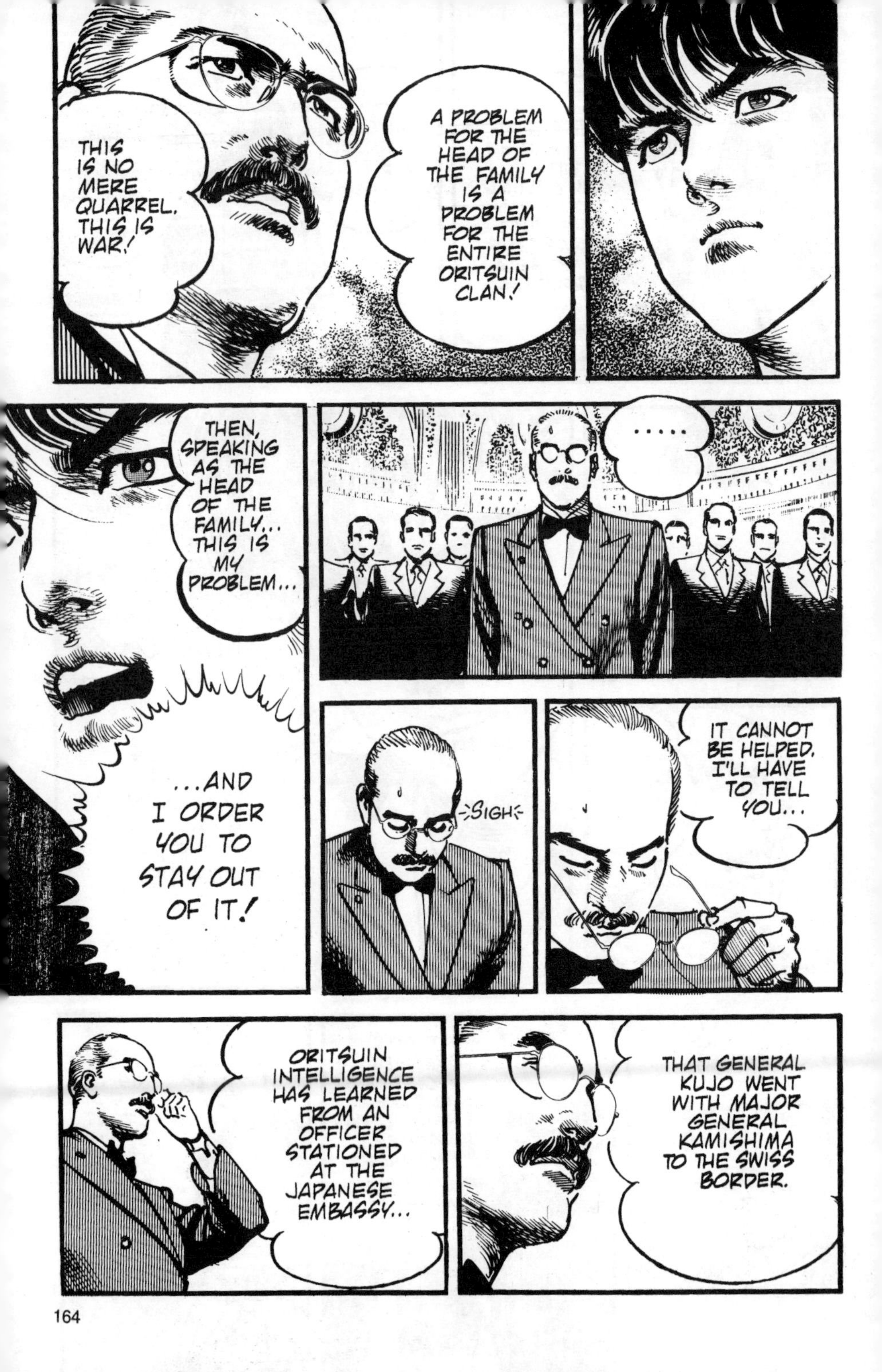
THIS IS NO MERE QUARREL. THIS IS WAR!
A PROBLEM FOR THE HEAD OF THE FAMILY IS A PROBLEM FOR THE ENTIRE ORITSUIN CLAN!
THEN, SPEAKING AS THE HEAD OF THE FAMILY... THIS IS MY PROBLEM...
...AND I ORDER YOU TO STAY OUT OF IT!
.....
SIGH
IT CANNOT BE HELPED. I'LL HAVE TO TELL YOU...
ORITSUIN INTELLIGENCE HAS LEARNED FROM AN OFFICER STATIONED AT THE JAPANESE EMBASSY...
THAT GENERAL KUJO WENT WITH MAJOR GENERAL KAMISHIMA TO THE SWISS BORDER.

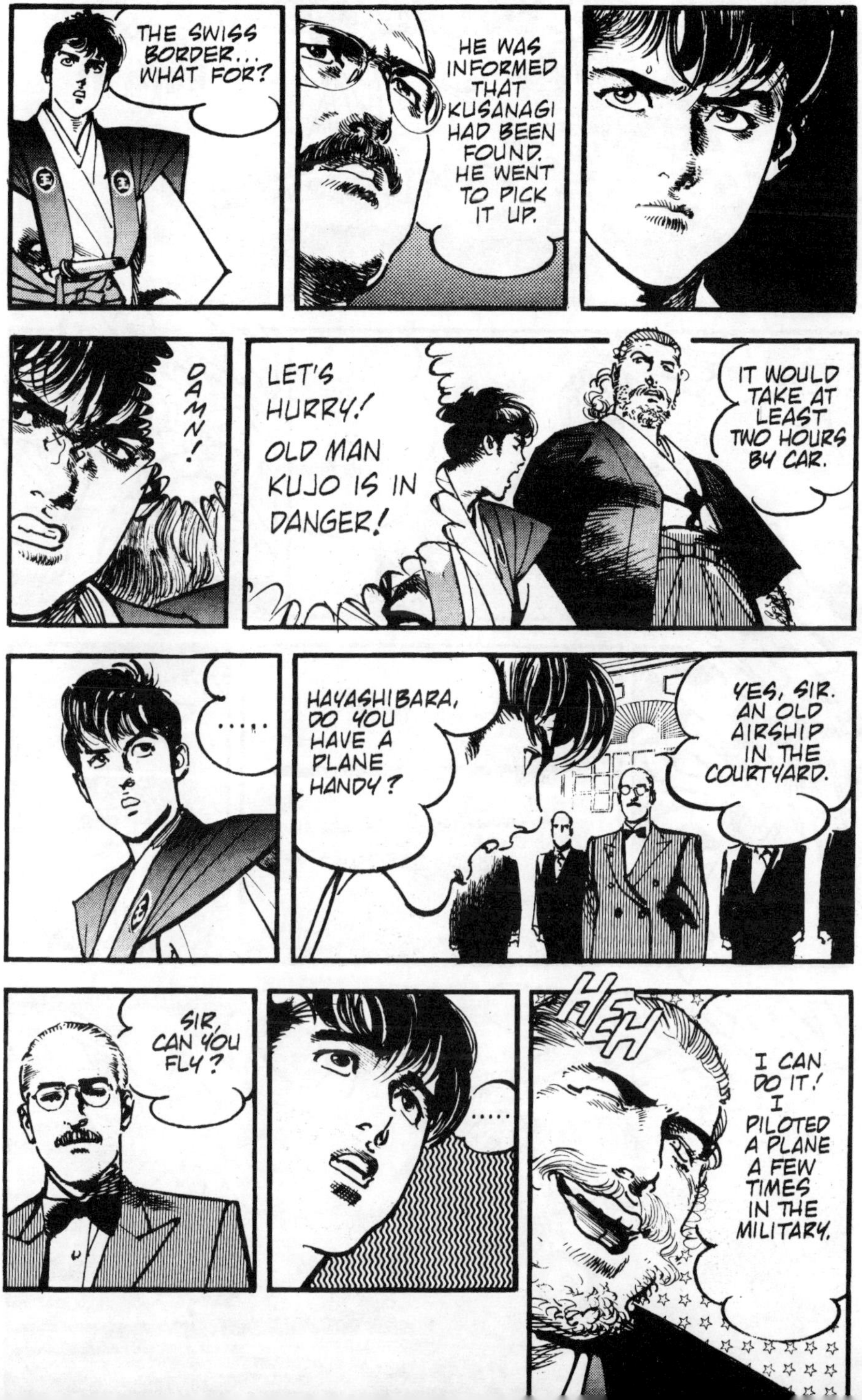
THE SWISS BORDER... WHAT FOR?
HE WAS INFORMED THAT KUSANAGI HAD BEEN FOUND. HE WENT TO PICK IT UP.
DAMN!
LET'S HURRY!
OLD MAN KUJO IS IN DANGER!
IT WOULD TAKE AT LEAST TWO HOURS BY CAR.
.....
HAYASHIBARA, DO YOU HAVE A PLANE HANDY?
YES, SIR. AN OLD AIRSHIP IN THE COURTYARD.
SIR, CAN YOU FLY?
.....
HEH
I CAN DO IT! I PILOTED A PLANE A FEW TIMES IN THE MILITARY.

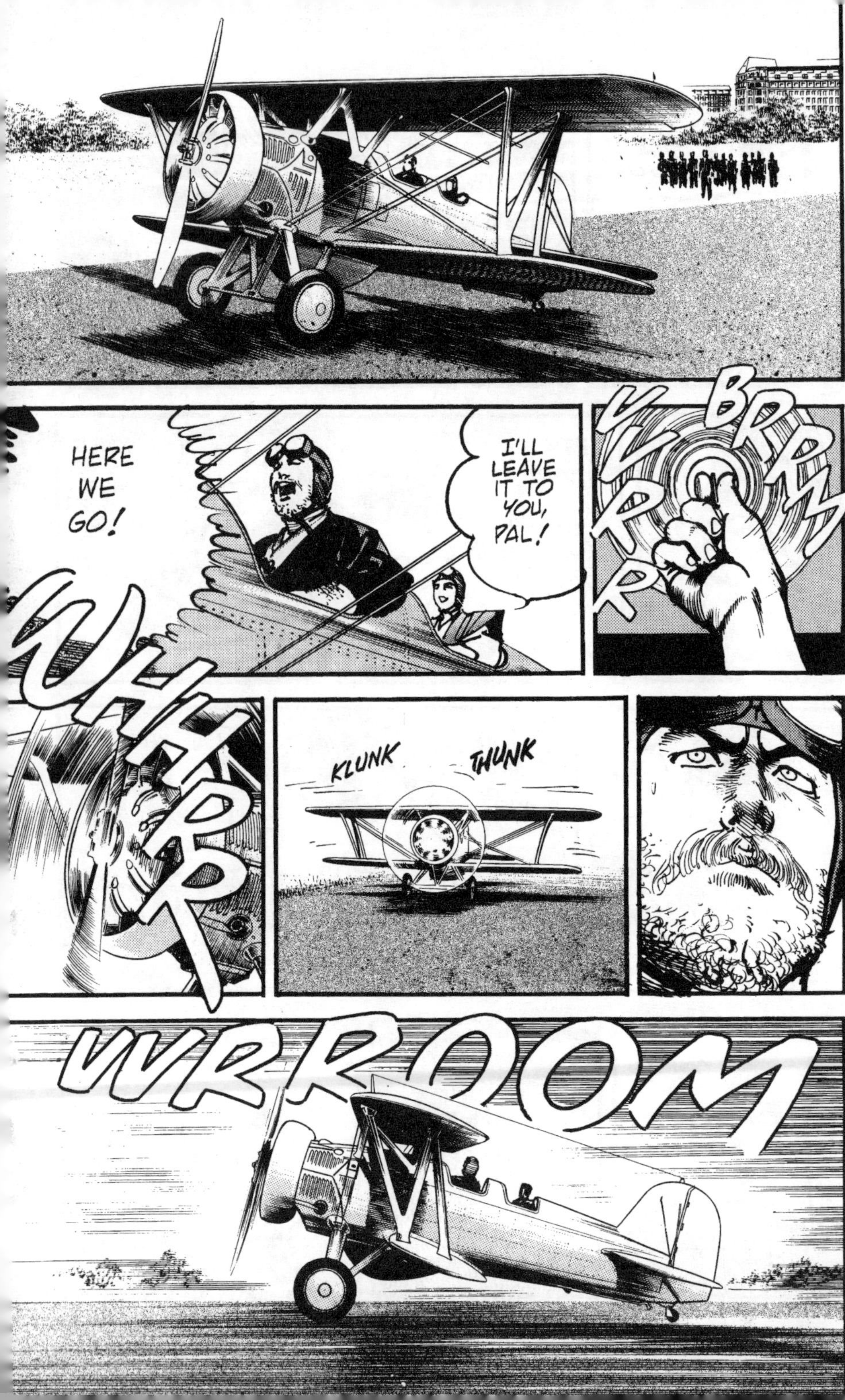
HERE WE GO!
I'LL LEAVE IT TO YOU, PAL!
WHHRR
VVRR
BRRM
KLUNK
THUNK
VVROOM

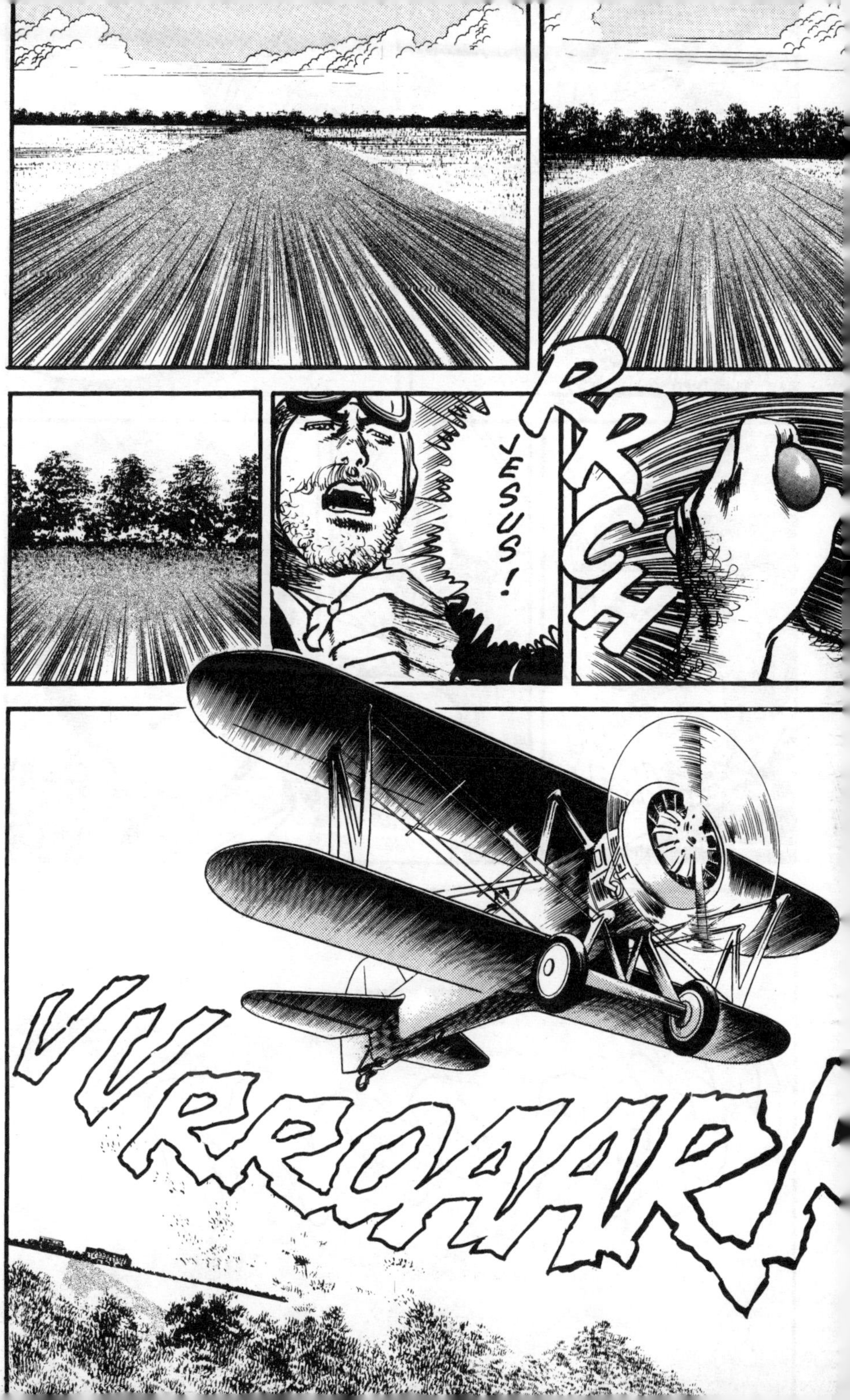
JESUS!
RRRCH
VRROAARR

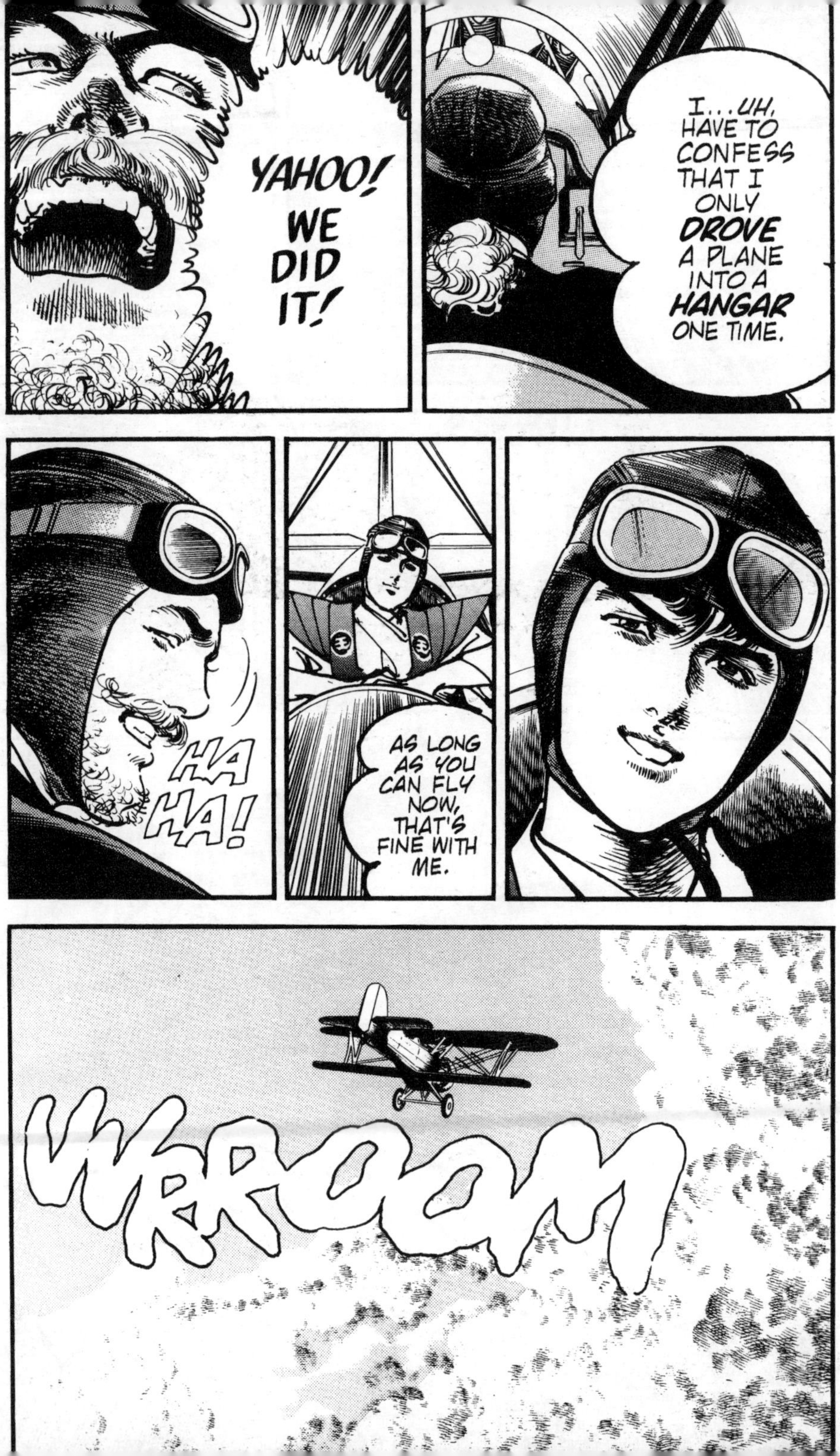
YAHOO! WE DID IT!
I...UH, HAVE TO CONFESS THAT I ONLY DROVE A PLANE INTO A HANGAR ONE TIME.
HA HA!
AS LONG AS YOU CAN FLY NOW, THAT'S FINE WITH ME.
VRROOM

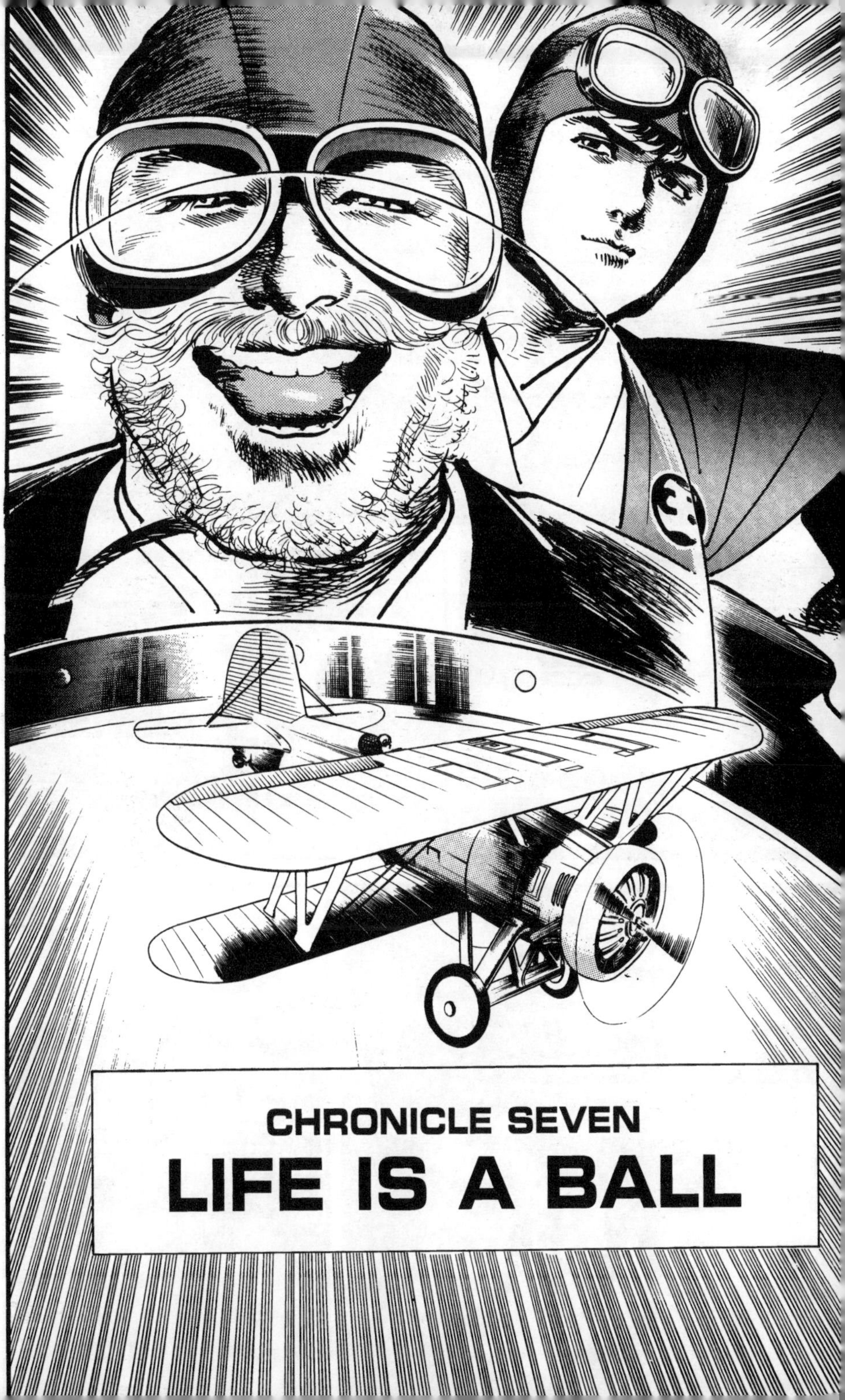
CHRONICLE SEVEN
LIFE IS A BALL

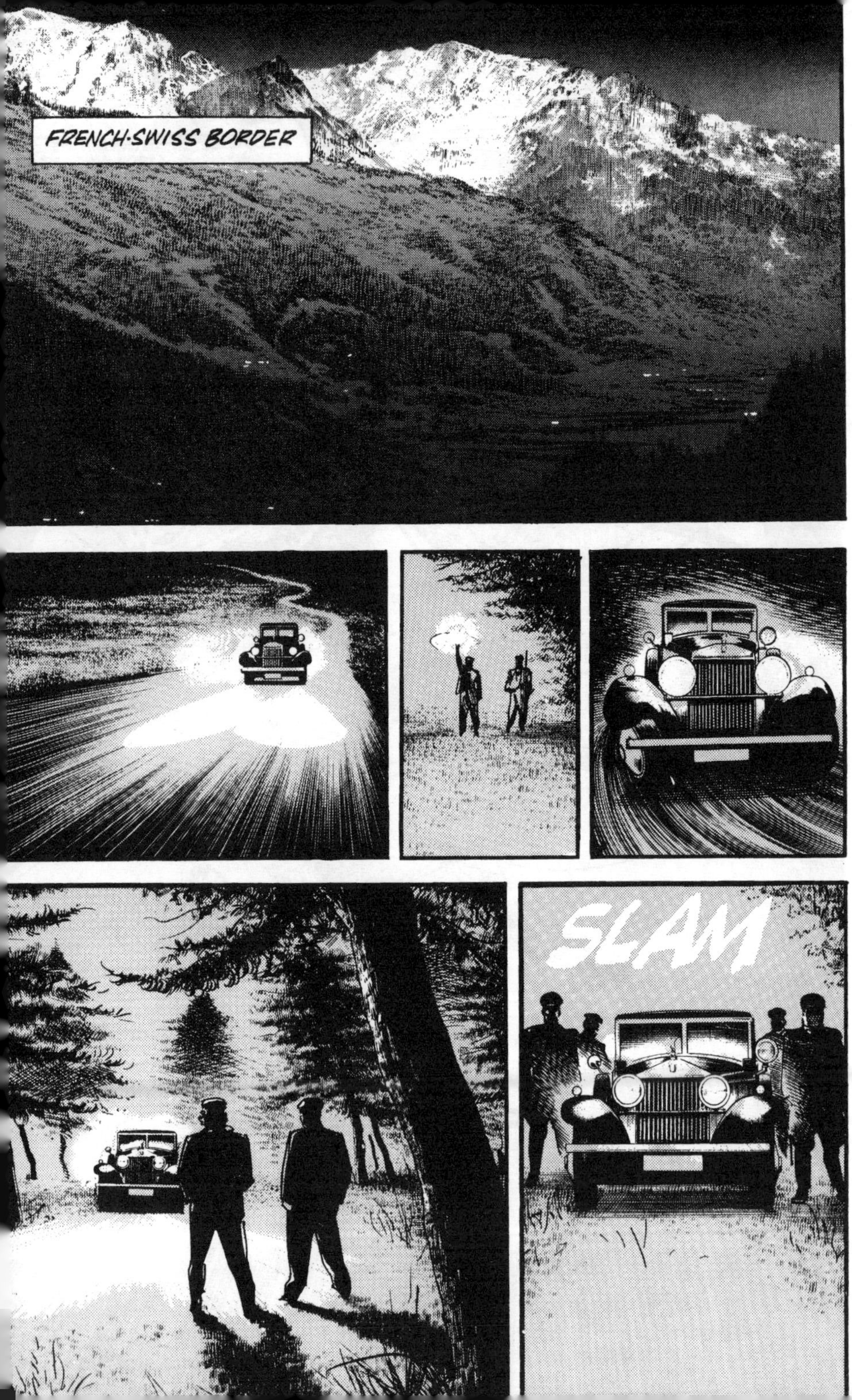
FRENCH-SWISS BORDER
SLAM

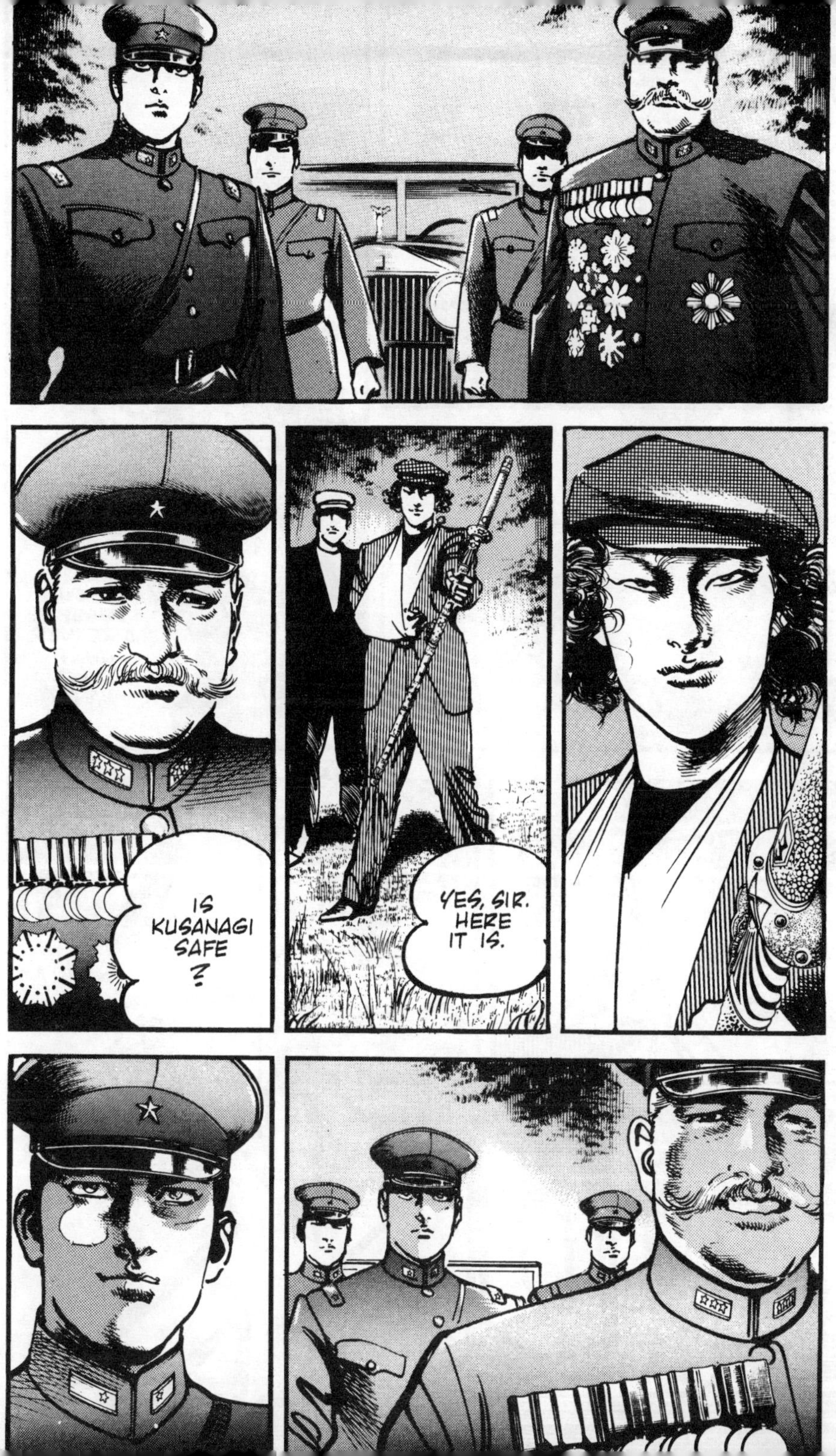
IS KUSANAGI SAFE ?
YES, SIR. HERE IT IS.

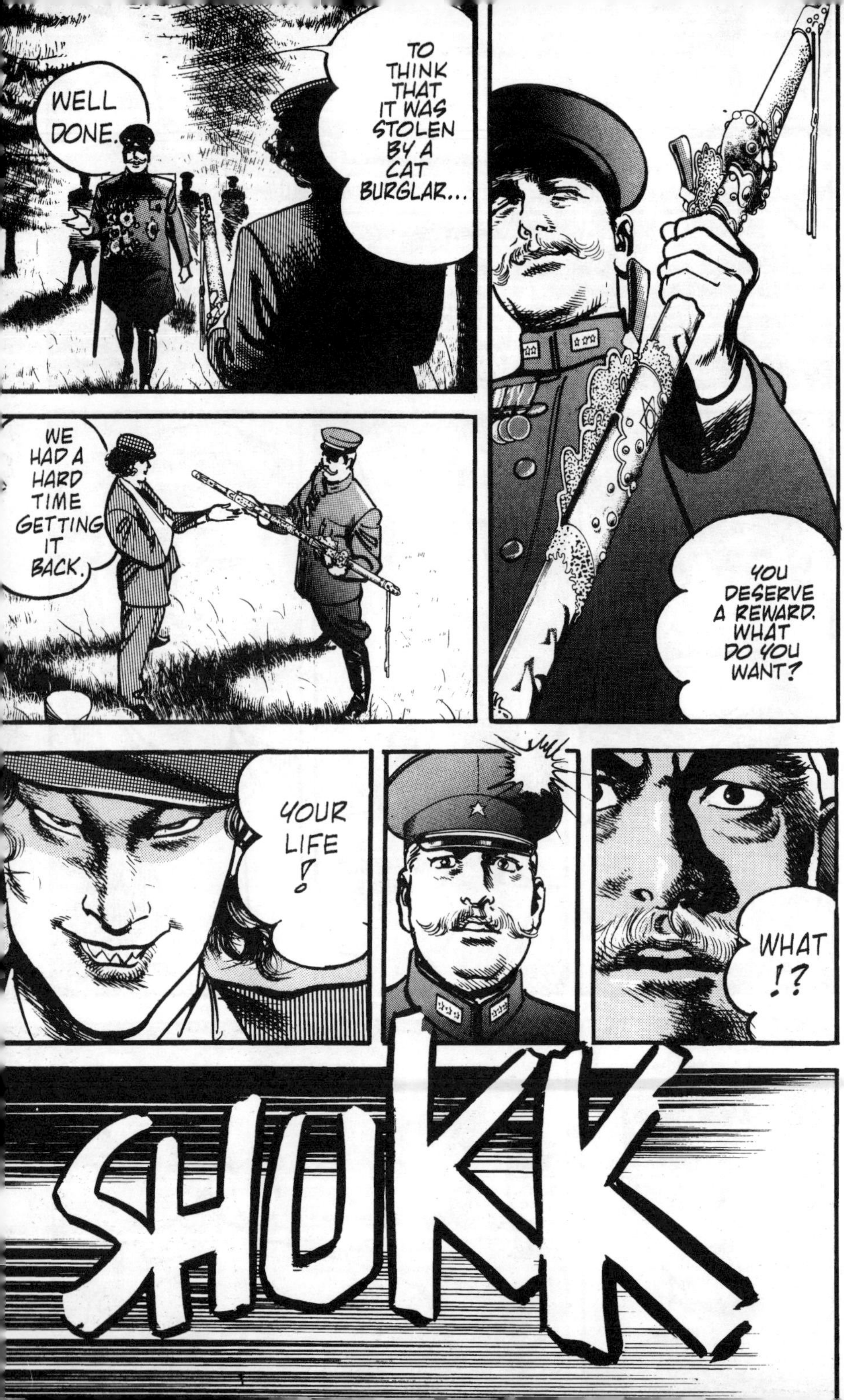
WELL DONE.
TO THINK THAT IT WAS STOLEN BY A CAT BURGLAR...
WE HAD A HARD TIME GETTING IT BACK.
YOU DESERVE A REWARD. WHAT DO YOU WANT?
YOUR LIFE!
WHAT!?
SHUKK

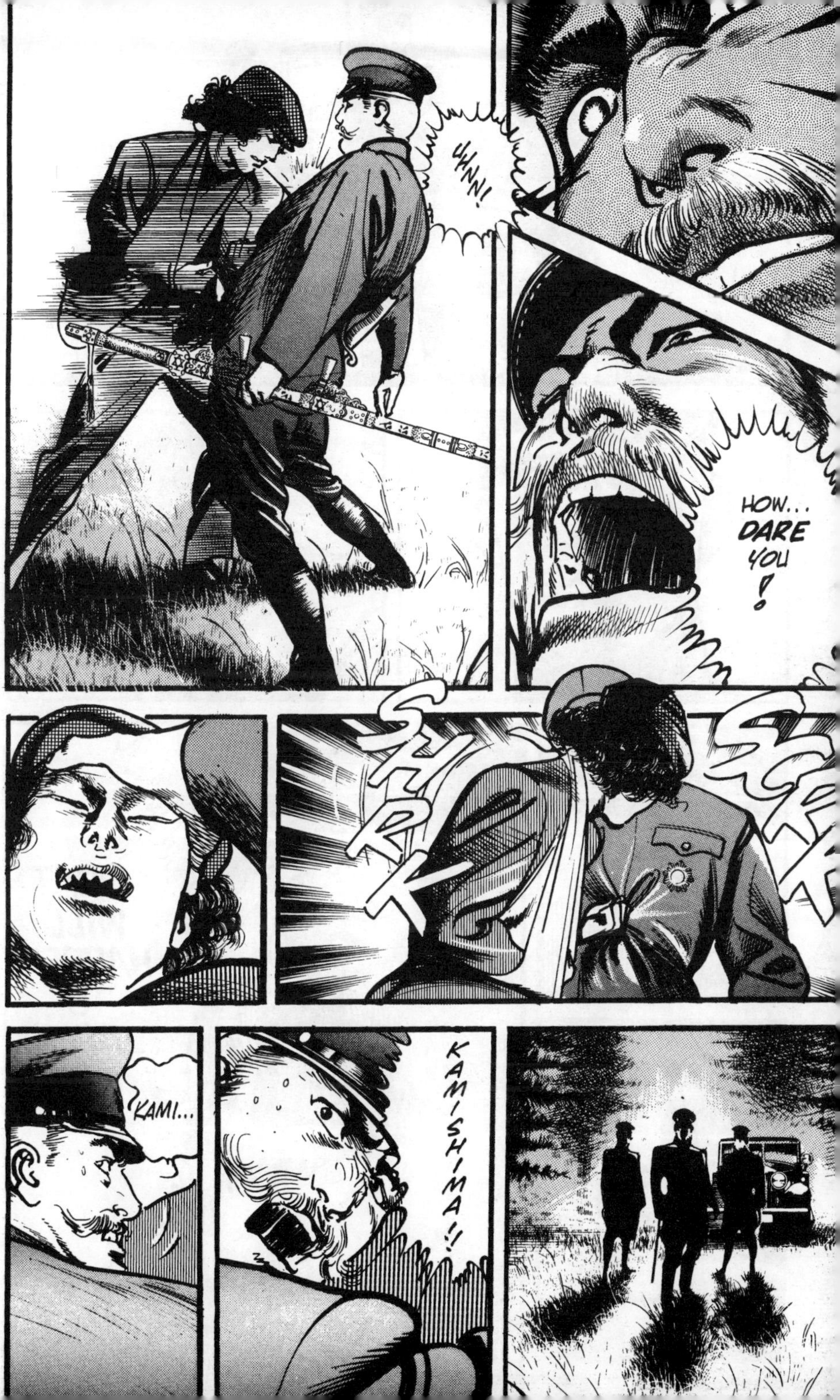
UHNN!
HOW... DARE YOU!
SHRRK
KAMI...
KAMISHIMA!!

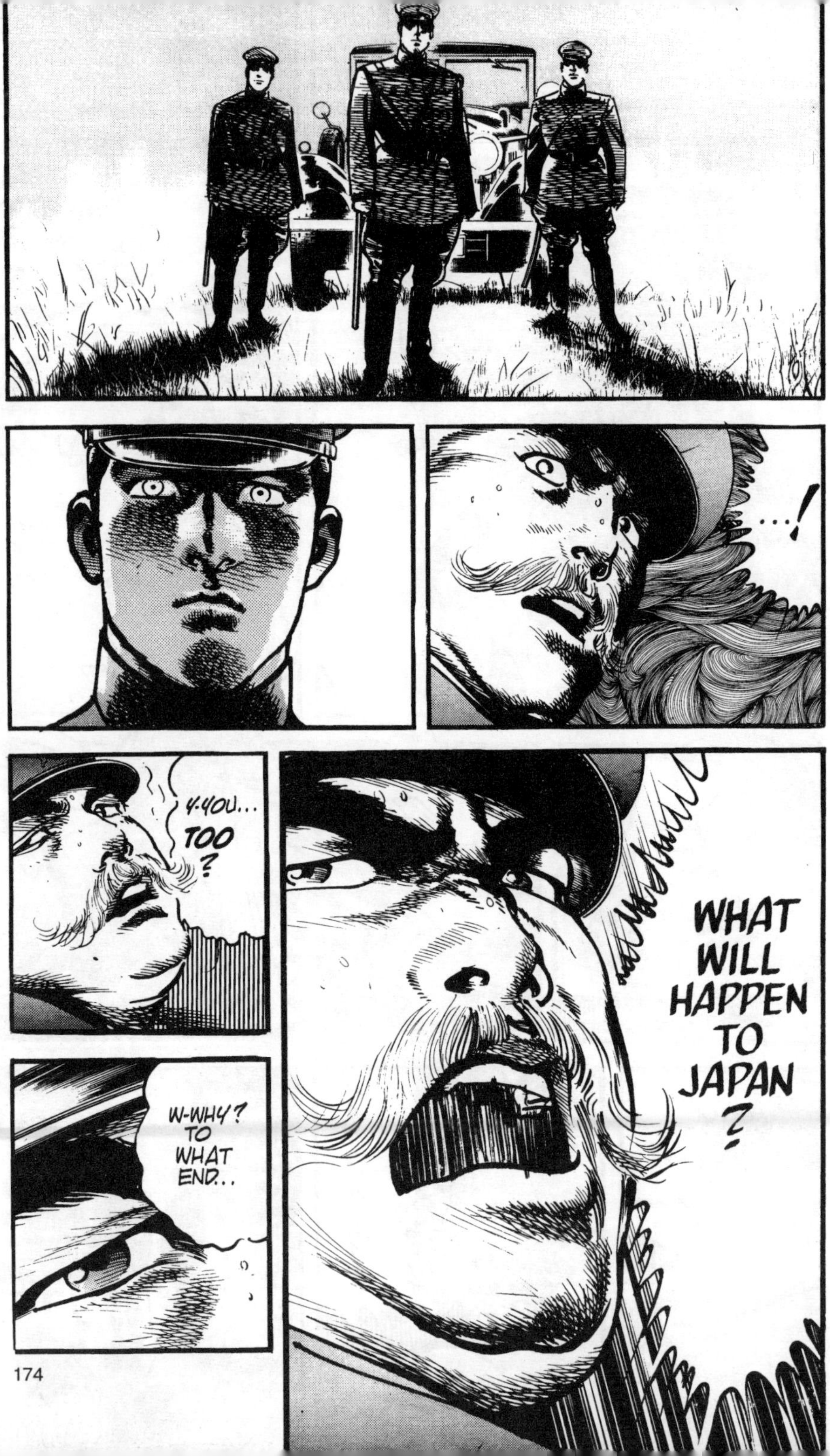
...!
Y-YOU... TOO?
W-WHY? TO WHAT END...
WHAT WILL HAPPEN TO JAPAN?

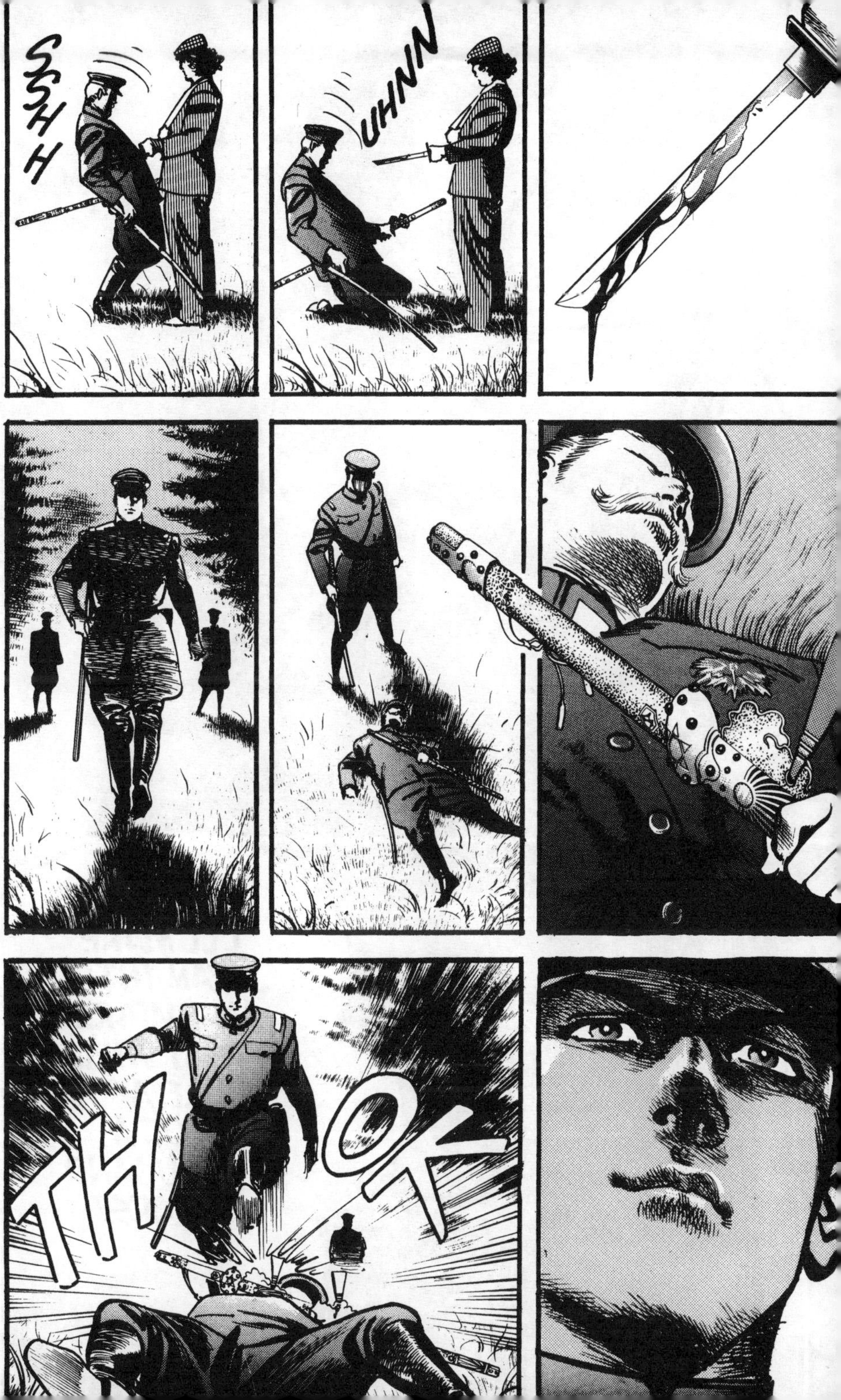
SSHH
UHNN
THOK

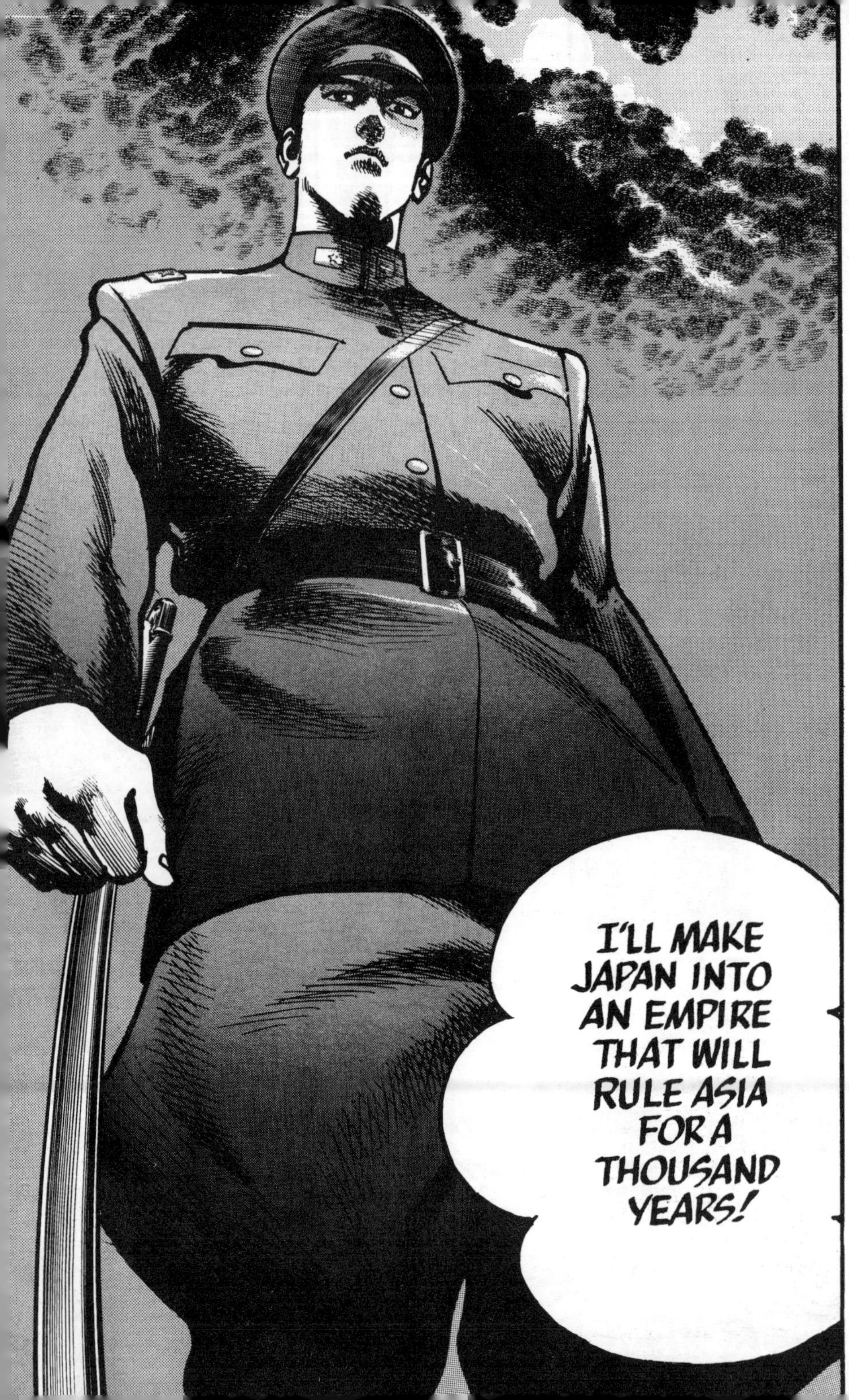
I'LL MAKE JAPAN INTO AN EMPIRE THAT WILL RULE ASIA FOR A THOUSAND YEARS!

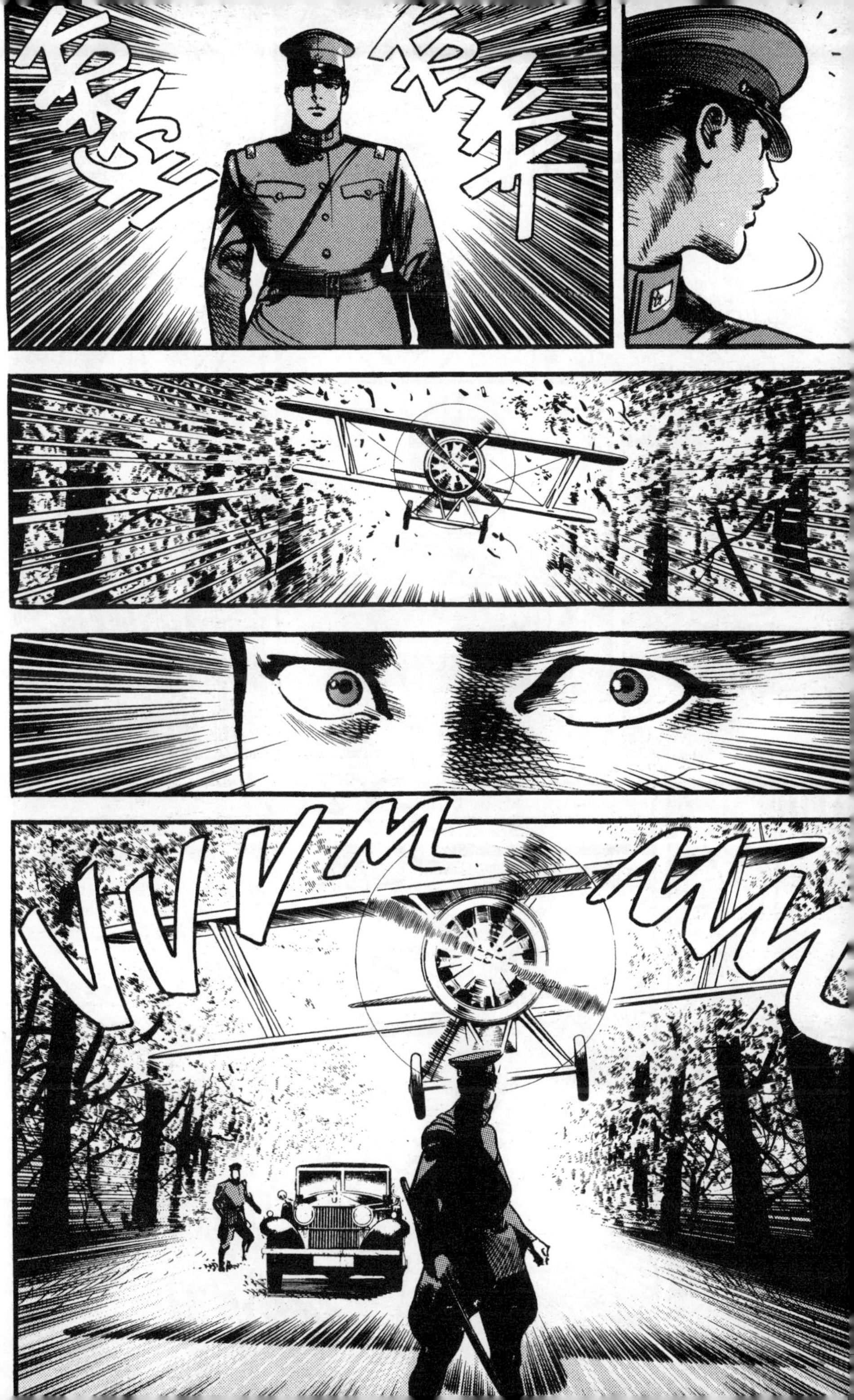
KRASH
KRAKK
VVVMMMM

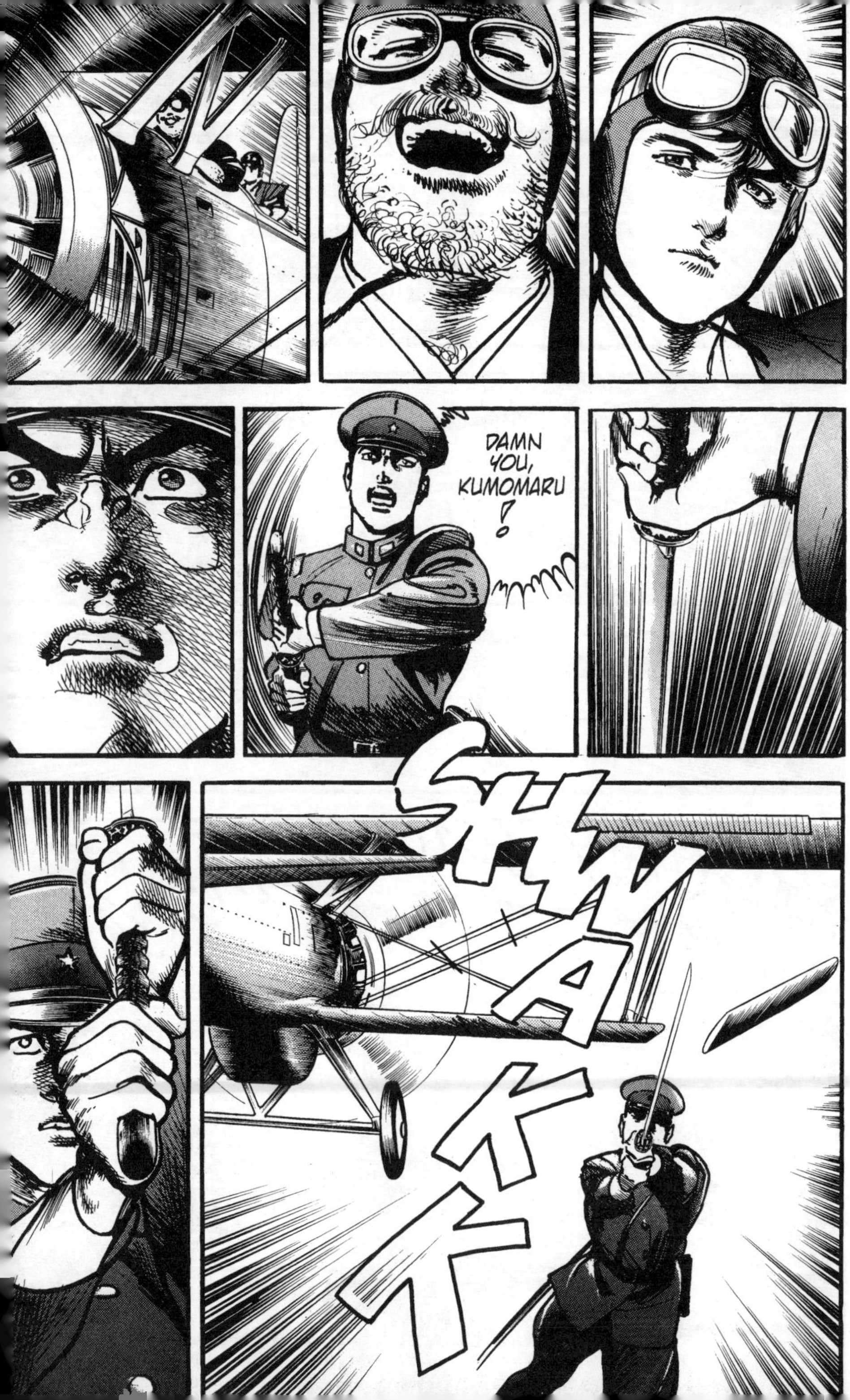
DAMN YOU, KUMOMARU!
SHWAKK

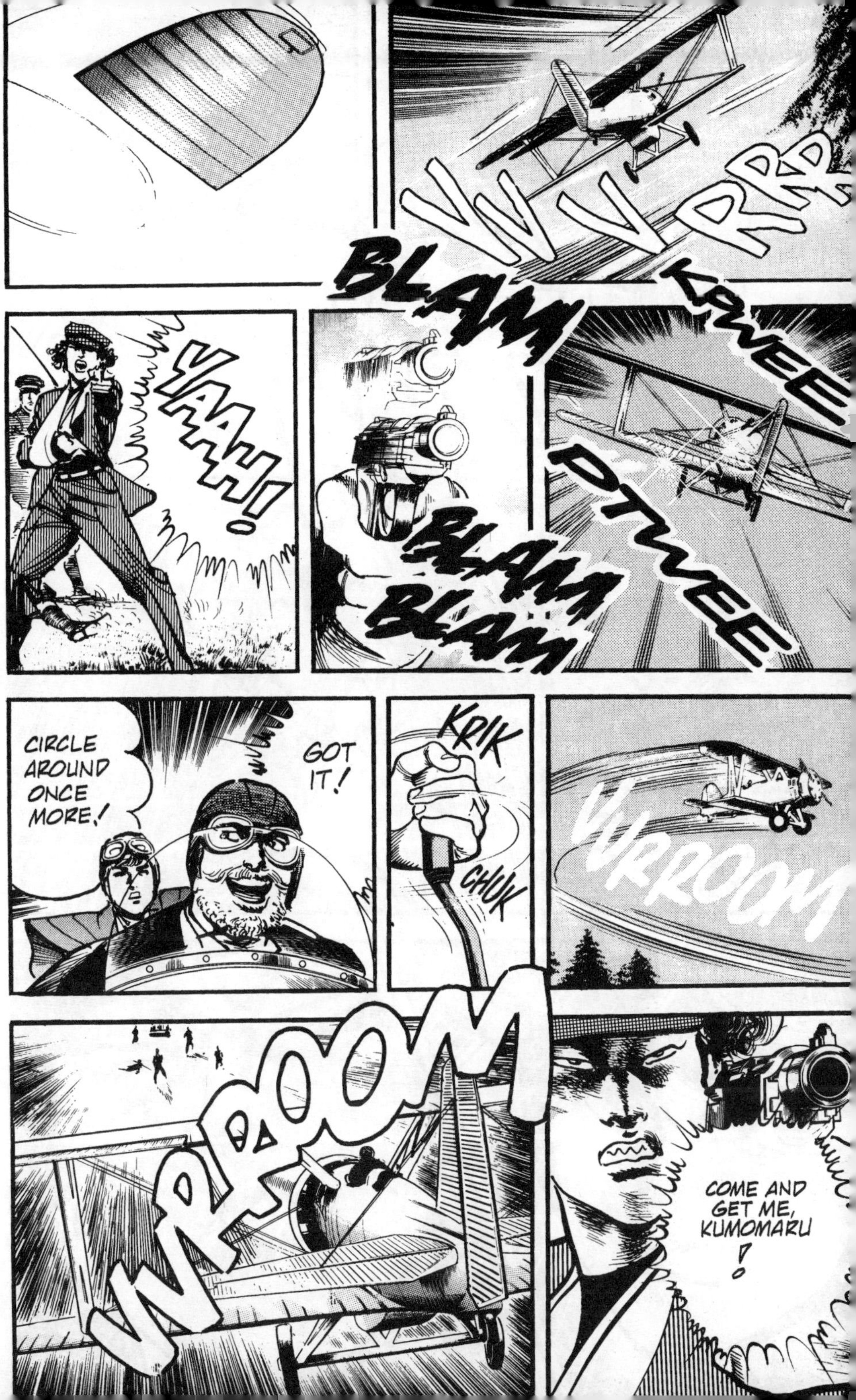
VVVRRR
BLAM
KRWEE
YAAH!
BLAM BLAM
PTWEE
CIRCLE AROUND ONCE MORE!
GOT IT!
KRIK
CHUK
VRROOM
VRROOM
COME AND GET ME, KUMOMARU!

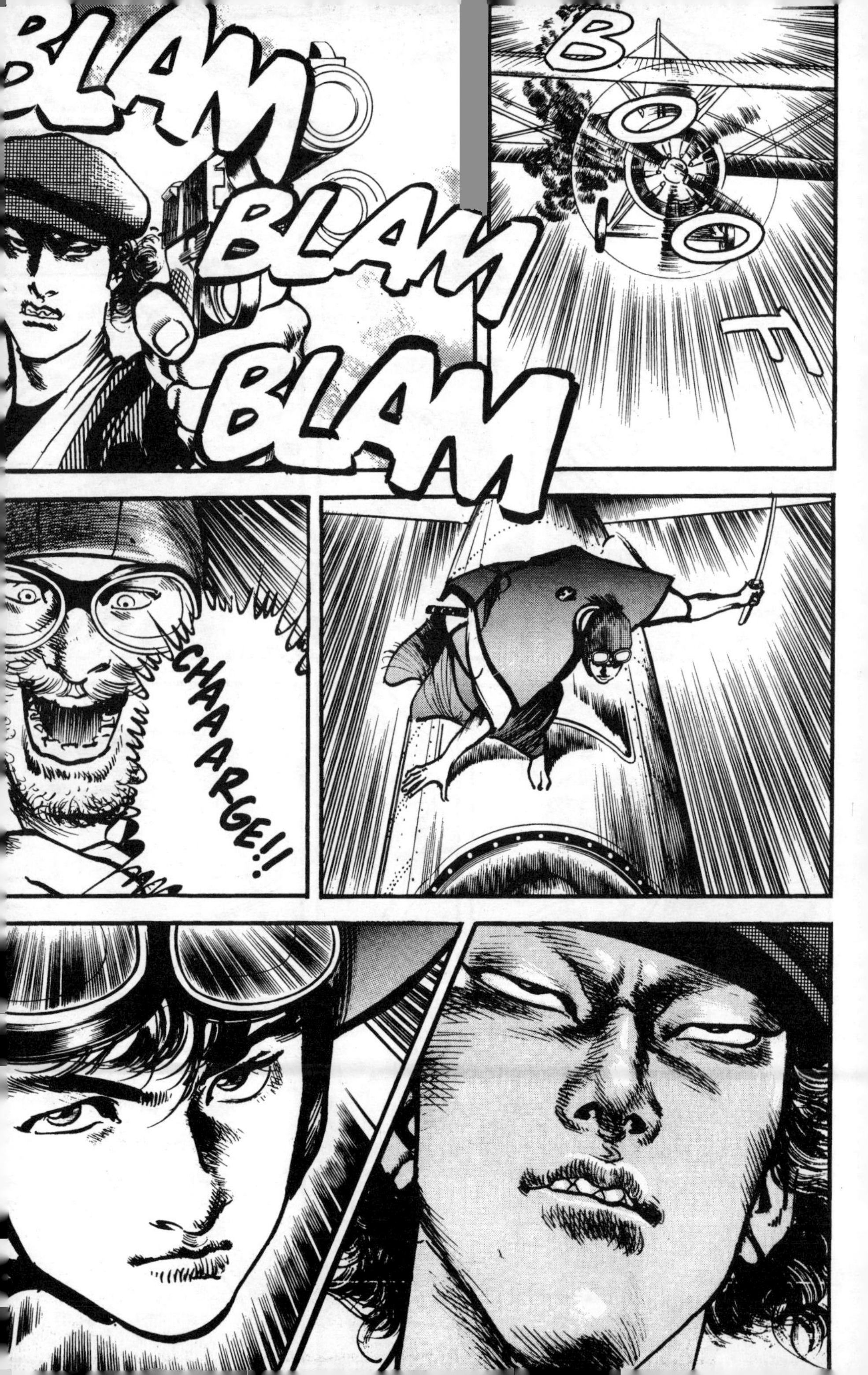
BLAM
BLAM
BLAM
BOOOF
CHAAAARGE!!

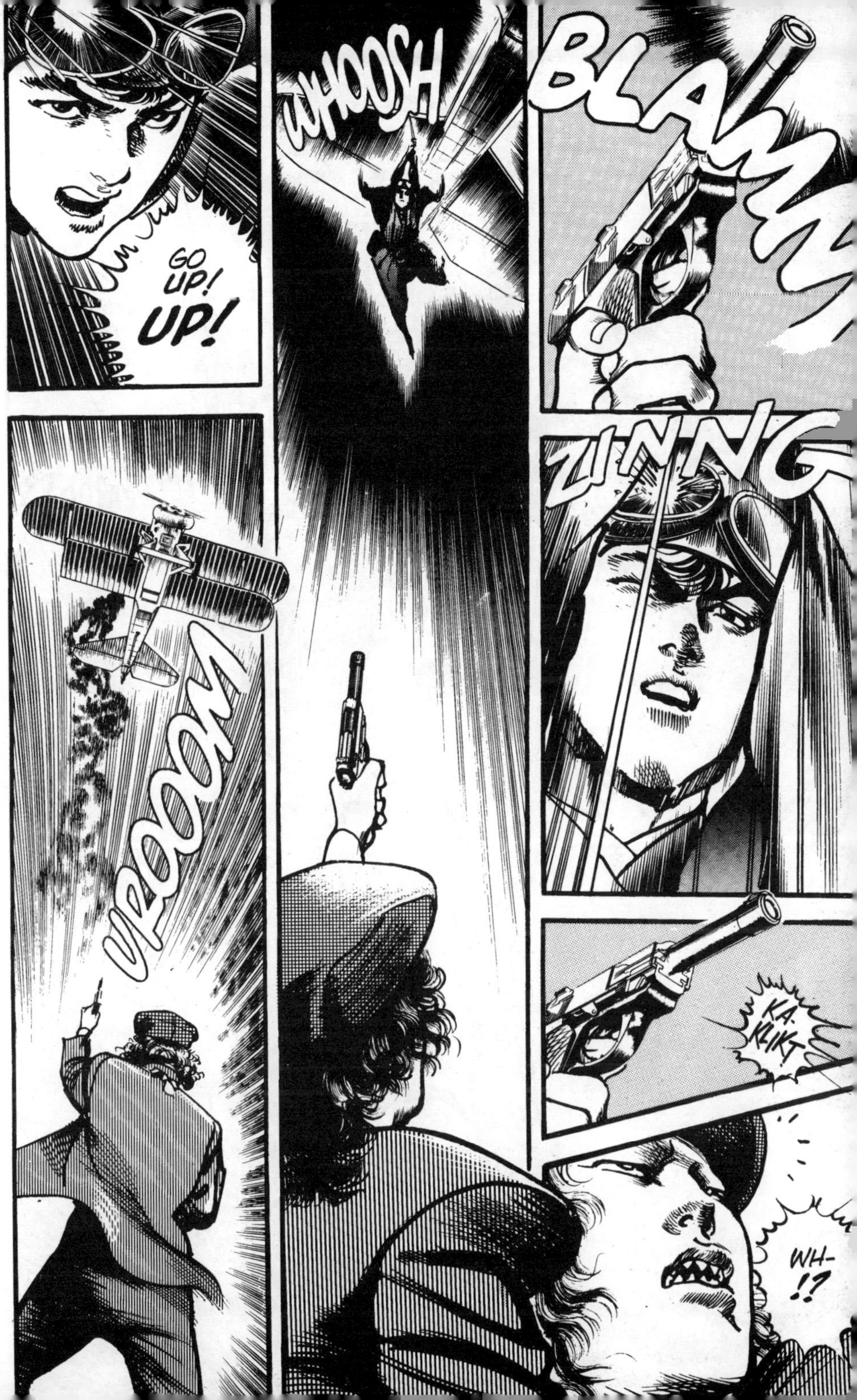
GO UP! UP!
WHOOSH
BLAM
VROOOM
ZINNG
KA-KLIKT
WH- !?

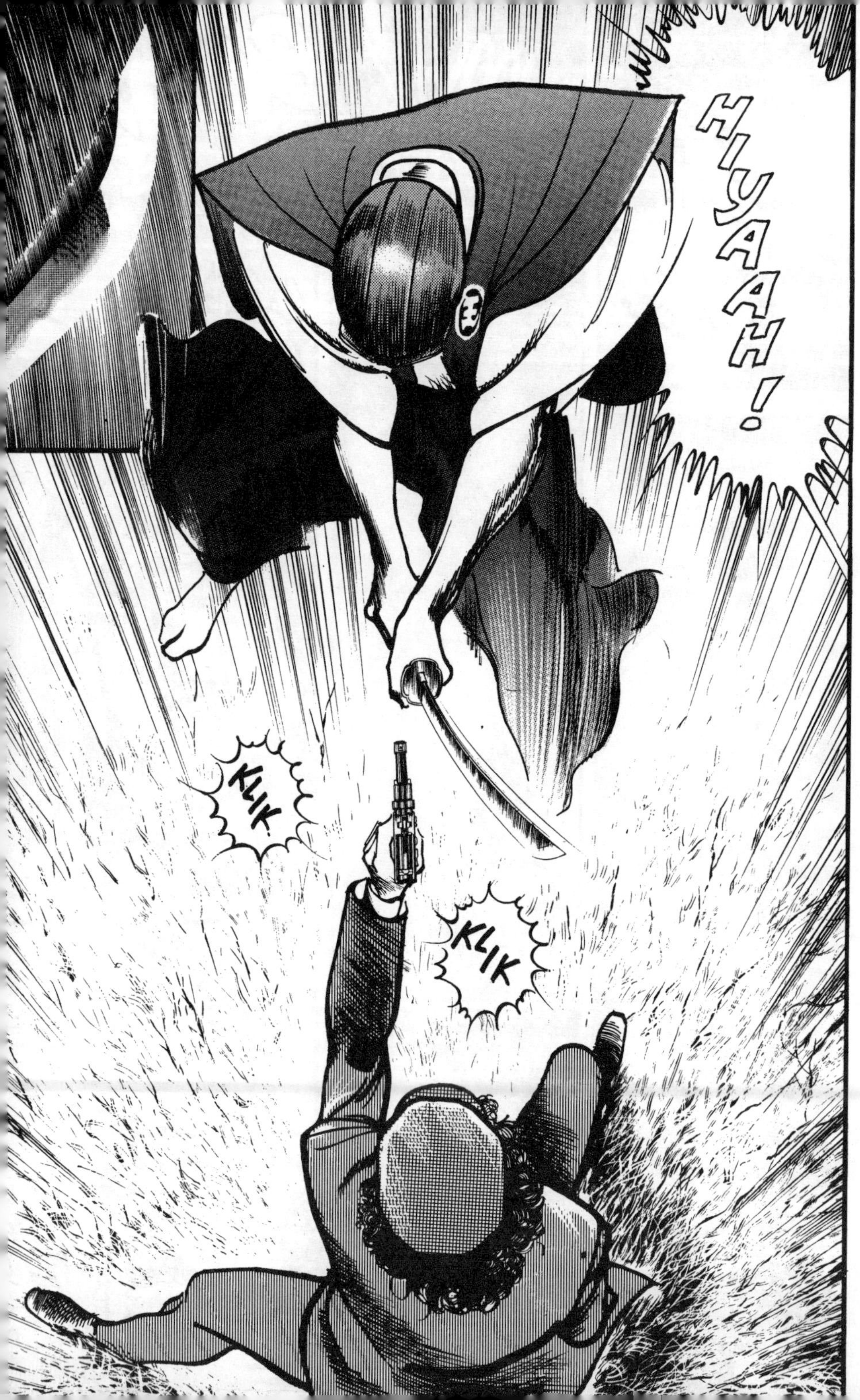
HIYAAAH!
KLIK
KLIK

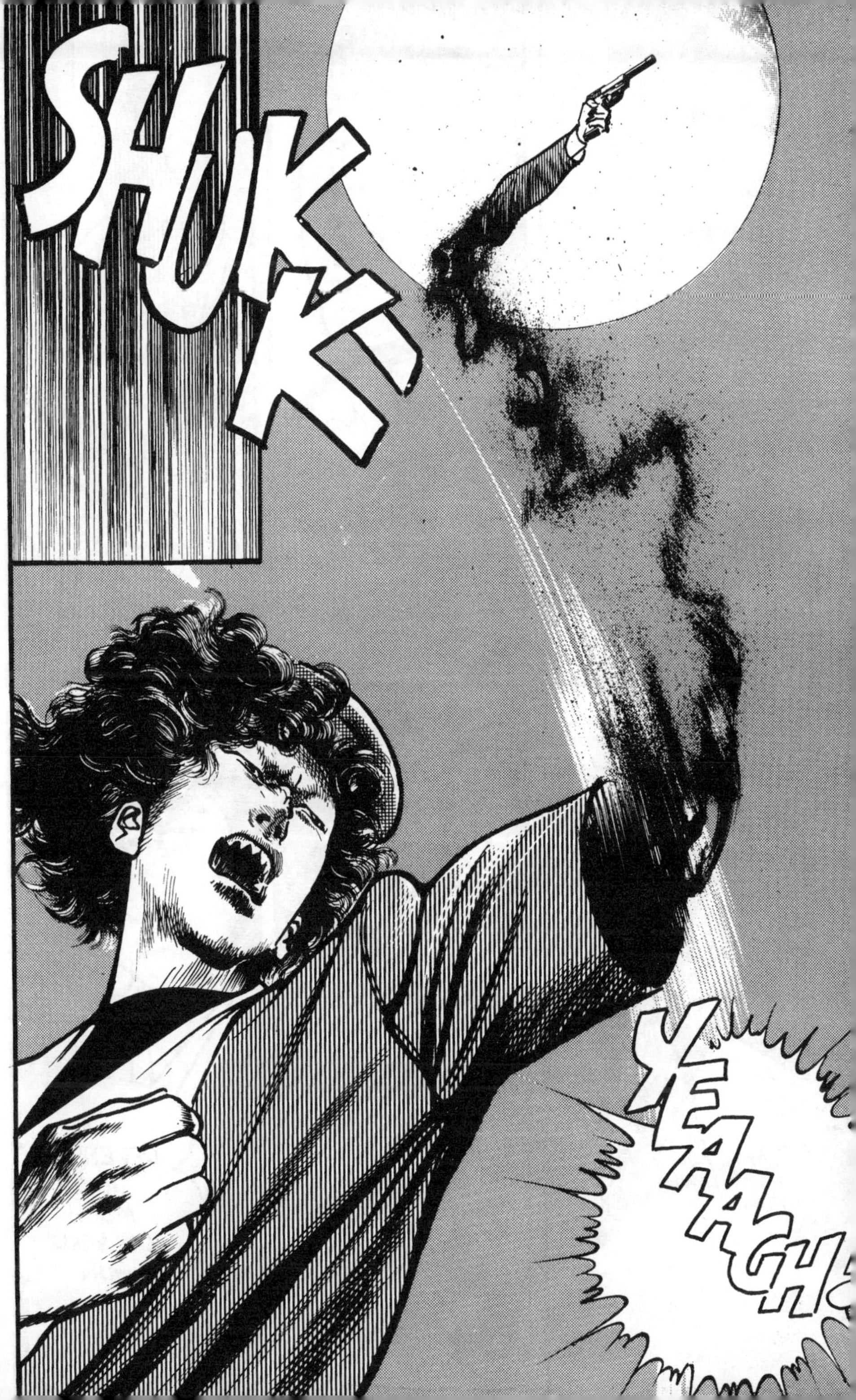
SHUKK
YEAAGH

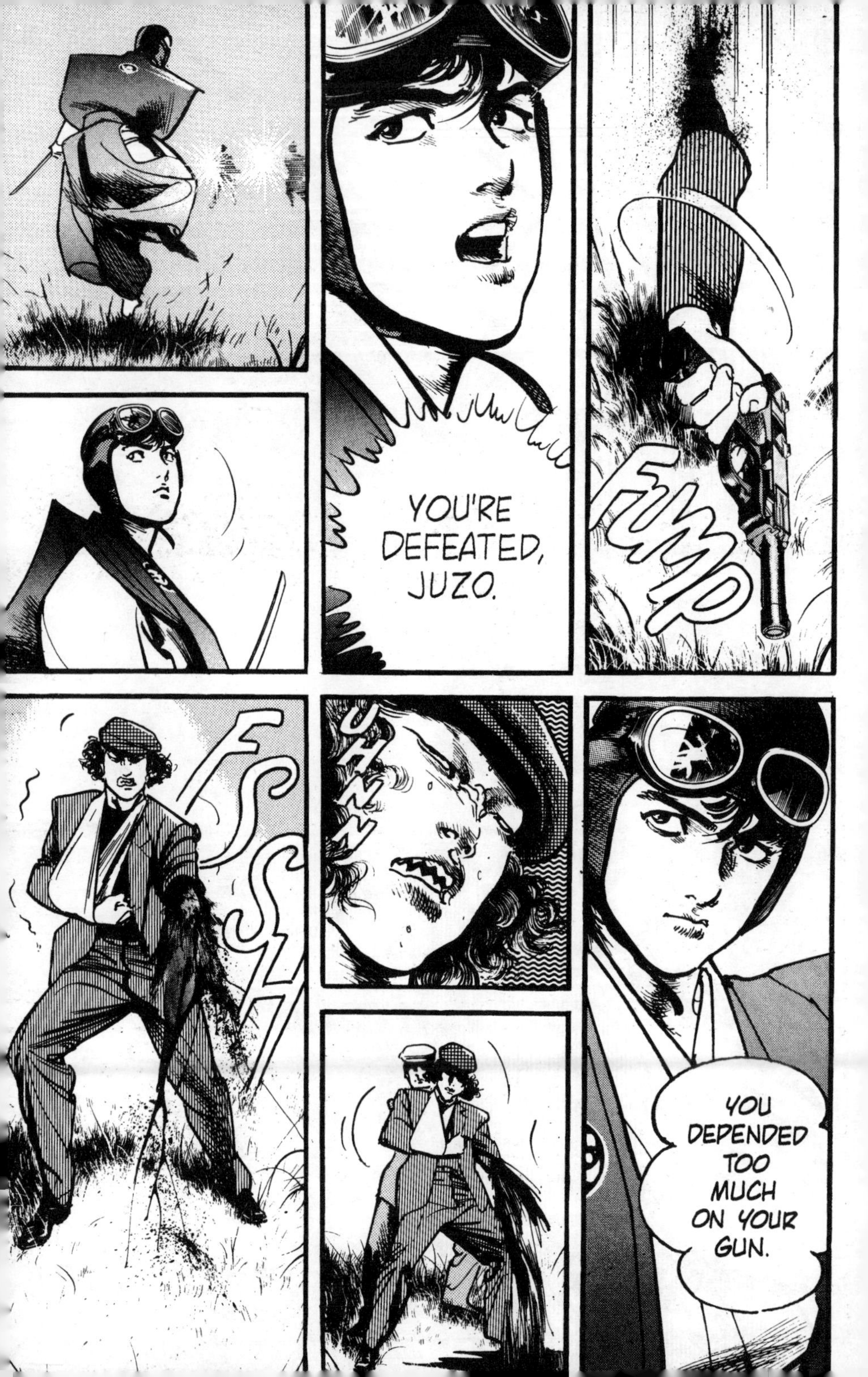
YOU'RE DEFEATED, JUZO.
YOU DEPENDED TOO MUCH ON YOUR GUN.

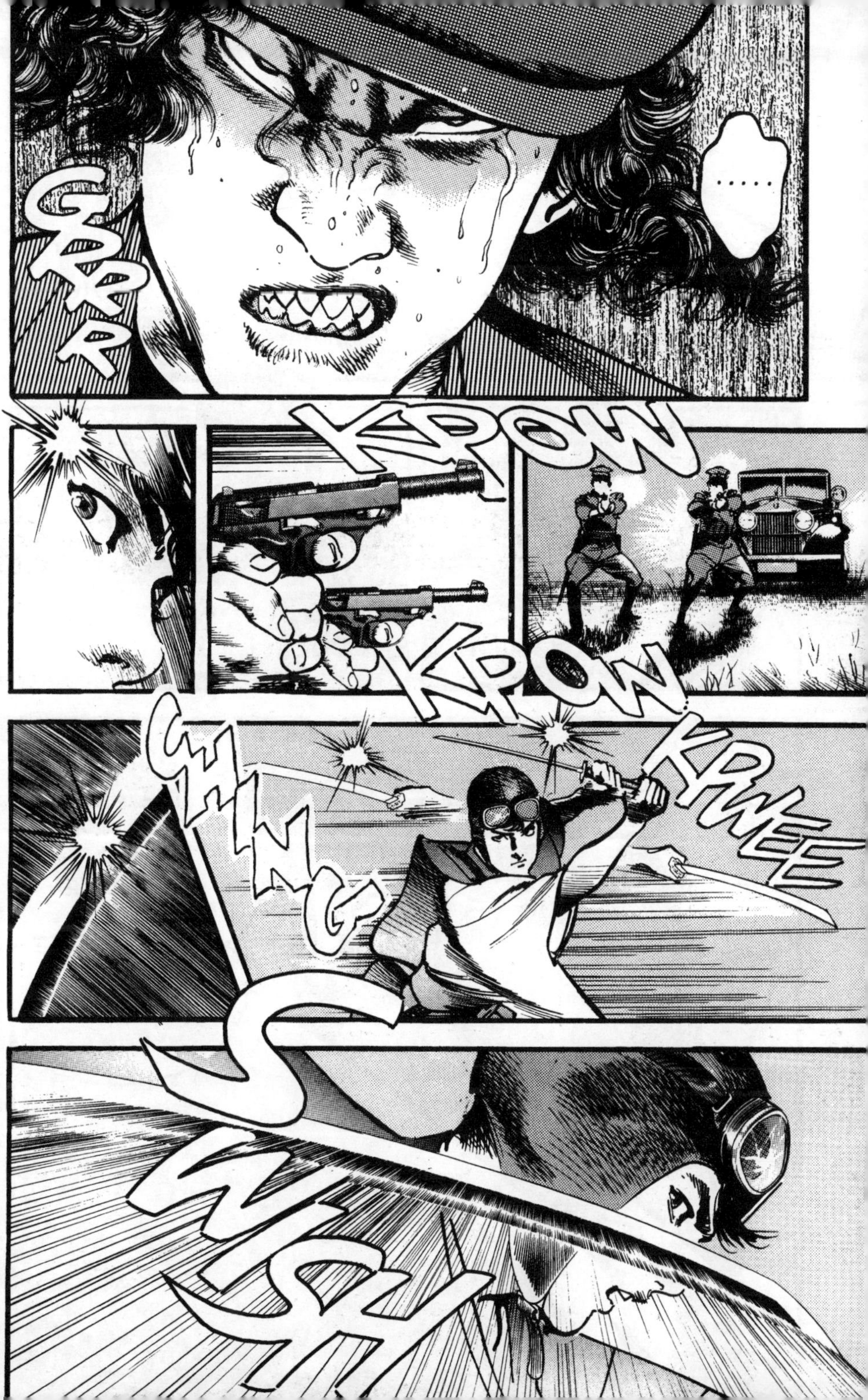
GRRR
......
KPOW
KPOW
CHING
KYWEE
SWISH

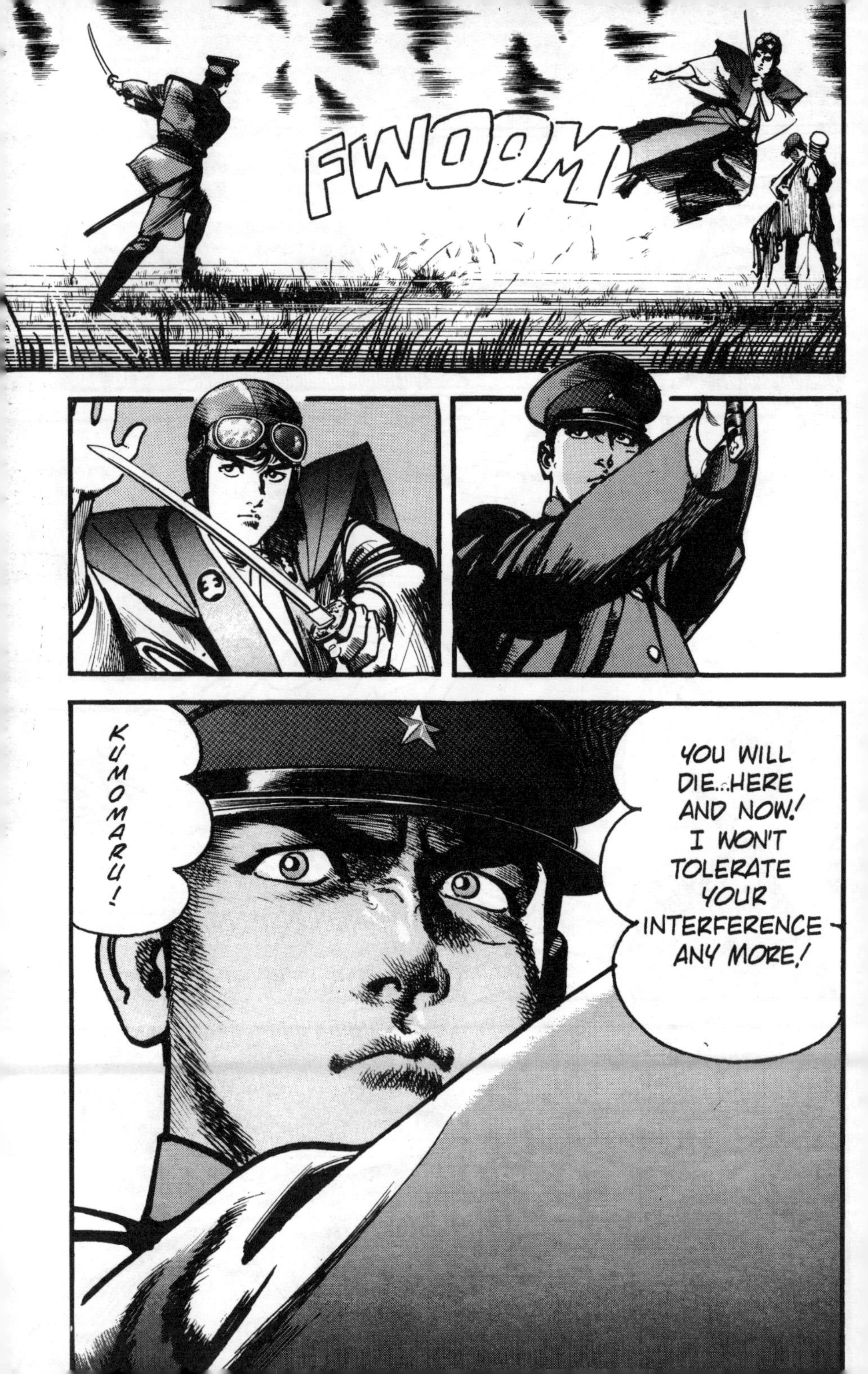
FWOOM
KUMOMARU!
YOU WILL DIE...HERE AND NOW! I WON'T TOLERATE YOUR INTERFERENCE ANY MORE!

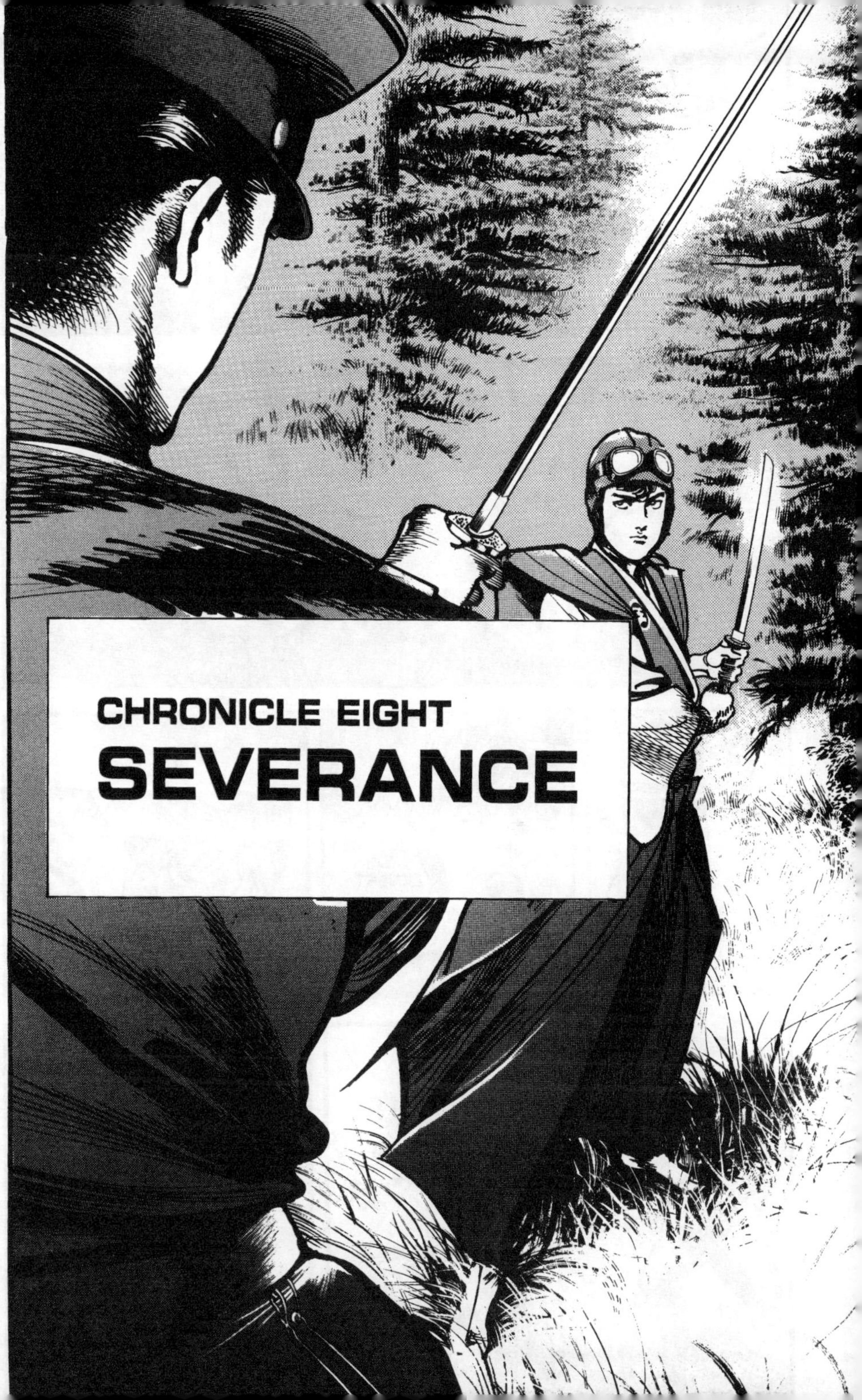
CHRONICLE EIGHT
SEVERANCE

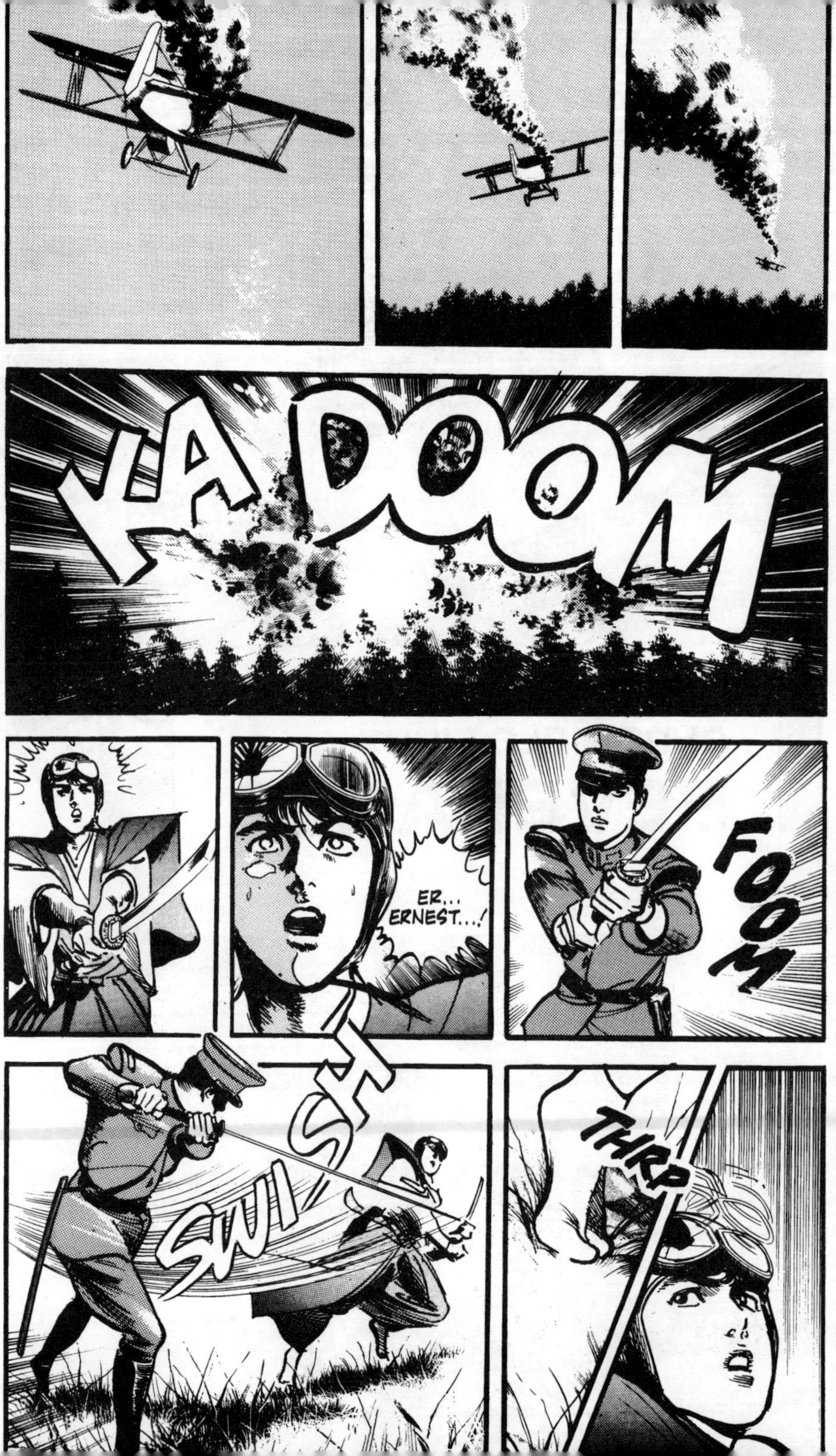
KADOOM
ER... ERNEST...!
FOOM
SHI
SWI
THRP

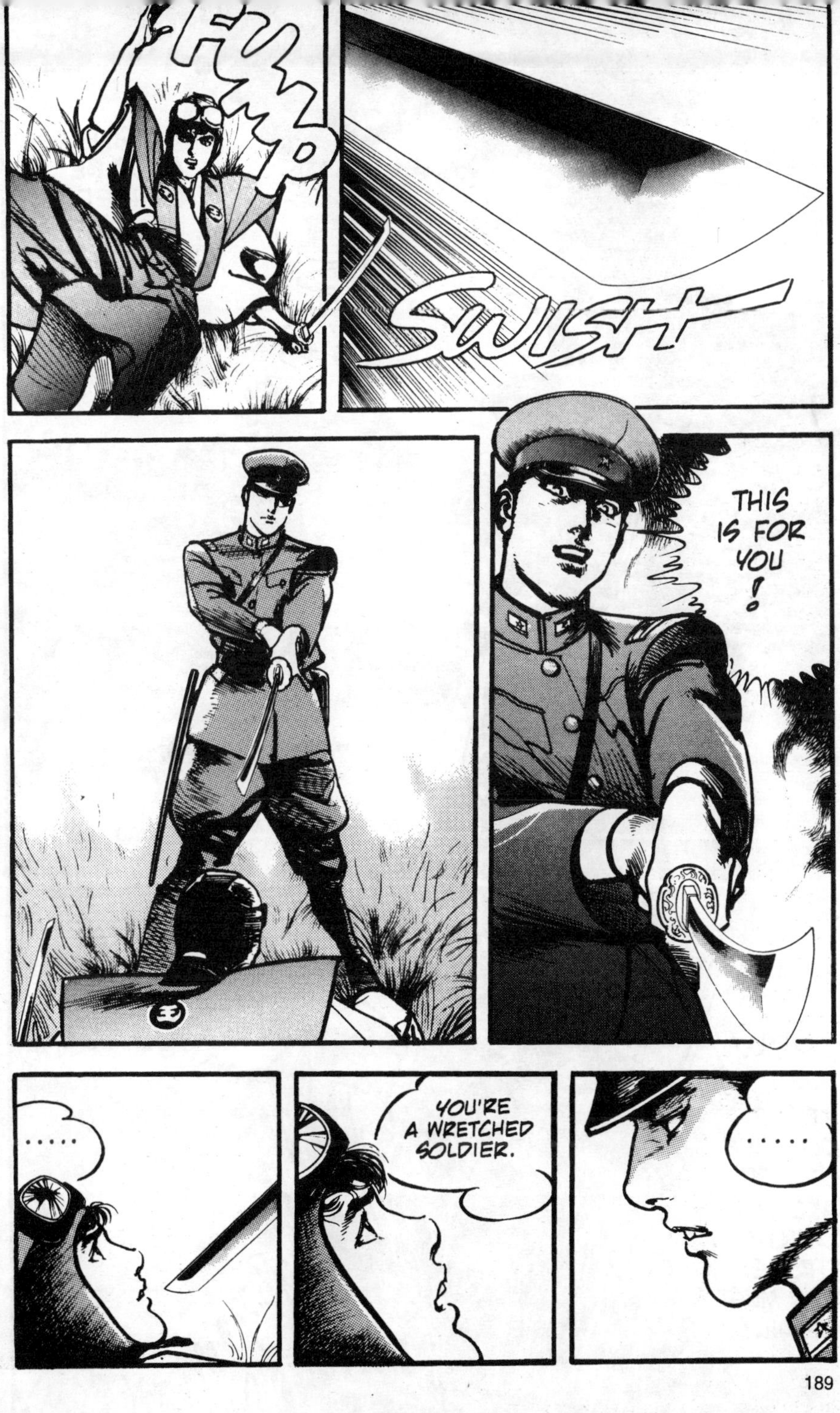
FUMP
SWISH
THIS IS FOR YOU!
.....
YOU'RE A WRETCHED SOLDIER.
.....

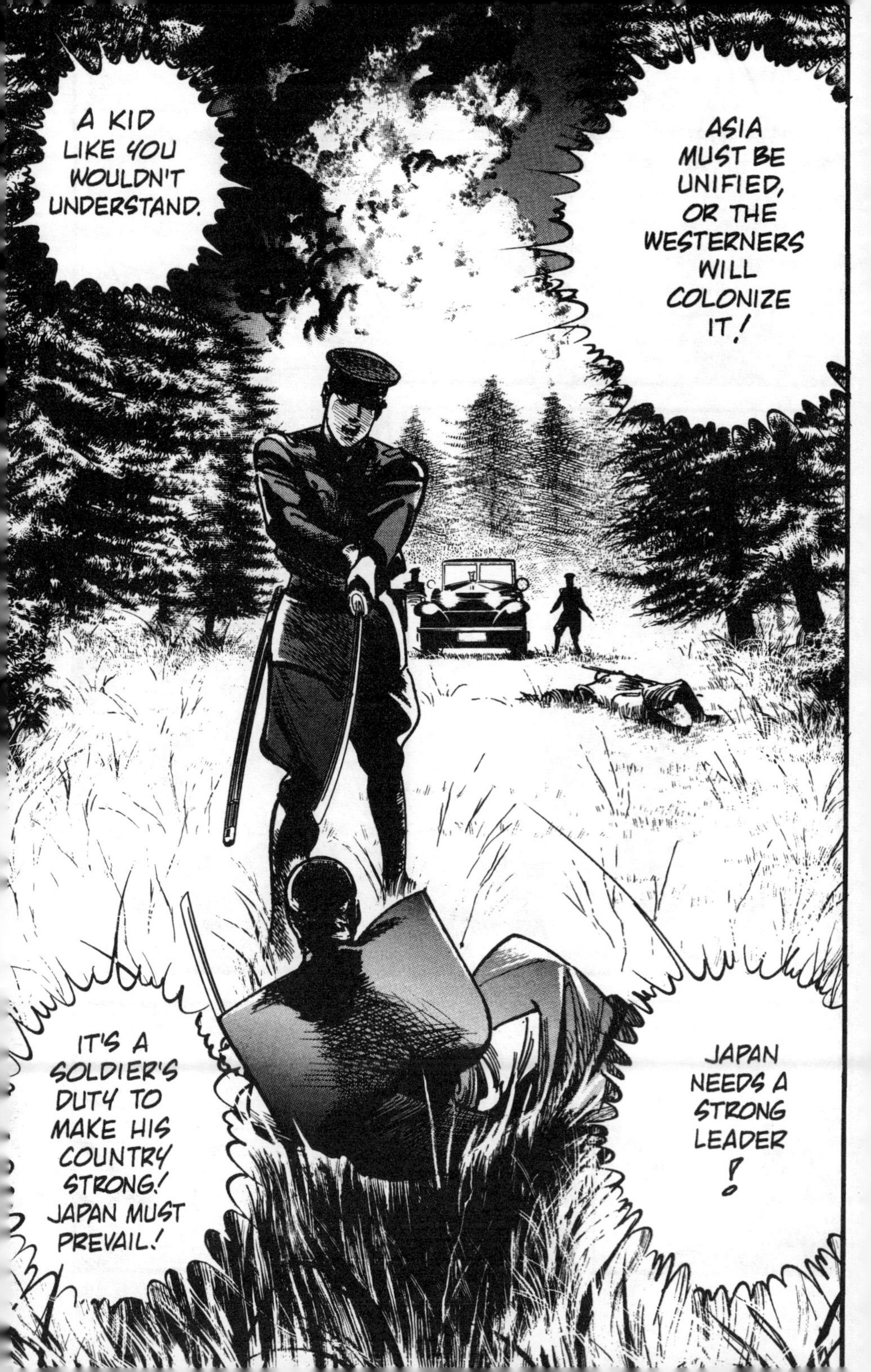
A KID LIKE YOU WOULDN'T UNDERSTAND.
ASIA MUST BE UNIFIED, OR THE WESTERNERS WILL COLONIZE IT!
IT'S A SOLDIER'S DUTY TO MAKE HIS COUNTRY STRONG! JAPAN MUST PREVAIL!
JAPAN NEEDS A STRONG LEADER!

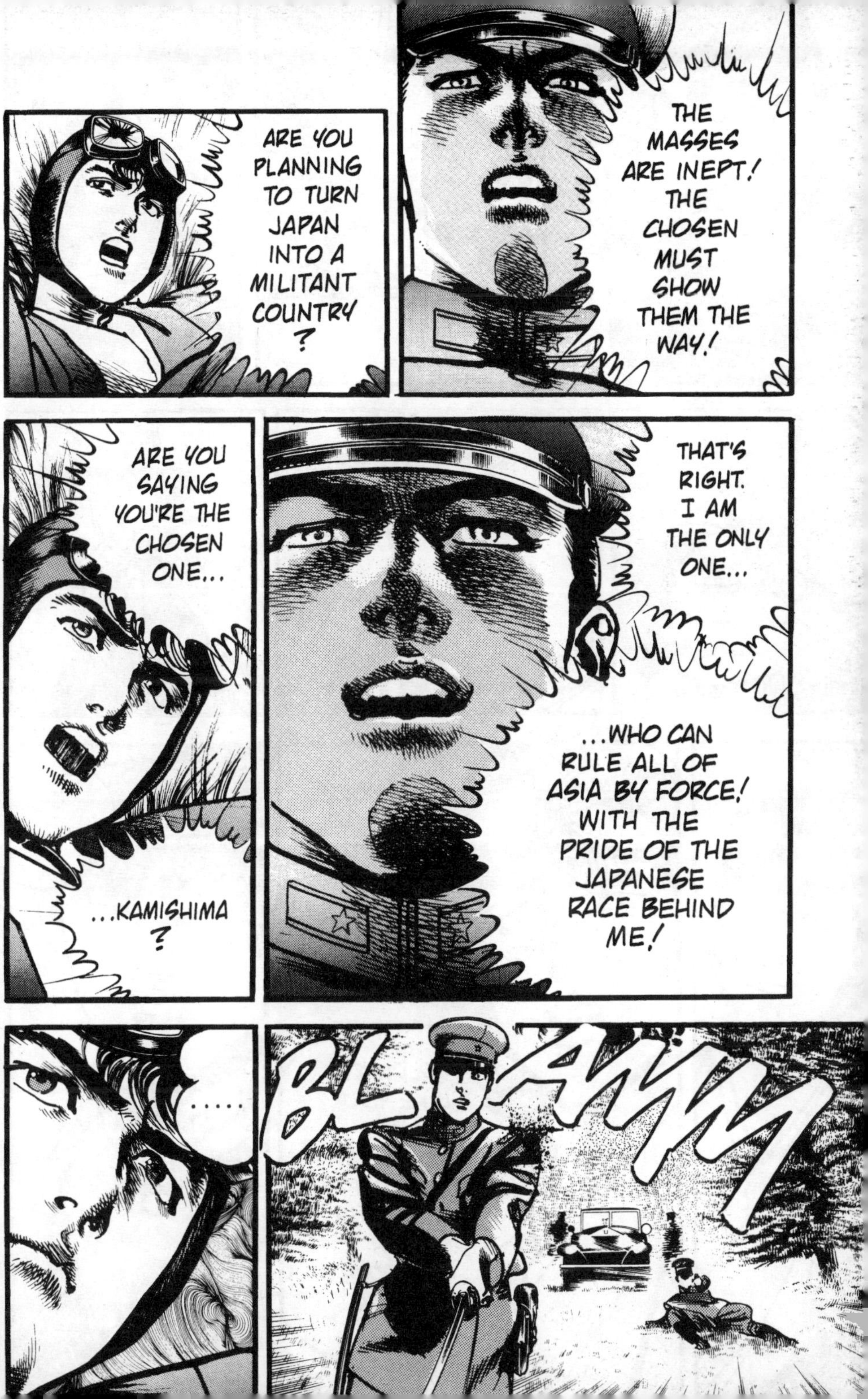
ARE YOU PLANNING TO TURN JAPAN INTO A MILITANT COUNTRY?
THE MASSES ARE INEPT! THE CHOSEN MUST SHOW THEM THE WAY!
ARE YOU SAYING YOU'RE THE CHOSEN ONE...
...KAMISHIMA?
THAT'S RIGHT. I AM THE ONLY ONE...
...WHO CAN RULE ALL OF ASIA BY FORCE! WITH THE PRIDE OF THE JAPANESE RACE BEHIND ME!
.....
BLAMM

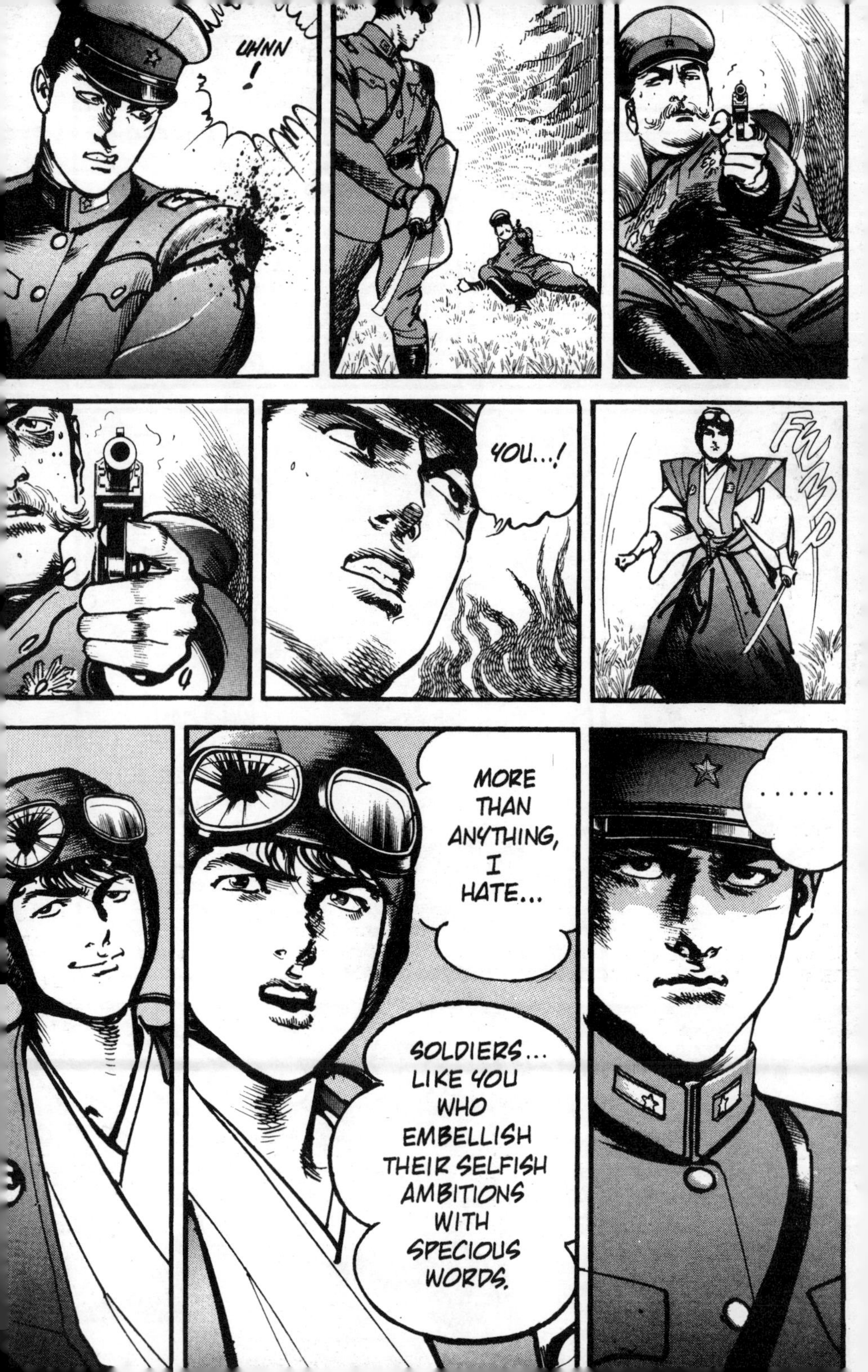
UHNN
!
YOU...!
FWUMP
MORE THAN ANYTHING, I HATE...
SOLDIERS... LIKE YOU WHO EMBELLISH THEIR SELFISH AMBITIONS WITH SPECIOUS WORDS.
......

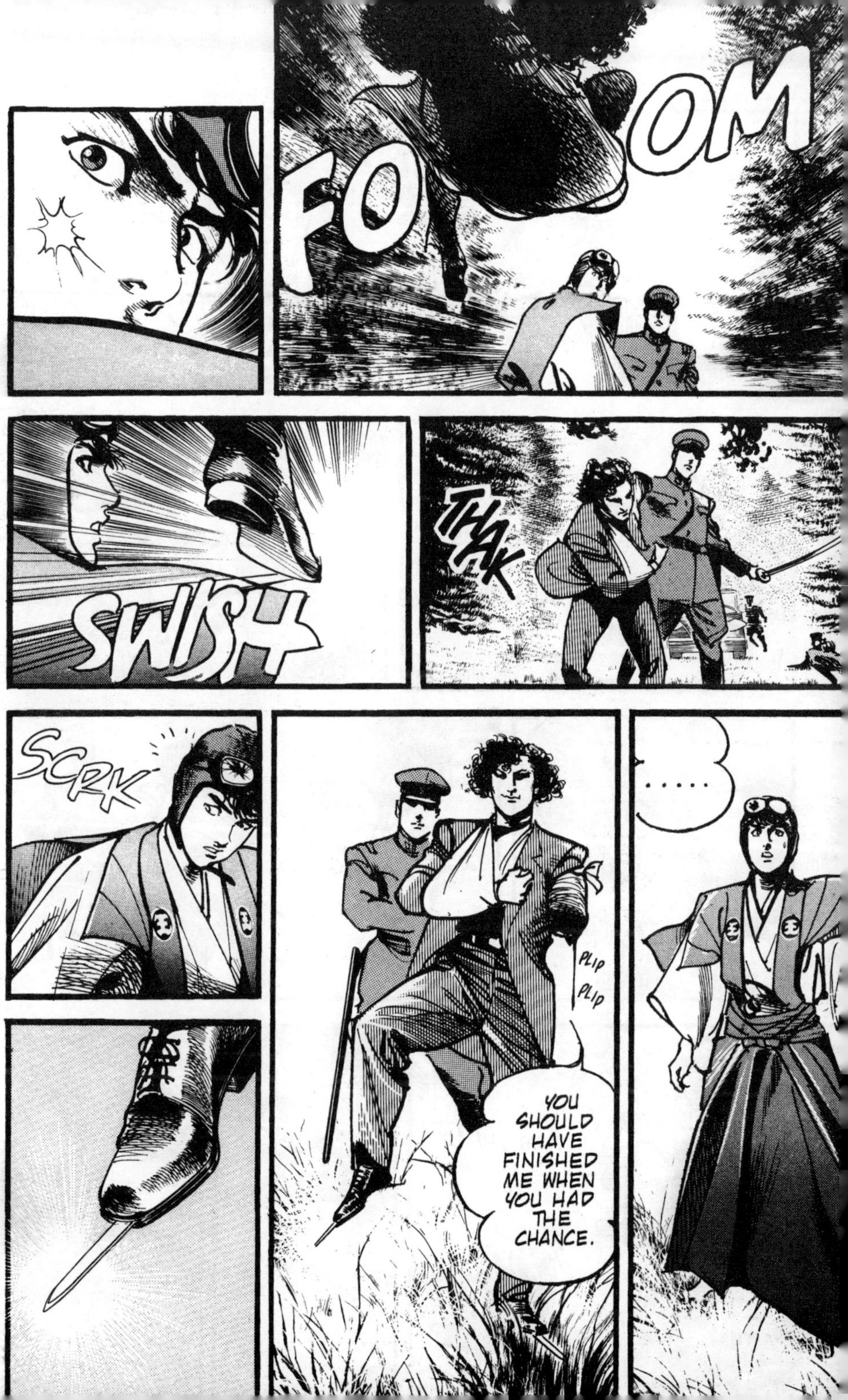
FOOM
SWISH
THAK
SCRK
PLIP
PLIP
YOU SHOULD HAVE FINISHED ME WHEN YOU HAD THE CHANCE.
.....

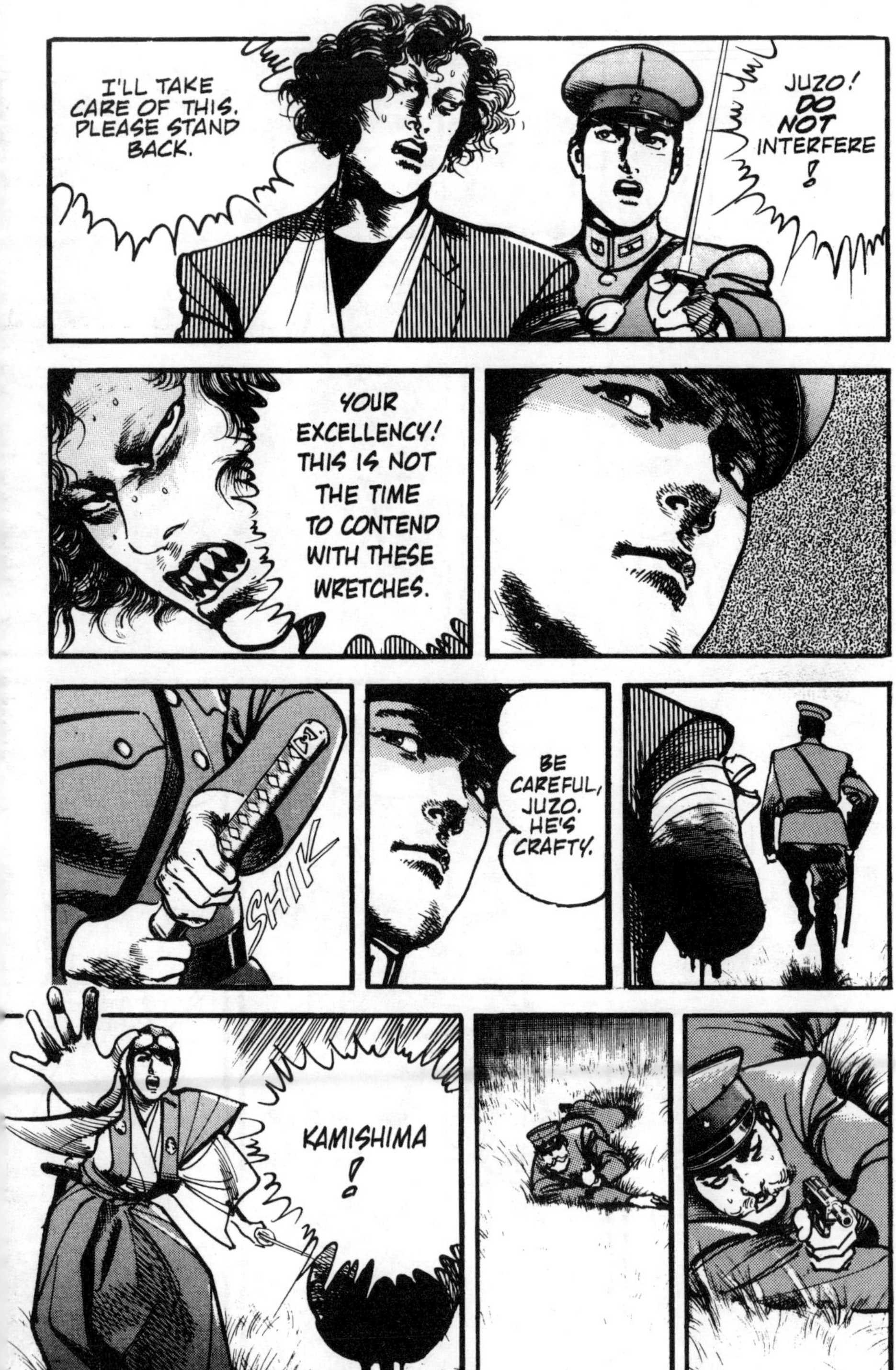
I'LL TAKE CARE OF THIS. PLEASE STAND BACK.
JUZO! DO NOT INTERFERE!
YOUR EXCELLENCY! THIS IS NOT THE TIME TO CONTEND WITH THESE WRETCHES.
SHIK
BE CAREFUL, JUZO. HE'S CRAFTY.
KAMISHIMA!

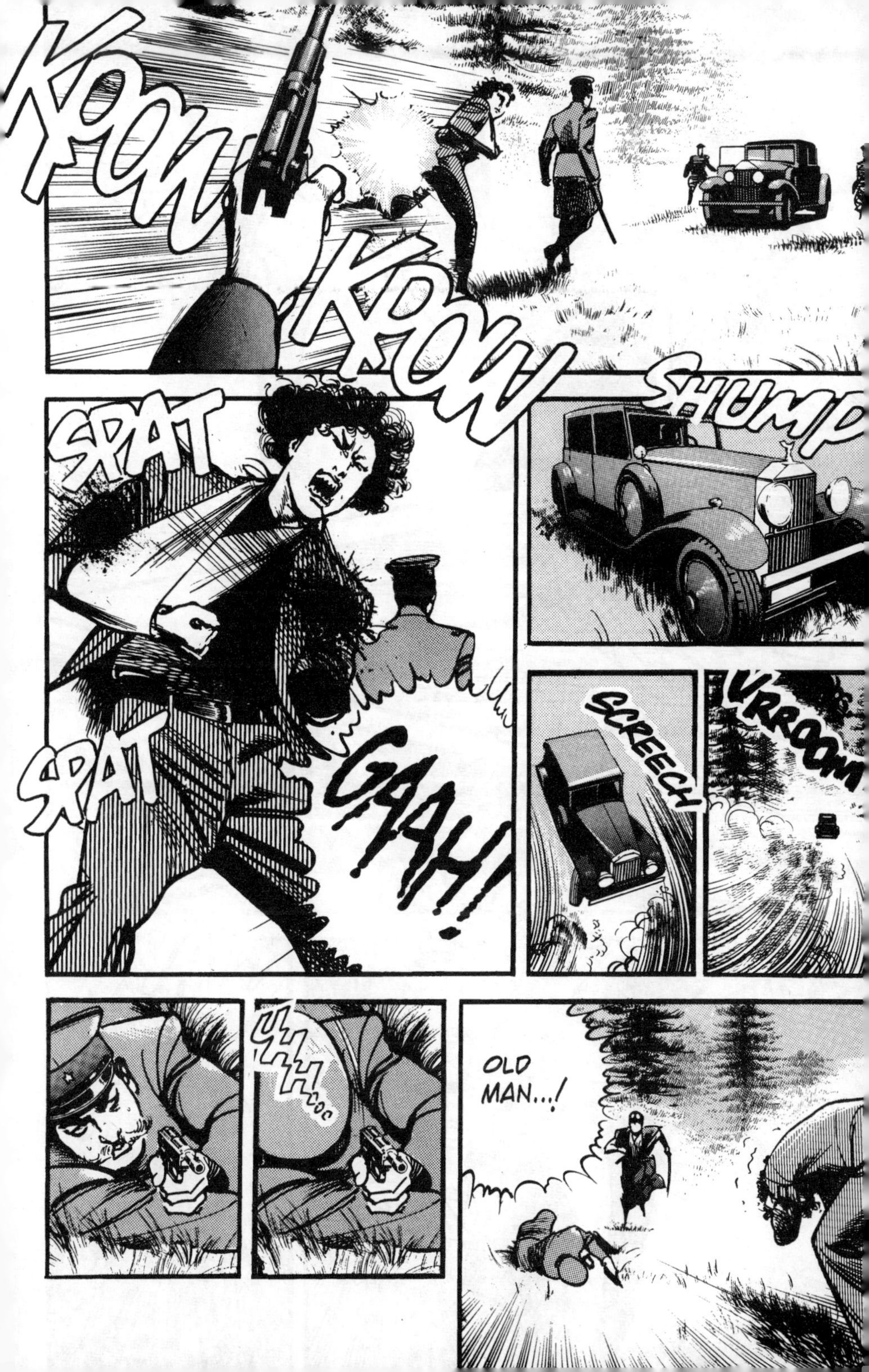
KPOW
KPOW
SHUMP
SPAT
SPAT
GAAH!!
SCREECH
VRROOOM
SHH
COC
OLD MAN...!

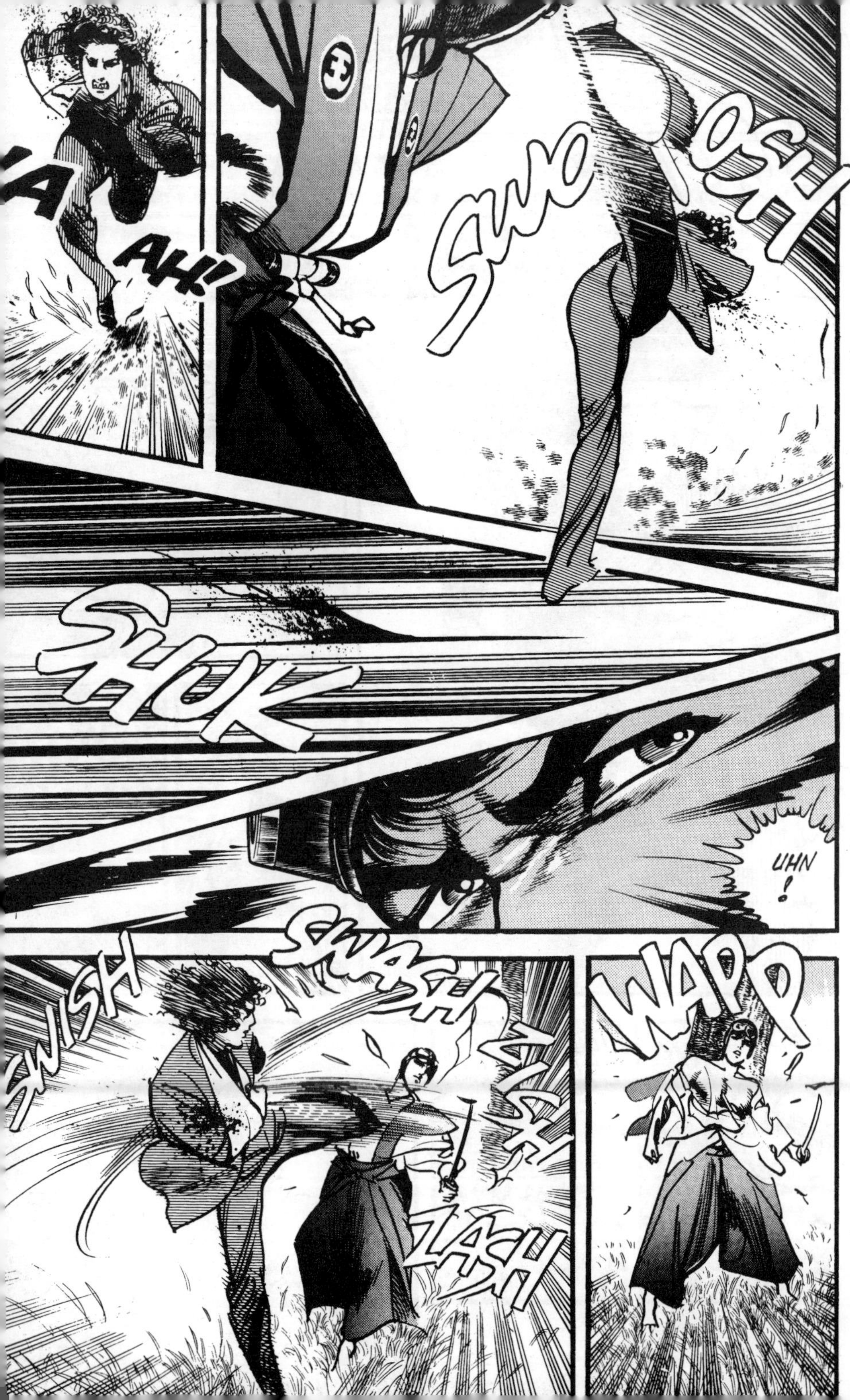
'A
AH!
SWOOSH
SHUK
UHN !
SWISH
SWASH
ZISH
ZLASH
WAPP

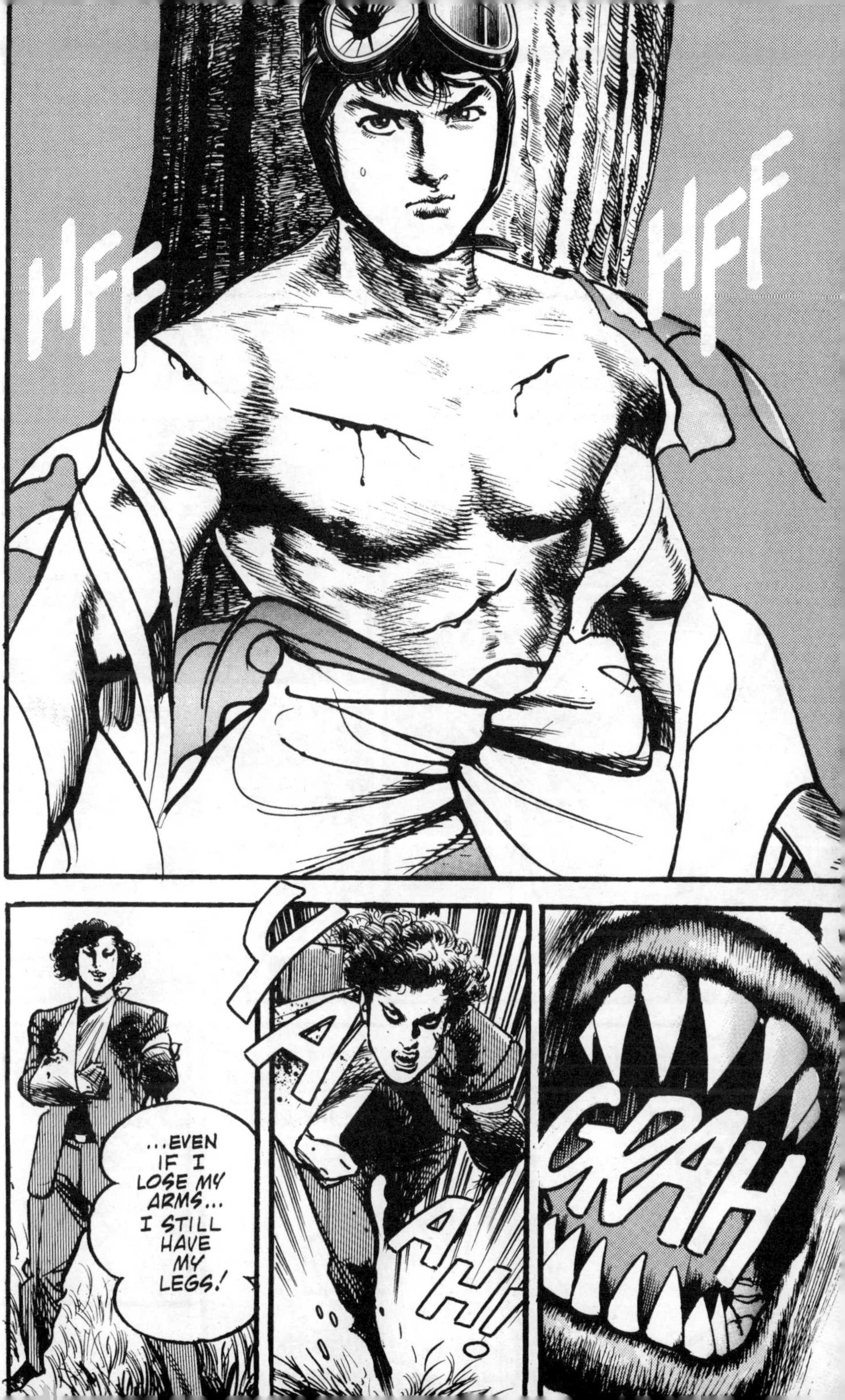
HFF HFF
...EVEN IF I LOSE MY ARMS... I STILL HAVE MY LEGS!
YAAH!
GRAH

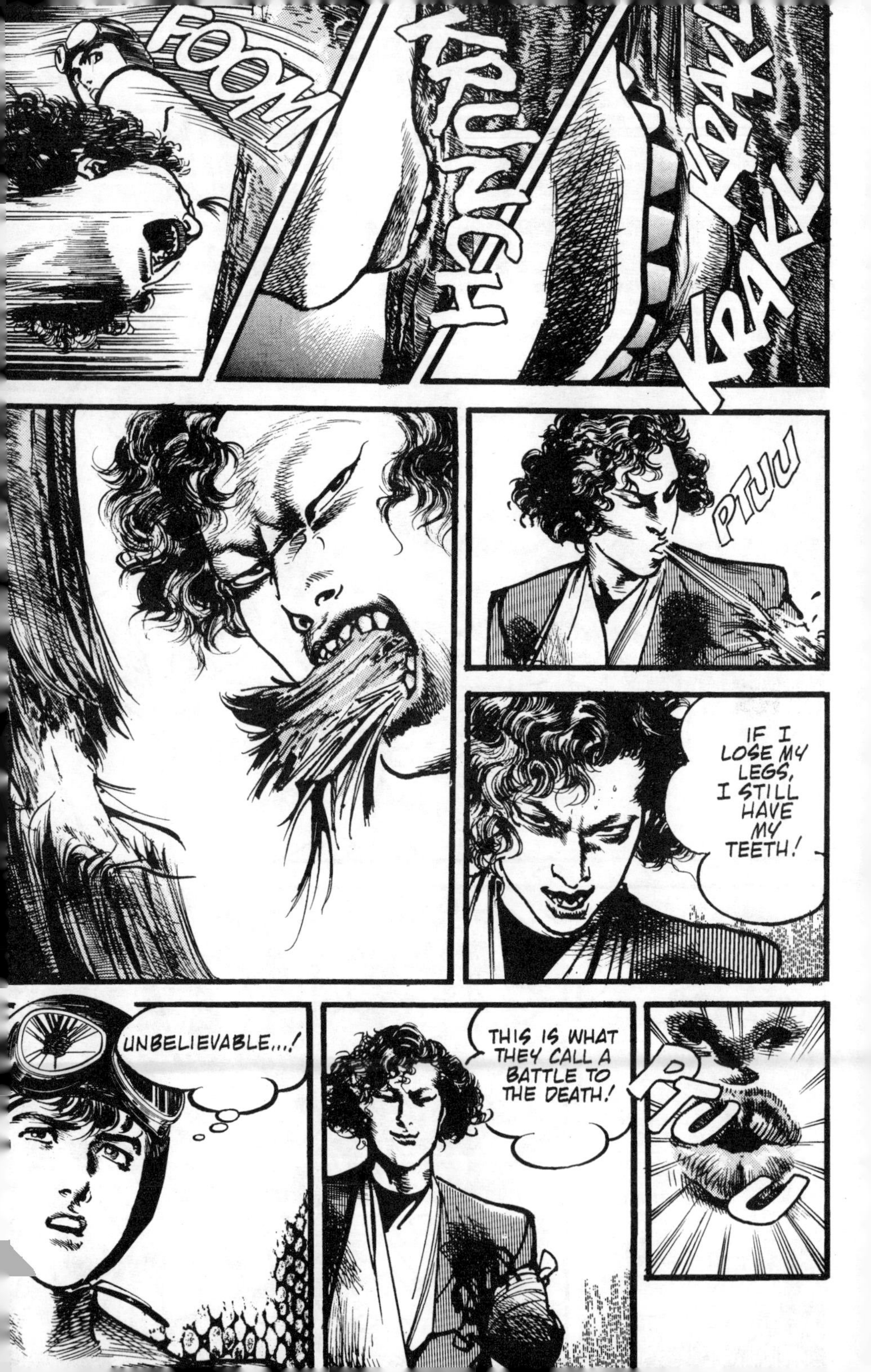
FOOM
KRUNCH
KRAK KRAK
PTUU
IF I LOSE MY LEGS, I STILL HAVE MY TEETH!
UNBELIEVABLE...!
THIS IS WHAT THEY CALL A BATTLE TO THE DEATH!
PTUU

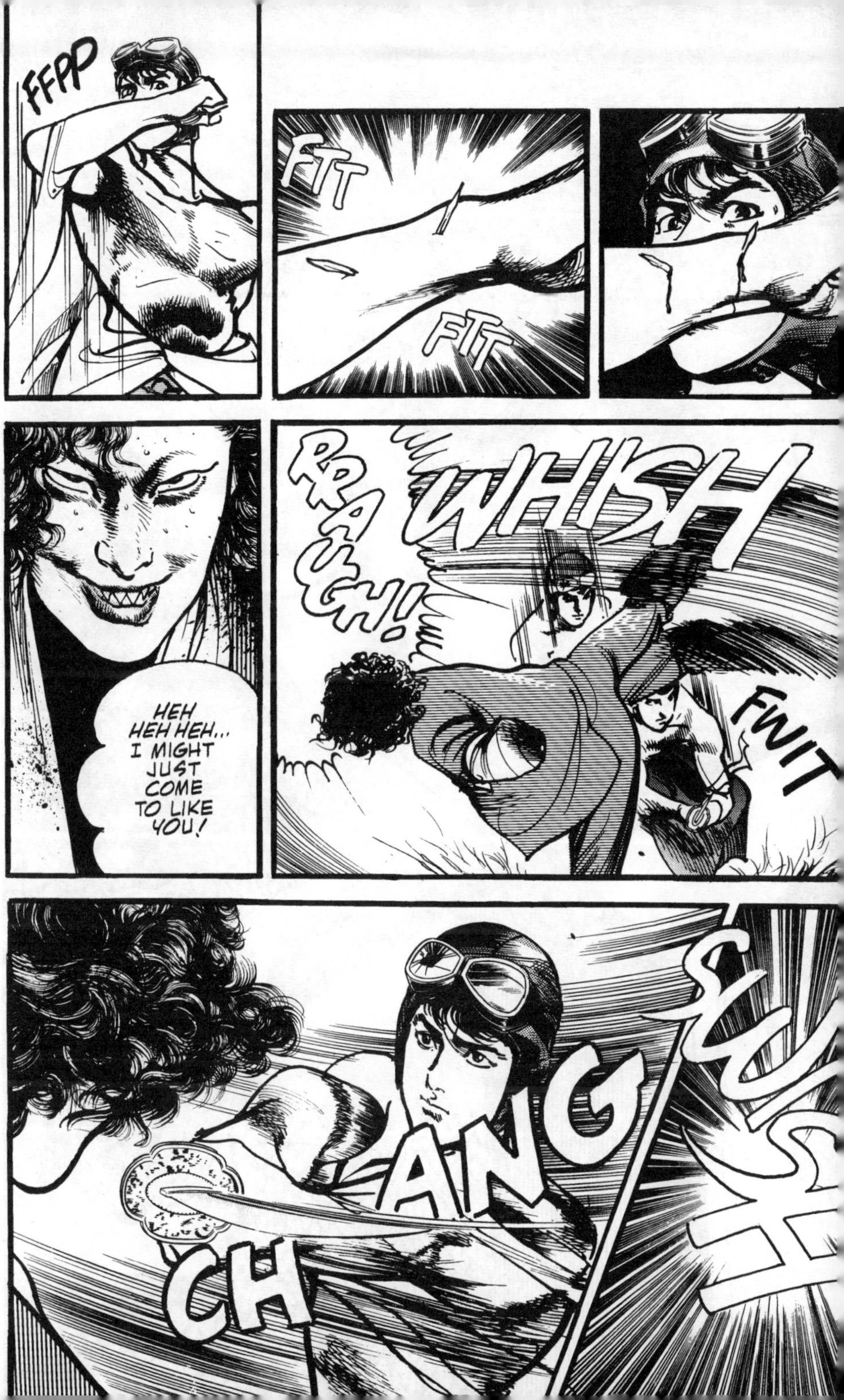
FFPP
FTT
FTT
HEH HEH HEH... I MIGHT JUST COME TO LIKE YOU!
RRAUGH!
WHISH
FWIT
CHANG
SWISH

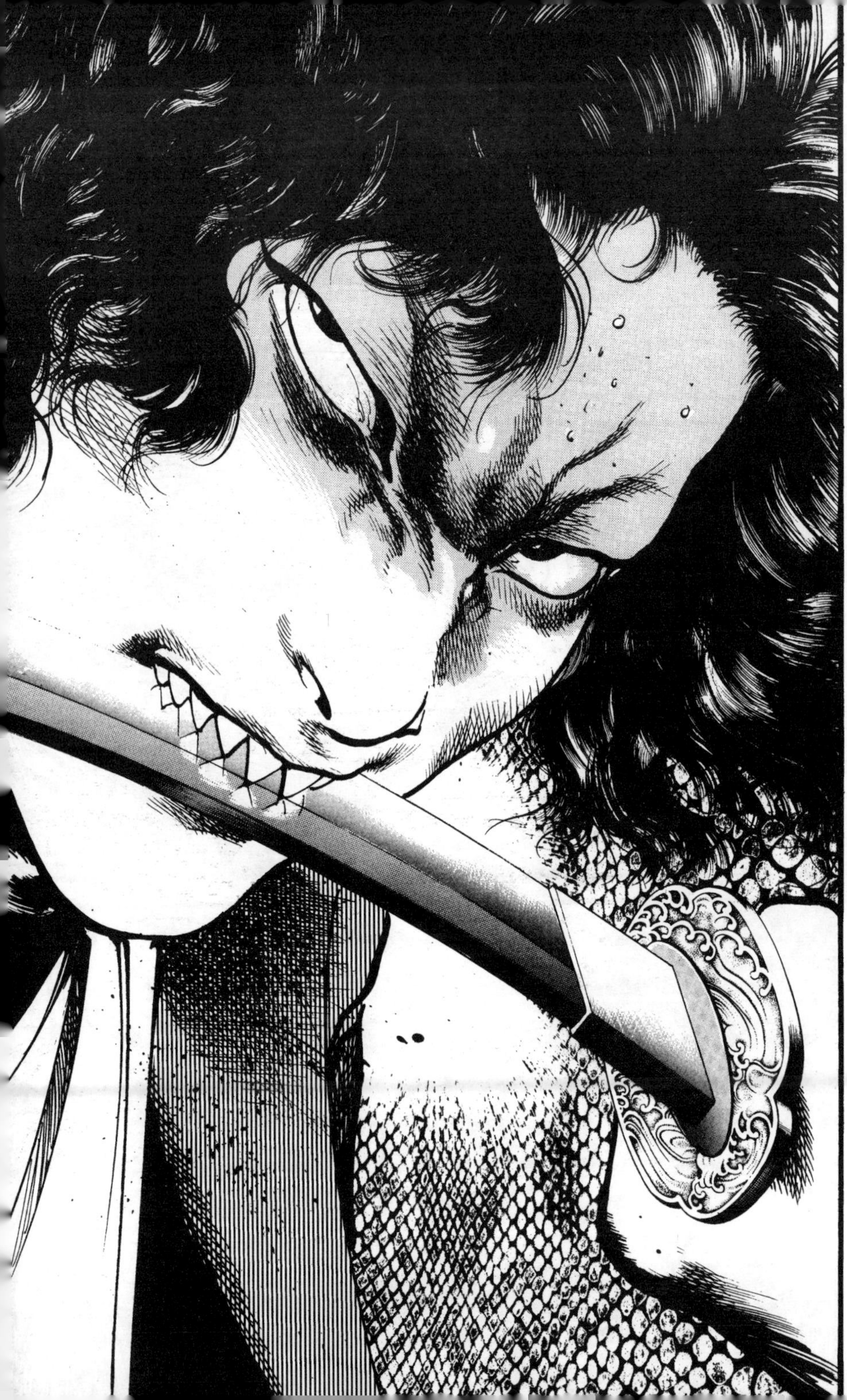

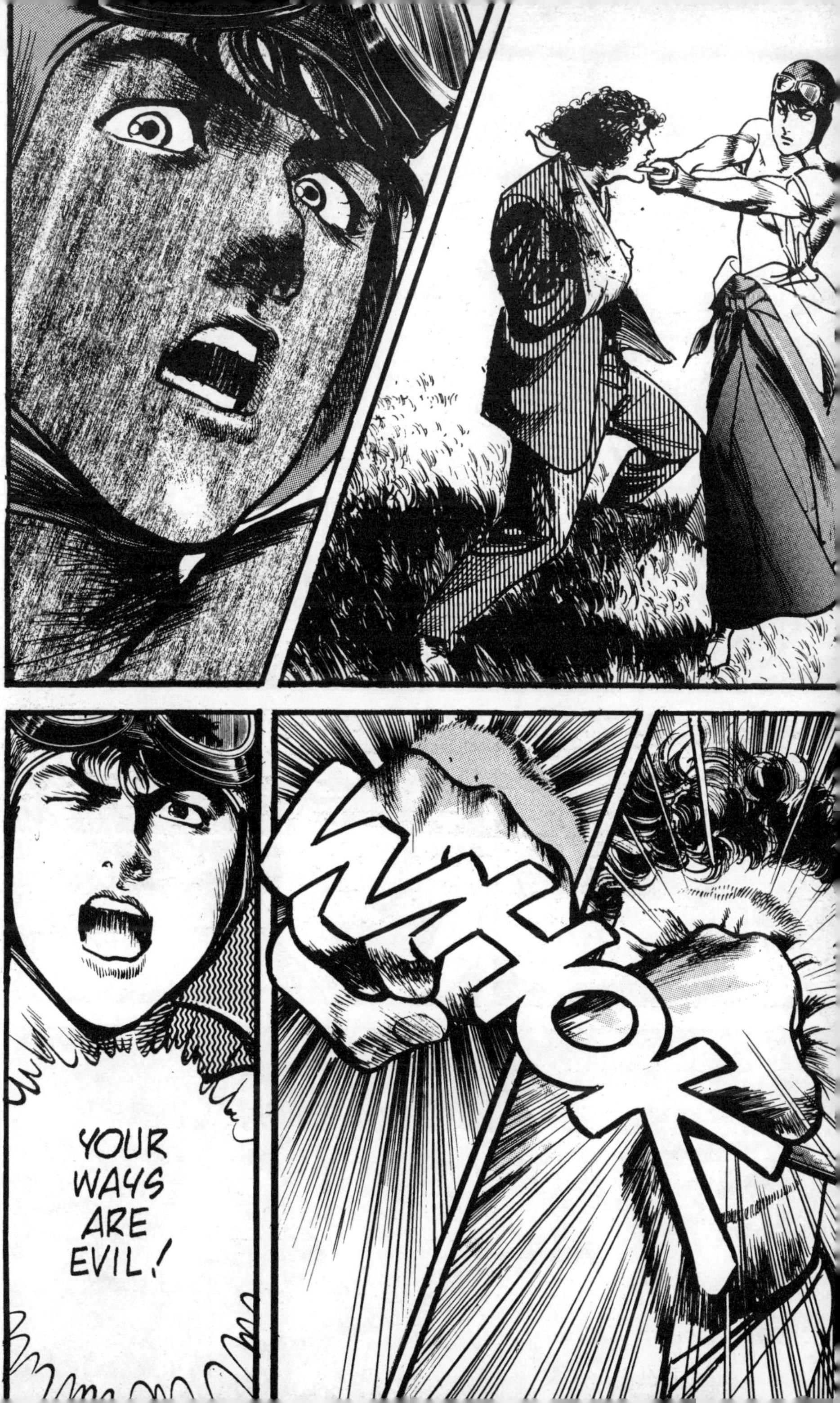
YOUR WAYS ARE EVIL!
WHOK

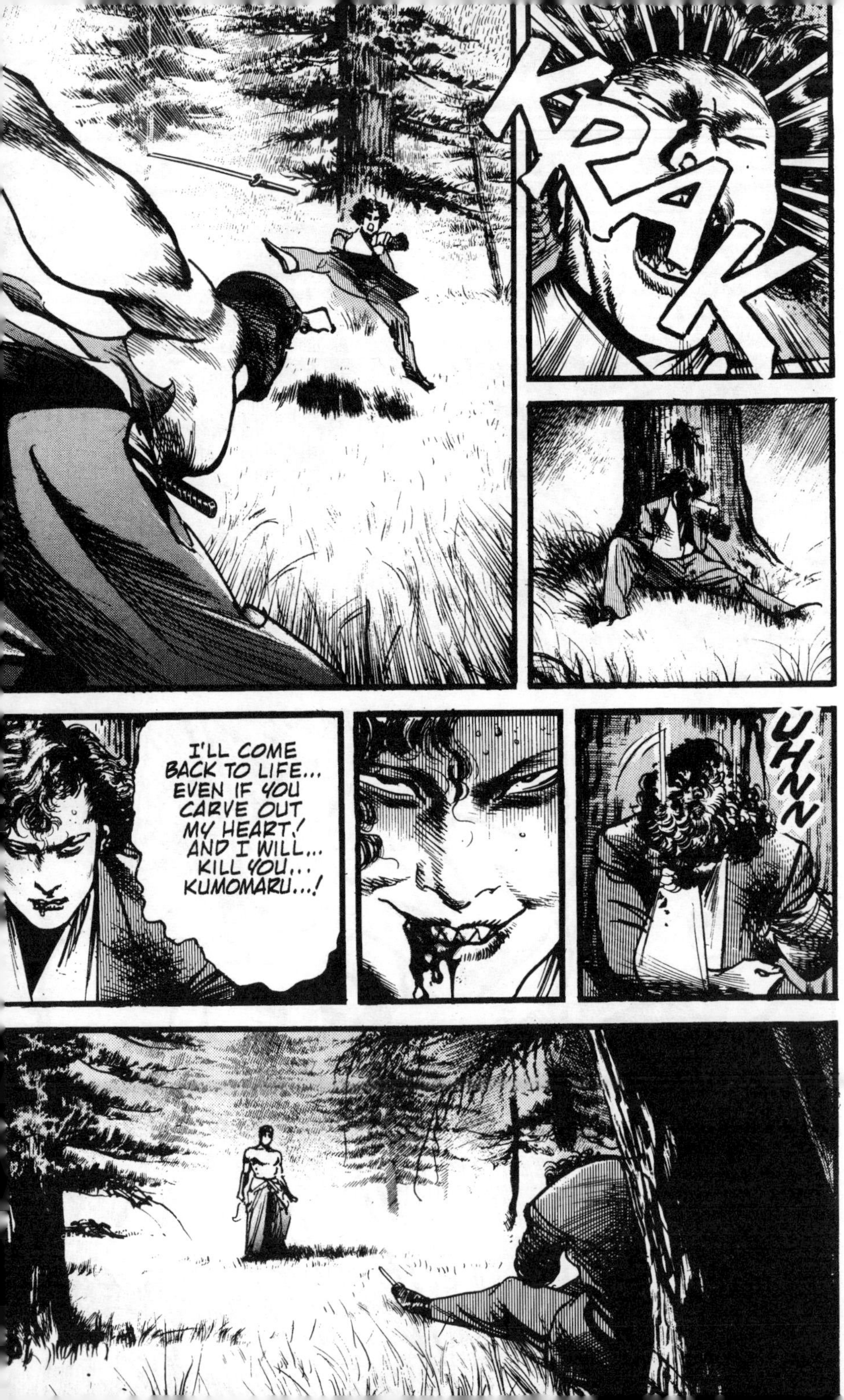
KRAK
I'LL COME BACK TO LIFE... EVEN IF YOU CARVE OUT MY HEART! AND I WILL... KILL YOU... KUMOMARU...!
UHNN

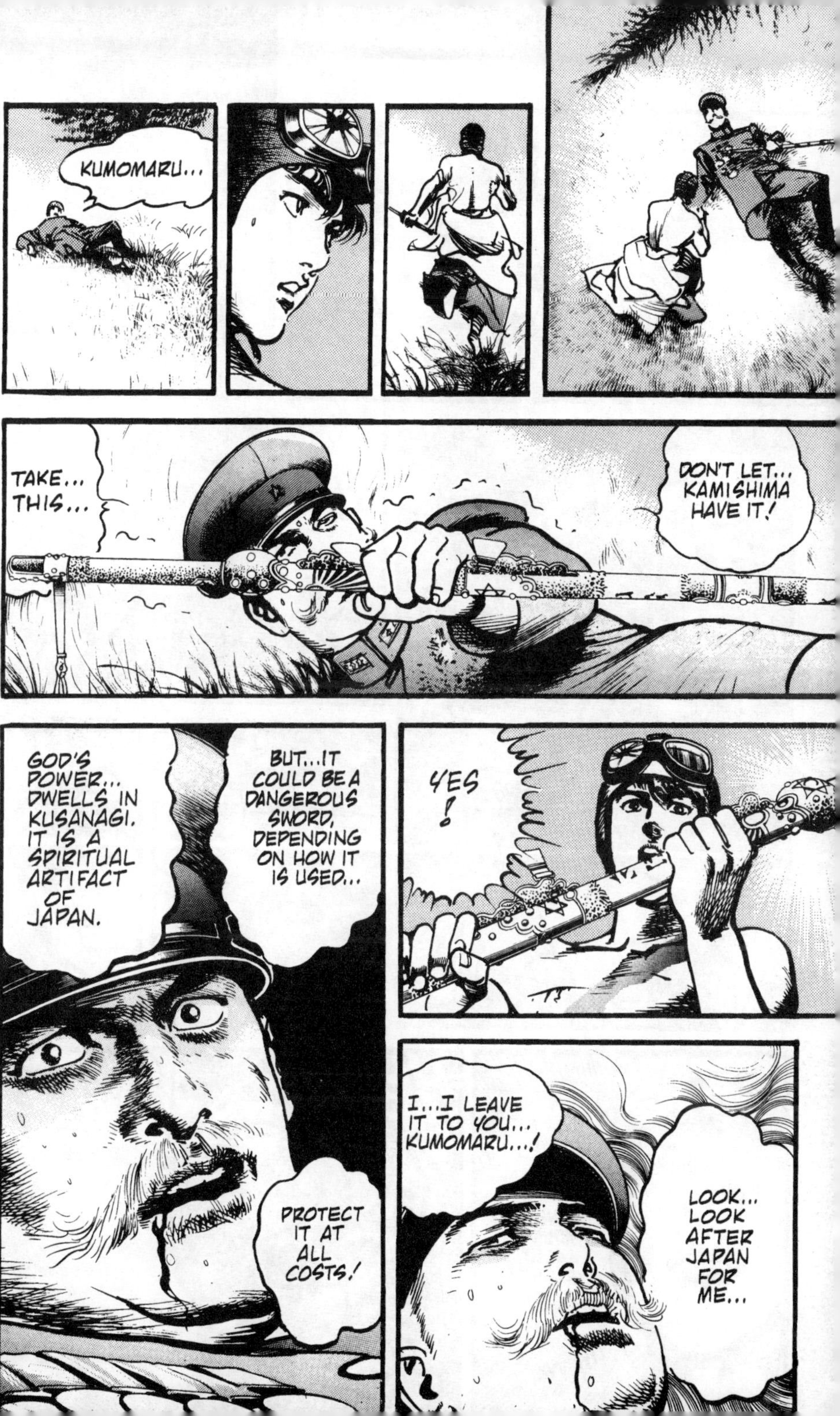
KUMOMARU...
TAKE... THIS...
DON'T LET... KAMISHIMA HAVE IT!
GOD'S POWER... DWELLS IN KUSANAGI. IT IS A SPIRITUAL ARTIFACT OF JAPAN.
BUT...IT COULD BE A DANGEROUS SWORD, DEPENDING ON HOW IT IS USED...
PROTECT IT AT ALL COSTS!
YES!
I...I LEAVE IT TO YOU... KUMOMARU...!
LOOK... LOOK AFTER JAPAN FOR ME...

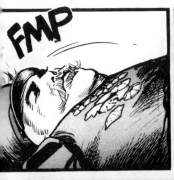

OLD MAN!

HEY!

ERNEST! YOU'RE ALL RIGHT!

...THEY CALL ME "IMMORTAL ERNEST"...

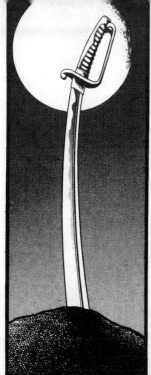

IS IT ALL RIGHT TO BURY HIM HERE...?

OLD MAN KUJO DOESN'T HAVE ANY FAMILY... AND HE ALWAYS SAID HE WANTED TO BECOME PART OF THE SOIL OF FRANCE...

KUSANAGI IS BACK IN YOUR HANDS AGAIN.

YEAH...

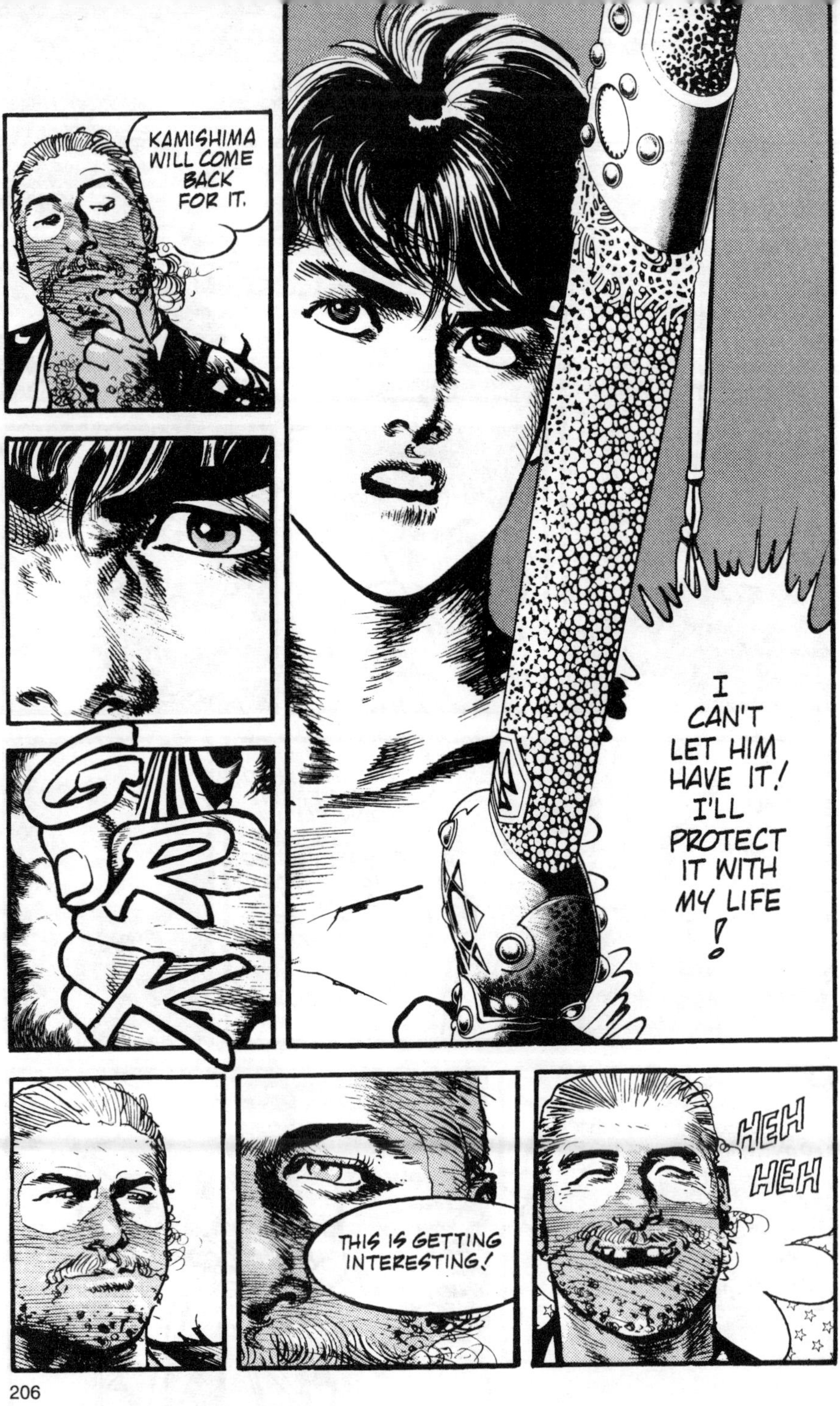
KAMISHIMA WILL COME BACK FOR IT.
GRK
I CAN'T LET HIM HAVE IT! I'LL PROTECT IT WITH MY LIFE!
THIS IS GETTING INTERESTING!
HEH HEH

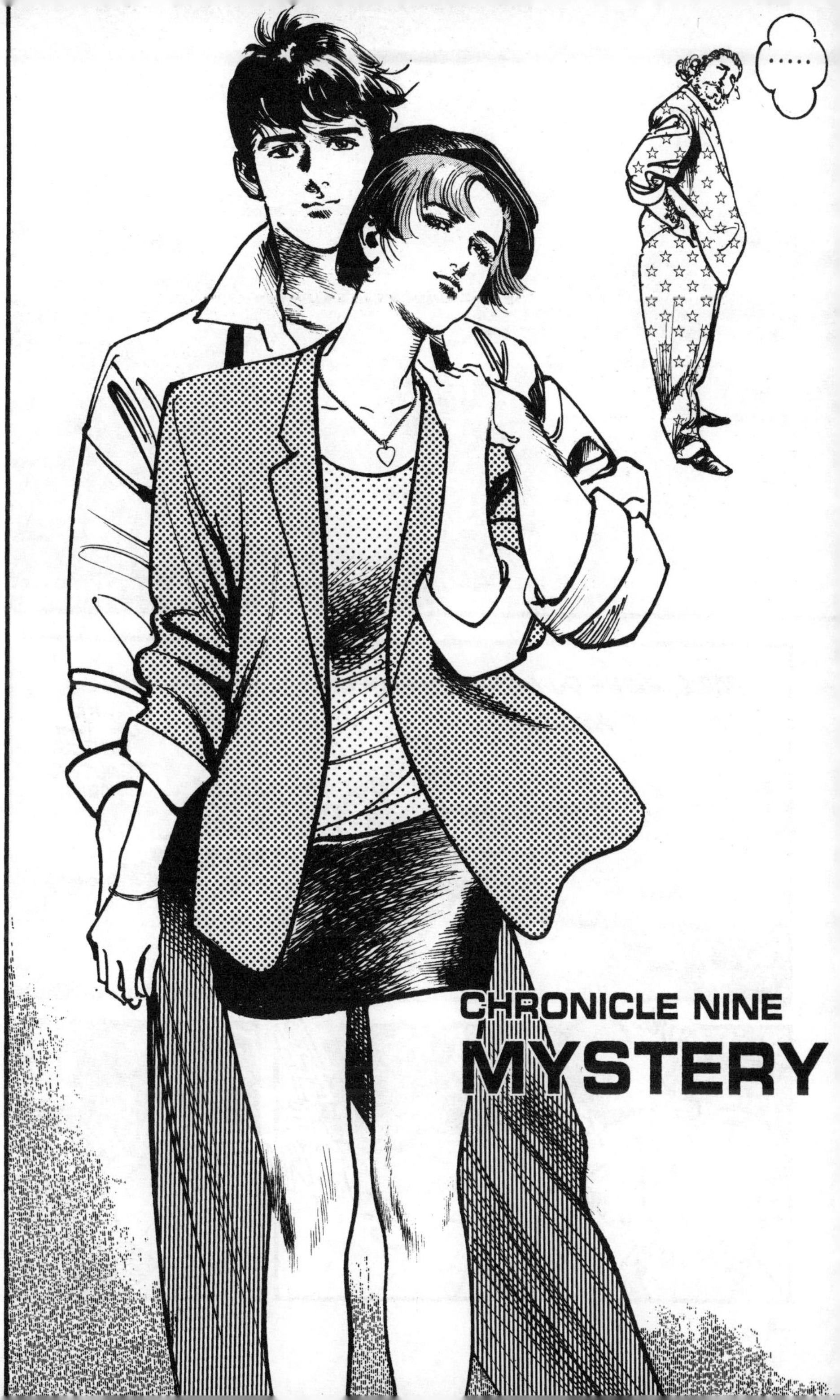
......
CHRONICLE NINE
MYSTERY

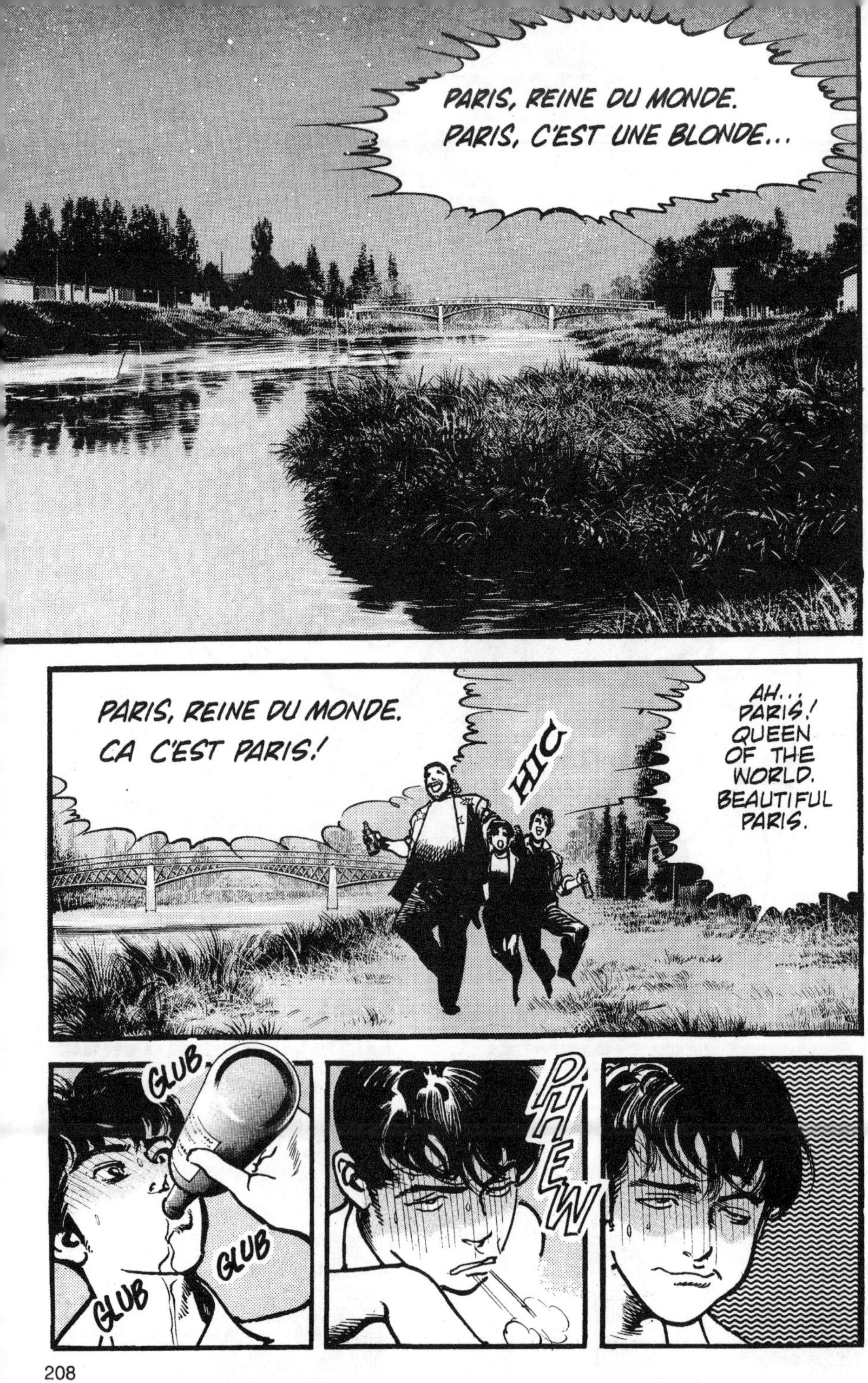
PARIS, REINE DU MONDE.
PARIS, C'EST UNE BLONDE...
PARIS, REINE DU MONDE.
CA C'EST PARIS!
HIC
AH... PARIS! QUEEN OF THE WORLD. BEAUTIFUL PARIS.
GLUB
GLUB
GLUB
PHEW

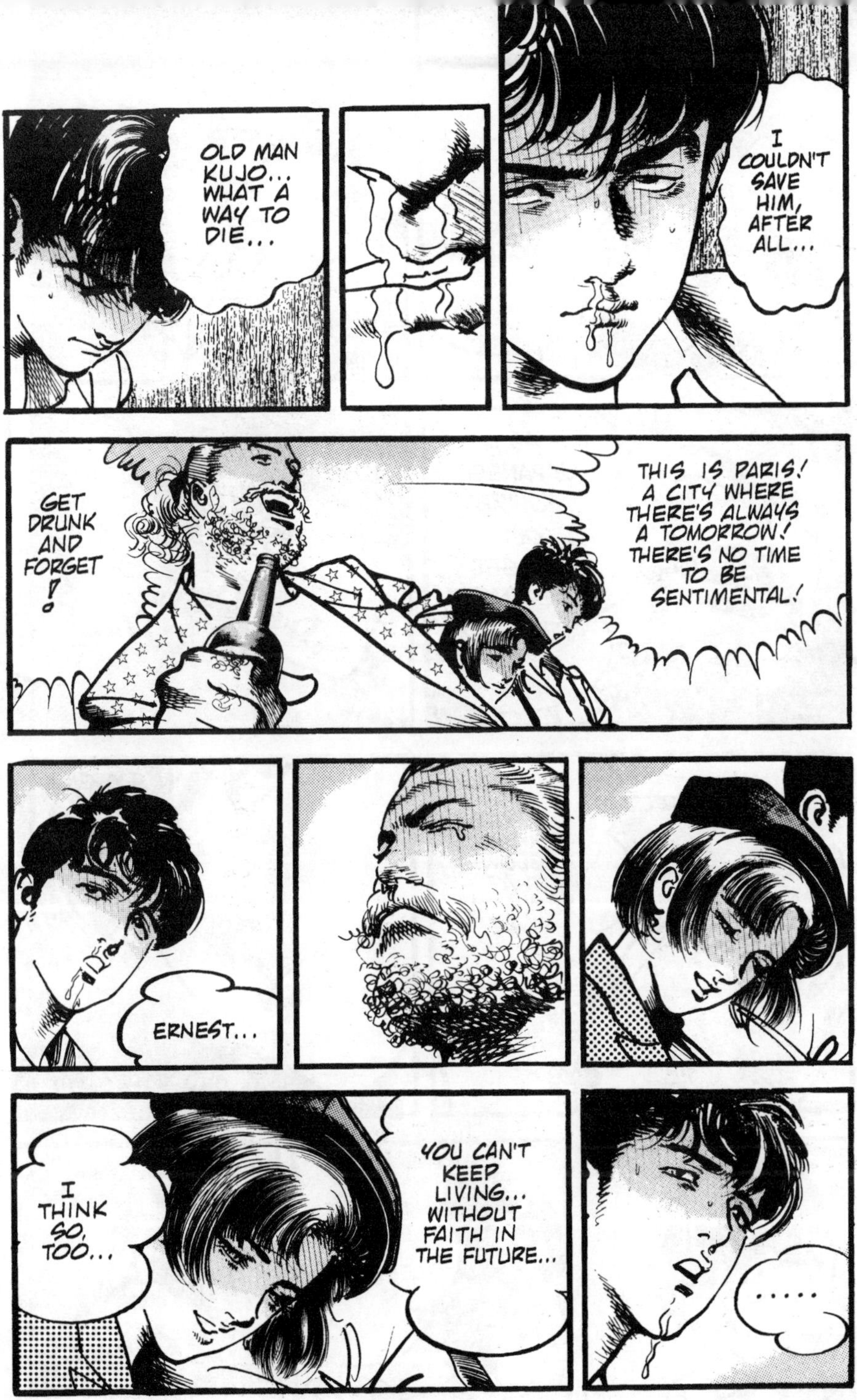
OLD MAN KUJO... WHAT A WAY TO DIE...
I COULDN'T SAVE HIM, AFTER ALL...
GET DRUNK AND FORGET!
THIS IS PARIS! A CITY WHERE THERE'S ALWAYS A TOMORROW! THERE'S NO TIME TO BE SENTIMENTAL!
ERNEST...
I THINK SO, TOO...
YOU CAN'T KEEP LIVING... WITHOUT FAITH IN THE FUTURE...
.....

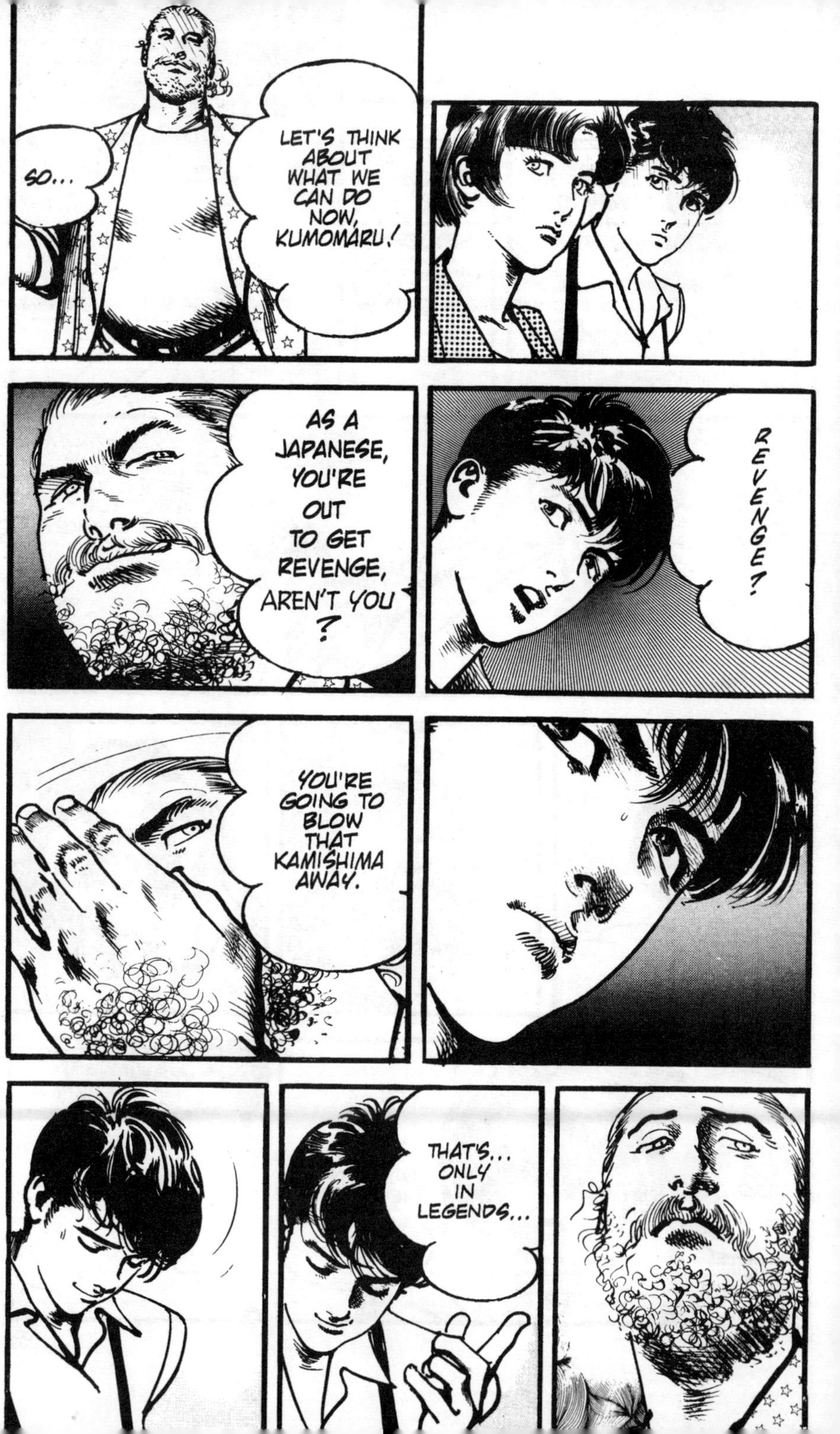
SO...
LET'S THINK ABOUT WHAT WE CAN DO NOW, KUMOMARU!
AS A JAPANESE, YOU'RE OUT TO GET REVENGE, AREN'T YOU?
REVENGE?
YOU'RE GOING TO BLOW THAT KAMISHIMA AWAY.
THAT'S... ONLY IN LEGENDS...

HE'S IN LONDON !

I SAW IT IN THE EVENING PAPER.

AREN'T YOU GOING AFTER HIM ?!

......

NO !

HE'S NOT! KUMOMARU'S GOING TO LIVE IN PARIS, RIGHT ?!

......

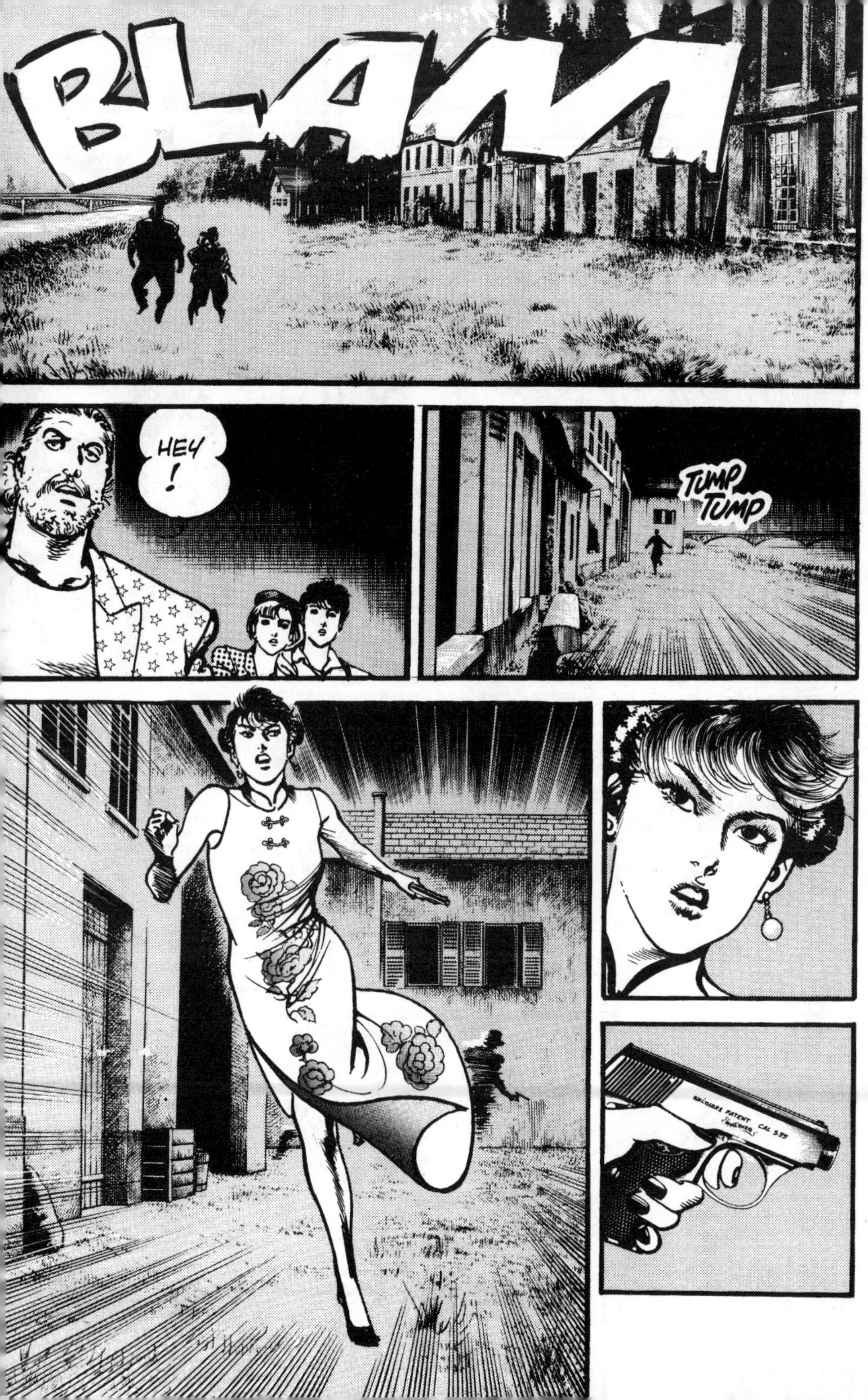
BLAM
HEY!
TUMP TUMP

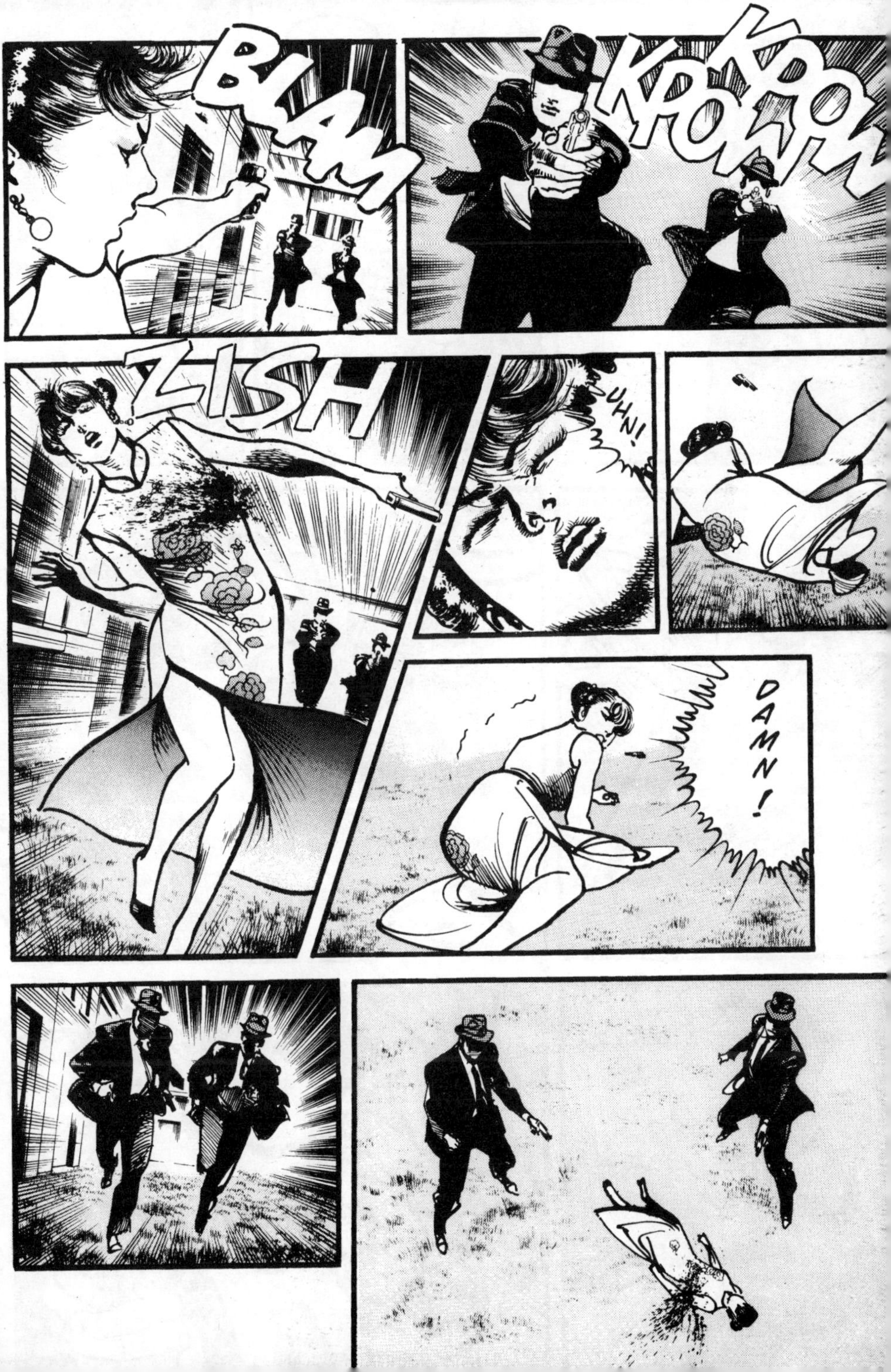
BLAM
KOOWW
KPOWW
ZISH
UHN!
DAMN!

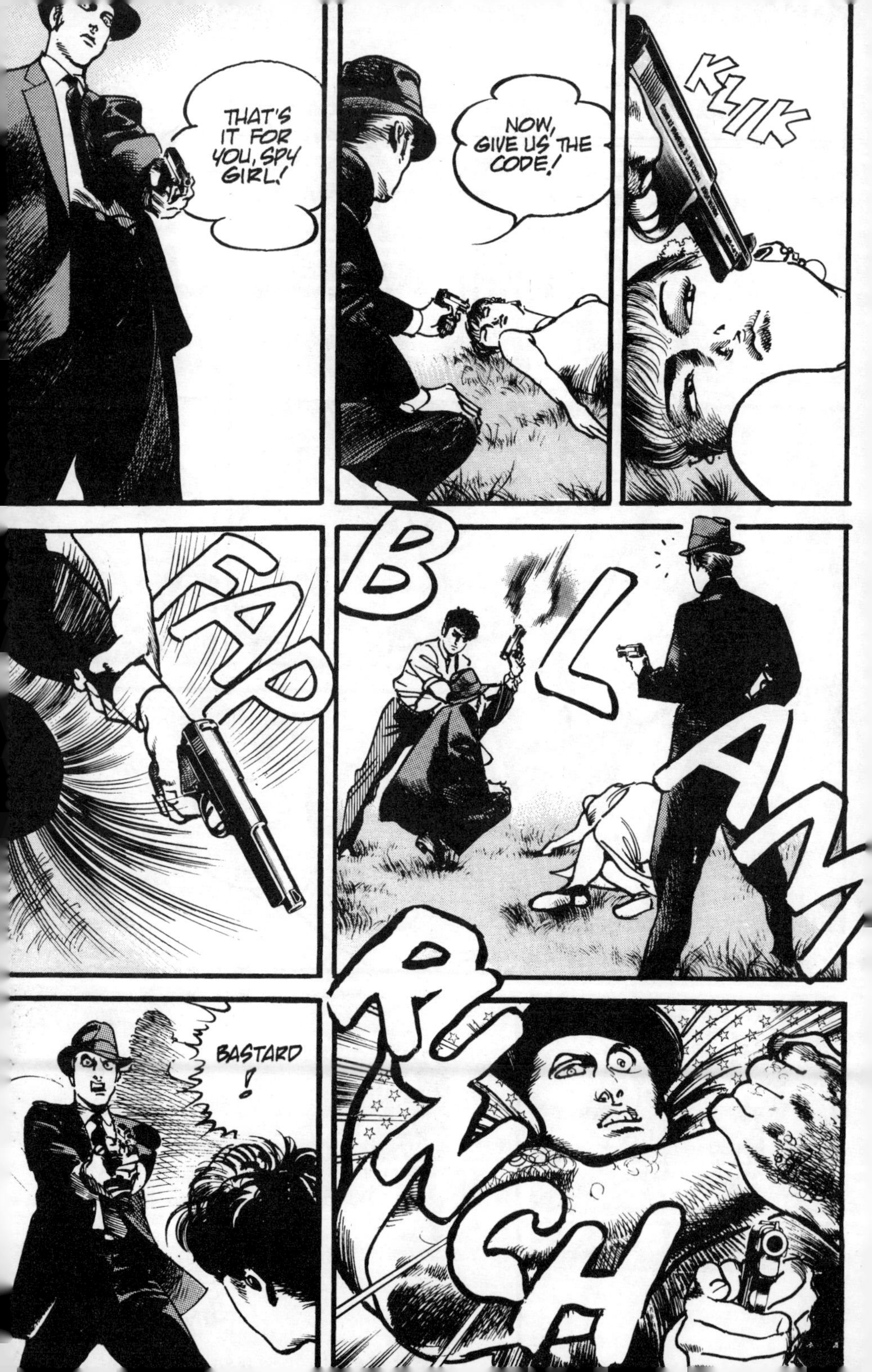
THAT'S IT FOR YOU, SPY GIRL!
NOW, GIVE US THE CODE!
KLIK
FAP
BLAM
BASTARD!
RNCH

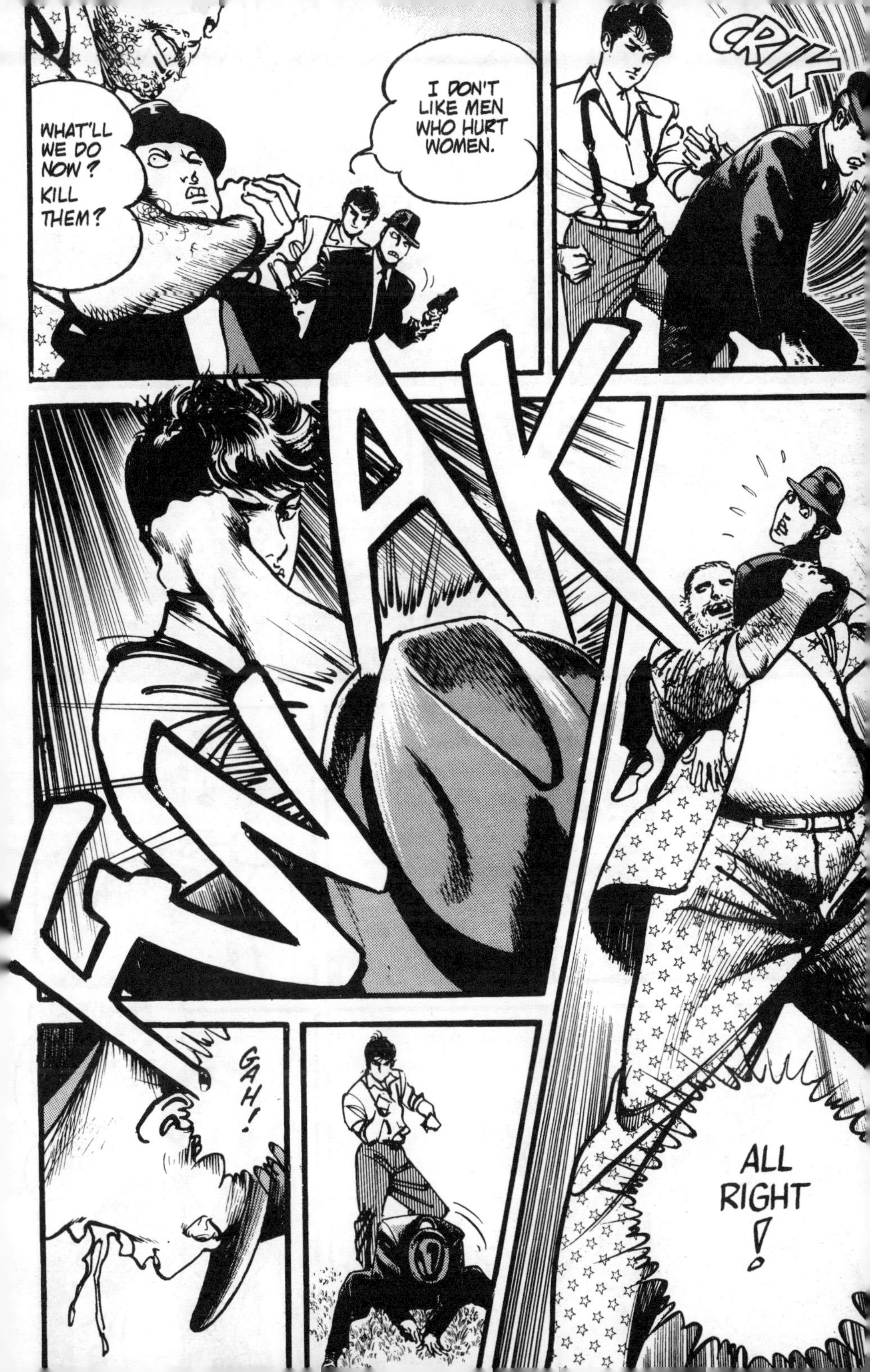
WHAT'LL WE DO NOW? KILL THEM?
I DON'T LIKE MEN WHO HURT WOMEN.
CRIK
WAK
GAH!
ALL RIGHT!

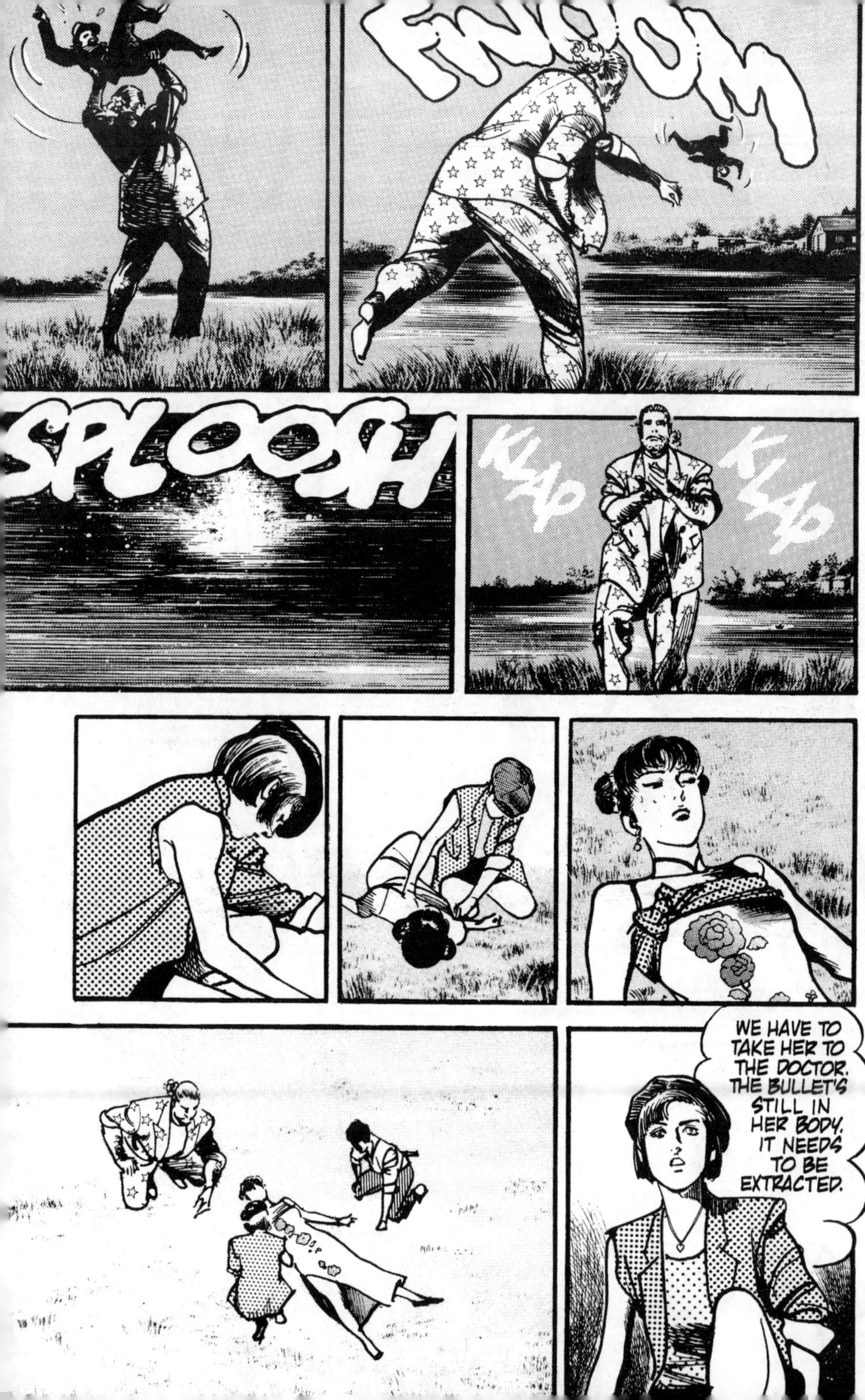
FWOOM
SPLOOSH
KLAP KLAP
WE HAVE TO TAKE HER TO THE DOCTOR. THE BULLET'S STILL IN HER BODY, IT NEEDS TO BE EXTRACTED.

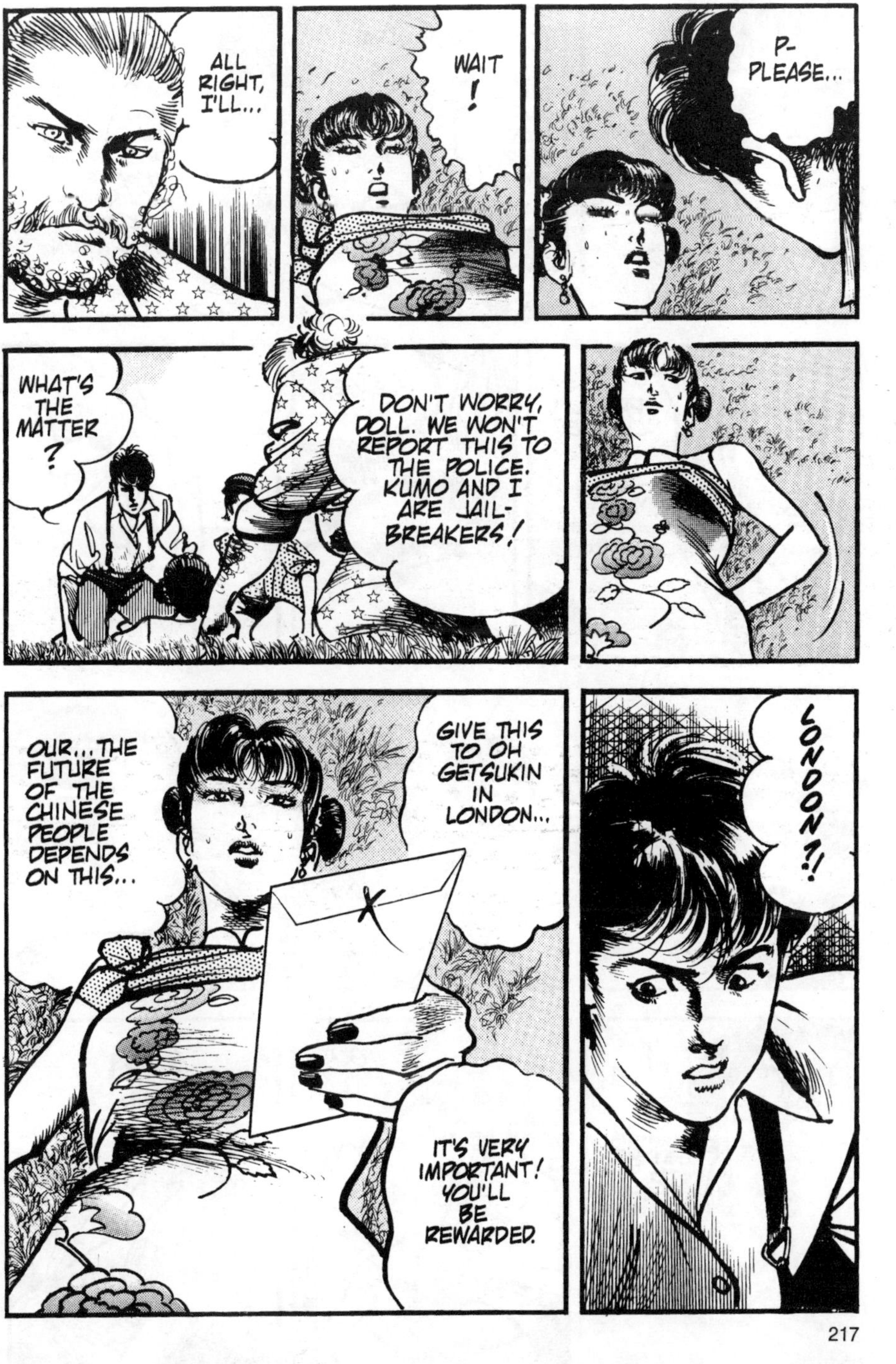

ALL RIGHT, I'LL...
WAIT!
P-PLEASE...
WHAT'S THE MATTER?
DON'T WORRY, DOLL. WE WON'T REPORT THIS TO THE POLICE. KUMO AND I ARE JAIL-BREAKERS!
OUR... THE FUTURE OF THE CHINESE PEOPLE DEPENDS ON THIS...
GIVE THIS TO OH GETSUKIN IN LONDON...
IT'S VERY IMPORTANT! YOU'LL BE REWARDED.
LONDON?!

ACROSS FROM WATERLOO STATION, THE TOBACCO SHOP...

TELL THE OLD MAN THERE...

≈KOFF≈ THAT YOU WANT TO EAT... DRAGON NOODLES MADE BY THE ≈KOFF≈ CHINESE CHEF ASSOCIATION.

DRAGON NOODLES...?

PLEASE...

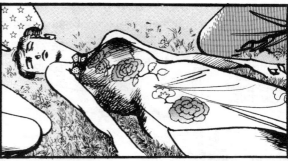

QUICK! GET HER TO THE HOSPITAL!

GOT IT!

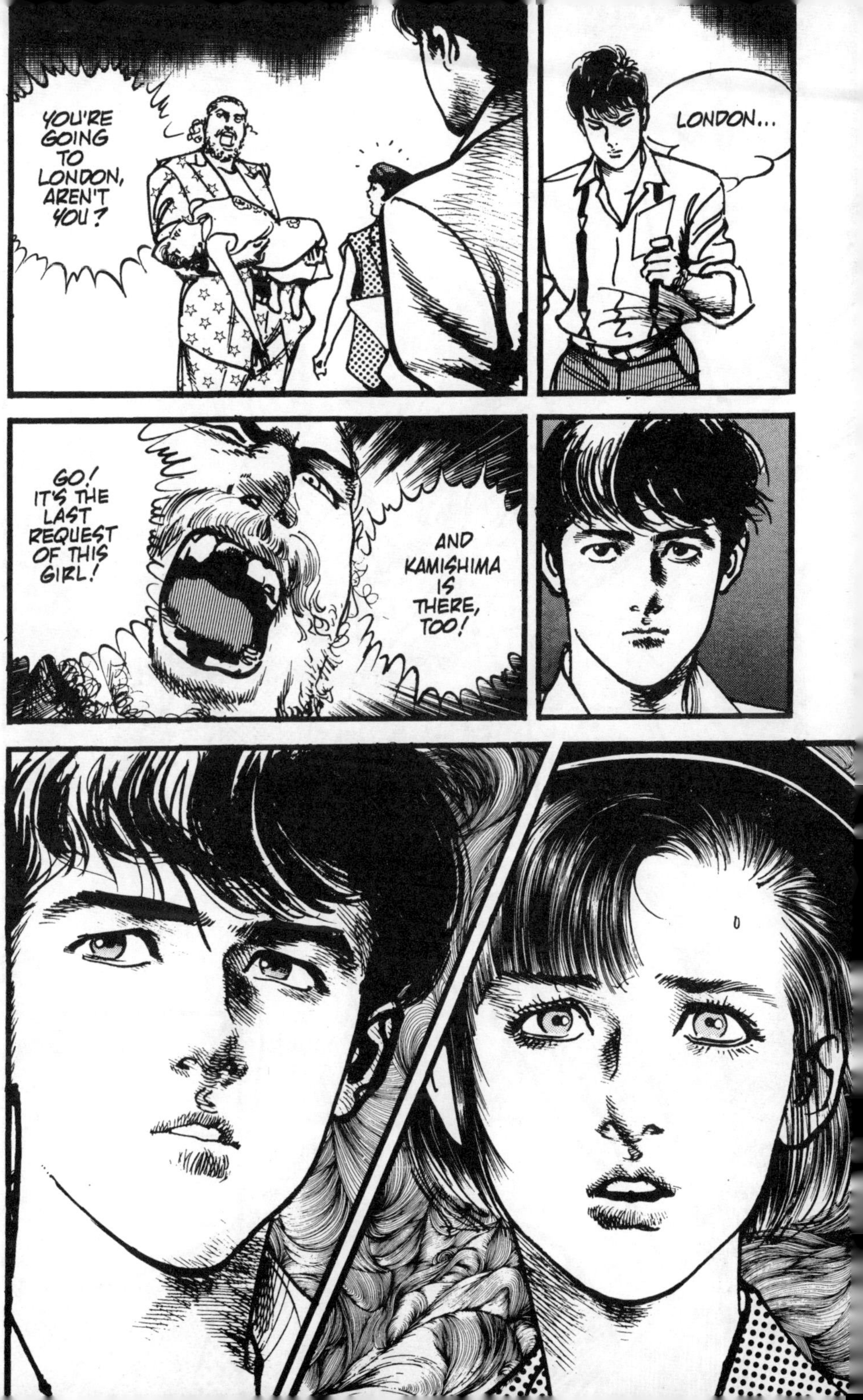
YOU'RE GOING TO LONDON, AREN'T YOU?
LONDON...
GO! IT'S THE LAST REQUEST OF THIS GIRL!
AND KAMISHIMA IS THERE, TOO!

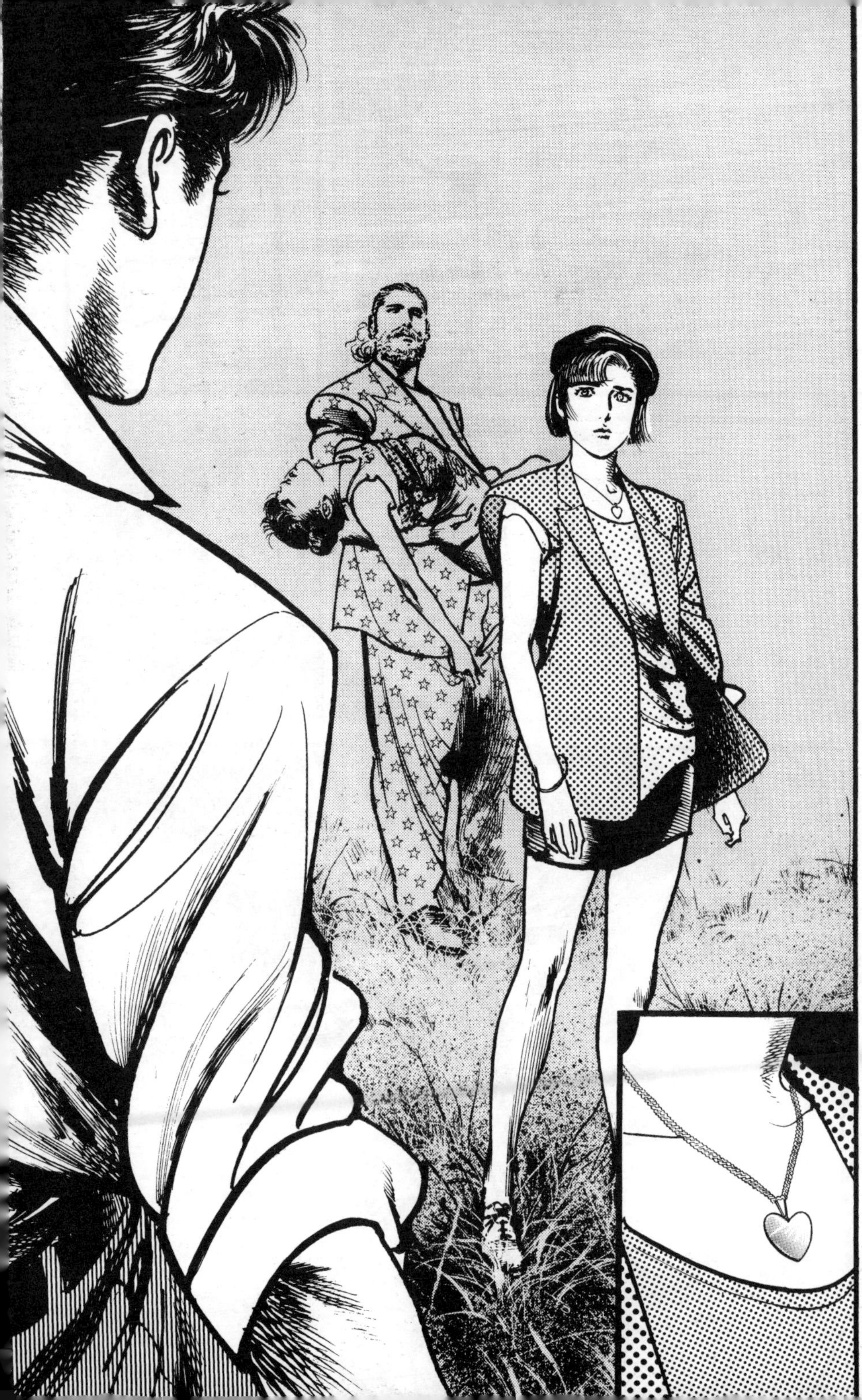

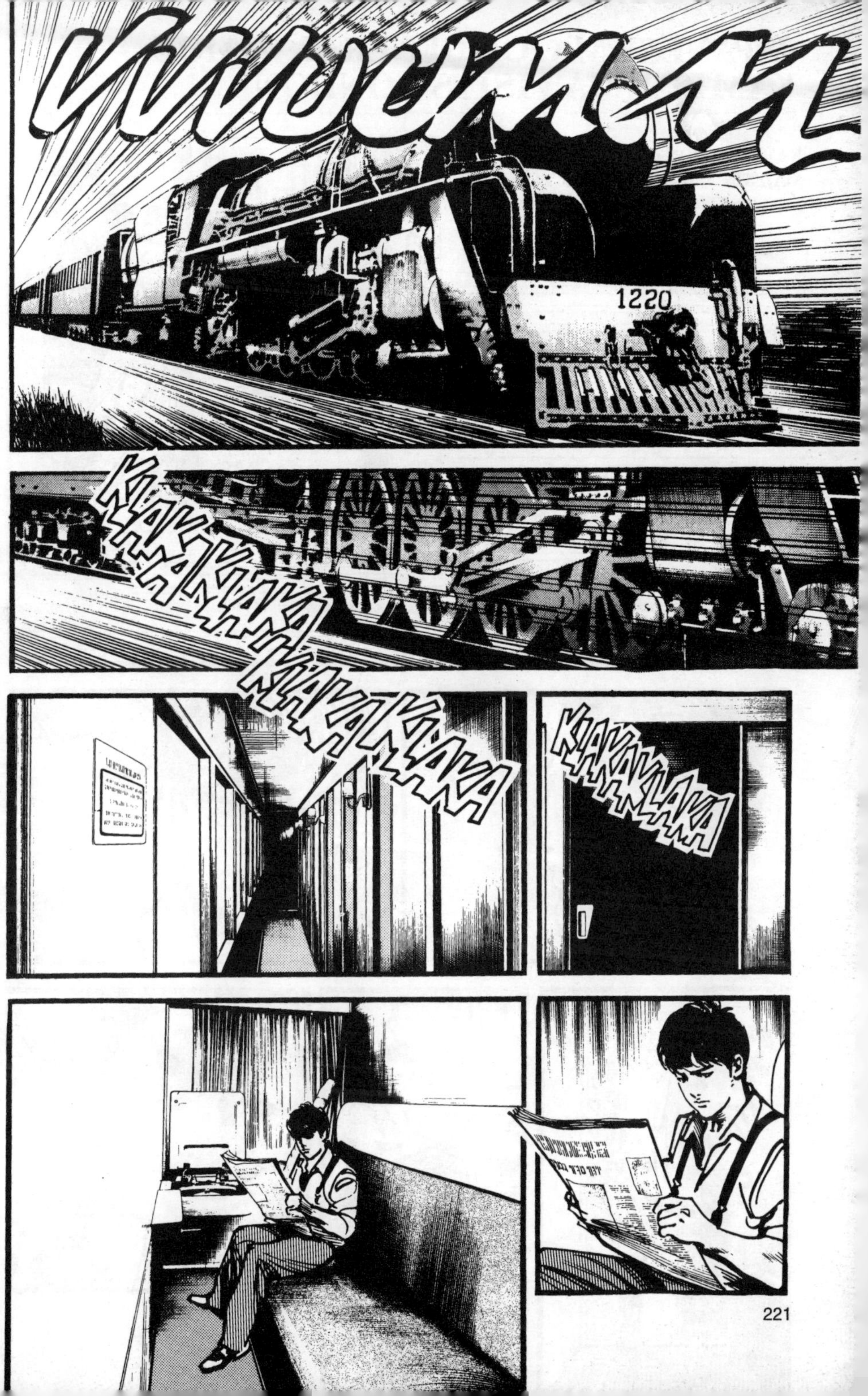
1220
KLAKAKLAKA
KLAKAKLAKA
KLAKAKLAKA

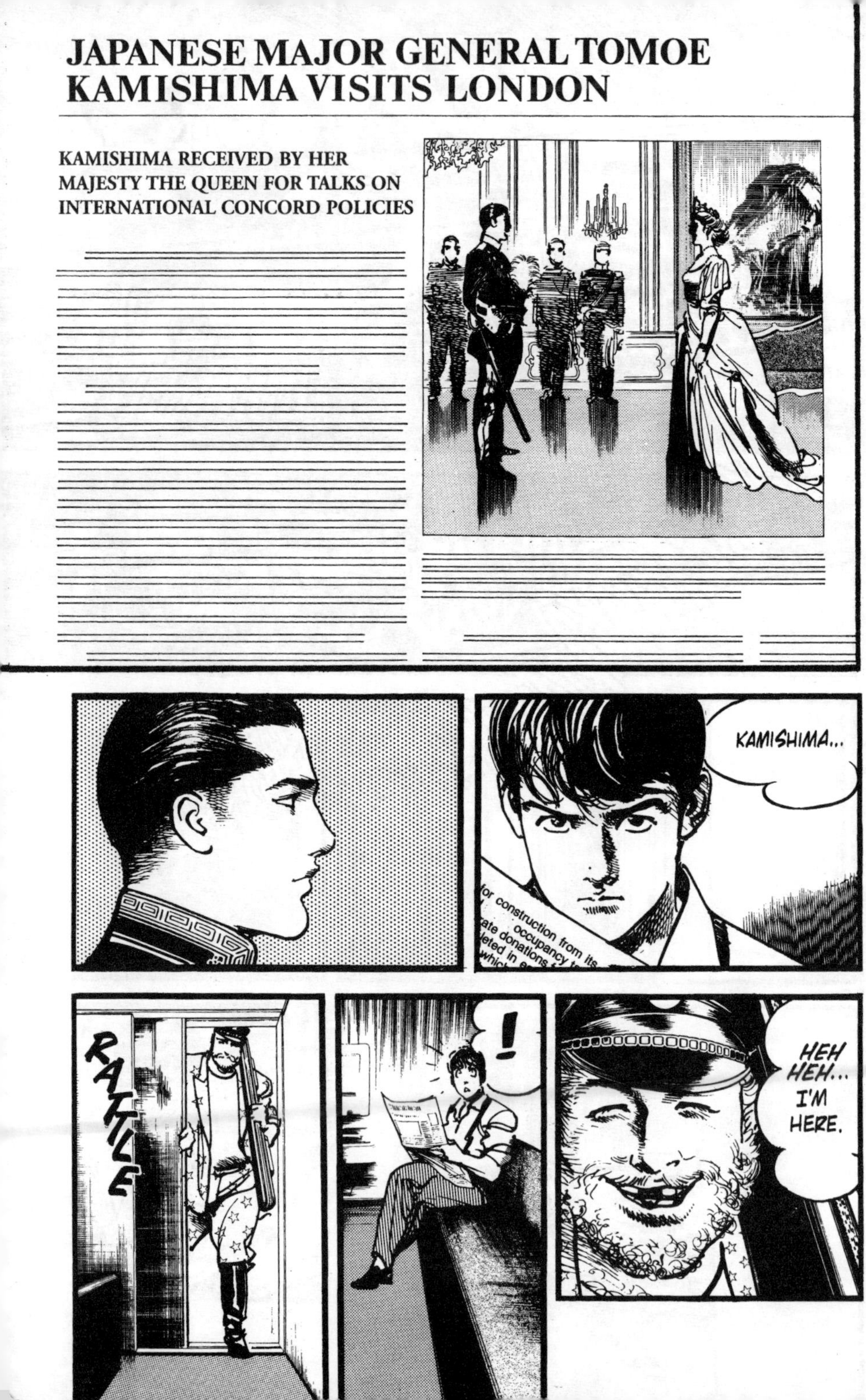
JAPANESE MAJOR GENERAL TOMOE KAMISHIMA VISITS LONDON
KAMISHIMA RECEIVED BY HER MAJESTY THE QUEEN FOR TALKS ON INTERNATIONAL CONCORD POLICIES
KAMISHIMA...
RATTLE
!
HEH HEH... I'M HERE.

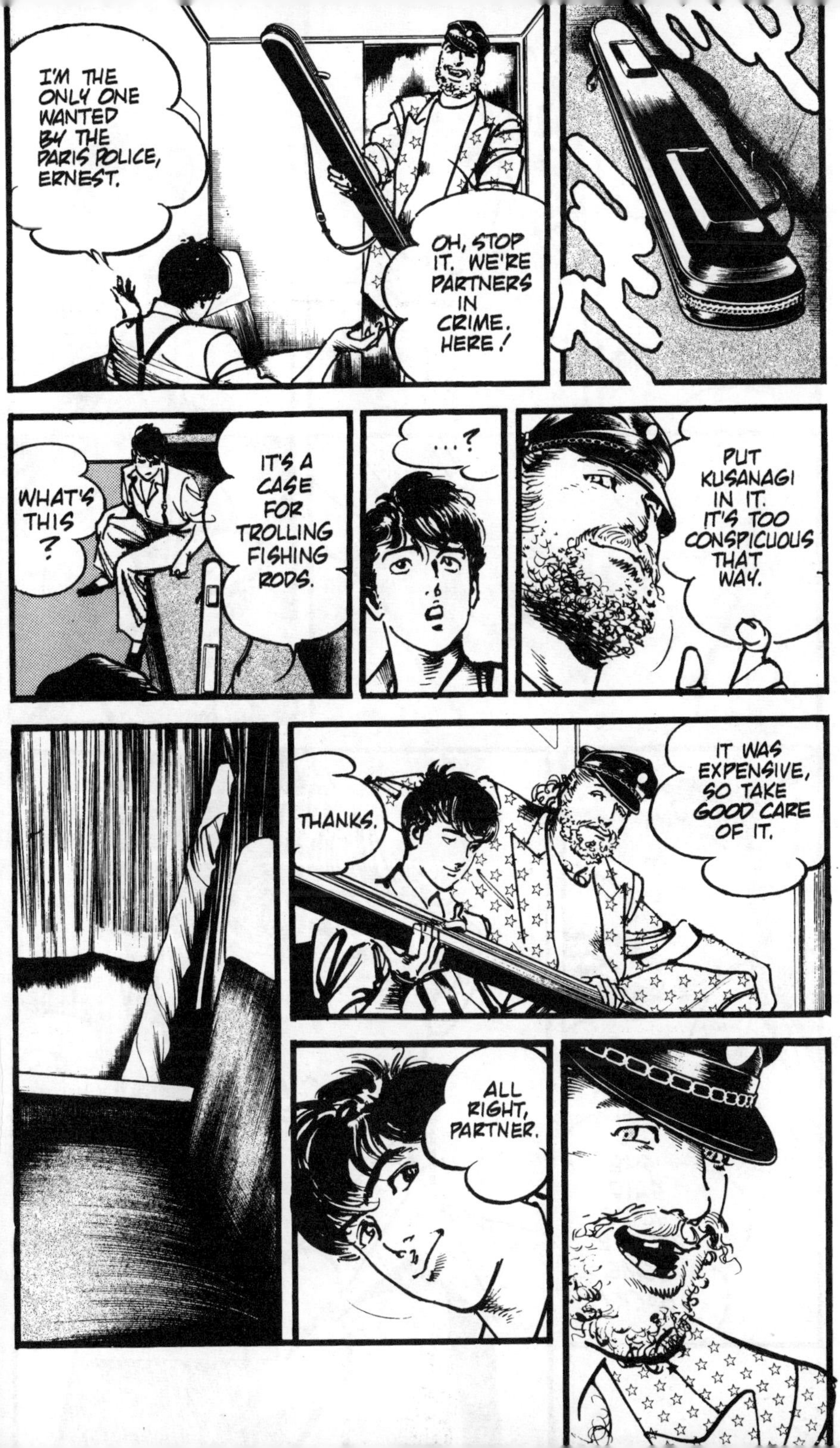
I'M THE ONLY ONE WANTED BY THE PARIS POLICE, ERNEST.
OH, STOP IT. WE'RE PARTNERS IN CRIME. HERE!
WHAT'S THIS?
IT'S A CASE FOR TROLLING FISHING RODS.
...?
PUT KUSANAGI IN IT. IT'S TOO CONSPICUOUS THAT WAY.
THANKS.
IT WAS EXPENSIVE, SO TAKE GOOD CARE OF IT.
ALL RIGHT, PARTNER.

OH, I ALMOST FORGOT.

THIS IS FROM GIGI.

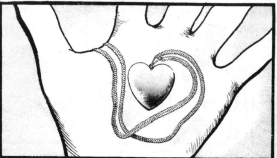

SHE SAID YOU'D BETTER COME BACK!

I WILL.

TO BE CONTINUED...